Languages and Machines

An Introduction to the
Theory of Computer Science

Thomas A. Sudkamp

Wright State University

ADDISON-WESLEY PUBLISHING COMPANY, INC.
Reading, Massachusetts • Menlo Park, California • New York
Don Mills, Ontario • Wokingham, England • Amsterdam
Bonn • Sydney • Singapore • Tokyo • Madrid • San Juan

This book is in the Addison-Wesley series in Computer Science
Michael A. Harrison/Consulting Editor

Library of Congress Cataloging-in-Publication Data

Sudkamp, Thomas A.
    Languages and machines.

    Includes bibliographies and index.
    1. Formal languages.   2. Machine theory.   3. Computational complexity.   I. Title.
QA267.3.S83   1988   004   87-19482
ISBN 0-201-15768-3

Reprinted with corrections November, 1988

ISBN 0-201-15768-3

CDEFGHIJ-DO-898

⟨*dedication*⟩ → ⟨*parents*⟩
⟨*parents*⟩ → ⟨ *first name*⟩ ⟨*last name*⟩
⟨ *first name*⟩ → *Donald* | *Mary*
⟨*last name*⟩ → *Sudkamp*

Preface

As computer science matures as an academic discipline, the theoretical foundations of computing are assuming a prominent and deserved position in the undergraduate curriculum. The primary objective of this book is to give a mathematically sound presentation of the theory of computing at a level suitable for junior- and senior-level computer science majors. The topics covered include the theory of formal languages and automata, computability, computational complexity, and deterministic parsing of context-free languages.

To make these topics accessible to the undergraduate student, no special mathematical prerequisites are assumed. Instead, Chapter 1 introduces the mathematical tools of the theory of computing: naive set theory, recursive definitions, and proof by mathematical induction.

The presentation of formal language theory and automata develops the relationships between the grammars and abstract machines that comprise the Chomsky hierarchy. Parsing context-free languages is presented in Chapter 4 via standard graph-searching algorithms. Introducing parsing at this point reinforces the need for a formal approach to language definition and motivates the development of normal forms in Chapter 5.

Finite-state automata and Turing machines provide the framework for the study of effective computation. Topics covered include decidability, the Church-Turing thesis, and the equivalence of Turing computability and μ-recursive functions. The classes $\mathcal{P}$ and $\mathcal{NP}$ of solvable decision problems and the theory of NP-completeness are introduced by analyzing the time complexity of Turing machines.

Chapters on LL and LR grammars are included to permit a presentation of formal language theory that serves as a foundation to a course in compiler design.

Since most students at this level have had little or no background in abstract mathematics, the presentation is designed not only to introduce the foundations of computer science but also to increase the student's mathematical sophistication. This is accomplished by a rigorous presentation of the concepts and theorems interspersed with a generous supply of examples and exercises.

Each chapter contains a set of exercises that reinforces and augments the material covered in the chapter. A student solutions manual is available that presents fully worked-out solutions for approximately one-third of the exercises. The exercises in the manual were chosen to complement the examples in the text. The number of an exercise whose solution is included in the manual is given in boldface.

The entire text can be comfortably covered in two semesters. However, since courses on the foundations of computing may emphasize different topics, the text was organized to allow the flexibility needed to design one-term courses that concentrate on one or two specific areas. Suggested outlines for such courses are:

Formal language and automata theory —
Chapters 1, 2, 3, 4, 5, 6, 7, 8, 9, 10

Computability and complexity theory —
Chapters 1, 2, 6, 9, 11, 12, 13, 14

Language design and parsing —
Chapters 1, 2, 3, 4, 5, 6, 15, 16

The following prerequisite table indicates the dependence of each chapter upon the preceding material.

Chapter	Prerequisite Chapters
1	—
2	1
3	2
4	3
5	3
6	2
7	3, 6
8	5, 7
9	2
10	8, 9
11	9
12	11
13	12
14	13
15	4, 5, 6
16	15

A number of people made significant contributions to this book. Professors Andrew Astromoff (San Francisco State University), Michael Harrison (University of California at Berkeley), David Hemmendinger (Wright State University), D. T. Lee (Northwestern University), C. L. Liu (University of Illinois at Urbana-Champaign), Kenneth Williams (Western Michigan University), and Hsu-Chun Yen (Iowa State University) reviewed the manuscript and offered many helpful suggestions. As usual, the unsung heroes of this book are the students who endured the preliminary versions of the manuscript.

I would also like to acknowledge the support received from the staff of Addison-Wesley Publishing Company. In particular, the assistance and congeniality of David Jackson and Judi Veoukas were greatly appreciated.

Thomas A. Sudkamp

Contents

PART III
Automata and Languages

CHAPTER 6
Finite Automata

CHAPTER 7
Regular Languages and Sets

CHAPTER 8

Pushdown Automata and Context-Free Languages

CHAPTER 9

Turing Machines

CHAPTER 10

The Chomsky Hierarchy

PART IV
Decidability and Computability

CHAPTER 14

Computational Complexity

PART V

Deterministic Parsing

CHAPTER 15

LL(*k*) Grammars

PART I

Introduction

CHAPTER 1

Mathematical Preliminaries

The study of formal languages has its roots in linguistics, mathematical logic and computer science. Phrase-structure grammars were developed to provide a mechanism for describing natural (spoken) languages. Mathematicians interested in algorithmic computation designed abstract machines to study the capabilities and limitations of the computational process. The principles of computer language definition and compiler design have their foundations in these linguistic and mathematical studies.

The terminology and notation of formal languages is influenced by each of these disciplines. Because of the need for clarity and precision, mathematical notation is used extensively. This chapter introduces the mathematical concepts that will be used throughout this book.

1.1 Set Theory

We assume that the reader is familiar with the notions of elementary set theory. In this section, the concepts and notation of that theory are briefly reviewed. The symbol $\in$ signifies membership; $x \in X$ indicates that x is a member or element of the set X. A slash through a symbol represents *not*, so $x \notin X$ signifies that x is not a member of X. Two sets are equal if they contain the same members. Throughout this book, sets are denoted by capital letters. In particular, X, Y, and Z are used to represent arbitrary sets. Italics are used to denote the elements of a set. For example, symbols and strings of the form *a, b, A, B,* and *abc* represent elements of sets.

The brackets { } are used to indicate a set definition. Sets with a small number of members can be defined explicitly; that is, their members can be listed. The sets

$$X = \{1, 2, 3\}$$
$$Y = \{a, b, c, d, e\}$$

are defined in an explicit manner. Sets having a large finite or infinite number of members must be defined implicitly. A set is defined by specifying conditions that describe the elements of the set. The set consisting of all perfect squares is defined by

$$\{n \mid n = m^2 \text{ for some natural number } m\}.$$

The vertical bar | in an implicit definition is read "such that." The entire definition is read "the set of n such that n equals m squared for some natural number m."

The previous example mentions the set of **natural numbers.** This important set, denoted N, consists of the numbers 0, 1, 2, 3, ... The **empty set,** denoted Ø, is the set that has no members and can be defined explicitly by Ø = { }.

A set is determined completely by its membership; the order in which the elements are presented in the definition is immaterial. The explicit definitions of X, Y, and Z describe the same set.

$$X = \{1, 2, 3\}$$
$$Y = \{2, 1, 3\}$$
$$Z = \{1, 3, 2, 2, 2\}$$

The definition of Z contains multiple instances of the number 2. Repetition in the definition of a set does not affect the membership. Set equality requires that the sets have exactly the same members, and this is the case; each of the sets X, Y, and Z has the natural numbers 1, 2, and 3 as its members.

Set Y is a **subset** of X, written $Y \subseteq X$, if every member of Y is also a member of X. The empty set is trivially a subset of every set. Every set X is a subset of itself. If Y is a subset of X and $Y \neq X$, then Y is called a **proper subset** of X. The set of all subsets of X is called the **power set** of X and is denoted $\mathcal{P}(X)$.

Example 1.1.1

Let X = {1, 2, 3}. The subsets of X are

Ø   {1}   {2}   {3}
{1, 2}   {2, 3}   {3, 1}   {1, 2, 3}.   □

Set operations are used to construct new sets from existing ones. The **union** of two sets is defined by

$$X \cup Y = \{z \mid z \in X \text{ or } z \in Y\}.$$

The *or* is inclusive. This means that z is a member of $X \cup Y$ if it is a member of X or

Y or both. The **intersection** of two sets is the set of elements common to both. This is defined by

$$X \cap Y = \{z \mid z \in X \text{ and } z \in Y\}.$$

Two sets whose intersection is empty are said to be **disjoint**. The union and intersection of n sets, $X_1, X_2, \ldots, X_n$, are defined by

$$\bigcup_{i=1}^{n} X_i = X_1 \cup X_2 \cup \cdots \cup X_n = \{x \mid x \in X_i, \text{ for some } i = 1, 2, \ldots, n\}$$

$$\bigcap_{i=1}^{n} X_i = X_1 \cap X_2 \cap \cdots \cap X_n = \{x \mid x \in X_i, \text{ for all } i = 1, 2, \ldots, n\}$$

respectively.

Subsets $X_1, X_2, \ldots, X_n$ of a set X are said to **partition** X if

i) $X = \bigcup_{i=1}^{n} X_i$

ii) $X_i \cap X_j = \emptyset$, for $1 \leq i, j \leq n$, and $i \neq j$.

For example, the set of even natural numbers (zero is considered even) and the set of odd natural numbers partition **N**.

The **difference** of sets X and Y, $X - Y$, consists of the elements of X that are not in Y.

$$X - Y = \{z \mid z \in X \text{ and } z \notin Y\}$$

Let X be a subset of U. The **complement** of X with respect to U is the set of elements in U but not in X. In other words, the complement of X with respect to U is the set $U - X$. When the set U is known, the complement of X with respect to U is denoted $\bar{X}$. The following identities, known as DeMorgan's laws, exhibit the relationships between union, intersection, and complement when X and Y are subsets of a set U and complementation is taken with respect to U.

i) $\overline{(X \cup Y)} = \bar{X} \cap \bar{Y}$

ii) $\overline{(X \cap Y)} = \bar{X} \cup \bar{Y}$

Example 1.1.2

Let $X = \{0, 1, 2, 3\}$ and $Y = \{2, 3, 4, 5\}$. $\bar{X}$ and $\bar{Y}$ denote the complement of X and Y with respect to **N**.

$$X \cup Y = \{0, 1, 2, 3, 4, 5\} \qquad \bar{X} = \{n \mid n > 3\}$$
$$X \cap Y = \{2, 3\} \qquad \bar{Y} = \{0, 1\} \cup \{n \mid n > 5\}$$
$$X - Y = \{0, 1\} \qquad \overline{(X \cup Y)} = \{n \mid n > 5\}$$
$$Y - X = \{4, 5\} \qquad \bar{X} \cap \bar{Y} = \{n \mid n > 5\} \qquad \square$$

Set equality is usually defined using set inclusion. Two sets X and Y are equal if $X \subseteq Y$ and $Y \subseteq X$. This simply states that every element of X is also an element of Y and vice versa. When establishing the equality of two sets, the two inclusions are usually proved separately and combined to yield the equality.

Example 1.1.3

We prove that the sets

$$X = \{n \mid n = m^2 \text{ for some natural number } m > 0\},$$
$$Y = \{n^2 + 2n + 1 \mid n \geq 0\}$$

are equal. First we show that every element of X is also an element of Y. Let $x \in X$; then $x = m^2$ for some natural number $m > 0$. Let m_0 be that number. Then x can be written

$$x = m_0^2$$
$$= (m_0 - 1 + 1)^2$$
$$= (m_0 - 1)^2 + 2(m_0 - 1) + 1.$$

Consequently, x is a member of the set Y.

We now establish the opposite inclusion. Let $y = n_0^2 + 2n_0 + 1$ be an element of Y. Factoring yields $y = (n_0 + 1)^2$. Thus y is the square of a natural number greater than zero and therefore an element of X.

Since $X \subseteq Y$ and $Y \subseteq X$, we conclude that $X = Y$. □

1.2   Cartesian Product, Relations, and Functions

The **Cartesian product** is a set operation that builds a set consisting of ordered pairs of elements from two existing sets. The Cartesian product of sets X and Y, denoted $X \times Y$, is defined by

$$X \times Y = \{[x, y] \mid x \in X \text{ and } y \in Y\}.$$

The Cartesian product of a set X with itself is denoted X^2.

A **binary relation** on X and Y is a subset of $X \times Y$. The ordering of the natural numbers can be used to generate a relation LT (less than) on the set $\mathbf{N} \times \mathbf{N}$. This relation is the subset of $\mathbf{N} \times \mathbf{N}$ defined by

$$LT = \{[i, j] \mid i < j \text{ and } i, j \in \mathbf{N}\}.$$

The notation $[i, j] \in LT$ indicates that i is less than j. For example, $[0, 1], [0, 2] \in LT$ and $[1, 1] \notin LT$.

The Cartesian product can be generalized to construct new sets from any finite number of sets. If $x_1, x_2, \ldots, x_n$ are n elements, then $[x_1, x_2, \ldots, x_n]$ is called an **ordered n-tuple.** An ordered pair is simply another name for an ordered 2-tuple. Ordered

3-tuples, 4-tuples, and 5-tuples are commonly referred to as triples, quadruples, and quintuples, respectively. The Cartesian product of n sets $X_1, X_2, \ldots, X_n$ is defined by

$$X_1 \times X_2 \times \cdots \times X_n = \{[x_1, x_2, \ldots, x_n] \mid x_i \in X_i \text{ for } i = 1, 2, \ldots, n\}.$$

The Cartesian product of a set X with itself n times is denoted X^n. An **n-ary relation** on $X_1, X_2, \ldots, X_n$ is a subset of $X_1 \times X_2 \times \cdots \times X_n$. 1-ary, 2-ary, and 3-ary relations are called unary, binary, and ternary, respectively.

Example 1.2.1

Let X = {1, 2, 3} and Y = {a, b}.

a) $X \times Y = \{[1, a], [1, b], [2, a], [2, b], [3, a], [3, b]\}$

b) $Y \times X = \{[a, 1], [a, 2], [a, 3], [b, 1], [b, 2], [b, 3]\}$

c) $Y \times Y = Y^2 = \{[a, a], [a, b], [b, a], [b, b]\}$

d) $X \times Y \times Y = X \times Y^2 =$
$$\{[1, a, a], [1, b, a], [2, a, a], [2, b, a], [3, a, a], [3, b, a]$$
$$[1, a, b], [1, b, b], [2, a, b], [2, b, b], [3, a, b], [3, b, b]\} \qquad \square$$

Informally, a **function** from a set X to a set Y is a mapping of elements of X to elements of Y. Each member of X is mapped to at most one element of Y. A function f from X to Y is denoted $f: X \to Y$. The element of Y assigned by the function f to an element $x \in X$ is denoted $f(x)$. The set X is called the **domain** of the function. The **range** of f is the subset of Y consisting of the members of Y that are assigned to elements of X. The range of a function f is the set $\{y \in Y \mid y = f(x) \text{ for some } x \in X\}$.

The relationship that assigns to each person his or her age is a function from the set of people to the natural numbers. Note that an element in the range may be assigned to more than one element of the domain—there are many people who have the same age. Moreover, not all natural numbers are in the range of the function; it is unlikely that the number 1000 is assigned to anyone.

The domain of a function is a set, but this set is often the Cartesian product of two or more sets. A function

$$f: X_1 \times X_2 \times \cdots \times X_n \to Y$$

is said to be an **n-variable function** or operation. The value of the function with variables $x_1, x_2, \ldots, x_n$ is denoted $f(x_1, x_2, \ldots, x_n)$. Functions with one, two, and three variables are often referred to as unary, binary, and ternary operations. The variables $x_1, x_2, \ldots, x_n$ are also called the arguments of the functions. The function $sq: N \to N$ that assigns n^2 to each natural number is a unary operation. When the domain of a function consists of the Cartesian product of a set X with itself, the function is simply said to be a binary operation on X. Addition and multiplication are examples of binary operations on **N**.

A function f relates members of the domain to members of the range of f. A natural definition of function is in terms of this relation. A **total function** f from X to Y is a binary relation on X × Y that satisfies the following two properties:

i) For each $x \in$ X there is a $y \in$ Y such that $[x, y] \in f$.

ii) If $[x, y_1] \in f$ and $[x, y_2] \in f$ then $y_1 = y_2$.

Condition i) guarantees that each element of X is assigned a member of Y, hence the term total. The second condition ensures that this assignment is unique. The previously defined relation LT is not a total function since it does not satisfy the second condition. A relation on N × N representing *greater than* fails to satisfy either of the conditions. Why?

Example 1.2.2

Let X = {1, 2, 3} and Y = {a, b}. The eight total functions from X to Y are listed below.

x	$f(x)$		x	$f(x)$		x	$f(x)$		x	$f(x)$
1	a		1	a		1	a		1	b
2	a		2	a		2	b		2	a
3	a		3	b		3	a		3	a

x	$f(x)$		x	$f(x)$		x	$f(x)$		x	$f(x)$
1	a		1	b		1	b		1	b
2	b		2	a		2	b		2	b
3	b		3	b		3	a		3	b

A **partial function** f from X to Y is a relation on X × Y in which $y_1 = y_2$ whenever $[x, y_1] \in f$ and $[x, y_2] \in f$. A partial function f is defined for an argument x if there is a $y \in$ Y such that $[x, y] \in f$. Otherwise, f is undefined for x. A total function is simply a partial function defined for all elements of the domain.

Although functions have been formally defined in terms of relations, we will use the standard function notation $f(x) = y$ to indicate that y is the value assigned to x by the function f, that is, that $[x, y] \in f$. The notation $f(x)\uparrow$ indicates that the partial function f is undefined for the argument x. The notation $f(x)\downarrow$ is used to show that $f(x)$ is defined without explicitly giving its value.

Integer division defines a binary partial function *div* from N × N to N. The quotient obtained from the division of i by j, when defined, is assigned to $div(i, j)$. For example, $div(3, 2) = 1$, $div(4, 2) = 2$, and $div(1, 2) = 0$. Using the previous notation, $div(i, 0)\uparrow$ and $div(i, j)\downarrow$ for all other values of j.

A total function f: X → Y is said to be **one-to-one** if each element of X maps to a distinct element in the range. Formally, f is one-to-one if $x_1 \neq x_2$ implies $f(x_1) \neq f(x_2)$. A function f: X → Y is said to be **onto** if the range of f is the entire set Y. A total function that is both one-to-one and onto defines a correspondence between the elements of domain and the range.

Example 1.2.3

The functions f, g, and h are defined from N to $N - \{0\}$, the set of positive natural numbers.

a) $f(n) = 2n + 1$

b) $g(n) = \begin{cases} 1 & \text{if } n = 0 \\ n & \text{otherwise} \end{cases}$

c) $s(n) = n + 1$

The function f is one-to-one but not onto. The range of f consists of the odd numbers. The mapping from N to $N - \{0\}$ defined by g is clearly onto but not one-to-one. The function s is both one-to-one and onto, defining a correspondence that maps each natural number to its successor. □

1.3 Countable and Uncountable Sets

Cardinality is a measure that compares the size of sets. Intuitively, the cardinality of a set is the number of elements in the set. This informal definition is sufficient when dealing with finite sets, the cardinality can be obtained by counting the elements of the set. There are obvious difficulties in extending this approach to infinite sets.

Two finite sets can be shown to have the same number of elements by constructing a one-to-one correspondence between the elements of the sets. For example, the mapping

$$
\begin{array}{ccc}
a & \longrightarrow & 1 \\
b & \longrightarrow & 2 \\
c & \longrightarrow & 3
\end{array}
$$

demonstrates that the sets $\{a, b, c\}$ and $\{1, 2, 3\}$ have the same size. This approach, comparing sets using mappings, works equally well for sets with a finite or infinite number of members.

Definition 1.3.1

i) Two sets X and Y have the same cardinality if there is a total one-to-one function from X onto Y.

ii) The cardinality of a set X is less than or equal to the cardinality of a set Y if there is total one-to-one function from X into Y.

The cardinality of a set X is denoted $card(X)$. The relationships in i) and ii) are denoted $card(X) = card(Y)$ and $card(X) \leq card(Y)$, respectively. The cardinality of X is said to be strictly less than that of Y, written $card(X) < card(Y)$, if $card(X) \leqslant card(Y)$ and $card(X) \neq card(Y)$.

The cardinality of a finite set is denoted by the number of elements in the set. Thus $card(\{a, b\}) = 2$. A set that has the same cardinality as the set of natural numbers is said to be **countably infinite** or **denumerable**. The term **countable** refers to sets that are either finite or denumerable. A set that is not countable is said to be **uncountable.**

The set $N - \{0\}$ is countably infinite; the function $s(n) = n + 1$ defines a one-to-one mapping from N onto $N - \{0\}$. It may seem paradoxical that the set $N - \{0\}$, obtained by removing an element from N, has the same number of elements of N. Clearly, there is no one-to-one mapping of a finite set onto a proper subset of itself. It is this property that differentiates finite and infinite sets.

Definition 1.3.2
A set is **infinite** if it has a proper subset of the same cardinality.

Example 1.3.1

The set of odd natural numbers is denumerable. The function $f(n) = 2n + 1$ from Example 1.2.3 establishes the one-to-one correspondence between N and the odd numbers.   □

A set is countably infinite if its elements can be put in a one-to-one correspondence with the natural numbers. A diagram of a mapping from N onto a set graphically exhibits the countability of the set. The one-to-one correspondence between the natural numbers and the set of all integers

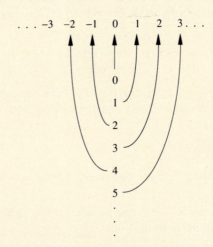

exhibits the countability of the set of integers. This correspondence is defined by the function

$$f(n) = \begin{cases} div(n,\ 2) + 1 & \text{if } n \text{ is odd} \\ -div(n,\ 2) & \text{if } n \text{ is even.} \end{cases}$$

Example 1.3.2

The points of an infinite two-dimensional grid can be used to show that $\mathbf{N} \times \mathbf{N}$, the set of ordered pairs of natural numbers, is denumerable. The grid is constructed by labeling the axes with the natural numbers. The position defined by row i and column j represents the ordered pair $[i,\ j]$.

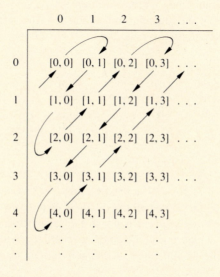

The elements of the grid can be listed sequentially by following the arrows in the diagram. This creates the correspondence

0	1	2	3	4	5	6	7	...
↓	↓	↓	↓	↓	↓	↓	↓	
[0, 0]	[0, 1]	[1, 0]	[2, 0]	[1, 1]	[0, 2]	[0, 3]	[1, 2]	...,

which demonstrates the countability of $\mathbf{N} \times \mathbf{N}$.   □

The sets of interest in language theory and computability are almost exclusively finite or denumerable. We state, without proof, several closure properties of countable sets.

Theorem 1.3.3

i) The union of two countable sets is countable.

ii) The Cartesian product of two countable sets is countable.

iii) The set of finite subsets of a countable set is countable.

iv) The set of finite-length sequences consisting of elements of a nonempty countable set is countably infinite.

Two total functions $f: \mathbf{N} \to \mathbf{N}$ and $g: \mathbf{N} \to \mathbf{N}$ are equal if they assume the same value for every element in the domain. That is, $f = g$ if $f(n) = g(n)$ for all $n \in \mathbf{N}$. To show that two functions are distinct, it suffices to find a single input value for which the functions differ. We will show that the set of total functions from $\mathbf{N}$ to $\mathbf{N}$ is uncountable.

A set is uncountable if it is impossible to sequentially list its members. The following proof technique, originated by Cantor, is known as the diagonalization argument. Assume that the set is denumerable. Then there is a sequence $f_0, f_1, f_2, \ldots$ that contains all the functions. The values of the functions are exhibited in the two-dimensional grid with the input values on the horizontal axis and the functions on the vertical axis.

	0	1	2	3	4	$\cdots$
f_0	$f_0(0)$	$f_0(1)$	$f_0(2)$	$f_0(3)$	$f_0(4)$	$\cdots$
f_1	$f_1(0)$	$f_1(1)$	$f_1(2)$	$f_1(3)$	$f_1(4)$	$\cdots$
f_2	$f_2(0)$	$f_2(1)$	$f_2(2)$	$f_2(3)$	$f_2(4)$	$\cdots$
f_3	$f_3(0)$	$f_3(1)$	$f_3(2)$	$f_3(3)$	$f_3(4)$	$\cdots$
f_4	$f_4(0)$	$f_4(1)$	$f_4(2)$	$f_4(3)$	$f_4(4)$	$\cdots$

Consider the function $f: \mathbf{N} \to \mathbf{N}$ defined by $f(n) = f_n(n) + 1$. The values of f are obtained by adding one to the values on the diagonal of the grid. By the definition of f, $f(i) \neq f_i(i)$ for every i. Consequently, f is not in the sequence $f_0, f_1, f_2, \ldots$. This is a contradiction since the sequence was assumed to contain all the total functions. The assumption that the number of functions is countably infinite leads to a contradiction. It follows that the set is uncountable.

Example 1.3.3

$\mathcal{P}(\mathbf{N})$, the set of subsets of $\mathbf{N}$, is uncountable. Assume that the subsets of $\mathbf{N}$ are countable. Then they can be listed $N_0, N_1, N_2, \ldots$. Define a subset D of $\mathbf{N}$ as follows: for every natural number j,

$$j \in D \text{ if, and only if, } j \notin N_j.$$

D is clearly a subset of $\mathbf{N}$. By our assumption, $N_0, N_1, N_2, \ldots$ is an exhaustive listing of the subsets of $\mathbf{N}$. Hence, $D = N_i$ for some i. Is the number i in the set D? By definition of D,

$$i \in D \text{ if, and only if, } i \notin N_i.$$

But since $D = N_i$, this becomes

$$i \in N_i \text{ if, and only if, } i \notin N_i.$$

We have shown that $i \in D$ if, and only if, $i \notin D$, which is a contradiction. Thus our assumption, that $\mathcal{P}(\mathbf{N})$ is countable, must be false and we conclude that $\mathcal{P}(\mathbf{N})$ is uncountable.

To appreciate the "diagonal" technique, consider a two-dimensional grid with the natural numbers on the horizontal axis and the vertical axis labeled by the sets N_0, N_1, N_2, ... The position of the grid designated by row N_i and column j contains *yes* if $j \in N_i$. Otherwise, the position defined by N_i and j contains *no*. The set D is constructed by considering the relationship between the entries along the diagonal of the grid: the number j and the set N_j. The number j is an element of D if, and only if, the entry at position N_j, j is *no*.   □

1.4   Recursive Definitions

Many of the sets involved in the generation of languages contain an infinite number of elements. We must be able to define an infinite set in a manner that allows its members to be constructed and manipulated. The description of the natural numbers avoided this by utilizing ellipsis dots (. . .). This seemed reasonable since everyone reading this text is familiar with the natural numbers and knows what comes after 0, 1, 2, 3. However, an alien unfamiliar with our base 10 arithmetic system and numeric representations would have no idea that the symbol 4 is the next element in the sequence.

In the development of a mathematical theory, such as the theory of languages or automata, the theorems and proofs may utilize only the definitions of the concepts of that theory. This requires precise definitions of both the objects of the domain and the operations. A method of definition must be developed that enables our friend the alien, or a computer that has no intuition, to generate and "understand" the properties of the elements of a set.

A **recursive definition** of a set X specifies a method for constructing the elements of the set. The definition utilizes two components: the basis elements and a finite set of operators. The basis consists of a set of elements that are explicitly designated as members of X. The operators are used to construct new elements of the set from the previously defined members. The recursively defined set X consists of all elements that can be generated from the basis elements by a finite number of applications of the operators.

The key word in the process of recursively defining a set is *generate*. Clearly, no process can list the complete set of natural numbers. Any particular number, however, can be obtained by beginning with zero and constructing an initial sequence of the natural numbers. This intuitively describes the process of recursively defining the natural numbers. This idea is formalized in the following definition.

Definition 1.4.1

A recursive definition of $\mathbf{N}$, the set of natural numbers, is constructed using the successor function s.

i) Basis: $0 \in \mathbf{N}$.

ii) Recursive step: If $n \in \mathbf{N}$, then $s(n) \in \mathbf{N}$.

iii) Closure: $n \in \mathbf{N}$ only if it can be obtained from 0 by a finite number of applications of the operation s.

The basis explicitly states that 0 is a natural number. In ii), a new natural number is defined in terms of a previously defined number and the successor operation. The closure section guarantees that the set contains only those members that can be obtained from 0 using the successor operator. Definition 1.4.1 generates an infinite sequence $0, s(0), s(s(0)), s(s(s(0))), \ldots$. This sequence is usually abbreviated $0, 1, 2, 3, \ldots$. However, anything that can be done with the familiar Arabic numerals could also be done with the more cumbersome unabbreviated representation.

The essence of a recursive procedure is to define complicated processes or structures in terms of simpler instances of the same process or structure. In the case of the natural numbers, simpler often means smaller. The recursive step of Definition 1.4.1 defines a number in terms of its predecessor.

The natural numbers have now been defined, but what does it mean to understand their properties? We usually associate operations of addition, multiplication, and subtraction with the natural numbers. We may have learned these by brute force, by either memorization or tedious repetition. For the alien or a computer to perform addition, the meaning of "add" must be appropriately defined. One cannot memorize the sum of all possible combinations of natural numbers, but we can use recursion to establish a method by which the sum of any two numbers can be mechanically calculated. The successor function is the only operation on the natural numbers that has been introduced. Thus the definition of addition may use only 0 and s.

Definition 1.4.2

Recursive definition of the sum of m and n. The recursion is done on n, the second member of the sum.

i) Basis: If $n = 0$, then $m + n = m$.

ii) Recursive step: $m + s(n) = s(m + n)$.

iii) Closure: $m + n = k$ only if this equality can be obtained from $m + 0 = m$ using finitely many applications of the operation in ii).

The closure step is often omitted from a recursive definition of an operation on a given domain. In this case, it is assumed that the operation is defined on all the elements of the domain. The addition operation given above is defined for all elements of $\mathbf{N} \times \mathbf{N}$.

The sum of m and the successor of n is defined in terms of the simpler case, the sum of m and n, and the successor operation. The choice of n as the recursive operand was arbitrary; the operation could also have been defined in terms of m with n fixed.

With this definition, the sum of any two natural numbers can be computed using 0 and s, the primitives used in the definition of the natural numbers, and Definition 1.4.2. Example 1.4.1 traces the recursive computation of $3 + 2$.

Example 1.4.1

The numbers 3 and 2 abbreviate $s(s(s(0)))$ and $s(s(0))$, respectively. The sum is computed recursively by

$$
\begin{aligned}
&s(s(s(0))) + s(s(0)) \\
=\ &s(s(s(s(0))) + s(0)) \\
=\ &s(s(s(s(s(0))) + 0)) \\
=\ &s(s(s(s(s(0))))) \qquad \text{'basis case.'}
\end{aligned}
$$

This final value is the representation of the number 5. □

Figure 1.1 illustrates the process of recursively generating a set X from basis X_0. Each of the concentric circles represents a stage of the construction. X_1 represents the basis elements and the elements that can be obtained from them using a single application of an operator. X_i contains the elements that can be constructed with i or fewer operations. The generation process in the recursive portion of the definition produces a countably infinite sequence of nested sets. The set X can be thought of as the infinite union of the X_i's. Let x be an element of X and let X_j be the first set in which x occurs. This means that x can be constructed from the basis elements using exactly j applications of the operators. Although each element of X can be generated in a finite number of applications of the operators, there is no upper bound on the number of applications needed to generate the entire set X. This property, generation using a finite but unbounded number of operations, is a fundamental property of recursive definitions.

The successor operator can be used recursively to define relations on the $N \times N$. The Cartesian product $N \times N$ is often portrayed by the grid of points representing the ordered pairs. Following the standard conventions, the horizontal axis represents the first component of the ordered pair and the vertical axis the second. The shaded area in Fig. 1.2(a) contains the ordered pairs $[i, j]$ in which $i < j$. This set is the relation LT, less than, which was described in Section 1.3.

Example 1.4.2

The relation LT is defined as follows:

i) Basis: $[0, 1] \in$ LT.

ii) Recursive step: If $[n, m] \in$ LT then $[n, s(m)] \in$ LT and $[s(n), s(m)] \in$ LT.

iii) Closure: $[n, m] \in$ LT only if it can be obtained from $[0, 1]$ by a finite number of applications of the operations in ii).

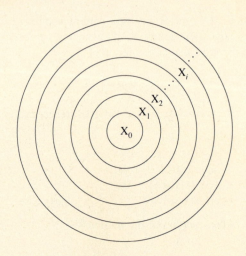

Recursive generation of X:

$X_0 = \{x \mid x \text{ is a basis element}\}$

$X_{i+1} = X_i \cup \{x \mid x \text{ can be generated by } i + 1 \text{ operations}\}$

$X = \{x \mid x \in X_j \text{ for some } j \geq 0\}$

FIGURE 1.1 Nested sequence of sets in recursive definition.

Using the infinite union description of recursive generation, the definition of LT generates the sequence LT_i of nested sets where

$$LT_0 = \{[0, 1]\}$$
$$LT_1 = \{[0, 2], [1, 2]\} \cup LT_0$$
$$LT_2 = \{[0, 3], [1, 3], [2, 3]\} \cup LT_1$$
$$LT_3 = \{[0, 4], [1, 4], [2, 4], [3, 4]\} \cup LT_2$$

$$\vdots$$

$$LT_i = \{[j, i + 1] \mid j = 0, 1, \ldots, i\} \cup LT_{i-1}$$

$$\vdots$$

□

The generation of an element in a recursively defined set may not be unique. The ordered pair $[1, 3] \in LT_2$ is generated by two distinct sequences of operations.

Basis: [0, 1]   [0,1]

1:    $[0, s(1)] = [0, 2]$ $[s(0), s(1)] = [1, 2]$

2:    $[s(0), s(2)] = [1, 3]$ $[1, s(2)] = [1, 3]$

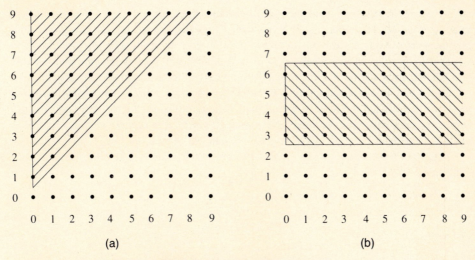

FIGURE 1.2   Relations on **N** × **N**.

Example 1.4.3

The shaded area in Fig. 1.2(b) contains all the ordered pairs with second component 3, 4, 5, or 6. A recursive definition of this set, call it X, is given below.

   i) Basis: [0, 3], [0, 4], [0, 5], and [0, 6] are in X.
  ii) Recursive step: If $[n, m] \in$ X, then $[s(n), m] \in$ X.
 iii) Closure: $[n, m] \in$ X only if it can be obtained from i) by a finite number of applications of the operations in ii).

The sequence of sets X_i generated by this recursive process are defined by

$$X_i = \{[j, 3], [j, 4], [j, 5], [j, 6] \mid j = 0, 1, \ldots, i\}. \qquad \Box$$

1.5   Directed Graphs

A mathematical structure consists of functions and relations on a set or sets and distinguished elements from the sets. A distinguished element is an element of a set that has special properties that distinguish it from the other elements. The natural numbers, as defined in Definition 1.4.1, can be expressed as a structure (**N**, s, 0). The set **N** contains the natural numbers; s is a unary function on **N**, and 0 is a distinguished element of **N**. Zero is distinguished because of its explicit role in the definition of the natural numbers.

A **directed graph** is a mathematical structure consisting of a set N and a binary relation A on N. The elements of N are called the nodes or vertices of the graph, and the members of A are called arcs or edges. A is referred to as the adjacency relation and y is said to be adjacent to x when $[x, y] \in A$. The ability to portray the essential features of a mathematical entity in a diagram aids the intuitive understanding of the concept. An arc from x to y in a directed graph is depicted by an arrow from x to y. Using the arrow metaphor, y is called the head of the arc and x the tail. The **in-degree** of a node x is the number of arcs with x as the head. The **out-degree** of x is the number of arcs with x as the tail. Node a in Fig. 1.3 has in-degree two and out-degree one.

A **path** of length n from x to y in a directed graph is a sequence of nodes $x_0, x_1, \ldots, x_n$ satisfying

i) x_i is adjacent to x_{i-1}, for $i = 1, 2, \ldots, n$

ii) $x = x_0$

iii) $y = x_n$.

The node x is the initial node of the path and y is the terminal node. There is a path of length zero from any node to itself called the **null path**. A path of length one or more that begins and ends with the same node is called a **cycle**. A cycle is **simple** if it does not contain a cyclic subpath. The path a, b, c, d, a in Fig. 1.3 is a simple cycle of length four. A directed graph containing at least one cycle is said to be **cyclic**. A graph with no cycles is said to be **acyclic**.

The arcs of a directed graph often designate more than the adjacency of the nodes. A labeled directed graph is a structure (N, L, A) where L is the set of labels and A is a relation on N × N × L. An element $[x, y, v] \in A$ is an arc from x to y labeled by v. The label on an arc specifies a relationship between the adjacent nodes. The labels on the graph in Fig. 1.4 indicate the distances of the legs of a trip from Chicago to Minneapolis, Seattle, San Francisco, Dallas, St. Louis, and back to Chicago.

N = {a, b, c, d}

A = [(a, b), (b, a), (b, c), (b, d), (c, b), (c, d), (d, a), (d, d)]

Node	In-degree	Out-degree
a	2	1
b	2	3
c	1	2
d	3	2

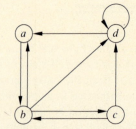

FIGURE 1.3 Directed graph.

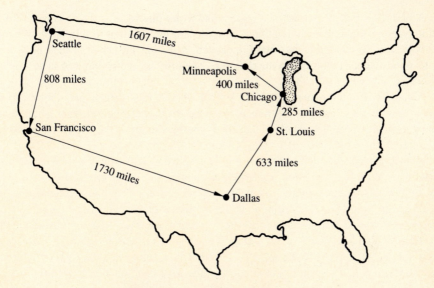

FIGURE 1.4 Labeled directed graph.

An **ordered tree,** or simply a tree, is an acyclic directed graph in which each node is connected by a unique path from a distinguished node called the **root** of the tree. The root has in-degree zero and all other nodes have in-degree one. A tree is a structure (N, A, r) where N is the set of nodes, A is the adjacency relation, and $r \in$ N is the root of the tree. The terminology of trees combines a mixture of references to family trees and to those of the arboreal nature. Although a tree is a directed graph, the arrows on the arcs are usually omitted in the illustrations of trees. Figure 1.5 gives a tree T with root x_1.

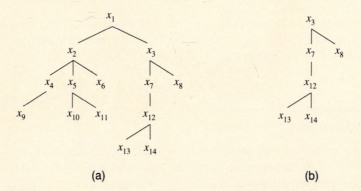

(a)   (b)

FIGURE 1.5 Ordered trees. (a) Tree T. (b) Subtree generated by x_3.

A node y is called a **child** of a node x and x the **parent** of y if y is adjacent to x. Accompanying the adjacency relation is an order on the children of any node. When a tree is drawn, this ordering is usually indicated by listing the children of a node in a left-to-right manner according to the ordering. The order of the children of x_2 in T is x_4, x_5, and x_6.

A node with out-degree zero is called a **leaf**. All other nodes are referred to as internal nodes. The **depth** of the root is zero; the depth of any other node is the depth of its parent plus one. The depth of the tree is the maximum of the depths of the nodes in the tree.

A node y is called a **descendant** of a node x and x an **ancestor** of y if there is a path from x to y. With this definition, each node is an ancestor and descendant of itself. The ancestor and descendant relations can be defined recursively using the adjacency relation (Exercises 24 and 25). The **minimal common ancestor** of two nodes x and y is an ancestor of both and a descendant of all other common ancestors. The minimal common ancestor of x_{10} and x_{11} is x_5, of x_{10} and x_6 is x_2, and of x_{10} and x_{14} is x_1.

A subtree of a tree T is a subgraph of T that is a tree in its own right. The set of descendants of a node x and the restriction of the adjacency relation to this set form a subtree with root x. This tree is called the subtree generated by x.

The ordering of siblings in the tree can be extended to a relation LEFTOF on N $\times$ N. LEFTOF attempts to capture the property of one node being to the left of another in the diagram of a tree. For two nodes x and y, neither of which is an ancestor of the other, the relation LEFTOF is defined in terms of the subtrees generated by the minimal common ancestor of the nodes. Let z be the minimal common ancestor of x and y and let $z_1, z_2, \ldots, z_n$ be the children of z in their correct order. Then x is in the subtree generated by one of the children of z, call it z_i. Similarly, y is in the subtree generated by z_j for some j. Since z is the minimal common ancestor of x and y, $i \neq j$. If $i < j$, then LEFTOF(x, y); LEFTOF(y, x) otherwise. With this definition, no node is LEFTOF one of its ancestors. If x_{13} were to the left of x_{12}, then x_{10} must also be to the left of x_5, since they are both the first child of their parent. The appearance of being to the left or right of an ancestor is a feature of the diagram, not a property of the ordering of the nodes.

The relation LEFTOF can be used to order the set of leaves of a tree. The **frontier** of a tree is constructed from the leaves in the order generated by the relation LEFTOF. The frontier of T is the sequence $x_9, x_{10}, x_{11}, x_6, x_{13}, x_{14}, x_8$.

1.6 Mathematical Induction

Establishing the relationships between the sets and the operations of a structure requires the capability of constructing proofs to verify the hypothesized properties. It is impossible to prove a property holds for every member in an infinite set by considering each element individually. The principle of mathematical induction gives sufficient conditions for proving that a property holds for every element in a recursively defined set. Induction uses the family of nested sets generated by the recursive process to extend a property from the basis to the entire set.

Principle of mathematical induction   Let X be a set defined by recursion from the basis X_0 and let $X_0, X_1, X_2, \ldots, X_i, \ldots$ be the sequence of sets generated by the recursive process. Also let **P** be a property defined on the elements of X. If it can be shown that

i) **P** holds for each element in X_0,

ii) whenever **P** holds for every element in $X_0, X_1, \ldots, X_i$, **P** also holds for every element in X_{i+1},

then, by the principle of mathematical induction, **P** holds for every element in X.

The soundness of the principle of mathematical induction can be intuitively exhibited using the sequence of sets constructed by a recursive definition. Shading the circle X_i indicates that **P** holds for every element of X_i. The first condition requires that the interior set be shaded. Condition ii) states that the shading can be extended from any circle to the next concentric circle. Figure 1.6 illustrates how this process eventually shades the entire set X.

The justification for the principle of mathematical induction should be clear from the preceding argument. Another justification can be obtained by assuming that conditions i) and ii) are satisfied but **P** is not true for every element in X. If **P** does not hold for all elements of X, then there is at least one set X_i for which **P** does not universally hold. Let X_j be the first such set. Since condition i) asserts that **P** holds for all elements of X_0, j cannot be zero. Now **P** holds for all elements of X_{j-1} by our choice of j. Condition ii) then requires that **P** hold for all elements in X_j. This implies that there is no first set in the sequence for which the property **P** fails. Consequently, **P** must be true for all the X_i's, and therefore for X.

An inductive proof consists of three distinct steps. The first step is proving that the property **P** holds for each element of a basis set. This corresponds to establishing condition i) in the definition of the principle of mathematical induction. The second is the statement of the inductive hypothesis. The inductive hypothesis is the assumption that the property **P** holds for every element in the sets $X_0, X_1, \ldots, X_n$. The inductive step then proves, using the inductive hypothesis, that **P** can be extended to each element in X_{n+1}. Completing the inductive step satisfies the requirements of the principle of mathematical induction. Thus, it can be concluded that **P** is true for all elements of X.

To illustrate the steps of an inductive proof we use the natural numbers as the underlying recursively defined set. It is often the case that the basis consists of the single natural number zero. Example 1.6.2 shows that this is not necessary; an inductive proof can be initiated using any number n as the basis. The principle of mathematical induction then allows us to conclude that the property holds for all natural numbers greater than or equal to n.

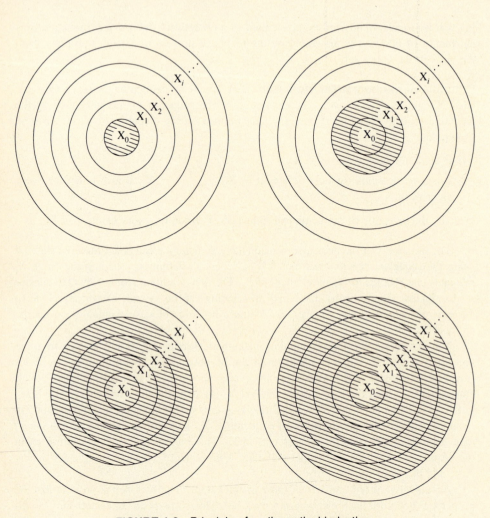

FIGURE 1.6 Principle of mathematical induction.

Example 1.6.1

Induction is used to prove that $0 + 1 + \cdots + n = n(n + 1)/2$. We will use the standard summation notation

$$\sum_{i=n_0}^{n_1} f(i) = f(n_0) + f(n_0 + 1) + \cdots + f(n_1),$$

where $n_0 \leq n_1$. Using this notation, the preceding expression can be written

$$\sum_{i=0}^{n} i = n(n + 1)/2.$$

Basis: The basis is $n = 0$. The relationship is explicitly established by computing the values of each of the sides of the equality.

$$\sum_{i=0}^{0} i = 0 = 0(0 + 1)/2.$$

Inductive Hypothesis: Assume for all values $k = 1, 2, \ldots, n$ that

$$\sum_{i=0}^{k} i = k(k + 1)/2.$$

Inductive Step: We need to prove that

$$\sum_{i=0}^{n+1} i = (n + 1)(n + 1 + 1)/2 = (n + 1)(n + 2)/2.$$

The inductive hypothesis must be used in the proof in the inductive step. The hypothesis establishes the result of the sum of the sequence containing n or fewer integers.

$$
\begin{aligned}
\sum_{i=0}^{n+1} i &= \sum_{i=0}^{n} i + (n + 1) && \text{'associativity of } +\text{'} \\
&= n(n + 1)/2 + (n + 1) && \text{'inductive hypothesis'} \\
&= (n + 1)(n/2 + 1) && \text{'distributive property'} \\
&= (n + 1)(n + 2)/2
\end{aligned}
$$

The conditions of the principle of mathematical induction have been established. Thus, we conclude that the result holds for all natural numbers. $\square$

Each step in the proof must follow from previously established properties of the operators or the inductive hypothesis. The strategy of an inductive proof is to manipulate the formula to contain an instance of the property applied to a simpler case. When this is accomplished, the inductive hypothesis may be invoked. After the application of the inductive hypothesis, the remainder of the proof often consists of algebraic operations to manipulate the result into the desired form.

Example 1.6.2

$n! > 2^n$, for $n \geq 4$.

Basis: $n = 4$. $4! = 24 > 16 = 2^4$.

Inductive Hypothesis: Assume that $k! > 2^k$ for all values $k = 4, 5, \ldots, n$.

Inductive Step: We need to prove that $(n + 1)! > 2^{n+1}$.

$$
\begin{aligned}
(n + 1)! &= n!(n + 1) \\
&> 2^n(n + 1) && \text{'inductive hypothesis'} \\
&> 2^n 2 && \text{'since } n + 1 > 2\text{'} \\
&= 2^{n+1}
\end{aligned}
$$
$\square$

The application of the inductive hypothesis in the preceding examples used only the assumption that the property in question was true for the previous natural number. This type of proof is sometimes referred to as **simple induction**. When the inductive step utilizes the full strength of the inductive hypothesis, that the property holds for all the preceding elements, the proof technique is called **strong induction**.

Example 1.6.3

A tree is called a **strictly binary tree** if every node either is a leaf or has precisely two children. A strictly binary tree can be defined recursively as follows:

 i) Basis: A directed graph $T = (\{r\}, \emptyset, r)$ is a strictly binary tree.

 ii) Recursive step: If $T_1 = (N_1, A_1, r_1)$ and $T_2 = (N_2, A_2, r_2)$ are strictly binary trees, N_1 and N_2 are disjoint, and $r \notin N_1 \cup N_2$, then

$$T = (N_1 \cup N_2 \cup \{r\}, A_1 \cup A_2 \cup \{[r, r_1], [r, r_2]\}, r)$$

is a strictly binary tree.

 iii) Closure: T is a strictly binary tree only if it can be obtained from the basis elements by a finite number of applications of the construction outlined in ii).

A strictly binary tree is either a single node or constructed from two distinct strictly binary trees by the addition of a root and arcs to the two subtrees. Let $lv(T)$ and $arc(T)$ denote the number of leaves and arcs in a strictly binary tree T. We prove, by induction on the number of leaves, that $2lv(T) - 2 = arc(T)$ for all strictly binary trees.

Basis: The basis consists of strictly binary trees containing a single leaf, the trees defined by the basis condition of the recursive definition. The equality clearly holds for these trees.

Inductive Hypothesis: Assume that every strictly binary tree T with n or fewer leaves satisfies $2lv(T) - 2 = arc(T)$.

Inductive Step: Let T be a strictly binary tree with $n + 1$ leaves. T is constructed from a node r and two strictly binary trees T_1 and T_2 with roots r_1 and r_2, respectively.

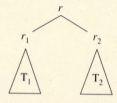

The node r is not a leaf since it has arcs to the roots of T_1 and T_2. Consequently, $lv(T) = lv(T_1) + lv(T_2)$. The arcs of T consist of the arcs of the component trees plus the two arcs from r.

Both of the subtrees of T are strictly binary trees with n or fewer leaves. Since each tree contains fewer than $n + 1$ leaves, we may employ strong induction to establish the desired equality. By the inductive hypothesis,

$$2lv(T_1) - 2 = arc(T_1)$$
$$2lv(T_2) - 2 = arc(T_2).$$

Now,

$$arc(T)$$
$$= arc(T_1) + arc(T_2) + 2$$
$$= 2lv(T_1) - 2 + 2lv(T_2) - 2 + 2$$
$$= 2(lv(T_1) + lv(T_2)) - 2$$
$$= 2(lv(T)) - 2$$

as desired.   □

The finite subsets of a set can be defined recursively using the binary operation union (Exercise 19). In Example 1.6.4, induction is used to establish the relationship between the cardinality of a finite set and that of its power set.

Example 1.6.4

Induction on the cardinality of X is used to show that $card(\mathscr{P}(X)) = 2^{card(X)}$ for any finite set X.

Basis: $card(X) = 0$. Then $X = \varnothing$ and $\mathscr{P}(X) = \{\varnothing\}$. So $2^{card(X)} = 2^0 = 1 = card(\mathscr{P}(X))$.

Inductive Hypothesis: Assume that $card(\mathscr{P}(X)) = 2^{card(X)}$ for all sets of cardinality $0, 1, \ldots, n$.

Inductive Step: Let X be any set of cardinality $n + 1$. The proof is completed by showing that $card(\mathscr{P}(X)) = 2^{card(X)}$. Since X is nonempty, it must contain at least one element. Choose an element $a \in X$. Let $Y = X - \{a\}$. Then $card(Y) = n$ and $card(\mathscr{P}(Y)) = 2^{card(Y)}$ by the inductive hypothesis.

The set of subsets of X can be partitioned into two disjoint subsets, those that contain the element a and those that do not contain a. The subsets of X that do not contain a are precisely the sets in $\mathscr{P}(Y)$. A subset of X containing a can be obtained by augmenting a subset of Y with the element a. Thus,

$$\mathscr{P}(X) = \mathscr{P}(Y) \cup \{Y_0 \cup \{a\} \mid Y_0 \in \mathscr{P}(Y)\}.$$

Since the two components of the union are disjoint, the cardinality of the union is the sum of the cardinalities of each of the sets.

$$card(\mathscr{P}(X)) = card(\mathscr{P}(Y)) + card(\{Y_0 \cup \{a\} \mid Y_0 \in \mathscr{P}(Y)\})$$
$$= card(\mathscr{P}(Y)) + card(\mathscr{P}(Y))$$
$$= 2^n + 2^n$$
$$= 2^{n+1}$$
$$= 2^{card(X)}$$

                                                                    □

Exercises

1. Let $X = \{1, 2, 3, 4\}$ and $Y = \{0, 2, 4, 6\}$. Explicitly define sets described in a) to e).
   a) $X \cup Y$
   b) $X \cap Y$
   c) $X - Y$
   d) $Y - X$
   e) $\mathcal{P}(X)$

2. Let $X = \{a, b, c\}$ and $Y = \{1, 2\}$.
   a) List all the subsets of X.
   b) List the members of $X \times Y$.
   c) List all total functions from Y to X.

3. Let $X = \{n^3 + 3n^2 + 3n \mid n \geqslant 0\}$ and $Y = \{n^3 - 1 \mid n > 0\}$. Prove that $X = Y$.

4. Prove DeMorgan's laws. Use the definition of set equality to establish the identities.

5. Prove that the set of even natural numbers is denumerable.

6. Prove that the set of nonnegative rational numbers is denumerable.

7. Prove that the union of two disjoint countable sets is countable.

8. Prove that the set of real numbers in the interval [0, 1] is uncountable. Hint: use the diagonalization argument on the decimal expansion of real numbers. Be sure that each number is represented by only one infinite decimal expansion.

9. Prove that there are an uncountable number of total functions from N to $\{0, 1\}$.

10. A total function f from N to N is said to be nonrepeating $f(n) \neq f(n + 1)$ for all $n \in N$. Otherwise, f is said to be repeating. Prove that there are an uncountable number of nonrepeating functions. Also, prove that there are an uncountable number of repeating functions.

11. A total function f from N to N is monotone increasing if $f(n) < f(n + 1)$ for all $n \in N$. Prove that there are an uncountable number of monotone increasing functions.

12. Give a recursive definition of the relation "greater than" on $N \times N$ using the successor operator s.

13. Give a recursive definition of the relation "is equal to" on $N \times N$ using the operator s.

14. Give a recursive definition of the operation of multiplication of natural numbers using the operations s and addition.

15. Give a recursive definition of the predecessor operation

$$pd(n) = \begin{cases} 0 & \text{if } n = 0 \\ n - 1 & \text{otherwise} \end{cases}$$

using the operator s.

16. Subtraction on the set of natural numbers is defined by

$$n \div m = \begin{cases} n - m & \text{if } n \geq m \\ 0 & \text{otherwise.} \end{cases}$$

This operation is often called **proper subtraction**. Give a recursive definition of proper subtraction using the operations s and pd.

17. Give a recursive definition of the set of points $[m, n]$ that lie on the line $n = 3m$ in $N \times N$. Use s as the operator in the definition.

18. Give a recursive definition of the set of points $[m, n]$ that lie on or under the line $n = 3m$ in $N \times N$. Use s as the operator in the definition.

19. Give a recursive definition of the set of finite subsets of N. Use union as the operator in the definition.

20. Prove that $2 + 5 + 8 + \cdots + (3n - 1) = n(3n+1)/2$ for all $n > 0$.

21. Prove that $1 + 2 + 2^2 + \cdots + 2^n = 2^{n+1} - 1$ for all $n \geq 0$.

22. Prove $1 + 2^n < 3^n$ for all $n > 2$.

23. Prove that 3 is a factor of $n^3 - n + 3$ for all $n \geq 0$.

24. Give a recursive definition of all the nodes in a directed graph that can be reached by paths from a given node x. Use the adjacency relation as the operation in the definition. This definition also defines the set of descendants of a node in a tree.

25. Give a recursive definition of the set of ancestors of a node x in a tree.

26. List the members of the relation LEFTOF for the tree in Fig. 1.5(a).

27. Using the tree below, give the values of each of the items in parts a) to e).

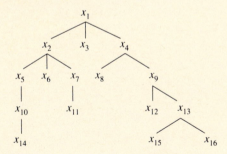

a) the depth of the tree
b) the ancestors of x_{11}
c) the minimal common ancestor of x_{14} and x_{11}, of x_{15} and x_{11}
d) the subtree generated by x_2
e) the frontier of the tree

28. Prove that a strictly binary tree with n leaves contains $2n - 1$ nodes.

29. A **complete binary tree** of depth n is a strictly binary tree in which every node on levels $1, 2, \ldots, n - 1$ is a parent and each node on level n is a leaf. Prove that a complete binary tree of depth n has $2^{n+1} - 1$ nodes.

Bibliographic Notes

This chapter reviews the topics normally covered in a first course in discrete mathematics. Introductory texts in discrete mathematics include Kolman and Busby [1984], Johnson-baugh [1984], Gersting [1982], Sahni [1981], and Tremblay and Manohar [1975]. A more sophisticated presentation of the discrete mathematical structures important to the foundations of computer science can be found in Bobrow and Arbib [1974].

There are a number of books that provide detailed presentations of the topics introduced in this chapter. An introduction to naive set theory can be found in Halmos [1974] and Stoll [1963]. The texts by Wilson [1985], Ore [1962], Bondy and Murty [1977], and Busacker and Saaty [1965] introduce the theory of graphs. The original presentation of Cantor's diagonalization argument is reproduced in Cantor [1947]. Induction, recursion, and their relationship to theoretical computer science are covered in Wand [1980].

CHAPTER 2

Languages

The concept of language includes a variety of seemingly distinct categories: natural languages, computer languages, and mathematical languages. A general definition of language must encompass these various types of languages. In this chapter, a purely set theoretic definition is presented. This is the broadest possible definition of language; there are no inherent restrictions on the form of the elements that comprise a language.

2.1 Strings and Languages

A **string** over a set X is a finite sequence of elements from X. Strings are the fundamental objects used in the definition of languages. The set of elements from which the strings are built is called the **alphabet** of the language. An alphabet consists of a finite set of indivisible elements. The alphabet of a language is denoted Σ.

The alphabet of a natural language, like English or French, consists of the words of the language. The words of the language are considered to be indivisible objects. The word *language* cannot be divided into *lang* and *uage*. The word *format* has no relation to the words *for* and *mat;* these are all distinct members of the alphabet. A string over this alphabet is a sequence of words. The sentence that you have just read, omitting the punctuation, is such a string. The alphabet of a computer language consists of the permissible keywords, variables, and symbols of the language. A string over this language is a sequence of computer code.

Because the elements of the alphabet of a language are indivisible, they are generally denoted by single characters. Letters *a, b, c, d, e,* with or without subscripts, are used to represent the elements of an alphabet. Strings over an alphabet are represented by letters occurring near the end of the alphabet. In particular *p, q, u, v, w, x, y, z* are used to denote strings. The notation used for natural languages and computer languages provides an exception to this convention. In these cases, the alphabet consists of elements of the particular language.

A string has been defined informally as a sequence of elements from an alphabet. In order to establish the properties of strings, the set of strings over an alphabet is defined recursively. The basis consists of the string containing no elements. This string is called the **null string** and denoted λ. The primitive operator used in the definition consists of adjoining a single element from the alphabet to the right-hand side of an existing string.

Definition 2.1.1

Let Σ be an alphabet. Σ^*, the set of strings over Σ, is defined recursively as follows:

  i) Basis: $\lambda \in \Sigma^*$.

  ii) Recursive step: If $w \in \Sigma^*$ and $a \in \Sigma$ then $wa \in \Sigma^*$.

  iii) Closure: $w \in \Sigma^*$ only if it can be obtained from λ by a finite number of applications of the operator in ii).

For any nonempty alphabet Σ, Σ^* contains infinitely many elements. If $\Sigma = \{a\}$, Σ^* contains the strings $\lambda, a, aa, aaa, \ldots$. The length of a string w, intuitively the number of elements in the string or formally the number of applications of the operator needed to construct the string, is denoted $length(w)$. If Σ contains n elements, then there are n^k strings of length k in Σ^*.

Example 2.1.1

Let $\Sigma = \{a, b, c\}$. The elements of Σ^* include

> Length 0: λ
> Length 1: *a b c*
> Length 2: *aa ab ac ba bb bc ca cb cc*
> Length 3: *aaa aab aac aba abb abc aca acb acc*
>   *baa bab bac bba bbb bbc bca bcb bcc*
>   *caa cab cac cba cbb cbc cca ccb ccc*   □

A language consists of strings over an alphabet. Usually some restrictions are placed on the strings that comprise the language. The English language consists of those strings of words that we call sentences. Not all strings of words form sentences in a language, only those satisfying certain conditions on the order and type of the constituent words. Consequently, a language consists of a subset of the set of all possible strings over the alphabet.

Definition 2.1.2
A **language** over an alphabet Σ is a subset of Σ^*.

Since strings are the elements of a language, we must examine the properties of strings and the operations on them. Concatenation is the binary operation of taking two strings and "gluing them together" to construct a new string. Concatenation is the fundamental operation in the generation of strings. A formal definition is given by recursion on the length of the second string in the concatenation. At this point, the primitive operation of adjoining a single character to the right-hand side of a string is the only operation on strings that has been introduced. Thus any new operation must be defined in terms of it.

Definition 2.1.3
Let $u, v \in \Sigma^*$. The **concatenation** of u and v, written uv, is a binary operation on Σ^* defined as follows:

   i) Basis: If $length(v) = 0$ then $v = \lambda$ and $uv = u$.
   ii) Recursive step: Let v be a string with $length(v) = n > 0$. Then $v = wa$, for some string w with length $n - 1$ and $a \in \Sigma$, and $uv = (uw)a$.

Example 2.1.2
Let $u = ab$, $v = ca$, and $w = bb$.

$$uv = abca \qquad\qquad vw = cabb$$
$$(uv)w = abcabb \qquad\qquad u(vw) = abcabb \qquad\qquad \square$$

The result of the concatenation of u, v, and w is independent of the order in which the operations are performed. Mathematically, this property is known as associativity. Theorem 2.1.4 proves that concatenation is an associative binary operation.

Theorem 2.1.4
Let $u, v, w \in \Sigma^*$. Then $(uv)w = u(vw)$.

Proof   The proof is by induction on the length of the string w. The string w was chosen for compatibility with the recursive definition of strings, which builds on the right-hand side of an existing string.

Basis: $length(w) = 0$. Then $w = \lambda$, and $(uv)w = uv$ by the definition of concatenation. On the other hand, $u(vw) = u(v) = uv$.

Inductive Hypothesis: Assume that $(uv)w = u(vw)$ for all strings w of length n or less.

Inductive Step: We need to prove that $(uv)w = u(vw)$, for all strings w of length $n + 1$. Let w be such a string. Then $w = xa$ for some string x of length n and $a \in \Sigma$.

$$
\begin{aligned}
(uv)w &= (uv)(xa) & \text{`substitution, } w = xa\text{'} \\
&= ((uv)x)a & \text{`definition of concatenation'} \\
&= (u(vx))a & \text{`inductive hypothesis'} \\
&= u((vx)a) & \text{`definition of concatenation'} \\
&= u(v(xa)) & \text{`definition of concatenation'} \\
&= u(vw) & \text{`substitution, } xa = w\text{'} \quad \blacksquare
\end{aligned}
$$

Since associativity guarantees the same result regardless of the order of the operations, parentheses are omitted from a sequence of applications of concatenation. Exponents are used to abbreviate the concatenation of a string with itself. The operation of concatenation is not commutative. For strings $u = ab$ and $v = ba$, $uv = abba$ and $vu = baab$. Note that $u^2 = abab$ and not $aabb = a^2b^2$.

Substrings can be defined using the operation of concatenation. Intuitively, u is a substring of v if u "occurs inside of" v. Formally, u is a **substring** of v if there are strings x and y such that $v = xuy$. A **prefix** of v is a substring u in which x is the null string in the decomposition of v. That is, $v = uy$. Similarly, u is a **suffix** of v if $v = xu$.

The reversal of a string is the string written backward. The reversal of $abbc$ is $cbba$. Like concatenation, this unary operation is also defined recursively on the length of the string. Removing an element from the right-hand side of a string constructs a smaller string that can then be used in the recursive step of the definition. Theorem 2.1.6 establishes the relationship between the operations of concatenation and reversal.

Definition 2.1.5

Let w be a string in Σ^*. The **reversal** of w, denoted w^R, is defined as follows:

i) Basis: $length(w) = 0$. Then $w = \lambda$ and $\lambda^R = \lambda$.

ii) Recursive step: If $length(w) = n \geq 1$, then $w = ua$, for some string u with length $n - 1$, $a \in \Sigma$, and $w^R = au^R$.

Theorem 2.1.6

Let $u, v \in \Sigma^*$. Then $(uv)^R = v^R u^R$.

Proof   The proof is by induction on the length of the string v.

Basis: $length(v) = 0$. Then $v = \lambda$ and $(uv)^R = u^R$. Similarly, $v^R u^R = \lambda^R u^R = u^R$.

Inductive Hypothesis: Assume $(uv)^R = v^R u^R$ for all strings v of length n or less.

Inductive Step: We must prove, for any string v of length $n + 1$, that $(uv)^R = v^R u^R$. Let v be a string of length $n + 1$. Then $v = wa$, where w is a string of length n and $a \in \Sigma$.

$$
\begin{aligned}
(uv)^R &= (u(wa))^R \\
&= ((uw)a)^R & \text{`associativity of concatenation'} \\
&= a(uw)^R & \text{`definition of reversal'} \\
&= a(w^R u^R) & \text{`inductive hypothesis'}
\end{aligned}
$$

$$= (aw^R)u^R \qquad \text{'associativity of concatenation'}$$
$$= (wa)^R u^R \qquad \text{'definition of reversal'}$$
$$= v^R u^R$$

∎

2.2 Finite Specification of Languages

A language has been defined as a set of strings over an alphabet. The specification of a language requires an unambiguous description of the strings that comprise the language. A finite language can be explicitly defined by enumerating its elements. An operation defined on strings can be extended to an operation on sets, hence on languages. Descriptions of infinite languages can be constructed from finite sets using the set operations.

Definition 2.2.1

The concatenation of languages X and Y, denoted XY, is the language

$$XY = \{uv \mid u \in X \text{ and } v \in Y\}.$$

The concatenation of X with itself n times is denoted X^n. X^0 is defined as $\{\lambda\}$.

Example 2.2.1

Let $X = \{a, b, c\}$ and $Y = \{abb, ba\}$.

$$XY = \{aabb, babb, cabb, aba, bba, cba\}.$$
$$X^0 = \{\lambda\}.$$
$$X^1 = X = \{a, b, c\}.$$
$$X^2 = XX = \{aa, ab, ac, ba, bb, bc, ca, cb, cc\}.$$
$$X^3 = X^2X = \{aaa, aab, aac, aba, abb, abc, aca, acb, acc,$$
$$baa, bab, bac, bba, bbb, bbc, bca, bcb, bcc,$$
$$caa, cab, cac, cba, cbb, cbc, cca, ccb, ccc\}.$$

□

The sets in the previous example should look familiar. For each i, X^i contains the strings of length i in Σ^* given in Example 2.1.1. This observation leads to another set operation, the Kleene star of a set X, denoted X^*. The strings over a set can now be defined using the operations of concatenation and union, rather than the primitive operation of Definition 2.1.1.

Definition 2.2.2

Let X be a set. Then

$$X^* = \bigcup_{i=0}^{\infty} X^i \qquad \text{and} \qquad X^+ = \bigcup_{i=1}^{\infty} X^i.$$

X^* contains all strings over the set X. X^+ is the set of nonnull strings over X. Set operations can be used to construct new languages from existing ones over a fixed alphabet. Let $X = \{a, b, bb\}$ and $Y = \{a\}^*$ be languages over $\{a, b\}$. Concatenating the languages produces the new languages

$$XY = \{aa^i, ba^i, bba^i \mid i \geq 0\},$$
$$YX = \{a^ia, a^ib, a^ibb \mid i \geq 0\}.$$

Defining languages requires the unambiguous specification of the strings that belong to the language. Describing languages informally lacks the rigor required for a precise definition. Consider the language over $\{a, b\}$ consisting of all strings that contain the substring bb. Does this mean they contain exactly one occurrence of bb, or are multiple substrings bb permitted? This could be answered by describing the strings as containing exactly one or at least one occurrence of bb. However, these types of questions are inherent in the imprecise medium provided by natural languages.

The precision afforded by the set operations can be used to give an unambiguous description of the strings of a language. The result of a unary operation on a language or a binary operation on two languages defines another language. Example 2.2.2 gives a set theoretic definition of the strings that contain the substring bb. In this definition, it is clear that the language contains all strings in which bb occurs at least once.

Example 2.2.2

The language $L = \{a, b\}^*\{bb\}\{a, b\}^*$ consists of the strings over $\{a, b\}$ that contain the substring bb. The concatenation of the set $\{bb\}$ ensures the presence of bb in every string in L. The sets $\{a, b\}^*$ permit any number of a's and b's, in any order, to precede and follow the occurrence of bb.   □

Example 2.2.3

Concatenation can be used to specify the order of components of strings. Let L be the language that consists of all strings that begin with aa or end with bb. The set $\{aa\}\{a, b\}^*$ describes the strings with prefix aa. Similarly, $\{a, b\}^*\{bb\}$ is the set of strings with suffix bb. Thus $L = \{aa\}\{a, b\}^* \cup \{a, b\}^*\{bb\}$.   □

Example 2.2.4

Let $L_1 = \{bb\}$ and $L_2 = \{\lambda, bb, bbbb\}$ be languages over $\{b\}$. The languages L_1^* and L_2^* both contain precisely the strings consisting of an even number of b's. Note that λ, with length zero, is an element of L_1^* and L_2^*.   □

Example 2.2.5

The set $\{aa, bb, ab, ba\}^*$ consists of all even-length strings over $\{a, b\}$. The repeated concatenation constructs strings by adding two elements at a time. The set of strings of odd length is $\{a, b\}^* - \{aa, bb, ab, ba\}^*$. This set can also be obtained by concatenating a single element to the even-length strings. Thus the odd-length strings are also defined by $\{a, b\}\{aa, bb, ab, ba\}^*$. □

2.3 **Regular Sets and Expressions**

A set is regular if it can be generated from the elements of the alphabet using union, concatenation, and the Kleene star operation. The regular sets are an important family of languages, occurring in both formal language theory and the theory of finite-state machines. A regular set is defined by combining the empty set and singleton sets with the allowed set operations.

Definition 2.3.1

Let Σ be an alphabet. The **regular sets** over Σ are defined recursively as follows:

i) Basis: $\emptyset$, $\{\lambda\}$ and $\{a\}$, for every $a \in \Sigma$, are regular sets over Σ.

ii) Recursive step: Let X and Y be regular sets over Σ. The sets

$$X \cup Y$$
$$XY$$
$$X^*$$

are regular sets over Σ.

iii) Closure: X is a regular set over Σ only if it can be obtained from the basis elements by a finite number of applications of the operations in ii).

Example 2.3.1

The language from Example 2.2.2, the set of strings containing the substring bb, is a regular set over $\{a, b\}$. From the basis of the definition, $\{a\}$ and $\{b\}$ are regular sets. Applying union and the Kleene star operation produces $\{a, b\}^*$, the set of all strings over $\{a, b\}$. Using concatenation, $\{b\}\{b\} = \{bb\}$ is regular. Applying concatenation twice yields $\{a, b\}^*\{bb\}\{a, b\}^*$. □

Example 2.3.2

The set of strings that begin and end with an a and contain at least one b is regular over $\{a, b\}$. The strings in this set could be described intuitively as "an a, followed by any string, followed by a b, followed by any string, followed by an a." The concatenation

$$\{a\}\{a, b\}^*\{b\}\{a, b\}^*\{a\}$$

exhibits the regularity of the set. □

By definition, regular sets are those that can be built from the empty set, the singleton sets containing the null string, and the elements of the alphabet using the operations of union, concatenation, and Kleene star. Regular expressions are used to abbreviate the descriptions of regular sets. The regular set $\{b\}$ is represented by b, removing the need for the set brackets $\{\ \}$. The set operations of union, Kleene star, and concatenation are designated by $\cup$, *, and juxtaposition, respectively. Parentheses are used to indicate the order of the operations.

Definition 2.3.2

Let Σ be an alphabet. The **regular expressions** over Σ are defined recursively as follows:

i) Basis: $\emptyset$, λ, and a, for every $a \in \Sigma$, are regular expressions over Σ.

ii) Recursive step: Let u and v be regular expressions over Σ. The expressions

$$(u \cup v)$$
$$(uv)$$
$$(u^*)$$

are regular expressions over Σ.

iii) Closure: u is a regular expression over Σ only if it can be obtained from the basis elements by a finite number of applications of the operations in ii).

Since union and concatenation are associative, parentheses can be omitted from expressions consisting of a sequence of one of these operations. To further reduce the number of parentheses, a precedence is assigned to the operators. The priority designates the Kleene star operation as the most binding operation, followed by concatenation and union. The regular expressions for sets in Examples 2.3.1 and 2.3.2 are $(a \cup b)^*bb(a \cup b)^*$ and $a(a \cup b)^*b(a \cup b)^*a$, respectively.

The notation u^+ is used to abbreviate the expression uu^*. Similarly, u^2 denotes the regular expression uu, u^3 denotes u^2u, etc.

Example 2.3.3

The set $\{bawab \mid w \in \{a, b\}^*\}$ is regular over $\{a, b\}$. The following table demonstrates the recursive generation of a regular set and the corresponding regular expression. The column on the right gives the justification for the regularity of each of the components used in the recursive operations.

Set	Expression	Justification
1. $\{a\}$	a	Basis
2. $\{b\}$	b	Basis
3. $\{a\}\{b\} = \{ab\}$	ab	1, 2, concatenation
4. $\{a\} \cup \{b\} = \{a, b\}$	$a \cup b$	1, 2, union
5. $\{b\}\{a\} = \{ba\}$	ba	1, 2, concatenation
6. $\{a, b\}^*$	$(a \cup b)^*$	4, Kleene star
7. $\{ba\}\{a, b\}^*$	$ba(a \cup b)^*$	5, 6, concatenation
8. $\{ba\}\{a, b\}^*\{ab\}$	$ba(a \cup b)^*ab$	3, 7, concatenation

Example 2.3.4

The regular expressions $(a \cup b)^* aa(a \cup b)^*$ and $(a \cup b)^* bb(a \cup b)^*$ represent the regular sets with strings containing aa and bb, respectively. Combining these two expressions with the $\cup$ operator yields the expression $(a \cup b)^* aa(a \cup b)^* \cup (a \cup b)^* bb(a \cup b)^*$ representing the set of strings over $\{a, b\}$ that contain the substring aa or bb. □

Example 2.3.5

A regular expression for the set of strings over $\{a, b\}$ that contain exactly two b's must explicitly ensure the presence of two b's. Any number of a's may occur before, between, and after the b's. Concatenating the required subexpressions produces $a^* b a^* b a^*$. □

Example 2.3.6

The regular expressions

i) $a^* b a^* b(a \cup b)^*$

ii) $(a \cup b)^* b a^* b a^*$

iii) $(a \cup b)^* b(a \cup b)^* b(a \cup b)^*$

define the set of strings over $\{a, b\}$ containing two or more b's. As in Example 2.3.5, the presence of at least two b's is ensured by the two instances of the expression b in the concatenation. □

Example 2.3.7

Consider the regular set defined by the expression $a^* (a^* b a^* b a^*)^*$. The expression inside the parentheses is the regular expression from Example 2.3.5 representing the strings with exactly two b's. The Kleene star generates the concatenation of any number of these strings. The result is the set containing all strings with an even number of b's. Another expression for this set is $a^* (b a^* b a^*)^*$. □

The previous examples show that the regular expression definition of a set is not unique. Two expressions that represent the same set are called **equivalent**. The identities in Table 2.3.1 can be used to algebraically manipulate regular expressions to construct equivalent expressions. These identities are the regular expression formulation of the set theoretic properties of union, concatenation, and the Kleene star operation.

Identity 5 follows from the commutativity of union. Identities 9 and 10 are the distributive laws translated to the regular expression notation. The final set of expressions specify all sequences of elements from the sets represented by u and v.

Example 2.3.8

A regular expression is constructed to represent the set of strings over $\{a, b\}$ that do not contain the substring aa. A string in this set may contain a prefix of any number of b's.

TABLE 2.3.1   Regular Expression Identities

1. $\emptyset u = u\emptyset = \emptyset$	8. $u^* = (u^*)^*$
2. $\lambda u = u\lambda = u$	9. $u(v \cup w) = uv \cup uw$
3. $\emptyset^* = \emptyset$	10. $(u \cup v)w = uw \cup vw$
4. $\lambda^* = \lambda$	11. $(uv)^*u = u(vu)^*$
5. $u \cup v = v \cup u$	12. $(u \cup v)^* = (u^* \cup v)^*$
6. $u \cup \emptyset = u$	$= u^*(u \cup v)^* = (u \cup vu^*)^*$
7. $u \cup u = u$	$= (u^*v)^* = u^*(vu^*)^*$
	$= (u^*vu^*)^*$

All a's must be followed by at least one b or terminate the string. The regular expression $b^*(ab^+)^* \cup b^*(ab^+)^*a$ generates the desired set by partitioning it into two disjoint sets, those ending in b and those ending in a. Using the identities from Table 2.3.1, this expression can be simplified as follows:

$$b^*(ab^+)^* \cup b^*(ab^+)^*a$$
$$= b^*(ab^+)^*(\lambda \cup a)$$
$$= b^*(abb^*)^*(\lambda \cup a)$$
$$= (b \cup ab)^*(\lambda \cup a) \qquad \square$$

Example 2.3.9

The regular expression $(a \cup b \cup c)^*bc(a \cup b \cup c)^*$ defines the set of strings containing the substring bc. The expression $(a \cup b \cup c)^*$ is the set of all strings over $\{a, b, c\}$. Following the technique of Example 2.3.5, the substring bc is placed in the string, preceded and followed by any sequence of a's, b's, and c's. $\qquad \square$

Example 2.3.10

Let L be the language defined by $c^*(b \cup (ac^*))^*$. The outer c^* and the ac^* inside the parentheses allow any number of a's and c's to occur in any order. A b can be followed by another b or a string from ac^*. When an element from ac^* occurs, any number of a's or b's, in any order, can follow. Putting these observations together, we see that L consists of all strings that do not contain the substring bc. To help develop your understanding of the representation of sets by expressions, convince yourself that both $acabacc$ and $bbaaacc$ are in the set represented by $c^*(b \cup (ac^*))^*$. $\qquad \square$

The previous two examples show that it is often easier to build a regular set (expression) in which every member satisfies a given condition than one consisting of all elements that do not satisfy the condition. Techniques for constructing a regular expression for a set from an expression defining its complement will be given in Chapter 6.

It is important to note that there are languages that cannot be defined by regular expressions. We will see that there is no regular expression that defines the language $\{a^n b^n \mid n \geq 0\}$.

Exercises

1. Give a recursive definition of the set of strings over {a, b} that contains all and only those strings with an equal number of a's and b's. Use concatenation as the operator.

2. Give a recursive definition of the length of a string over Σ. Use the primitive operation from the definition of string.

3. A **palindrome** over an alphabet Σ is a string in Σ^* that is spelled the same forward and backward. The set of palindromes over Σ can be defined recursively as follows:

   i) Basis: λ and a, for all $a \in \Sigma$, are palindromes.

   ii) Recursive step: If w is a palindrome and $a \in \Sigma$, then awa is a palindrome.

   iii) Closure: w is a palindrome only if it can be obtained from the basis elements by a finite number of applications of ii).

   The set of palindromes can also be defined by $\{w \mid w = w^R\}$. Prove that these two definitions generate the same set.

4. Prove that $(w^R)^i = (w^i)^R$ for all strings w and all $i \geq 0$.

5. Prove, using induction on the length of the string, that $(w^R)^R = w$.

For Exercises 6–25, give a regular expression that represents the described set.

6. The set of strings over {a, b, c} in which all the a's precede the b's, which in turn precede the c's.

7. The same set as Exercise 6 without the null string.

8. The set of strings over {a, b} in which the substring aa occurs exactly once.

9. The set of strings over {a, b} that do not contain the substring aaa.

10. The set of strings over {a, b, c} that do not contain the substring aa.

11. The set of strings over {a, b, c} that begin with a, contain exactly two b's, and end with cc.

12. The set of strings over {a, b, c} in which the total number of b's and c's is three.

13. The set of strings over {a, b, c} in which every b is followed by at least one c.

14. The set of strings over {a, b} that contain the substring aa and the substring bb.

15. The set of strings over {a, b, c} that contain the substrings aa, bb, and cc.

16. The set of strings over {a, b, c} with length three.

17. The set of strings over {a, b, c} with length less than three.

18. The set of strings over {a, b, c} with length greater than three.

19. The set of strings over {a, b} in which the number of a's is divisible by three.

20. The set of strings over {a, b} in which every a is either preceded or followed by b, for example, $baab$, aba, and b.

21. The set of strings over {a, b} with an even number of a's or an odd number of b's.

22. The set of strings over {a, b} with an even number of a's and an even number of b's.

23. The set of strings of odd length over $\{a, b\}$ that contain exactly two b's.

24. The set of strings of odd length over $\{a, b, c\}$ that contain exactly one a.

25. The set of strings over $\{a,b,c\}$ with an odd number of occurrences of the substring ab.

26. Use the regular expression identities in Table 2.3.1 to establish the following identities:

   a) $(ba)^+(a^*b^* \cup a^*) = (ba)^*ba^+(b^* \cup \lambda)$

   b) $b^+(a^*b^* \cup \lambda)b = b(b^*a^* \cup \lambda)b^+$

   c) $(a \cup b)^* = (a \cup b)^*b^*$

   d) $(a \cup b)^* = (a^* \cup ba^*)^*$

   e) $(a \cup b)^* = (b^*(a \cup \lambda)b^*)^*$

Bibliographic Notes

Regular expressions were developed by Kleene [1956] for studying the properties of neural networks. McNaughton and Yamada [1960] proved that the regular sets are closed under the operations of intersection and complementation. An axiomatization of the algebra of regular expressions can be found in Salomaa [1966].

PART II

Context-Free Grammars and Parsing

CHAPTER 3

Context-Free Grammars

A language has been defined as a set of strings over an alphabet. Languages of interest are not comprised of arbitrary sets of strings but rather of strings having specified forms. The acceptable forms define the syntax of the language. A correctly formed string in a natural language is called a sentence. Syntactically correct strings in a computer language are called programs.

The alphabet of a language consists of the indecomposable elements from which the strings are constructed. These elements are called the **terminal symbols** of the language. The alphabet of a natural language consists of the words of the language. The terminal symbols of a computer language are often referred to as tokens. The set of tokens for the programming language Pascal includes keywords, identifiers, and special symbols such as $+$, [, and $:=$.

In this chapter, a formal approach is developed for generating the strings of a language. Borrowing the terminology of natural languages, a syntactically correct string is called a **sentence** of the language. A small subset of the English language is presented to illustrate the components of the string-generation process. The alphabet of our miniature language is the set {*a, the, John, Jill, hamburger, car, drives, eats, slowly, frequently, big, juicy, brown*}. Capitalization, punctuation, and other important features of written languages are ignored in this example.

The sentence-generation procedure should construct the strings *John eats a hamburger* and *Jill drives frequently*. Strings of the form *Jill* and *car John rapidly* should not result from this process. Additional symbols are used during the construction of sentences to enforce the syntactic restrictions of the language. These intermediate symbols, known as **variables** or **nonterminals**, are represented by enclosing them in the brackets ⟨ ⟩.

Since the generation procedure constructs sentences, the initial variable is named ⟨*sentence*⟩. The generation process consists of replacing variables by strings of a specific form. Syntactically correct replacements are given by a set of transformation rules. Two possible rules for the variable ⟨*sentence*⟩ are

1. ⟨*sentence*⟩ → ⟨*noun-phrase*⟩ ⟨*verb-phrase*⟩
2. ⟨*sentence*⟩ → ⟨*noun-phrase*⟩ ⟨*verb*⟩ ⟨*direct-object-phrase*⟩.

An informal interpretation of rule 1 is that a sentence may be formed by a noun phrase followed by a verb phrase. At this point, of course, neither of the variables ⟨*noun-phrase*⟩ nor ⟨*verb-phrase*⟩ has been defined. The second rule gives an alternative definition of sentence, a noun phrase followed by a verb followed by a direct object phrase. The existence of multiple transformations indicates that syntactically correct sentences may have several different forms.

A noun phrase may contain either a proper or a common noun. A common noun is preceded by a determiner while a proper noun stands alone. This feature of the syntax of the English language is represented by rules 3 and 4.

Rules for the variables that generate noun and verb phrases are given below. Rather than rewriting the left-hand side of alternative rules for the same variable, the right-hand sides of the rules are listed sequentially. Numbering the rules is not a feature of the generation process, merely a notational convenience.

3. ⟨*noun-phrase*⟩ → ⟨*proper-noun*⟩
4.   → ⟨*determiner*⟩ ⟨*common-noun*⟩

5. ⟨*proper-noun*⟩ → *John*
6.   → *Jill*

7. ⟨*common-noun*⟩ → *car*
8.   → *hamburger*

9. ⟨*determiner*⟩ → *a*
10.   → *the*

11. ⟨*verb-phrase*⟩ → ⟨*verb*⟩ ⟨*adverb*⟩
12.   → ⟨*verb*⟩

13. ⟨*verb*⟩ → *drives*
14.   → *eats*

15. ⟨*adverb*⟩ → *slowly*
16.   → *frequently*

With the exception of ⟨*direct-object-phrase*⟩, rules have been defined for each of the variables that have been introduced. The generation of a sentence consists of repeated rule applications to transform the variable ⟨*sentence*⟩ into a string of terminal symbols. For example, the sentence *Jill drives frequently* is generated by the following transformations:

Derivation	Rule Applied
⟨*sentence*⟩ ⟹ ⟨*noun-phrase*⟩ ⟨*verb-phrase*⟩	1
⟹ ⟨*proper-noun*⟩ ⟨*verb-phrase*⟩	3
⟹ *Jill* ⟨*verb-phrase*⟩	6
⟹ *Jill* ⟨*verb*⟩ ⟨*adverb*⟩	11
⟹ *Jill drives* ⟨*adverb*⟩	13
⟹ *Jill drives frequently*	16

The symbol → is used in the definition of a rule and ⟹ is used in its application. The application of a rule transforms one string to another. The symbol ⟹ is read "derives." The column on the right indicates the number of the rule that was applied to achieve the transformation. The derivation of a sentence terminates when all variables have been removed from the derived string. The set of terminal strings derivable from the variable ⟨*sentence*⟩ is the language generated by the rules of the example.

To complete the set of rules, the transformations for ⟨*direct-object-phrase*⟩ must be given. Before designing rules, we must decide upon the form of the strings that we wish to generate. In our language we will allow the possibility of any number of adjectives, including repetitions, to precede the direct object. This requires a set of rules capable of generating each of the following strings:

> *John eats a hamburger*
> *John eats a big hamburger*
> *John eats a big juicy hamburger*
> *John eats a big brown juicy hamburger*
> *John eats a big big brown juicy hamburger*

The rules of the grammar must be capable of generating strings of arbitrary length. The use of a recursive definition allows the elements of an infinite set to be generated by a finite specification. Following that example, recursion is introduced into the string-generation process, that is, into the rules.

17. ⟨*adjective-list*⟩ → ⟨*adjective*⟩ ⟨*adjective-list*⟩

18.   → λ

19. ⟨*adjective*⟩ → *big*

20.   → *juicy*

21.   → *brown*

The definition of ⟨*adjective-list*⟩ follows the standard recursive pattern. Rule 17 defines ⟨*adjective-list*⟩ in terms of itself while rule 18 provides the basis of the recursive definition.

The λ on the right-hand side of rule 18 indicates that the application of this rule replaces ⟨adjective-list⟩ with the null string. Repeated applications of rule 17 generate a sequence of adjectives. Rules for ⟨direct-object-phrase⟩ are constructed using ⟨adjective-list⟩.

22. ⟨direct-object-phrase⟩ → ⟨adjective-list⟩ ⟨proper-noun⟩

23.   → ⟨determiner⟩ ⟨adjective-list⟩ ⟨common-noun⟩

The sentence *John eats a big juicy hamburger* can be derived by the following sequence of rule applications:

Derivation	Rule Applied
⟨sentence⟩ ⇒ ⟨noun-phrase⟩ ⟨verb⟩ ⟨direct-object-phrase⟩	2
⇒ ⟨proper-noun⟩ ⟨verb⟩ ⟨direct-object-phrase⟩	3
⇒ John ⟨verb⟩ ⟨direct-object-phrase⟩	5
⇒ John eats ⟨direct-object-phrase⟩	14
⇒ John eats ⟨determiner⟩ ⟨adjective-list⟩ ⟨common-noun⟩	23
⇒ John eats a ⟨adjective-list⟩ ⟨common-noun⟩	9
⇒ John eats a ⟨adjective⟩ ⟨adjective-list⟩ ⟨common-noun⟩	17
⇒ John eats a big ⟨adjective-list⟩ ⟨common-noun⟩	19
⇒ John eats a big ⟨adjective⟩ ⟨adjective-list⟩ ⟨common-noun⟩	17
⇒ John eats a big juicy ⟨adjective-list⟩ ⟨common-noun⟩	20
⇒ John eats a big juicy ⟨common-noun⟩	18
⇒ John eats a big juicy hamburger	8

The generation of sentences is strictly a function of the rules. The string *the car eats slowly* is a sentence in the language since it has the form ⟨noun-phrase⟩ ⟨verb-phrase⟩ outlined by rule 1. This illustrates the important distinction between syntax and semantics; the generation of sentences is concerned with the form of the derived string without regard to any underlying meaning that may be associated with the terminal symbols.

By rules 3 and 4, a noun phrase consists of a proper noun or a common noun preceded by a determiner. The variable ⟨adjective-list⟩ may be incorporated into the ⟨noun-phrase⟩ rules, permitting adjectives to modify the noun.

3'. ⟨noun-phrase⟩ → ⟨adjective-list⟩ ⟨proper-noun⟩

4'.   → ⟨determiner⟩ ⟨adjective-list⟩ ⟨common-noun⟩

With this modification, the string *big John eats frequently* can be derived from the variable ⟨sentence⟩.

3.1   Context-Free Grammars and Languages

We will now define a formal system, the context-free grammar, that is used to generate the strings of a language. The natural language example was presented to motivate the components and features of generation in a context-free grammar.

Definition 3.1.1

A **context-free grammar** is a quadruple (V, Σ, P, S) where V is a finite set of variables, Σ (the alphabet) is a finite set of terminal symbols, S is a distinguished element of V called the start symbol, and P is a finite set of rules. The sets V and Σ are assumed to be disjoint.

A **rule** is often called a production and is an element of the set $V \times (V \cup \Sigma)^*$. The production $[A, w]$ is usually written $A \rightarrow w$. A rule of this form is called an **A rule**, referring to the variable on the left-hand side. Since the null string is in $(V \cup \Sigma)^*$, λ may occur on the right-hand side of a rule. A rule of the form $A \rightarrow \lambda$ is called a **null** or **lambda rule**.

Italics are used to denote the variables and terminals of a context-free grammar. Terminals are represented by lowercase letters occurring at the beginning of the alphabet, i.e., a, b, c . . . . Following the conventions introduced for strings, the letters p, q, u, v, w, x, y, z, with or without subscripts, represent arbitrary members of $(V \cup \Sigma)^*$.

Grammars are used to generate properly formed strings over the prescribed alphabet. The fundamental step in the generation process consists of transforming a string by the application of a rule. The application of $A \rightarrow w$ to the variable A in uAv produces the string uwv. This is denoted $uAv \Rightarrow uwv$. The grammars are called context-free because of the general applicability of the rules. An A rule can be applied to a variable A whenever and wherever it occurs. The rule can be applied regardless of the form of the remainder of the string, the context. A string w is derivable from v if there is a finite sequence of rule applications that transforms v to w, that is, if a sequence of transformations

$$v \Rightarrow w_1 \Rightarrow w_2 \Rightarrow \cdots \Rightarrow w_n = w$$

can be constructed from the rules of the grammar. The derivability of w from v is denoted $v \overset{*}{\Rightarrow} w$. The set of strings derivable from v, being constructed by a finite but (possibly) unbounded number of rule applications, can be defined recursively.

Definition 3.1.2

Let G = (V, Σ, P, S) be a context-free grammar and $v \in (V \cup \Sigma)^*$. The set of strings derivable from v is defined recursively as follows:

i) v is derivable from v.

ii) If $u = xAy$ is derivable from v and $A \rightarrow w \in P$, then xwy is derivable from v.

iii) Precisely those strings constructed from v by finitely many applications of ii) are derivable from v.

Note that the definition of a rule uses the $\rightarrow$ notation while its application uses $\Rightarrow$. This is because the two are relations on different sets. A rule is a member of a relation on $V \times (V \cup \Sigma)^*$, while an application of a rule is a member of $(V \cup \Sigma)^+ \times (V \cup \Sigma)^*$. The symbol $\overset{+}{\Rightarrow}$ designates derivability utilizing one or more rule applications. The length of a derivation is the number of rule applications employed. A derivation of w from v of length n is denoted $v \stackrel{n}{\Rightarrow} w$. When more than one grammar is being considered, the notation $v \stackrel{*}{\underset{G}{\Rightarrow}} w$ will be used to explicitly indicate that the derivation utilizes the rules of the grammar G.

A language has been defined as a set of strings over an alphabet. A grammar consists of an alphabet and a method of generating strings. These strings may contain both variables and terminals. The start symbol of the grammar, assuming the role of ⟨sentence⟩ in the natural language example, initiates the procedure of generating acceptable strings. The language of the grammar G is the set of terminal strings derivable from the start symbol. We now state this as a definition.

Definition 3.1.3

Let $G = (V, \Sigma, P, S)$ be a context-free grammar.

i) A string $w \in (V \cup \Sigma)^*$ is a **sentential form** of G if there is a derivation $S \stackrel{*}{\Rightarrow} w$ in G.

ii) A string $w \in \Sigma^*$ is a **sentence** of G if there is a derivation $S \stackrel{*}{\Rightarrow} w$ in G.

iii) The **language** of G, denoted L(G), is the set $\{w \in \Sigma^* \mid S \stackrel{*}{\Rightarrow} w\}$.

The sentential forms are the strings derivable from the start symbol of the grammar. The sentences are the sentential forms that contain only terminal symbols. The language of a grammar is the set of sentences generated by the grammar. A set of strings over an alphabet Σ is called a **context-free language** if there is a context-free grammar that generates it. Two grammars are said to be equivalent if they generate the same language.

Recursion is necessary for a finite set of rules to generate infinite languages and strings of arbitrary length. An A rule of the form $A \rightarrow uAv$ is called **directly recursive.** This rule can generate any number of copies of the string u followed by an A and an equal number of v's. Another, nonrecursive A rule may then be employed to halt the recursion. A variable A is called recursive if there is a derivation $A \stackrel{+}{\Rightarrow} uAv$. A derivation $A \Rightarrow w \stackrel{+}{\Rightarrow} uAv$, where A is not in w, is said to be **indirectly recursive.**

A grammar G and four distinct derivations of the terminal string *ababaa* are given in Fig. 3.1. The definition of derivation permits the transformation of any variable in the string. Each rule application in derivations (a) and (b) transforms the first variable occurring in a left-to-right reading of the string. Derivations with this property are called **leftmost.** Derivation (c) is **rightmost,** since the rightmost variable has a rule applied to it. Derivation (d) is neither, the rules being applied in no particular order. These derivations demonstrate that there may be more than one derivation of a string in a context-free grammar.

Figure 3.1 exhibits the flexibility of derivations in a context-free grammar. The essential feature of a derivation is not the order in which the rules are applied, but the manner in which each variable is decomposed. This decomposition can be graphically depicted by a derivation or parse tree. The tree structure specifies the rule that is applied to each variable but does not designate the order of the rule applications. The leaves of the derivation tree can be ordered to yield the result of a derivation represented by the tree.

$$G = (V, \Sigma, P, S)$$
$$V = \{S, A\}$$
$$\Sigma = \{a, b\}$$
P: $S \rightarrow AA$
      $A \rightarrow AAA \mid bA \mid Ab \mid a$

(a)	(b)	(c)	(d)
$S \Rightarrow AA$	$S \Rightarrow AA$	$S \Rightarrow AA$	$S \Rightarrow AA$
$\Rightarrow aA$	$\Rightarrow AAAA$	$\Rightarrow Aa$	$\Rightarrow aA$
$\Rightarrow aAAA$	$\Rightarrow aAAA$	$\Rightarrow AAAa$	$\Rightarrow aAAA$
$\Rightarrow abAAA$	$\Rightarrow abAAA$	$\Rightarrow AAbAa$	$\Rightarrow aAAa$
$\Rightarrow abaAA$	$\Rightarrow abaAA$	$\Rightarrow AAbaa$	$\Rightarrow abAAa$
$\Rightarrow ababAA$	$\Rightarrow ababAA$	$\Rightarrow AbAbaa$	$\Rightarrow abAbAa$
$\Rightarrow ababaA$	$\Rightarrow ababaA$	$\Rightarrow Ababaa$	$\Rightarrow ababAa$
$\Rightarrow ababaa$	$\Rightarrow ababaa$	$\Rightarrow ababaa$	$\Rightarrow ababaa$

FIGURE 3.1   Sample derivations of *ababaa* in G.

Definition 3.1.4

Let $G = (V, \Sigma, P, S)$ be a context-free grammar and $S \overset{*}{\underset{G}{\Rightarrow}} w$ a derivation. The **derivation tree**, DT. of $S \overset{*}{\underset{G}{\Rightarrow}} w$ is an ordered tree that can be built iteratively as follows:

i) Initialize DT with root S.

ii) If $A \rightarrow x_1 x_2 \ldots x_n$ with $x_i \in (V \cup \Sigma)$ is the ith rule in the derivation applied to the string uAv, then add $x_1, x_2, \ldots, x_n$ as the children of A in the tree.

iii) If $A \rightarrow \lambda$ is the ith rule in the derivation applied to the string uAv, then add λ as the only child of A in the tree.

The ordering of the leaves also follows this iterative process. Initially the only leaf is S and the ordering is obvious. When the rule $A \rightarrow x_1 x_2 \ldots x_n$ is used to generate the children of A, each x_i becomes a leaf and A is replaced in the ordering of the leaves by the sequence $x_1, x_2, \ldots, x_n$. The application of a rule $A \rightarrow \lambda$ simply replaces A by the null string. Figure 3.2 traces the construction of the tree corresponding to derivation (a) of Fig. 3.1. The ordering of the leaves is given along with each of the trees.

The order of the leaves in a derivation tree is independent of the derivation from which the tree was generated. The ordering provided by the iterative process is identical to the ordering of the leaves given by the relation LEFTOF in Section 1.5. The frontier of the derivation tree is the string generated by the derivation.

Figure 3.3 gives the derivation trees for each of the derivations in Fig. 3.1. The trees generated by derivations (a) and (d) are identical, indicating that each variable is decomposed in the same manner. The only difference between these derivations is the order of the rule applications.

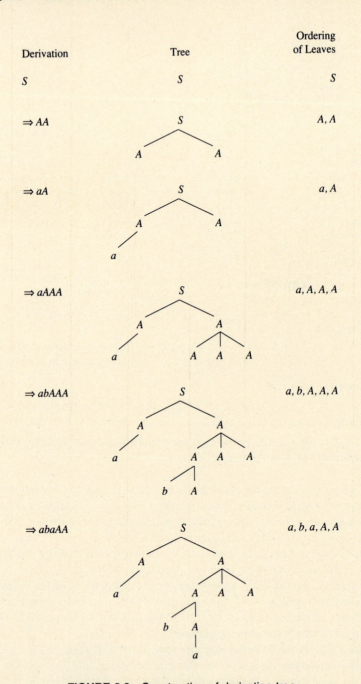

FIGURE 3.2 Construction of derivation tree.

Derivation	Tree	Ordering of Leaves

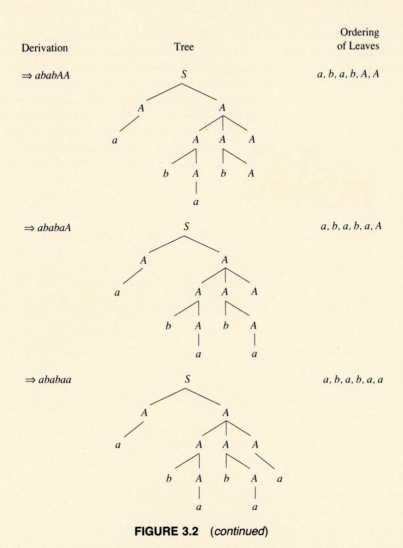

$\Rightarrow ababAA$ · a, b, a, b, A, A

$\Rightarrow ababaA$ · a, b, a, b, a, A

$\Rightarrow ababaa$ · a, b, a, b, a, a

FIGURE 3.2   (*continued*)

A derivation tree can be used to produce several derivations that generate the same string. For a node containing a variable A, the rule applied to A can be reconstructed from the children of A in the tree. The rightmost derivation

$$
\begin{aligned}
S &\Rightarrow AA \\
&\Rightarrow AAAA \\
&\Rightarrow AAAa \\
&\Rightarrow AAbAa \\
&\Rightarrow AAbaa \\
&\Rightarrow AbAbaa \\
&\Rightarrow Ababaa \\
&\Rightarrow ababaa
\end{aligned}
$$

is obtained from the derivation tree (a) in Fig. 3.3. Notice that this derivation is different from the rightmost derivation (c) in Fig. 3.1. In the latter derivation, the second variable in the string AA is transformed using the rule $A \rightarrow a$ while $A \rightarrow AAA$ is used in the derivation above. The two trees illustrate the distinct decompositions.

As we have seen, the context-free applicability of rules allows a great deal of flexibility in the construction of derivations. Lemma 3.1.5 shows that a derivation may be broken into subderivations from each variable in the string. Derivability was defined recursively, the length of derivations being finite but unbounded. Mathematical induction provides a proof technique for establishing that a property holds for all derivations from a given string.

Lemma 3.1.5

Let G be a context-free grammar and $v \overset{n}{\Rightarrow} w$ be a derivation in G where

$$v = w_1 A_1 w_2 A_2 \ldots w_k A_k w_{k+1},$$
$$w = w_1 p_1 w_2 p_2 \ldots w_k p_k w_{k+1},$$

and $w_i \in \Sigma^*$. Then there are derivations $A_i \overset{t_i}{\underset{G}{\Rightarrow}} p_i$ for each i with the sum of the t_i's equal to n.

Proof   The proof is by induction on the length of the derivation of w from v.

Basis: The basis consists of derivations of the form $v \overset{0}{\Rightarrow} w$. In this case, $w = v$ and each A_i is equal to the corresponding p_i. The desired derivations have the form $A_i \overset{0}{\Rightarrow} p_i$.

Inductive Hypothesis: Assume that all derivations $v \overset{n}{\Rightarrow} w$ can be decomposed into derivations from A_i, the variables of v, which together form a derivation of w from v of length n.

Inductive Step: Let $v \overset{n+1}{\Rightarrow} w$ be a derivation in G with

$$v = w_1 A_1 w_2 A_2 \ldots w_k A_k w_{k+1},$$
$$w = w_1 p_1 w_2 p_2 \ldots w_k p_k w_{k+1},$$

where $w_i \in \Sigma^*$. The derivation can be written $v \Rightarrow u \overset{n}{\Rightarrow} w$. This reduces the original derivation to a derivation of length n, which is in the correct form for the invocation of the inductive hypothesis, and the application of a single rule.

The derivation $v \Rightarrow u$ transforms one of the variables in v, call it A_j, with a rule

$$A_j \rightarrow u_1 B_1 u_2 B_2 \ldots u_m B_m u_{m+1}$$

where each $u_t \in \Sigma^*$. The string u is obtained from v by replacing A_j by the right-hand side of the A_j rule. Making this substitution, u can be written

$$w_1 A_1 \ldots A_{j-1} w_j u_1 B_1 u_2 B_2 \ldots u_m B_m u_{m+1} w_{j+1} A_{j+1} \ldots w_k A_k w_{k+1}.$$

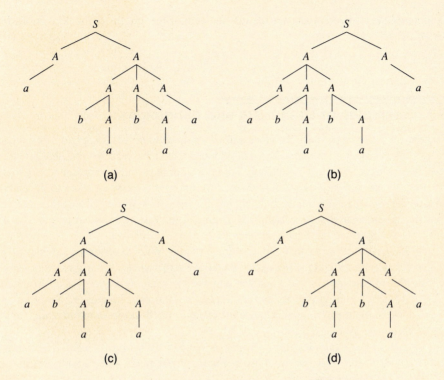

FIGURE 3.3   Trees corresponding to the derivations in Fig. 3.1.

Now p_j, the terminal string derived from A_j, can be written

$$p_j = u_1 q_1 u_2 q_2 \ldots u_m q_m u_{m+1}.$$

By the inductive hypothesis, the derivation $u \overset{n}{\Rightarrow} w$ consists of subderivations $A_i \overset{*}{\Rightarrow} p_i$, for all $i \neq j$, and $B_t \overset{*}{\Rightarrow} q_t$ whose lengths satisfy

$$\sum_{\substack{i=1 \\ i \neq j}}^{k} len(A_i \overset{*}{\Rightarrow} p_i) + \sum_{t=1}^{m} len(B_t \overset{*}{\Rightarrow} q_t) = n$$

where $len(A \overset{*}{\Rightarrow} v)$ denotes the length of the derivation $A \overset{*}{\Rightarrow} v$. The length of the derivation of p_j from A_j is the sum of the lengths of the derivations from the B_t's plus one, the rule that generated the B_t's.

$$len(A_j \overset{*}{\Rightarrow} p_j) = 1 + \sum_{t=1}^{m} len(B_t \overset{*}{\Rightarrow} q_t).$$

Combining the two equalities, we see that the sum of the lengths of the derivations from the A_i's is $n + 1$. ∎

3.2 Examples of Grammars and Languages

Context-free grammars have been described as generators of languages. Formal languages, like computer languages and natural languages, have requirements that the strings must satisfy in order to be syntactically correct. Grammars must be designed to generate precisely the desired strings and no others. Two approaches may be taken to develop the relationship between grammars and languages. One is to specify a language and then construct a grammar that generates it. Conversely, the rules of a given grammar can be analyzed to determine the language generated.

Initially both of these tasks may seem difficult. With experience, techniques will evolve for generating certain frequently occurring patterns. Building grammars and observing the interactions of the variables and the terminals is the only way to increase one's proficiency with grammars and the formal definition of languages. No proofs will be given in this section; the goal is to use the examples to develop an intuitive understanding of grammars and languages.

In each of the examples, the grammar is defined by listing its rules. The variables and terminals of the grammar are those occurring in the rules. The variable S is the start symbol of each grammar.

Example 3.2.1

Let G be the grammar given by the productions

$$S \rightarrow aSa \mid aBa$$
$$B \rightarrow bB \mid b.$$

Then $L(G) = \{a^n b^m a^n \mid n > 0, m > 0\}$. The rule $S \rightarrow aSa$ recursively builds an equal number of a's on each end of the string. When the rule $S \rightarrow aBa$ is applied, the recursion is terminated, ensuring at least one leading and one trailing a. The first B rule then generates any number of b's. To remove the variable B from the string and obtain a sentence of the language, the rule $B \rightarrow b$ must be applied, forcing the presence of at least one b. □

Example 3.2.2

Let G_1 and G_2 be the grammars

$$G_1: S \rightarrow AB \qquad\qquad G_2: S \rightarrow aS \mid aB$$
$$ A \rightarrow aA \mid a \qquad\qquad B \rightarrow bB \mid \lambda.$$
$$ B \rightarrow bB \mid \lambda$$

Both of these grammars generate the language a^+b^*. The A rules in G_1 provide the standard method of generating a nonnull string of a's. The use of the lambda rule to terminate the recursion allows the possibility of having no b's. Grammar G_2 builds the same language in a left-to-right manner. This example shows that there may be many grammars that generate the same language. There may not even be a best grammar. In later chapters, however, we will see that some rules have certain desirable forms that facilitate the mechanical generation of strings. □

Example 3.2.3

Consider the grammar

$$S \to abScB \mid \lambda$$
$$B \to bB \mid b.$$

The recursive S rule generates an equal number of ab's and cB's. The B rules generate b^+. The language of the grammar consists of the set $\{(ab)^n(cb^{m_n})^n \mid n \geq 0, m_n > 0\}$. The superscript m_n indicates that each occurrence of cB may produce a different number of b's. □

Example 3.2.4

The grammars G_1 and G_2 generate the strings over $\{a, b\}$ that contain exactly two b's. That is, the language of the grammars is $a^*ba^*ba^*$.

$$G_1: S \to AbAbA \qquad G_2: S \to aS \mid bA$$
$$A \to aA \mid \lambda \qquad A \to aA \mid bC$$
$$C \to aC \mid \lambda$$

G_1 requires only two variables, since the three instances of a^* are generated by the same A rules. The second builds the strings in a left-to-right manner, requiring a distinct variable for the generation of each sequence of a's. □

Example 3.2.5

The grammars from Example 3.2.4 can be easily modified to generate strings with at least two b's.

$$G_1: S \to AbAbA \qquad G_2: S \to aS \mid bA$$
$$A \to aA \mid bA \mid \lambda \qquad A \to aA \mid bC$$
$$C \to aC \mid bC \mid \lambda$$

□

Example 3.2.6

A grammar is given that generates the language consisting of even-length strings over $\{a, b\}$. The strategy can be generalized to construct strings of length divisible by three, by four, and so forth. The variables S and O serve as counters. An S occurs in a sentential form when an even number of terminals has been generated. An O records the presence of an odd number of terminals.

$$S \rightarrow aO \mid bO \mid \lambda$$
$$O \rightarrow aS \mid bS$$

The application of $S \rightarrow \lambda$ completes the derivation of a terminal string. Until this occurs, the derivation alternates between applications of the S and O rules.   □

Example 3.2.7

Let L be the language over $\{a, b\}$ consisting of all strings with an even number of b's. A grammar to generate L combines the techniques presented in the previous examples; Example 3.2.6 for the even number of b's and Example 3.2.4 for the arbitrary number of a's. Deleting all rules containing C yields another grammar that generates L.

$$S \rightarrow aS \mid bB \mid \lambda$$
$$B \rightarrow aB \mid bS \mid bC$$
$$C \rightarrow aC \mid \lambda$$ □

Example 3.2.8

The rules of a grammar are designed to impose a structure on the strings in the language. This structure may consist of ensuring the presence or absence of certain combinations of elements of the alphabet. We construct a grammar with alphabet $\{a, b, c\}$ whose language consists of all strings that do not contain the substring abc. The technique is similar to the generation of strings with even length. The variables are used to determine how far the derivation has progressed toward generating the string abc.

$$S \rightarrow bS \mid cS \mid aB \mid \lambda$$
$$B \rightarrow aB \mid cS \mid bC \mid \lambda$$
$$C \rightarrow aB \mid bS \mid \lambda$$

The strings are built in a left-to-right manner. At most one variable is present in a sentential form. If an S is present, no progress has been made toward deriving abc. The variable B occurs when the previous terminal is an a. The variable C is present only when preceded by ab. Thus, the C rules cannot generate the terminal c.   □

Example 3.2.9

The relationship between the number of leading a's and trailing d's in the language $\{a^n b^m c^m d^{2n} \mid n \geq 0, m > 0\}$ indicates that a recursive rule is needed to generate them. The same is true of the b's and c's. Derivations in the grammar

$$S \rightarrow aSdd \mid A$$
$$A \rightarrow bAc \mid bc$$

generate strings in an outside-to-inside manner. The *S* rules produce the *a*'s and *d*'s while the *A* rules generate the *b*'s and *c*'s. The rule $A \rightarrow bc$, whose application terminates the recursion, ensures the presence of the substring *bc* in every string in the language.   □

Example 3.2.10

A string *w* is a palindrome if $w = w^R$. A grammar is constructed to generate the set of palindromes over $\{a, b\}$. The rules of the grammar mimic the recursive definition given in Exercise 2.3. The basis of the set of palindromes consists of the strings λ, *a*, and *b*. The *S* rules

$$S \rightarrow a \mid b \mid \lambda$$

immediately generate these strings. The recursive part of the definition consists of adding the same symbol to each side of an existing palindrome. The rules

$$S \rightarrow aSa \mid bSb$$

capture the recursive generation process.   □

3.3   Regular Grammars

A context-free grammar is regular if the right-hand side of every rule satisfies certain prescribed conditions. The regular grammars comprise an important subclass of the context-free grammars.

Definition 3.3.1

A **regular grammar** is a context-free grammar in which each of the rules has the form

  i) $A \rightarrow a$

  ii) $A \rightarrow aB$

  iii) $A \rightarrow \lambda$

where $A, B \in V$, and $a \in \Sigma$.

A language is said to be regular if it can be generated by a regular grammar. A regular language may be generated by both regular and nonregular grammars. The grammars G_1 and G_2 from Example 3.2.2 generate the language a^+b^*. The grammar G_1 is not a regular because the rule $S \rightarrow AB$ does not have the specified form. G_2, however, is a regular grammar. A language is regular if it is generated by some regular grammar; the existence of nonregular grammars that also generate it is irrelevant. The grammars constructed in Examples 3.2.6, 3.2.7, and 3.2.8 provide additional examples of regular grammars.

Derivations in regular grammars have a particularly nice form. There is at most one variable present in a sentential form and that variable, if present, is the rightmost symbol in the string. Each rule application adds a terminal to the string until a rule of the form $A \rightarrow a$ or $A \rightarrow \lambda$ terminates the derivation.

Example 3.3.1

We will construct a regular grammar that generates the language of the grammar

$$G: S \rightarrow abSA \mid \lambda$$
$$A \rightarrow Aa \mid \lambda.$$

The language of G is given by the regular expression $(ab)^*a^*$. An equivalent regular grammar must generate the strings in a left-to-right manner. In the grammar below, the S and B rules generate a prefix from the set $(ab)^*$. If a string has a suffix of a's, the rule $B \rightarrow bA$ is applied. The A rules are used to generate the remainder of the string.

$$S \rightarrow aB \mid aA \mid \lambda$$
$$B \rightarrow bS \mid bA$$
$$A \rightarrow aA \mid \lambda$$

$\square$

3.4   Grammars and Languages Revisited

The grammars in the previous sections were built to generate specific languages. An intuitive argument was given to show that the grammar did indeed generate the correct set of strings. No matter how convincing the argument, the possibility of error exists. A proof is required to guarantee that a grammar generates precisely the desired strings.

To prove that the language of a grammar G is identical to a given set X, the inclusions $X \subseteq L(G)$ and $L(G) \subseteq X$ must be established. To demonstrate the techniques involved, we will prove that the language of the grammar

$$G: S \rightarrow AASB \mid AAB$$
$$A \rightarrow a$$
$$B \rightarrow bbb$$

is the set $\{a^{2n}b^{3n} \mid n > 0\}$.

A terminal string is in the language of a grammar if it can be derived from the start symbol using the rules of the grammar. The inclusion $X = \{a^{2n}b^{3n} \mid n > 0\} \subseteq L(G)$ is established by showing that every string in X is derivable in G. Since X has an infinite number of elements, we cannot construct a derivation for every element of X. Unfortunately, this is precisely what is required. The apparent dilemma is solved by providing a derivation schema. The schema consists of a pattern that can be followed to construct a derivation for any element in X. Every element of the form $a^{2n}b^{3n}$, for $n > 0$, can be derived by the following sequence of rule applications:

Derivation	Rule Applied
$S \overset{n-1}{\Longrightarrow} (AA)^{n-1}SB^{n-1}$	$S \to AASB$
$\Longrightarrow (AA)^n B^n$	$S \to AAB$
$\overset{2n}{\Longrightarrow} (aa)^n B^n$	$A \to a$
$\overset{n}{\Longrightarrow} (aa)^n (bbb)^n$	$B \to bbb$
$= a^{2n}b^{3n}$	

The opposite inclusion, $L(G) \subseteq \{a^{2n}b^{3n} \mid n > 0\}$, requires each terminal string derivable in G to have the form specified by the set X. The derivation of a string in the language is the result of a finite number of rule applications, indicating the suitability of a proof by induction. The first difficulty is to determine exactly what we need to prove. We wish to establish a relationship between the a's and b's in all terminal strings derivable in G. A necessary condition for a string w to be a member of X is that three times the number of a's in the string is equal to twice the number of b's. Letting $n_w(x)$ be the number of occurrences of the symbol x in the string w, this relationship can be expressed by $3n_w(a) = 2n_w(b)$.

This numeric relationship between the symbols in a terminal string clearly is not true for every string derivable from S. Consider the derivation

$$S \Rightarrow AASB$$
$$\Rightarrow aASB.$$

The string $aASB$, derivable in G, contains one a and no b's.

Relationships between the variables and terminals that hold for all steps in the derivation must be determined. When a terminal string is derived, no variables will remain and the relationships should yield the required structure of the string.

The interactions of the variables and the terminals in the rules of G must be examined to determine their effect on the derivations of terminal strings. The rule $A \to a$ guarantees that every A will eventually be replaced by a single a. The number of a's present at the termination of a derivation consists of those already in the string and the number of A's in the string. The sum $n_w(a) + n_w(A)$ represents the number of a's that must be generated in deriving a terminal string from w. Similarly, every B will be replaced by the string bbb. The number of b's in a terminal string derivable from w is $n_w(b) + 3n_w(B)$. These observations are used to construct condition i) establishing the correspondence of variables and terminals that holds for each step in the derivation.

i) $3(n_w(a) + n_w(A)) = 2(n_w(b) + 3n_w(B))$.

The string $aASB$, derived above, satisfies this condition since $n_w(a) + n_w(A) = 2$ and $n_w(b) + 3n_w(B) = 3$.

All strings in $\{a^{2n}b^{3n} \mid n > 0\}$ contain at least two a's and three b's. Conditions i) and ii) combine to yield this property.

ii) $n_w(A) + n_w(a) > 1$.

iii) The a's and A's in a sentential form precede the S that precedes the b's and B's.

Condition iii) prescribes the order of the symbols in a derivable string. Not all of the symbols must be present in each string; strings derivable from S by one rule application do not contain any terminal symbols.

After the appropriate relationships have been determined, we must prove that they hold for every string derivable from S. The basis of the induction consists of all strings that can be obtained by derivations of length one (the S rules). The inductive hypothesis asserts that the conditions are satisfied for all strings derivable by n or fewer rule applications. The inductive step consists of showing that the application of an additional rule preserves the relationships.

There are two derivations of length one, $S \Rightarrow AASB$ and $S \Rightarrow AAB$. For each of these strings, $3(n(a) + n(A)) = 2(n(b) + 3n(B)) = 6$. By observation, conditions ii) and iii) hold for the two strings.

Now assume that i), ii), and iii) hold for all strings derivable by n or fewer rule applications. Let w be a string derivable from S by a derivation of length $n + 1$. We must show that the three conditions hold for the string w. A derivation of length $n + 1$ consists of a derivation of length n followed by a single rule application. $S \overset{n+1}{\Longrightarrow} w$ can be written as $S \overset{n}{\Rightarrow} w' \Rightarrow w$. For any $u \in (V \cup \Sigma)^*$, let $j(u) = 3(n_u(a) + n_u(A))$ and $k(u) = 2(n_u(b) + 3n_u(B))$. By the inductive hypothesis, $j(w') = k(w')$ and $j(w')/3 > 1$. The effects of the application of an additional rule on the constituents of the string w' is given in the following table.

Rule	$j(w)$	$k(w)$	$j(w)/3$
$S \rightarrow AASB$	$j(w') + 6$	$k(w') + 6$	$j(w') + 2$
$S \rightarrow AAB$	$j(w') + 6$	$k(w') + 6$	$j(w') + 2$
$A \rightarrow a$	$j(w')$	$k(w')$	$j(w')$
$B \rightarrow bbb$	$j(w')$	$k(w')$	$j(w')$

Since $j(w') = k(w')$, we conclude that $j(w) = k(w)$ and $j(w)/3 > 1$. The ordering of the symbols is preserved by noting that each rule application either replaces S by an appropriately ordered sequence of variables or transforms a variable to the corresponding terminal.

We have shown that the three conditions hold for every string derivable in G. Since there are no variables in a string $w \in L(G)$, condition i) implies $3n_w(a) = 2n_w(b)$. Condition ii) guarantees the existence of a's and b's, while iii) prescribes the order. Thus $L(G) \subseteq \{a^{2n}b^{3n} \mid n > 0\}$.

Having established the opposite inclusions, we conclude that $L(G) = \{a^{2n}b^{3n} \mid n > 0\}$.

As illustrated by the preceding argument, proving a grammar generates a certain set is a complicated process. This, of course, was an extremely simple grammar with only a few rules. The inductive process is straightforward after the correct relationships have been determined. The relationships are sufficient if, when all references to the variables are removed, they yield the desired structure of the terminal strings.

Example 3.4.1

Let G be the grammar

$$S \rightarrow aSb \mid ab.$$

Then $\{a^n b^n \mid n > 0\} \subseteq L(G)$. An arbitrary string in this set has the form $a^n b^n$ with $n > 0$. A derivation for this string is

Derivation	Rule Applied
$S \overset{n-1}{\Longrightarrow} a^{n-1}Sb^{n-1}$	$S \rightarrow aSb$
$\Longrightarrow a^n b^n$	$S \rightarrow ab$

$\square$

Example 3.4.2

Let G be the grammar given in Example 3.2.7. We will prove that $L(G) = a^*(a^* ba^* ba^*)^*$, the set of all strings over $\{a, b\}$ with even number of b's.

$$S \rightarrow aS \mid bB \mid \lambda$$
$$B \rightarrow aB \mid bS \mid bC$$
$$C \rightarrow aC \mid \lambda$$

It is not true that every string derivable from S has an even number of b's. The derivation $S \Rightarrow bB$ produces a single b. To derive a terminal string, every B must eventually be transformed into a b. Consequently, we conclude that the desired relationship asserts that $n(b) + n(B)$ is even. When a terminal string w is derived, $n_w(B) = 0$ and we conclude that $n_w(b)$ is even.

Proof We will prove that $n(b) + n(B)$ is even for all strings derivable from S. The proof is by induction on the length of the derivations.

Basis: Derivations of length one. There are three such derivations:

$$S \Rightarrow aS$$
$$S \Rightarrow bB$$
$$S \Rightarrow \lambda$$

By inspection, $n(b) + n(B)$ is even for these strings.

Inductive Hypothesis: Assume that $n_w(b) + n_w(B)$ is even for all strings w that can be derived with n rule applications.

Inductive Step: Prove that if $S \overset{n+1}{\Longrightarrow} w$ then $n_w(b) + n_w(B)$ is even. The key step is to reformulate the derivation to apply the inductive hypothesis. The derivation of w can be written $S \overset{n}{\Rightarrow} w' \Rightarrow w$.

By the inductive hypothesis, $n_{w'}(b) + n_{w'}(B)$ is even. Let $k = n_{w'}(b) + n_{w'}(B)$. We show that the result of the application of any rule to w' preserves the parity of k. The table below indicates the value of $n_w(b) + n_w(B)$ when the corresponding rule is applied to w'.

Rule	$n_w(b) + n_w(B)$
$S \rightarrow aS$	k
$S \rightarrow bB$	$k + 2$
$S \rightarrow \lambda$	k
$B \rightarrow aB$	k
$B \rightarrow bS$	k
$B \rightarrow bC$	k
$C \rightarrow aC$	k
$C \rightarrow \lambda$	k

Each of the rules leaves the total number of B's and b's fixed, except the second, which adds two to the total. The table shows that the sum of the b's and B's in a string obtained from w' by the application of a rule is even. Since a terminal string contains no B's, we have shown that every string in L(G) has an even number of b's.

To complete the proof, the opposite inclusion, $L(G) \subseteq a^*(a^*ba^*ba^*)^*$, must also be established. To accomplish this, we show that every string in $a^*(a^*ba^*ba^*)^*$ is derivable in G. A string in $a^*(a^*ba^*ba^*)^*$ has the form

$$a^{n_1}ba^{n_2}ba^{n_3} \ldots a^{n_{2k}}ba^{n_{2k+1}}, \; k \geq 0.$$

Any string in a^* can be derived using the rules $S \rightarrow aS$ and $S \rightarrow \lambda$. All other strings in L(G) can be generated by a derivation of the form

Derivation	Rule Applied
$S \overset{n_1}{\Longrightarrow} a^{n_1}S$	$S \rightarrow aS$
$\Longrightarrow a^{n_1}bB$	$S \rightarrow bB$
$\overset{n_2}{\Longrightarrow} a^{n_1}ba^{n_2}B$	$B \rightarrow aB$
$\Longrightarrow a^{n_1}ba^{n_2}bS$	$B \rightarrow bS$
$\vdots$	
$\overset{n_{2k}}{\Longrightarrow} a^{n_1}ba^{n_2}ba^{n_3} \ldots a^{n_{2k}}B$	$B \rightarrow aB$
$\Longrightarrow a^{n_1}ba^{n_2}ba^{n_3} \ldots a^{n_{2k}}bC$	$B \rightarrow bC$
$\overset{n_{2k+1}}{\Longrightarrow} a^{n_1}ba^{n_2}ba^{n_3} \ldots a^{n_{2k}}ba^{n_{2k+1}}C$	$C \rightarrow aC$
$\Longrightarrow a^{n_1}ba^{n_2}ba^{n_3} \ldots a^{n_{2k}}ba^{n_{2k+1}}$	$C \rightarrow \lambda$

$\square$

Example 3.4.3

Let G be the grammar

$$S \rightarrow aASB \mid \lambda$$
$$B \rightarrow bb$$
$$A \rightarrow ad \mid d.$$

We show that every string in L(G) has at least as many b's as a's. The number of b's in a terminal string depends upon the b's and B's in the intermediate steps of the derivation. Each B generates two b's while an A generates at most one a. We will prove, for every sentential form of G, that $n(a) + n(A) \leq n(b) + 2n(B)$. Let $j(u) = n_u(a) + n_u(A)$ and $k(u) = n_u(b) + 2n_u(B)$.

Basis: There are two derivations of length one.

Rule	j	k
$S \Rightarrow aASB$	2	2
$S \Rightarrow \lambda$	0	0

and $j \leq k$ for both of the derivable strings.

Inductive Hypothesis: Assume that $j(w) \leq k(w)$ for all strings w derivable from S in n or fewer rule applications.

Inductive Step: We need to prove that $j(w) \leq k(w)$ whenever $S \overset{n+1}{\Longrightarrow} w$. The derivation of w can be rewritten $S \overset{n}{\Rightarrow} w' \Rightarrow w$. By the inductive hypothesis, $j(w') \leq k(w')$. We must show that the inequality is preserved by an additional rule application.

Rule	$j(w)$	$k(w)$
$S \rightarrow aASB$	$j(w') + 2$	$k(w') + 2$
$S \rightarrow \lambda$	$j(w')$	$k(w')$
$B \rightarrow bb$	$j(w')$	$k(w')$
$A \rightarrow ad$	$j(w')$	$k(w')$
$A \rightarrow d$	$j(w') - 1$	$k(w')$

The first rule adds 2 to each side of an inequality, maintaining the inequality. The final rule subtracts 1 from the smaller side, reinforcing the inequality. For a string $w \in L(G)$, the inequality yields $n_w(a) \leq n_w(b)$ as desired.   □

Example 3.4.4

The grammar

$$G: S \rightarrow aSdd \mid A$$
$$A \rightarrow bAc \mid bc$$

was constructed in Example 3.2.9 to generate the language $L = \{a^n b^m c^m d^{2n} \mid n \geq 0, m > 0\}$. We develop relationships among the variables and terminals that are sufficient to prove that $L(G) \subseteq L$. The S and the A rules enforce the numeric relationships between the a's and d's and the b's and c's. In a derivation of G, the start symbol is removed by an application of the rule $S \to A$. The presence of an A guarantees that a b will eventually be generated. These observations lead to the following three conditions:

i) $2n(a) = n(d)$

ii) $n(b) = n(c)$

iii) $n(S) + n(A) + n(b) > 0$.

The equalities guarantee that the terminals occur in correct numerical relationships. The description of the language demands more, that the terminals occur in a specified order. The additional requirement, that the a's (if any) precede the b's (if any) which precede the S or A (if present) which precede the c's (if any) which precede the d's, must be established to ensure the correct order of the components in a terminal string.   □

3.5   A Context-Free Grammar for Pascal

In the preceding sections context-free grammars were used to generate small "toy" languages. These examples were given to illustrate the use of context-free grammars as a tool for defining languages. The design of programming languages must contend with a complicated syntax and larger alphabets, increasing the complexity of the rules needed to generate the language. John Backus [1959] and Peter Naur [1963] used a system of rules to define the programming language ALGOL 60. The method of definition employed is now referred to as Backus-Naur form, or BNF. The syntax of the programming language Pascal, designed by Niklaus Wirth [1971], was also defined using this technique.

A BNF description of a language is a context-free grammar, the only difference being the notation used to define the rules. The definition of Pascal in its BNF form is given in Appendix II. The notational conventions are the same as the natural language example at the beginning of the chapter. The names of the variables are chosen to indicate the components of the language that they generate. Variables are enclosed in ⟨ ⟩. Terminals are represented by character strings delimited by blanks.

The design of a programming language, like the design of a complex program, is greatly simplified by utilizing modularity. The rules for modules, subsets of the grammar that are referenced repeatedly by other rules, can be developed independently. To illustrate the principles of language design and the importance of precise language definition, the syntax of several important constituents of the Pascal language is examined. The rules are given in the notation of context-free grammars.

Numeric constants in Pascal include positive and negative integers and real numbers. The simplest numeric constants, the unsigned integers, are defined first.

$\langle digit \rangle \rightarrow 0 \mid 1 \mid 2 \mid 3 \mid 4 \mid 5 \mid 6 \mid 7 \mid 8 \mid 9$

$\langle unsigned\ integer \rangle \rightarrow \langle digit \rangle \langle unsigned\ integer \rangle \mid \langle digit \rangle$

This definition places no limit on the size of an integer. Overflow conditions are properties of implementations, not of the language. Notice that this definition allows leading zeros in unsigned integers.

Real numbers are defined using the variable $\langle unsigned\ integer \rangle$. Real number constants in Pascal have several possible forms. Examples include 12.34, 1.1E23, and 2E−3. A separate rule is designed to generate each of these different forms.

$\langle unsigned\ real \rangle \rightarrow \langle unsigned\ integer \rangle\ .\ \langle unsigned\ integer \rangle \mid$

$\qquad \langle unsigned\ integer \rangle\ .\ \langle unsigned\ integer \rangle\ E\ \langle scale\ factor \rangle \mid$

$\qquad \langle unsigned\ integer \rangle\ E\ \langle scale\ factor \rangle$

$\langle scale\ factor \rangle \rightarrow \langle unsigned\ integer \rangle \mid \langle sign \rangle \langle unsigned\ integer \rangle$

$\langle sign \rangle \rightarrow + \mid -$

The rules for the numeric constants can be easily constructed, utilizing the Pascal definitions of integers and real numbers.

$\langle unsigned\ number \rangle \rightarrow \langle unsigned\ integer \rangle \mid \langle unsigned\ real \rangle$

$\langle unsigned\ constant \rangle \rightarrow \langle unsigned\ number \rangle$

$\langle constant \rangle \rightarrow \langle unsigned\ number \rangle \mid \langle sign \rangle \langle unsigned\ number \rangle$

Another independent portion of a programming language is the definition of identifiers. Identifiers have many uses: variable names, constant names, procedure and function names. A Pascal identifier consists of a letter followed by any string of letters and digits. These strings can be generated by the following rules:

$\langle letter \rangle \rightarrow a \mid b \mid c \mid \ldots \mid y \mid z$

$\langle identifier \rangle \rightarrow \langle letter \rangle \langle identifier\text{-}tail \rangle$

$\langle identifier\text{-}tail \rangle \rightarrow \langle letter \rangle \langle identifier\text{-}tail \rangle \mid \langle digit \rangle \langle identifier\text{-}tail \rangle \mid \lambda$

A constant is declared and its value assigned in the constant definition part of a block in Pascal. This is accomplished by the rule

$\langle constant\ definition \rangle \rightarrow \langle identifier \rangle = \langle constant \rangle .$

The string "*pi* = 3.1415" is a syntactically correct constant definition. What about the string "*plusone* = −−1"? Are two signs allowed in a constant definition? To determine your answer, attempt to construct a derivation of the string.

3.6　Arithmetic Expressions

The evaluation of expressions is the key to numeric computation. Expressions may be written in prefix, postfix, or infix notation. The postfix and prefix forms are computationally the most efficient since they require no parentheses. The precedence of the operators is determined completely by their position in the string. The more familiar infix notation utilizes a precedence relationship defined on the operators. Parentheses are used to override the positional properties. Many of the common programming languages, including Pascal, use the infix notation for arithmetic expressions.

We will examine the rules that define the syntax of expressions in Pascal. The interactions between the variables ⟨*term*⟩ and ⟨*factor*⟩ specify the relationship between subexpressions and the precedence of the operators. The derivations begin with the rules

$$\langle expression \rangle \to \langle simple\ expression \rangle$$
$$\langle simple\ expression \rangle \to \langle term \rangle \mid$$
$$\langle sign \rangle \langle term \rangle \mid$$
$$\langle simple\ expression \rangle \langle adding\ operator \rangle \langle term \rangle.$$

The arithmetic operators, for numeric computation, are defined by

$$\langle adding\ operator \rangle \to +\mid -$$
$$\langle multiplying\ operator \rangle \to *\mid /\mid \textbf{div} \mid \textbf{mod}.$$

A ⟨*term*⟩ represents a subexpression of an adding operator. The variable ⟨*term*⟩ follows ⟨*adding operator*⟩ and is combined with the result of the ⟨*simple expression*⟩. Since additive operators have the lowest priority of the infix operators, the computation within a term should be completed before the adding operator is invoked.

$$\langle term \rangle \to \langle factor \rangle \mid \langle term \rangle \langle multiplying\ operator \rangle \langle factor \rangle$$

When a multiplying operator is present, it is immediately evaluated. The rule for factor shows that its subexpressions are either variables, constants, or other expressions enclosed in parentheses.

$$\langle factor \rangle \to \langle variable \rangle \mid \langle unsigned\ constant \rangle \mid (\langle expression \rangle)$$

The subgrammar for generating expressions is used to construct the derivations of several expressions. Owing to the complexity of the infix notation, simple expressions often require lengthy derivations.

Example 3.6.1

The constant 5 is generated by the derivation

$$\langle expression \rangle \Rightarrow \langle simple\ expression \rangle$$
$$\Rightarrow \langle term \rangle$$
$$\Rightarrow \langle factor \rangle \qquad \text{'since no addition occurs'}$$
$$\Rightarrow \langle unsigned\ constant \rangle$$
$$\Rightarrow \langle unsigned\ number \rangle$$
$$\Rightarrow \langle unsigned\ integer \rangle$$
$$\Rightarrow \langle digit \rangle$$
$$\Rightarrow 5.$$

□

Example 3.6.2

The expression $x + 5$ consists of two subexpressions: x and 5. The existence of the adding operator dictates the decomposition of ⟨*simple expression*⟩, with the subexpressions x and 5 being the operands.

⟨*expression*⟩ ⟹ ⟨*simple expression*⟩
    ⟹ ⟨*simple expression*⟩ ⟨*adding operator*⟩ ⟨*term*⟩
    ⟹ ⟨*term*⟩ ⟨*adding operator*⟩ ⟨*term*⟩
    ⟹ ⟨*factor*⟩ ⟨*adding operator*⟩ ⟨*term*⟩
    ⟹ ⟨*variable*⟩ ⟨*adding operator*⟩ ⟨*term*⟩
    ⟹ ⟨*entire variable*⟩ ⟨*adding operator*⟩ ⟨*term*⟩
    ⟹ ⟨*variable identifier*⟩ ⟨*adding operator*⟩ ⟨*term*⟩
    ⟹ ⟨*identifier*⟩ ⟨*adding operator*⟩ ⟨*term*⟩
    ⟹ ⟨*letter*⟩ ⟨*identifier tail*⟩ ⟨*adding operator*⟩ ⟨*term*⟩
    ⟹ x ⟨*identifier tail*⟩ ⟨*adding operator*⟩ ⟨*term*⟩
    ⟹ x ⟨*adding operator*⟩ ⟨*term*⟩
    ⟹ $x + $ ⟨*term*⟩
    $\overset{*}{\Rightarrow} x + 5$ 'from Example 3.6.1'

The derivation of 5 from the variable ⟨*term*⟩ was given in the previous example.   □

Example 3.6.3

A derivation of the expression $5*(x + 5)$ can be constructed using the derivations of the subexpressions 5 and $x + 5$. This example illustrates the relationship between terms and factors. The operands of a multiplicative operator consist of a term and a factor.

   ⟨*expression*⟩ ⟹ ⟨*simple expression*⟩
      ⟹ ⟨*term*⟩
      ⟹ ⟨*term*⟩ ⟨*multiplying operator*⟩ ⟨*factor*⟩
      $\overset{*}{\Rightarrow}$ 5 ⟨*multiplying operator*⟩ ⟨*factor*⟩   'from 3.6.1'
      ⟹ $5*$⟨*factor*⟩
      ⟹ $5*($⟨*expression*⟩$)$
      $\overset{*}{\Rightarrow} 5*(x + 5)$ 'from 3.6.2'   □

Exercises

1. Let G be the grammar

$$S \rightarrow abSc \mid A$$
$$A \rightarrow cAd \mid cd.$$

 a) Give a derivation of *ababccddcc*.

 b) Build the derivation tree for the derivation in part a).

 c) Use set notation to define L(G).

2. Let G be the grammar

$$S \rightarrow ASB \mid \lambda$$
$$A \rightarrow aAb \mid \lambda$$
$$B \rightarrow bBa \mid ba.$$

a) Give a leftmost derivation of *aabbba*.

b) Give a rightmost derivation of *abaabbbabbaa*.

c) Build the derivation tree for the derivations in parts a) and b).

d) Use set notation to define L(G).

3. Let DT be the derivation tree

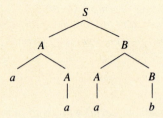

a) Give a leftmost derivation that generates the tree DT.

b) Give a rightmost derivation that generates the tree DT.

c) How many different derivations are there that generate DT?

4. Give the leftmost and rightmost derivations corresponding to each of the derivation trees given in Fig. 3.3.

5. For each of the following grammars, use set notation to define the language generated by the grammar.

a) $S \rightarrow aaSB \mid \lambda$
   $B \rightarrow bB \mid b$

b) $S \rightarrow aSbb \mid A$
   $A \rightarrow cA \mid c$

c) $S \rightarrow aS \mid bS \mid A$
   $A \rightarrow cA \mid c \mid S$

d) $S \rightarrow abSdc \mid A$
   $A \rightarrow cdAba \mid \lambda$

6–25 (**11, 14, 20, 21, 25**). For each of the languages described in Exercises 6–25 in Chapter 2, give a regular grammar G whose language is the specified set.

26. Construct a grammar over $\{a, b, c\}$ whose language is $\{a^n b^m c^{2n+m} \mid n, m > 0\}$.

27. Construct a grammar over $\{a, b, c\}$ whose language is $\{a^m b^n c^i \mid m > n + i\}$.

28. Construct a grammar over $\{a, b\}$ whose language contains precisely the strings with the same number of a's and b's.

29. The grammar in Fig. 3.1 generates $(b^* ab^* ab^*)^*$, the set of all strings with a positive, even number of a's. Prove this.

30. Let G be the grammar

$$S \rightarrow aSaa \mid B$$
$$B \rightarrow bbBdd \mid C$$
$$C \rightarrow bd.$$

a) What is L(G)?

b) Prove that L(G) is the set given in part a).

31. Prove that the grammar given in Example 3.2.9 generates the given language.

32. Let G be the grammar

$$S \rightarrow aSbS \mid aS \mid \lambda.$$

Prove that every prefix of a string in L(G) has at least as many a's as b's.

For Exercises 33–36, use the definition of Pascal in Appendix II to construct the derivations.

33. Construct a derivation of the string $x1y$ from the variable ⟨*variable*⟩.

34. Construct a derivation of $(x1y)$ from ⟨*expression*⟩.

35. Construct a derivation for the expression $(x*y*5)$ from the variable ⟨*expression*⟩.

36. For the not faint of heart, construct a derivation of the $(x+y*(12+z))$ from the variable ⟨*expression*⟩.

37. Let G_1 and G_2 be the following grammars:

$$G_1: S \rightarrow aABb \qquad G_2: S \rightarrow AABB$$
$$A \rightarrow aA \mid a \qquad A \rightarrow AA \mid a$$
$$B \rightarrow bB \mid b \qquad B \rightarrow BB \mid b$$

a) For each variable A, show that every A rule of G_1 is derivable from the corresponding variable A using the rules of G_2. Use this to conclude that $L(G_1) \subseteq L(G_2)$.

b) Prove that $L(G_1) = L(G_2)$.

38. A **right-linear grammar** is a context-free grammar each of whose rules is of the form

i) $A \rightarrow w$

ii) $A \rightarrow wB$

iii) $A \rightarrow \lambda$

where $w \in \Sigma^*$.

Prove that a language L is generated by a right-linear grammar if, and only if, L is generated by a regular grammar.

39. Try to construct a regular grammar that generates the language $\{a^n b^n \mid n \geq 0\}$. Explain why none of your attempts succeed.

40. Try to construct a context-free grammar that generates the language $\{a^n b^n c^n \mid n \geq 0\}$. Explain why none of your attempts succeed.

Bibliographic Notes

Context-free grammars were introduced by Chomsky [1956], [1959]. Backus-Naur form was developed by Backus [1959]. This formalism was used to define the programming language ALGOL; see Naur [1963]. The language Pascal, a descendant of ALGOL, was also defined using the BNF notation. The BNF definition of Pascal is given in Appendix II. The equivalence of context-free languages and the languages generated by BNF definitions was noted by Ginsburg and Rice [1962].

CHAPTER 4

Parsing:
An Introduction

Derivations in a context-free grammar provide a mechanism for the generation of the strings that comprise the language of the grammar. The language of the Backus-Naur definition of Pascal is the set of syntactically correct Pascal programs. An important question remains, how can we determine whether a sequence of Pascal code is a syntactically correct program? The syntax is correct if the string is derivable from the start symbol using the rules of the grammar. Algorithms must be designed to generate derivations for strings in the language of the grammar. When an input string is not in the language, these procedures should discover that no derivation exists. A procedure that performs this function is called a **parsing algorithm** or **parser**.

This chapter introduces several simple parsing algorithms. These parsers are variations of classical algorithms for traversing directed graphs. Grammars designed to define programming languages often require restrictions on the rules of the grammar to efficiently parse the strings of the language. Grammars specifically designed to facilitate the parsing process are presented in Chapters 15 and 16.

4.1 Leftmost Derivations and Ambiguity

The language of a grammar is the set of terminal strings that can be derived, in any manner, from the start symbol. A terminal string may be generated by a number of different derivations. Four distinct derivations of the string *ababaa* are given in the grammar presented in Fig. 3.1. Any one of these derivations is sufficient to exhibit the syntactic correctness of the string.

The sample derivations generating Pascal expressions in Chapter 3 were given in a leftmost form. This is a natural technique for readers of English since the leftmost variable is the first encountered when scanning a string. To reduce the number of derivations that must be considered by a parser, we prove that every string in the language of a grammar is derivable in a leftmost manner. It follows that a parser that constructs only leftmost derivations is sufficient for deciding whether a string is generated by a grammar.

Theorem 4.1.1

Let $G = (V, \Sigma, P, S)$ be a context-free grammar. A string w is in $L(G)$ if, and only if, there is a leftmost derivation of w from S.

Proof   Clearly, $w \in L(G)$ whenever there is a leftmost derivation of w from S. We must establish the "only if" clause of the equivalence, that is, that every string in the $L(G)$ is derivable in a leftmost manner. Let

$$S \Rightarrow w_1 \Rightarrow w_2 \Rightarrow w_3 \Rightarrow \cdots \Rightarrow w_n = w$$

be a, not necessarily leftmost, derivation of w in G. The independence of rule applications in a context-free grammar is used to build a leftmost derivation of w. Let w_k be the first sentential form in the derivation to which the rule application is not leftmost. If there is no such k, the derivation is already leftmost and there is nothing to show. If k is less than n, a new derivation of w with length n is constructed in which the first nonleftmost rule application occurs after step k. This procedure can be repeated, $n - k$ times if necessary, to produce a leftmost derivation.

By the choice of w_k, the derivation $S \overset{k}{\Rightarrow} w_k$ is leftmost. Assume that A is the leftmost variable in w_k and B is the variable transformed in the $k + 1$st step of the derivation. Then w_k can be written $u_1 A u_2 B u_3$ with $u_1 \in \Sigma^*$. The application of a rule $B \to v$ to w_k has the form

$$w_k = u_1 A u_2 B u_3 \Rightarrow u_1 A u_2 v u_3 = w_{k+1}.$$

Since w is a terminal string, an A rule must eventually be applied to the leftmost variable in w_k. Let the first rule application that transforms the A occur at the $j + 1$st step in the original derivation. Then the application of the rule $A \to p$ can be written

$$w_j = u_1 A q \Rightarrow u_1 p q = w_{j+1}.$$

The rules applied in steps $k + 2$ to j transform the string $u_2 v u_3$ into q. The derivation is completed by the subderivation

$$w_{j+1} \overset{*}{\Rightarrow} w_n = w.$$

The original derivation has been divided into five distinct subderivations. The first k rule applications are already leftmost, so they are left intact. To construct a leftmost derivation, the rule $A \to p$ is applied to the leftmost variable at step $k + 1$. The context-free nature of rule applications permits this rearrangement. A derivation of w that is leftmost for the first $k + 1$ rule applications is obtained as follows:

$$S \overset{k}{\Rightarrow} w_k = u_1 A u_2 B u_3$$
$$\Rightarrow u_1 p u_2 B u_3 \qquad \text{'applying } A \to p\text{'}$$
$$\Rightarrow u_1 p u_2 v u_3 \qquad \text{'applying } B \to v\text{'}$$
$$\overset{j-k-1}{\Longrightarrow} u_1 p q \qquad \text{'using the segment } w_{k+1} \overset{*}{\Rightarrow} w_j\text{'}$$
$$\overset{n-j-1}{\Longrightarrow} w_n \qquad \text{'using the segment } w_{j+1} \overset{*}{\Rightarrow} w_n\text{'}$$

Every time this procedure is repeated the derivation becomes "more" leftmost. If the length of a derivation is n, then at most n iterations are needed to produce a leftmost derivation of w. ∎

Theorem 4.1.1 does not guarantee that all sentential forms of the grammar can be generated by a leftmost derivation. Only leftmost derivations of terminal strings are assured. Consider the grammar

$$S \to AB$$
$$A \to aA \mid \lambda$$
$$B \to bB \mid \lambda$$

that generates a^*b^*. The string A can be obtained by the rightmost derivation $S \Rightarrow AB \Rightarrow A$. It is easy to see that there is no leftmost derivation of A.

A similar result (Exercise 2) establishes the sufficiency of using rightmost derivations for the generation of terminal strings. Leftmost and rightmost derivations of w from v are explicitly denoted $v \overset{*}{\underset{L}{\Rightarrow}} w$ and $v \overset{*}{\underset{R}{\Rightarrow}} w$.

Restricting our attention to leftmost derivations eliminates many of the possible derivations of a string. Is this reduction sufficient to establish a canonical derivation, that is, is there a unique leftmost derivation of every string in the language of a grammar? Unfortunately, the answer is no. Two distinct leftmost derivations of the string *ababaa* are given in Fig. 3.1.

The possibility of a string having several leftmost derivations introduces the notion of ambiguity. Ambiguity in formal languages is similar to ambiguity encountered frequently in natural languages. The sentence *Jack was given a book by Hemingway* has two distinct structural decompositions. The prepositional phrase *by Hemingway* can modify either *given* or *book*. Each of these structural decompositions represents a syntactically correct sentence.

The compilation of a computer program utilizes the derivation produced by the parser to generate machine language code. The compilation of a program that has two derivations uses only one of the possible interpretations to produce the executable code. An unfortunate programmer may then be faced with debugging a program that is completely correct according to the language definition but doesn't perform as expected. To avoid this possibility, and help maintain the sanity of programmers everywhere, the definitions of computer languages should be constructed so that no ambiguity can occur. The preceding discussion of ambiguity leads to the following definition.

Definition 4.1.2

A context-free grammar is **ambiguous** if there is a string $w \in L(G)$ that can be derived by two distinct leftmost derivations. A grammar that is not ambiguous is called **unambiguous.**

Example 4.1.1

Let G be the grammar

$$S \rightarrow aS \mid Sa \mid a.$$

G is ambiguous since the string aa has two distinct leftmost derivations.

$$
\begin{array}{ll}
S \Rightarrow aS & S \Rightarrow Sa \\
 \Rightarrow aa & \Rightarrow aa
\end{array}
$$

The language of G is a^+. This language is also generated by the unambiguous grammar

$$S \rightarrow aS \mid a.$$

This grammar, being regular, has the property that all strings are generated in a left-to-right manner. The variable S remains as the rightmost symbol of the string until the recursion is halted by the application of the rule $S \rightarrow a$.   □

The previous example demonstrates that ambiguity is a property of grammars, not of languages. When a grammar is shown to be ambiguous, it is often possible to construct an equivalent unambiguous grammar. This is not always the case. There are some context-free languages that cannot be generated by any unambiguous grammar. Such languages are called **inherently ambiguous.** The syntax of most programming languages, which require unambiguous derivations, is sufficiently restrictive to avoid generating inherently ambiguous languages.

Example 4.1.2

Let G be the grammar

$$S \rightarrow bS \mid Sb \mid a.$$

The language of G is b^*ab^*. The leftmost derivations

$$
\begin{array}{ll}
S \Rightarrow bS & S \Rightarrow Sb \\
 \Rightarrow bSb & \Rightarrow bSb \\
 \Rightarrow bab & \Rightarrow bab
\end{array}
$$

exhibit the ambiguity of G. The ability to generate the b's in either order must be eliminated to obtain an unambiguous grammar. L(G) is also generated by the unambiguous grammars

$$
\begin{array}{ll}
G_1\text{:}\ S \rightarrow bS \mid aA & G_2\text{:}\ S \rightarrow bS \mid A \\
\phantom{G_1\text{:}\ } A \rightarrow bA \mid \lambda & \phantom{G_2\text{:}\ } A \rightarrow Ab \mid a.
\end{array}
$$

In G_1, the sequence of rule applications in a leftmost derivation is completely determined by the string being derived. The only leftmost derivation of the string $b^n a b^m$ has the form

$$\begin{aligned}
S &\stackrel{n}{\Rightarrow} b^n S \\
&\Rightarrow b^n a A \\
&\stackrel{m}{\Rightarrow} b^n a b^m A \\
&\Rightarrow b^n a b^m.
\end{aligned}$$

A derivation in G_2 initially generates the leading b's, followed by the trailing b's and finally the a.　　　　　　　　　　　　　　　　　　　　　　　□

A grammar is unambiguous if, at each step in a leftmost derivation, there is only one rule whose application can lead to a derivation of the desired string. This does not mean that there is only one applicable rule, but that the application of any other rule makes it impossible to complete a derivation of the string.

Consider the possibilities encountered in constructing a leftmost derivation of the string $bbabb$ using the grammar G_2 from Example 4.1.2. There are two S rules that can initiate a derivation. Derivations initiated with the rule $S \rightarrow A$ generate strings beginning with a. Consequently, a derivation of $bbabb$ must begin with the application of the rule $S \rightarrow bS$. The second b is generated by another application of the same rule. At this point, the derivation continues using $S \rightarrow A$. Another application of $S \rightarrow bS$ would generate the prefix bbb. The suffix bb is generated by two applications of $A \rightarrow Ab$. The derivation is successfully completed with an application of $A \rightarrow a$. Since the terminal string specifies the exact sequence of rule applications, the grammar is unambiguous.

A derivation tree depicts the decomposition of the variables in a derivation. There is a natural one-to-one correspondence between leftmost (rightmost) derivations and derivation trees. Definition 3.1.4 outlines the construction of a derivation tree directly from a leftmost derivation. Conversely, a unique leftmost derivation of a string w can be extracted from a derivation tree with frontier w. Utilizing this correspondence, ambiguity is often defined in terms of derivation trees. Figure 3.3 shows that the two leftmost derivations of the string $ababaa$ in Fig. 3.1 generate distinct derivation trees.

4.2   The Graph of a Grammar

The leftmost derivations of a context-free grammar G can be represented by a labeled directed graph $g(G)$, the leftmost graph of the grammar G. The nodes of the graph are the left sentential forms of the grammar. A **left sentential form** is a string that can be derived from the start symbol by a leftmost derivation. A string w is adjacent to v in $g(G)$ if $v \underset{L}{\Rightarrow} w$, that is, if w can be obtained from v by one leftmost rule application.

Definition 4.2.1

Let G = (V, Σ, P, S) be a context-free grammar. The **leftmost graph of the grammar** G, g(G), is the labeled directed graph (N, P, A) where the nodes and arcs are defined by

i) $N = \{w \in (V \cup \Sigma)^* \mid S \underset{L}{\overset{*}{\Rightarrow}} w\}$

ii) $A = \{(v, w, r) \in N \times N \times P \mid v \underset{L}{\Rightarrow} w$ by application of rule $r\}$.

A path from S to w in g(G) represents a derivation of w from S in the G. The label on the arc from v to w specifies the rule applied to v to obtain w. The problem of deciding whether a string w is in L(G) is reduced to that of finding a path from S to w in g(G).

The relationship between leftmost derivations in a grammar and paths in the graph of the grammar can be seen in Fig. 4.1. The number of rules that can be applied to the leftmost variable of a sentential form determines the number of children of the node. Since a context-free grammar has finitely many rules, each node has only finitely many children. A graph with this property is called locally finite. Graphs of all interesting grammars, however, have infinitely many nodes. The repeated applications of the directly recursive S rule and the indirectly recursive S and B rules generate arbitrarily long paths in the graph of the grammar depicted in Fig. 4.1.

The graph of a grammar may take many forms. If every string in the graph has only one leftmost derivation, the graph is a tree with the start symbol as the root. Figure 4.2 gives the graphs of two ambiguous grammars. The lambda rules in (b) generate cycles in the graph.

A rightmost graph of a grammar G can be constructed by defining adjacency using rightmost rule applications. The complete graph of G is defined by replacing $v \underset{L}{\Rightarrow} w$ with $v \Rightarrow w$ in condition ii). Theorem 4.1.1 and Exercise 2 guarantee that every terminal string in the complete graph also occurs in both the leftmost and rightmost graphs. When referring to the graph of a grammar G, unless stated otherwise, we mean the leftmost graph defined in Definition 4.2.1.

Using the graph of a grammar, the generation of derivations is reduced to the construction of paths in a locally finite directed graph. Standard graph searching techniques will be used to develop several simple parsing algorithms. In graph searching terminology, the graph of a grammar is called an implicit graph since its nodes have not been constructed prior to the invocation of the algorithm. The search consists of building the graph as the paths are examined. An important feature of the search is to explicitly construct as little of the implicit graph as possible.

Two distinct strategies may be employed to find a derivation of w from S. The search can begin with the node S and attempt to find the string w. An algorithm utilizing this approach is called a **top-down parser**. An algorithm that begins with the terminal string w and searches for the start symbol is called a **bottom-up** parsing algorithm. An important difference between these strategies is the ease with which the adjacent nodes can be generated while constructing the explicit search structure.

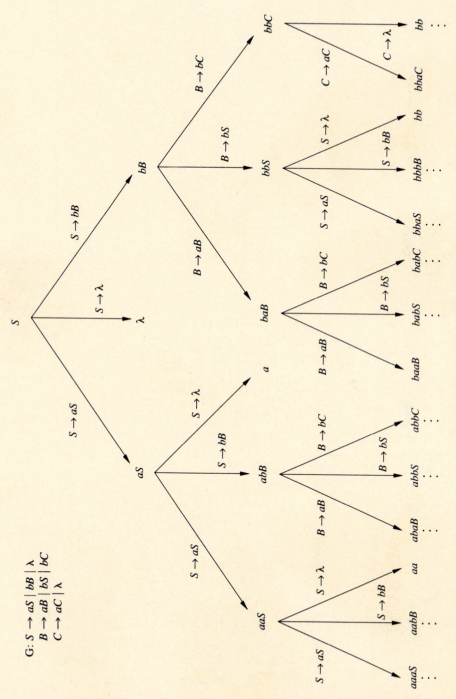

FIGURE 4.1   Graph of grammar G.

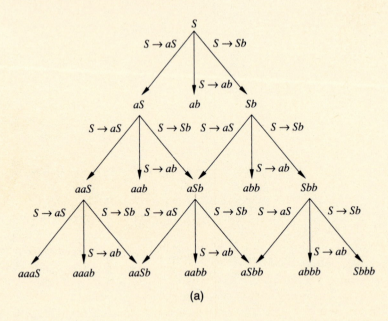

(a)

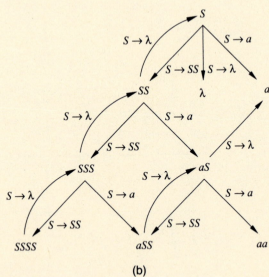

(b)

FIGURE 4.2   Graphs of ambiguous grammars. (a) $S \rightarrow aS \mid Sb \mid ab$. (b) $S \rightarrow SS \mid a \mid \lambda$.

4.3 A Breadth-First Top-down Parser

The objective of a parser is to determine whether an input string is derivable from the rules of a grammar. A top-down parser constructs derivations by applying rules to the leftmost variable of a sentential form. The application of a rule $A \rightarrow w$ in a leftmost derivation has the form $uAv \Rightarrow uwv$. The string u, consisting solely of terminals, is called the **terminal prefix** of the sentential form uAv. The parsing algorithm uses the terminal prefix of the derived string to identify dead-ends. A dead-end is a string that the parser can determine does not occur in a derivation of the input string.

Parsing is an inherently nondeterministic process. In constructing a derivation, there may be several rules that can be applied to a sentential form. It is not known whether the application of a particular rule will lead to a derivation of the input string, a dead-end, or an unending computation. A parse is said to terminate successfully when it produces a derivation of the input string.

Paths beginning with S in the graph of a grammar represent the leftmost derivations of the grammar. The arcs emanating from a node represent the possible rule applications. The parsing algorithm presented in Algorithm 4.3.1 employs a breadth-first search of the implicit graph of a grammar. The algorithm terminates by accepting or rejecting the input string. An input string p is accepted if the parser constructs a derivation of p. If the parser determines that no derivation of p is possible, the string is rejected.

To implement a breadth-first search, the parser builds a search tree T containing nodes from $g(G)$. The **search tree** is the portion of the implicit graph of the grammar that is explicitly examined during the parse. The rules of the grammar are numbered to facilitate the construction of the search tree. The children of a node uAv are added to the tree according to the ordering of the A rules. The search tree is built with directed arcs from each child to its parent (parent pointers).

A queue is used to implement the first-in, first-out memory management strategy required for a breadth-first graph traversal. The queue **Q** is maintained by three functions; $INSERT(x, \mathbf{Q})$ places the string x at the rear of the queue, $REMOVE(\mathbf{Q})$ returns the item at the front and deletes it from the queue, and $EMPTY(\mathbf{Q})$ is a Boolean function that returns true if the queue is empty, false otherwise.

Algorithm 4.3.1
Breadth-First Top-down Parsing Algorithm

input: context-free grammar $G = (V, \Sigma, P, S)$
      string $p \in \Sigma^*$
      queue **Q**

1. initialize T with root S
   $INSERT(S, \mathbf{Q})$

2. **repeat**
    2.1. $q := REMOVE(\mathbf{Q})$

2.2. $i := 0$
2.3. done $:= false$
Let $q = uAv$ where A is the leftmost variable in q.
2.4. **repeat**
    2.4.1. **if** there is no A rule numbered greater than i **then** done $:= true$
    2.4.2. **if** not done **then**
        Let $A \to w$ be the first A rule with number greater than i. Let j be
        the number of this rule.
        2.4.2.1. **if** $uwv \notin \Sigma^*$ and the terminal prefix of uwv matches a
            prefix of p **then**
            2.4.2.1.1. *INSERT*$(uwv, \mathbf{Q})$
            2.4.2.1.2. Add node uwv to T. Set a pointer from
                uwv to q.
        end if
    end if
    2.4.3. $i := j$
  until done **or** $p = uvw$
until *EMPTY*$(\mathbf{Q})$ **or** $p = uwv$
3. **if** $p = uwv$ **then** accept **else** reject

The search tree is initialized with root S since a top-down algorithm attempts to find a derivation of p from S. The repeat-until loop in step 2.4 generates the successors of the node with sentential form q in the order specified by the numbering of the rules. The process of generating the successors of a node and adding them to the search tree is called expanding the node. Utilizing the queue, nodes are expanded level by level, resulting in the breadth-first construction of T.

The terminal prefix of a string can be used to determine dead-ends in the search. Let uAv be a string in T with terminal prefix u. If u is not a prefix of p, no sequence of rule applications can derive p from uAv. The condition in step 2.4.2.1 checks each node for a prefix match before inserting it into the queue. The node expansion phase is repeated until the input string is generated or the queue is emptied. The latter occurs only when all possible derivations have been examined and have failed.

Throughout the remainder of this chapter, the grammar AE (additive expressions) is used to demonstrate the construction of derivations by the parsers presented in this chapter. The language of AE consists of arithmetic expressions with the single variable b, the $+$ operator, and parentheses. Strings generated by AE include b, (b), $(b + b)$, and $(b) + b$. The variable S is the start symbol of AE.

$$\text{AE: } V = \{S, A, T\}$$
$$\Sigma = \{b, +, (,)\}$$

P: 1. $S \to A$
       2. $A \to T$
       3. $A \to A + T$
       4. $T \to b$
       5. $T \to (A)$

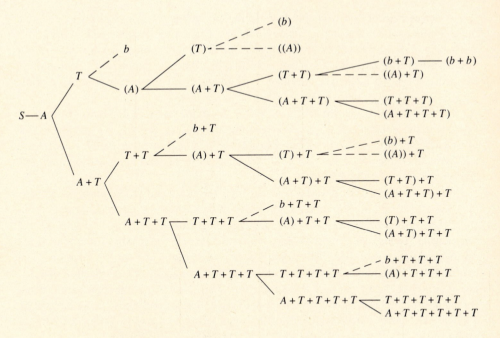

FIGURE 4.3 Breadth-first top-down parse of $(b + b)$.

The search tree constructed by the parse of $(b + b)$ using Algorithm 4.3.1 is given in Fig. 4.3. The sentential forms that are generated but not added to the search tree due to the prefix matching conditions are indicated by the dotted lines.

The comparison in step 2.4.1.1 matches the terminal prefix of the sentential form generated by the parser to the input string. To obtain the information required for the match, the parser "reads" the input string as it builds derivations. Like a human reading a string of text, the parser scans the input string in a left-to-right manner. The growth of the terminal prefix causes the parser to read the entire input string. The derivation of $(b + b)$ exhibits the correspondence between the initial segment of the string scanned by the parser and the terminal prefix of the derived string.

Derivation	Input Read by Parser
$S \Rightarrow A$	λ
$\Rightarrow T$	λ
$\Rightarrow (A)$	$($
$\Rightarrow (A + T)$	$($
$\Rightarrow (T + T)$	$($
$\Rightarrow (b + T)$	$(b +$
$\Rightarrow (b + b)$	$(b + b)$

A parser must not only be able to generate derivations for strings in the language; it must also determine when strings are not in the language. The bottom branch of the search tree in Fig. 4.3 can potentially grow forever. The direct recursion of the rule $A \rightarrow A + T$ builds strings with any number of $+T$'s as a suffix. While searching for a derivation of the string not in the language, the directly recursive A rule will never generate a prefix capable of terminating the search.

It may be argued that the string $A + T + T$ cannot lead to a derivation of $(b + b)$ and should be declared a dead-end. It is true that the presence of two $+$'s guarantees that no sequence of rule applications can transform $A + T + T$ to $(b + b)$. However, such a determination requires a knowledge of the input string beyond the initial segment that has been scanned by the parser.

More complicated parsers may scan the input string several times. Multipass parsers may use other criteria, such as the total length of the derived string, to determine dead-ends. An initial pass can be used to obtain the length of the input string. A sentential form derived by the parser containing more terminals than the length of the input string can be declared a dead-end. This condition can be strengthened for grammars without lambda rules. Derivations in these grammars are noncontracting; the application of a rule does not reduce the length of a sentential form. This implies that the input string is not derivable from any sentential form of greater length. These conditions cannot be used by a single-pass parser since the length of the input string is not known until the parse is completed.

Although the breadth-first algorithm succeeds in constructing a derivation for any string in the language, the practical application of this approach has several shortcomings. Lengthy derivations and grammars with a large number of rules cause the size of the search tree to increase rapidly. The exponential growth of the search tree is not limited to parsing algorithms but is a general property of breadth-first graph searches. If the grammar can be designed to utilize the prefix matching condition quickly or if other conditions can be developed to find dead-ends in the search, the combinatorial problems associated with growth of the search tree may be delayed.

4.4   A Depth-First Top-down Parser

A depth-first search of a graph avoids the combinatorial problems associated with a breadth-first search. The traversal moves through the graph examining a single path. In a graph defined by a grammar, this corresponds to exploring a single derivation at a time. When a node is expanded, only one successor is generated and added to the search structure. The choice of the descendant added to the path is arbitrary, and it is possible that the alternative chosen will not produce a derivation of the input string.

The possibility of incorrectly choosing a successor adds two complications to a depth-first parser. The algorithm must be able to determine that an incorrect choice has been made. When this occurs, the parser must have the ability to backtrack and generate the alternative

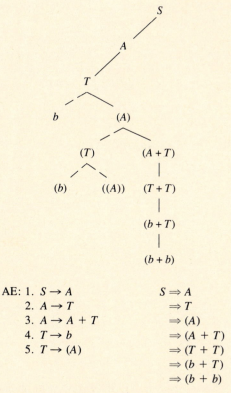

$$AE: \begin{array}{l} 1. \ S \rightarrow A \\ 2. \ A \rightarrow T \\ 3. \ A \rightarrow A + T \\ 4. \ T \rightarrow b \\ 5. \ T \rightarrow (A) \end{array} \qquad \begin{array}{l} S \Rightarrow A \\ \Rightarrow T \\ \Rightarrow (A) \\ \Rightarrow (A + T) \\ \Rightarrow (T + T) \\ \Rightarrow (b + T) \\ \Rightarrow (b + b) \end{array}$$

FIGURE 4.4   Path and derivation generated by depth-first search for $(b + b)$ in the graph of AE.

derivations. Figure 4.4 shows the sentential forms constructed by a depth-first parse of the string $(b + b)$ in the graph of the grammar AE. The sentential forms connected by dotted lines are those that have been generated and determined to be dead-ends. The prefix matching conditions introduced in Algorithm 4.3.1 are used to make these determinations.

The successors of a string are generated in the order specified by the numbering of the rules. In Fig. 4.4, the string T is initially expanded with the rule $T \rightarrow b$ since it precedes $T \rightarrow (A)$ in the ordering. When this choice results in a dead-end, the next T rule is applied. Using the prefix matching condition, the parser eventually determines that the rule $A \rightarrow T$ applied to (A) cannot lead to a derivation of $(b + b)$. At this point the search returns to the node (A) and constructs derivations utilizing the A rule $A \rightarrow A + T$.

Backtracking algorithms can be implemented by using a stack to store the information required for generating the alternative paths. A stack **S** is maintained using the procedures *PUSH*, *POP*, and *EMPTY*. A stack element is an ordered pair $[u, i]$ where u is a sentential form and i the number of the rule applied to u to generate the subsequent node in the path. *PUSH*$([u, i],$ **S**$)$ places the stack item $[u, i]$ on the top of the stack **S**. *POP*(**S**) returns the top item and deletes it from the stack. *EMPTY*(S) is a Boolean function that returns true if the stack is empty, false otherwise.

A stack provides a last-in first-out memory management strategy. A top-down back-tracking algorithm is given in Algorithm 4.4.1. The input string is p and q is the sentential form contained in the final node of the path currently being explored. When the parse successfully terminates, a derivation can be obtained from the elements stored in the stack.

Algorithm 4.4.1
Depth-First Top-down Parsing Algorithm

input: context-free grammar $G = (V, \Sigma, P, S)$
       string $p \in \Sigma^*$
       stack S

1. *PUSH*([S, 0], S)

2. **repeat**
    2.1. [q, i] := *POP*(S)
    2.2. dead-end := *false*
    2.3. **repeat**
        Let $q = uAv$ where A is the leftmost variable in q.
        2.3.1. **if** u is not a prefix of p **then** dead-end := *true*
        2.3.2. **if** there are no A rules numbered greater than i **then**
             dead-end := *true*
        2.3.3. **if not** dead-end **then**
             Let $A \rightarrow w$ be the first A rule with number greater than i.
             Let j be the number of this rule.
             2.3.3.1. *PUSH*([q, j], S)
             2.3.3.2. $q := uwv$
             2.3.3.3. $i := 0$
        end if
        until dead-end **or** $q \in \Sigma^*$
    until $q = p$ **or** *EMPTY*(S)

3. **if** $q = p$ **then** accept **else** reject

The algorithm consists of two repeat-until loops. The interior loop extends the current derivation by expanding the final node of the path. This loop terminates when the most recently constructed node completes the derivation of a terminal string or is determined to be a dead-end. There are three ways in which dead-ends can be detected. The terminal prefix of q may not match an initial substring of p (step 2.3.1). There may be no rules to apply to the leftmost variable in the q (step 2.3.2). This occurs when all the appropriate rules have been examined and have produced dead-ends. Finally, a terminal string other than p may be derived.

When a dead-end is discovered, the outer loop pops the stack to implement the backtracking. The order in which the rules are applied is determined by the numbering of the rules and the integer stored in the stack. When the stack is popped, step 2.1 restores the sentential form in the preceding node. If the top stack element is $[uAv, i]$, with A the leftmost variable in the string, the first A rule with number greater than i is applied to extend the derivation.

Example 4.4.1

The top-down backtracking algorithm is used to construct a derivation of $(b + b)$. The action of the parser is demonstrated by tracing the sequence of nodes generated. The strings at the bottom of each column, except the final one, are dead-ends that cause the parser to backtrack. The items popped from the stack are indicated by the slash. A stack item to the immediate right of a popped item is the alternative generated by backtracking. For example, the string T is expanded with rule 5, $T \rightarrow (A)$, after the expansion with rule 4 produces b.

$[S, 0]$	$[S, 1]$			
	$[A, 2]$			
	$[T, 4]$	$[T, 5]$		
	b	$[(A), 2]$		$[(A), 3]$
		$[(T), 4]$	$[(T), 5]$	$[(A +T), 2]$
		(b)	$((A))$	$[(T +T), 4]$
				$[(b +T), 4]$
				$(b + b)$

A derivation of the input string can be constructed from the items on the stack when the search successfully terminates. The first element is the sentential form being expanded and the second is the number of the rule applied to generate the successor.

Stack	Derivation
$[S, 1]$	$S \Rightarrow A$
$[A, 2]$	$\Rightarrow T$
$[T, 5]$	$\Rightarrow (A)$
$[(A), 3]$	$\Rightarrow (A + T)$
$[(A + T), 2]$	$\Rightarrow (T + T)$
$[(T + T), 4]$	$\Rightarrow (b + T)$
$[(b + T), 4]$	$\Rightarrow (b + b)$

The exhaustive nature of the breadth-first search guarantees that Algorithm 4.3.1 produces a derivation whenever the input is in the language of the grammar. We have already noted that prefix matching does not provide sufficient information to ensure that the breadth-first search terminates for strings not in the language. Unfortunately, the backtracking algorithm may fail to find derivations for strings in the language. Since it employs a depth-first strategy, the parser may explore an infinitely long path. If this exploration fails to trigger one of the dead-end conditions, the search will never backtrack to examine other paths in the graph. Example 4.4.2 shows that Algorithm 4.4.1 fails to terminate when attempting to parse the string $(b) + b$ using the rules of the grammar AE.

Example 4.4.2

The actions of the top-down backtracking algorithm are traced for input string $(b) + b$.

$[S,0]$ $[S,1]$
  $[A,2]$
  $[T,4]$ $[T,5]$
  b $[(A),2]$ $[(A),3]$
          $[(T),4]$ $[(T),5]$ $[(A+T),2]$ $[(A+T),3]$
          (b) $((A))$ $[(T+T),4]$ $[(T+T),5]$ $[(A+T+T),2]$
                               $(b+T)$ $((A)+T)$ $[(T+T+T),4]$ $[(T+T+T),5]$
                                                        $(b+T+T)$ $((A)+T+T)$

A pattern emerges in columns five and six and in columns seven and eight. The next step of the algorithm is to pop the stack and restore the string $(A+T+T)$. The stack item $[(A+T+T), 2]$ indicates that all A rules numbered two or less have previously been examined. Rule 3 is then applied to $(A+T+T)$, generating $(A+T+T+T)$. The directly recursive rule $A \rightarrow A+T$ can be applied repeatedly without increasing the length of the terminal prefix. The path consisting of (A), $(A+T)$, $(A+T+T)$, $(A+T+T+T)$, ... will be explored without producing a dead-end. The possibility of nonterminating computation is a consequence of left recursion in the grammar. This type of behavior must be eliminated to ensure the termination of a depth-first parse.   □

4.5 Bottom-up Parsing

A derivation of a string p is obtained by building a path from the start symbol S to p in the graph of a grammar. When the explicit search structure begins with input string p, the resulting algorithm is known as a bottom-up parser. To limit the size of the implicit graph, top-down parsers in Sections 4.3 and 4.4 generated only leftmost derivations. The bottom-up parsers that we examine will construct rightmost derivations. Thus, bottom-up parsing may be considered to be a search of the implicit rightmost graph of the grammar.

Let $G = (V, \Sigma, P, S)$ be a context-free grammar. The nodes of the rightmost graph of the grammar are the right sentential forms of G, that is, the strings w obtained by derivations $S \overset{*}{\underset{R}{\Rightarrow}} w$. A node w is adjacent to a node v in the rightmost graph if G contains a derivation $S \overset{*}{\underset{R}{\Rightarrow}} v \underset{R}{\Rightarrow} w$. That is, w is adjacent to v if $v = u_1 A u_2$ with rightmost variable A, $w = u_1 q u_2$, and $A \rightarrow q$ is a rule of the grammar. The process of obtaining v from w is known as a **reduction** because the substring q in w is reduced to the variable

A in *v*. A bottom-up parse repeatedly applies reductions until the input string is transformed into the start symbol of the grammar.

Example 4.5.1

A reduction of the string (*b*) + *b* to *S* is given using the rules of the grammar AE.

Reduction	Rule
(*b*) + *b*	
(*T*) + *b*	*T* → *b*
(*A*) + *b*	*A* → *T*
T + *b*	*T* → (*A*)
A + *b*	*A* → *T*
A + *T*	*T* → *b*
A	*A* → *A* + *T*
S	*S* → *A*

Reversing the order of the sentential forms that comprise the reduction of *w* to *S* produces the rightmost derivation

$$S \Rightarrow A$$
$$\Rightarrow A + T$$
$$\Rightarrow A + b$$
$$\Rightarrow T + b$$
$$\Rightarrow (A) + b$$
$$\Rightarrow (T) + b$$
$$\Rightarrow (b) + b.$$

For this reason, bottom-up parsers are often said to construct rightmost derivations in reverse.   □

To generate all possible reductions of a string *w*, a bottom-up parser utilizes a pattern matching scheme. The string *w* is divided into two substrings, *w* = *uv*. The initial division sets *u* to the null string and *v* to *w*. The right-hand side of each rule is compared with the suffixes of *u*. A match occurs when *u* can be written $u_1 q$ and *A* → *q* is a rule of the grammar. This combination produces the reduction of *w* to $u_1 Av$.

When all the rules have been compared with *u* for a given pair *uv*, *w* is divided into a new pair of substrings *u'v'* and the process is repeated. The new decomposition is obtained by setting *u'* to *u* concatenated with the first element of *v*; *v'* is *v* with its first element removed. The process of updating the division is known as a shift. The shift and compare operations are used to generate all possible reductions of the string (*A* + *T*) in the grammar AE.

	u	*v*	**Rule**	**Reduction**
	λ	$(A + T)$		
Shift	$($	$A + T)$		
Shift	$(A$	$+ T)$	$S \to A$	$(S + T)$
Shift	$(A +$	$T)$		
Shift	$(A + T$	$)$	$A \to A + T$	(A)
			$A \to T$	$(A + A)$
Shift	$(A + T)$	λ		

In generating the reductions of the string, the right-hand side of the rule must match a suffix of *u*. All other reductions of *u* would have been discovered prior to the most recent shift.

Algorithm 4.5.1 is a breadth-first bottom-up parser. Like the breadth-first top-down parser, a search tree T is constructed using the queue operations *INSERT, REMOVE,* and *EMPTY.*

Algorithm 4.5.1
Breadth-First Bottom-up Parser

input: context-free grammar $G = (V, \Sigma, P, S)$
      string $p \in \Sigma^*$
      queue **Q**

1. initialize T with root p
   INSERT$(p, $ **Q**$)$

2. **repeat**
     $q := REMOVE($**Q**$)$
     2.1. **for each** rule $A \to w$ in P **do**
         2.1.1. **if** $q = uwv$ with $v \in \Sigma^*$ **then**
             2.1.1.1. *INSERT*$(uAv, $ **Q**$)$
             2.1.1.2. Add node uAv to T. Set a pointer from uAv to q.
         end if
     end for
  until $q = S$ or *EMPTY*(**Q**)

3. **if** $q = S$ **then** accept **else** reject

Step 2.1.1.1 inserts reductions into the queue. Bottom-up parsers are designed to generate only rightmost derivations. A reduction of *uwv* to *uAv* is added to the search tree only if *v* is a terminal string. Like the top-down parser, the left-hand side of the string is transformed first. The bottom-up parser, however, is building the derivation "in reverse." The first reduction is the last rule application of the derivation. Consequently,

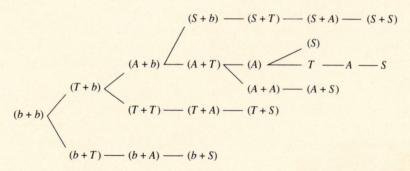

FIGURE 4.5   Breadth-first bottom-up parse of $(b + b)$.

the left side of the string is the last to be transformed when the rules are applied, resulting in a rightmost derivation.

Figure 4.5 shows the search tree built when the string $(b + b)$ is analyzed by the breadth-first bottom-up parsing algorithm. Following the path from S to $(b + b)$ yields the rightmost derivation

$$
\begin{aligned}
S &\Rightarrow A \\
&\Rightarrow T \\
&\Rightarrow (A) \\
&\Rightarrow (A + T) \\
&\Rightarrow (A + b) \\
&\Rightarrow (T + b) \\
&\Rightarrow (b + b).
\end{aligned}
$$

Does a breadth-first bottom-up parser halt for every possible input string or is it possible for the algorithm to loop indefinitely in the repeat-until loop? If the string p is in the language of the grammar, a rightmost derivation will be found. If the length of the right-hand side of each rule is greater than one, the reduction of a sentential form creates a new string of strictly smaller length. For grammars satisfying this condition, the depth of the search tree cannot exceed the length of the input string, assuring termination of a parse with either a derivation or a failure. This condition, however, is not satisfied by grammars with rules of the form $A \rightarrow B$, $A \rightarrow a$, and $A \rightarrow \lambda$.

4.6   A Shift-Reduce Parser

Bottom-up parsing can also be implemented in a depth-first manner. The reductions are generated by the shift and compare technique described for the breadth-first algorithm. The order in which the reductions are processed is determined by the number of shifts required to produce the match and the ordering of the rules. The right-hand sides of the rules $A \to T$ and $T \to b$ both occur in the string $(T + b)$. Reducing $(T + b)$ with the rule $A \to T$ produces $(A + b)$ with terminal suffix $+ b$). The other reduction produces the string to $(T + T)$ with terminal suffix). The parser examines the reduction to $(A + b)$ first since it is discovered after only two shifts while four shifts are required to find the other.

The stack elements of the backtracking bottom-up parser presented in Algorithm 4.6.1 are triples $[u, i, v]$ where $w = uv$ is the sentential form that was reduced and i the number of the rule used in the reduction. The strings u and v specify the decomposition of w created by the shifting process; u is the substring whose suffixes are compared with the right-hand side of the rules. There are two distinct reductions of the string $(b + b)$ using the rule $T \to b$. The reduction of the first b pushes $[(b, 4, + b)]$ onto the stack. The stack element $[(b + b, 4,)]$ is generated by the second reduction. The possibility of a string admitting several reductions demonstrates the need for storing the decomposition of the sentential form in the stack element.

Algorithm 4.6.1 is designed for parsing strings in a context-free grammar in which the start symbol is nonrecursive. The start symbol is nonrecursive if it does not occur on the right-hand side of any rule. A reduction using a rule $S \to w$ in a grammar with a nonrecursive start symbol is a dead-end unless $u = w$ and $v = \lambda$. In this case, the reduction successfully terminates the parse.

Algorithm 4.6.1 utilizes an auxiliary procedure *shift*. If v is not null, $shift(u, v)$ removes the first symbol from v and concatenates it to the end of u.

Algorithm 4.6.1
Depth-First Bottom-up Parsing Algorithm

input: context-free grammar $G = (V, \Sigma, P, S)$ with nonrecursive start symbol
      string $p \in \Sigma^*$
      stack **S**

1. *PUSH*($[\lambda, 0, p]$, **S**)

2. **repeat**
    2.1. $[u, i, v] := POP(\mathbf{S})$
    2.2. dead-end $:= false$
    2.3. **repeat**
        Find the first $j > i$ with rule number j that satisfies
        i) $A \to w$ with $u = qw$ and $A \neq S$ or
        ii) $S \to w$ with $u = w$ and $v = \lambda$
        2.3.1. **if** there is such a j **then**
            2.3.1.1. *PUSH*($[u, j, v]$, **S**)
            2.3.1.2. $u := qA$
            2.3.1.3. $i := 0$
        end if

2.3.2.   **if** there is no such j **and** $v \neq \lambda$ **then**
    2.3.2.1.   *shift(u, v)*
    2.3.2.2. $i := 0$
   end if
  2.3.3.   **if** there is no such j **and** $v = \lambda$ **then** dead-end := *true*
  until $(u = S)$ **or** dead-end
 until $(u = S)$ **or** *EMPTY*(S)
3.   **if** *EMPTY*(S) **then** reject **else** accept

The condition that detects dead-ends and forces the parser to backtrack occurs in step 2.3.3. When the string v is empty, an attempted shift indicates that all reductions of uv have been examined.

Algorithm 4.6.1 assumes that the grammar has a nonrecursive start symbol. This restriction does not limit the languages that can be parsed. In Section 5.1, we will see that any context-free grammar can easily be transformed into an equivalent grammar with nonrecursive start symbol. Algorithm 4.6.1 can be modified to parse arbitrary context-free grammars. This requires removing the condition that restricts the processing of reductions using S rules. The modification is completed by changing the terminating condition of the repeat-until loops from $(u = S)$ to $(u = S$ **and** $v = \lambda)$.

Example 4.6.1

Using Algorithm 4.6.1 and the grammar AE, a derivation of the string $(b + b)$ is constructed. The stack is given in the column on the left. The decomposition of the string and current rule numbers are in the columns labeled u, v, and i.

Stack	u	i	v	Operation
$[\lambda, 0, (b + b)]$				
	λ	0	$(b + b)$	pop
	$($	0	$b + b)$	shift
	$(b$	0	$+ b)$	shift
$[(b, 4, + b)]$	$(T$	0	$+ b)$	reduction
$[(T, 2, + b)]$				
$[(b, 4, + b)]$	$(A$	0	$+ b)$	reduction
$[(T, 2, + b)]$				
$[(b, 4, + b)]$	$(A +$	0	$b)$	shift
$[(T, 2, + b)]$				
$[(b, 4, + b)]$	$(A + b$	0	$)$	shift

Continued

Stack	u	i	v	Operation
$[(A + b, 4,)]$				
$[(T, 2, + b)]$				
$[(b, 4, + b)]$	$(A + T$	0	)	reduction
$[(A + T, 2,)]$				
$[(A + b, 4,)]$				
$[(T, 2, + b)]$				
$[(b, 4, + b)]$	$(A + A$	0	)	reduction
$[(A + T, 2,)]$				
$[(A + b, 4,)]$				
$[(T, 2, + b)]$				
$[(b, 4, + b)]$	$(A + A)$	0	λ	shift
$[(A + b, 4,)]$				
$[(T, 2, + b)]$				
$[(b, 4, + b)]$	$(A + T$	2	)	pop
$[(A + T, 3,)]$				
$[(A + b, 4,)]$				
$[(T, 2, + b)]$				
$[(b, 4, + b)]$	$(A$	0	)	reduction
$[(A + T, 3,)]$				
$[(A + b, 4,)]$				
$[(T, 2, + b)]$				
$[(b, 4, + b)]$	(A)	0	λ	shift
$[(A), 5, \lambda]$				
$[(A + T, 3,)]$				
$[(A + b, 4,)]$				
$[(T, 2, + b)]$				
$[(b, 4, + b)]$	T	0	λ	reduction
$[T, 2, \lambda]$				
$[(A), 5, \lambda]$				
$[(A + T, 3,)]$				
$[(A + b, 4,)]$				
$[(T, 2, + b)]$				
$[(b, 4, + b)]$	A	0	λ	reduction
$[A, 1, \lambda]$				
$[T, 2, \lambda]$				
$[(A), 5, \lambda]$				
$[(A + T, 3,)]$				
$[(A + b, 4,)]$				
$[(T, 2, + b)]$				
$[(b, 4, + b)]$	S	0	λ	reduction

The rightmost derivation produced by this parse is identical to that obtained by the breadth-first parse. □

Exercises

1. Build the subgraph of the grammar of G consisting of the left sentential forms that are generated by derivations of length three or less.

$$G: S \rightarrow aS \mid AB \mid B$$
$$A \rightarrow abA \mid ab$$
$$B \rightarrow BB \mid ba$$

2. Let G be a grammar and $w \in L(G)$. Prove that there is a rightmost derivation of w in G.

3. Let G be the grammar

$$S \rightarrow aS \mid Sb \mid ab \mid SS.$$

a) Give a regular expression for L(G).

b) Construct two leftmost derivations of the string *aabb*.

c) Build the derivation trees for the derivations from part b).

d) Construct an unambiguous grammar equivalent to G.

4. Let G be the grammar

$$S \rightarrow aSA \mid \lambda$$
$$A \rightarrow bA \mid \lambda.$$

a) Give a regular expression for L(G).

b) Show that G is ambiguous.

c) Construct an unambiguous grammar G' with $L(G') = L(G)$.

5. Show that the grammar

$$S \rightarrow bSc \mid bbSc \mid \lambda$$

is ambiguous.

6. Let G be the grammar

$$S \rightarrow ASB \mid ab \mid SS$$
$$A \rightarrow aA \mid \lambda$$
$$B \rightarrow bB \mid \lambda.$$

a) Give a leftmost derivation of *aaabb*.

b) Give a rightmost derivation of *aaabb*.

c) Show that G is ambiguous.

d) Construct an unambiguous grammar equivalent to G.

7. Let G be the grammar

$$S \rightarrow AaSbB \mid \lambda$$
$$A \rightarrow aA \mid a$$
$$b \rightarrow bB \mid \lambda.$$

a) Define L(G) using set notation.

b) Show that G is ambiguous.

c) Construct an unambiguous grammar equivalent to G.

8. Let G be the grammar

$$S \rightarrow ASB \mid AB$$
$$A \rightarrow aA \mid a$$
$$B \rightarrow bB \mid \lambda.$$

a) Give a regular expression for L(G).

b) Show that G is ambiguous.

c) Construct an unambiguous regular grammar equivalent to G.

9. Construct two regular grammars, one ambiguous and one unambiguous, that generate the language a^*.

10. Construct unambiguous grammars for the languages $L_1 = \{a^n b^n c^m \mid n, m > 0\}$ and $L_2 = \{a^n b^m c^m \mid n, m > 0\}$. Construct a grammar G that generates $L_1 \cup L_2$. Prove that G is ambiguous. This is an example of an inherently ambiguous language. Explain, intuitively, why every grammar generating $L_1 \cup L_2$ must be ambiguous.

In Exercises 11–19, trace the actions of the algorithm as it parses the input string. For the breadth-first algorithms, build the tree constructed by the parser. For the depth-first algorithms, trace the stack as in Examples 4.4.1 and 4.6.1. If the input string is in the language, give the derivation constructed by the parser.

11. Algorithm 4.3.1 with input $(b) + b$.

12. Algorithm 4.3.1 with input $b + (b)$.

13. Algorithm 4.3.1 with input $((b))$.

14. Algorithm 4.4.1 with input $((b))$.

15. Algorithm 4.4.1 with input $b + (b)$.

16. Algorithm 4.5.1 with input $(b) + b$.

17. Algorithm 4.5.1 with input $(b))$.

18. Algorithm 4.6.1 with input $(b) + b$.

19. Algorithm 4.6.1 with input $(b))$.

20. Construct a grammar G and string $p \in \Sigma^*$ such that Algorithm 4.5.1 loops indefinitely in attempting to parse p.

21. Construct a grammar G and string $p \in L(G)$ such that Algorithm 4.6.1 loops indefinitely in attempting to parse p.

Bibliographic Notes

Properties of ambiguity are examined in Floyd [1962], Cantor [1962], and Chomsky and Schutzenberger [1963]. Inherent ambiguity was first noted in Parikh [1966]. A proof that the language in Exercise 10 is inherently ambiguous can be found in Harrison [1978]. Closure properties for ambiguous and inherently ambiguous languages were established by Ginsburg and Ullian [1966a, 1966b].

The nondeterministic parsing algorithms are essentially graph searching algorithms modified for this particular application. The depth-first algorithms presented here are from Denning, Dennis, and Qualitz [1978]. A thorough exposition of graph and tree traversals is given in Knuth [1968], Tremblay and Sorenson [1984], and most data structures texts.

The analysis of the syntax of a string is an essential feature in the construction of compilers for computer languages. Grammars amenable to deterministic parsing techniques are presented in Chapters 15 and 16. For references to parsing, see the bibliographic notes following those chapters.

CHAPTER 5

Normal Forms

A normal form is defined by imposing restrictions on the form of the rules allowed in the grammar. Two important normal forms for context-free grammars, the Chomsky and Greibach normal forms, are introduced in this chapter. The grammars in a normal form generate the entire set of context-free languages. The restrictions on the rules often reduce the complexity of derivations in the grammar.

Transformations are developed to convert an arbitrary context-free grammar into an equivalent grammar in normal form. The transformations consist of employing a series of techniques that add and delete rules. Each of these replacement schema preserves the language generated by the grammar.

5.1   Elimination of Lambda Rules

The transformation of a grammar begins by imposing a restriction of the start symbol of the grammar. Given a grammar G, an equivalent grammar G′ is constructed in which the role of the start symbol is limited to the initiation of derivations. A recursive derivation of the form $S \overset{*}{\Rightarrow} uSv$ permits the start symbol to occur in sentential forms in intermediate steps of a derivation. The restriction is satisfied whenever the start symbol of G′ is a nonrecursive variable.

Lemma 5.1.1

Let G = (V, Σ, P, S) be a context-free grammar. There is a grammar G′ = (V′, Σ, P′, S′) satisfying the following conditions:

i) $L(G) = L(G')$.

ii) The rules of P′ are of the form

$$A \to w$$

where $A \in V'$ and $w \in ((V - \{S'\}) \cup \Sigma)^*$.

Proof   If the start symbol S does not occur on the right-hand side of a rule of G, then G′ = G. If S is a recursive variable, the recursion of the start symbol must be removed. The alteration is accomplished "taking a step backward" with the start of a derivation. The grammar G′ = (V ∪ {S′}, Σ, P ∪ {S′ → S}, S′) is constructed by designating a new start symbol, S′, and adding S′ → S to the rules of G. The two grammars generate the same language since any string u derivable in G by $S \underset{G}{\overset{*}{\Rightarrow}} u$ can be obtained by the derivation $S' \underset{G'}{\Rightarrow} S \underset{G'}{\overset{*}{\Rightarrow}} u$ in G′. The only role of the rule added to P′ is to initiate a derivation in G′ the remainder of which is identical to a derivation in G.   ■

Example 5.1.1

The start symbol of the grammar G is recursive. The technique outlined in Lemma 5.1.1 is used to construct an equivalent grammar G′ with a nonrecursive start symbol. The start symbol of G′ is the variable S′.

$$
\begin{array}{ll}
\text{G: } S \to aS \mid AB \mid AC & \text{G′: } S' \to S \\
\quad A \to aA \mid \lambda & \quad S \to aS \mid AB \mid AC \\
\quad B \to bB \mid bS & \quad A \to aA \mid \lambda \\
\quad C \to cC \mid \lambda & \quad B \to bB \mid bS \\
& \quad C \to cC \mid \lambda
\end{array}
$$

The variable S is still recursive in G′, but it is not the start symbol of the new grammar.   □

In the derivation of a terminal string, the intermediate sentential forms may contain variables that do not generate terminal symbols. These variables are removed from the sentential form by applications of lambda rules. This property is illustrated by the derivation of the string *aaaa* in the grammar

$$
\begin{array}{l}
S \to SaB \mid aB \\
B \to bB \mid \lambda.
\end{array}
$$

The language generated by this grammar is $(a^+b^*)^+$. The leftmost derivation *aaaa* generates four B's, each of which is removed by the application of the rule $B \to \lambda$.

$$
\begin{array}{l}
S \Rightarrow SaB \\
 \Rightarrow SaBaB
\end{array}
$$

$$\Rightarrow SaBaBaB$$
$$\Rightarrow aBaBaBaB$$
$$\Rightarrow aaBaBaB$$
$$\Rightarrow aaaBaB$$
$$\Rightarrow aaaaB$$
$$\Rightarrow aaaa$$

A more efficient approach would be to avoid the generation of variables that are subsequently removed by lambda rules. Another grammar, without lambda rules, that generates $(a^+b^*)^+$ is given below. The string $aaaa$ is generated using half the number of rule applications. This efficiency is gained at the expense of increasing the number of rules of the grammar.

$$S \rightarrow SaB \mid Sa \mid aB \mid a \qquad S \Rightarrow Sa$$
$$B \rightarrow bB \mid b \qquad\qquad\quad \Rightarrow Saa$$
$$\Rightarrow Saaa$$
$$\Rightarrow aaaa$$

A variable that can derive the null string is called **nullable**. The length of a sentential form can be reduced by a sequence of rule applications if the string contains nullable variables. A grammar without nullable variables is called **noncontracting** since the application of a rule cannot decrease the length of the sentential form. Algorithm 5.1.2 iteratively constructs the set of nullable variables in G. The algorithm utilizes two sets; the set NULL collects the nullable variables and PREV triggers the halting condition.

Algorithm 5.1.2
Construction of the Set of Nullable Variables

input: context-free grammar $G = (V, \Sigma, P, S)$

1. NULL := $\{A \mid A \rightarrow \lambda \in P\}$

2. **repeat**
   2.1. PREV := NULL
   2.2. **for** each variable $A \in V$ **do**
        if there is an A rule $A \rightarrow w$ and $w \in$ PREV* **then**
            NULL := NULL $\cup \{A\}$
   until NULL = PREV

The set PREV is initialized with the variables that derive the null string in one rule application. A variable A is added to NULL if there is an A rule whose right-hand side consists entirely of variables that have previously been determined to be nullable. The algorithm halts when an iteration fails to find a new nullable variable. The repeat-until loop must terminate since the number of variables is finite. The definition of nullable, based on the notion of derivability, is recursive. Induction is used to show that the set NULL contains exactly the nullable variables G at the termination of the computation.

Lemma 5.1.3

Let $G = (V, \Sigma, P, S)$ be a context-free grammar. Algorithm 5.1.2 generates the set of nullable variables of G.

Proof   Induction on the number of iterations of the algorithm is used to show that every variable in NULL derives the null string. If A is added to NULL in step 1, then G contains the rule $A \rightarrow \lambda$ and the derivation is obvious.

Assume that all the variables in NULL after n iterations are nullable. We must prove that any variable added in iteration $n + 1$ is nullable. If A is such a variable, then there is a rule

$$A \rightarrow A_1 A_2 \ldots A_k$$

with each A_i in PREV at the $n + 1$st iteration. By the inductive hypothesis, $A_i \overset{*}{\Rightarrow} \lambda$ for $i = 1, 2, \ldots, k$. These derivations can be used to construct the derivation

$$\begin{aligned}
A &\Rightarrow A_1 A_2 \ldots A_k \\
&\overset{*}{\Rightarrow} A_2 \ldots A_k \\
&\overset{*}{\Rightarrow} A_3 \ldots A_k \\
&\quad\vdots \\
&\overset{*}{\Rightarrow} A_k \\
&\overset{*}{\Rightarrow} \lambda
\end{aligned}$$

exhibiting the nullability of A.

Now we show that every nullable variable is eventually added to NULL. If n is the length of the minimal derivation of the null string from the variable A, then A is added to the set NULL on or before iteration n of the algorithm. The proof is by induction on the length of the derivation of the null string from the variable A.

If $A \overset{1}{\Rightarrow} \lambda$, then A is added to NULL in step 1. Suppose that all variables whose minimal derivations of the null string have length n or less are added to NULL on or before iteration n. Let A be a variable that derives the null string by a derivation of length $n + 1$. The derivation can be written

$$\begin{aligned}
A &\Rightarrow A_1 A_2 \ldots A_k \\
&\overset{n}{\Rightarrow} \lambda.
\end{aligned}$$

Each of the variables A_i is nullable with minimal derivations of length n or less. By the inductive hypothesis, each A_i is in NULL prior to iteration $n + 1$. Let $m \leq n$ be the iteration in which all of the A_i's first appear in NULL. On iteration $m + 1$ the rule

$$A \rightarrow A_1 A_2 \ldots A_k$$

adds A to NULL.   ∎

The language generated by a grammar contains the null string only if it can be derived from the start symbol of the grammar, that is, if the start symbol is nullable. Thus Algorithm 5.1.2 provides a decision procedure for determining whether the null string is in the language of a grammar.

Example 5.1.2

The set of nullable variables of the grammar

$$G: S \rightarrow ACA$$
$$A \rightarrow aAa \mid B \mid C$$
$$B \rightarrow bB \mid b$$
$$C \rightarrow cC \mid \lambda$$

is constructed using Algorithm 5.1.2. The action of the algorithm is traced by giving the contents of the sets NULL and PREV after each iteration of the repeat-until loop. Iteration zero specifies the composition of NULL prior to entering the loop.

Iteration	NULL	PREV
0	$\{C\}$	
1	$\{A, C\}$	$\{C\}$
2	$\{S, A, C\}$	$\{A, C\}$
3	$\{S, A, C\}$	$\{S, A, C\}$

The algorithm halts after three iterations. The nullable variables of G are S, A, and C.   □

Example 5.1.3

The set of nullable variables of the grammars G and G′ from Example 5.1.1 are $\{S, A, C\}$ and $\{S', S, A, C\}$, respectively. The start symbol S' obtained by removing recursion is nullable only if the start symbol of the original grammar is nullable.   □

The process of transforming grammars into the normal forms consists of removing and adding rules to the grammar. With each alteration, the language generated by the grammar should remain unchanged. Lemma 5.1.4 establishes a simple criterion by which rules may be added to a grammar without altering the language.

Lemma 5.1.4

Let $G = (V, \Sigma, P, S)$ be a context-free grammar. If $A \overset{*}{\underset{G}{\Rightarrow}} w$, then the grammar $G' = (V, \Sigma, P \cup \{A \rightarrow w\}, S)$ is equivalent to G.

Proof   Clearly, $L(G) \subseteq L(G')$ since every rule in G is also in G′. The other inclusion results from the observation that the application of the rule $A \rightarrow w$ in a derivation in G′ can be simulated in G by the derivation $A \overset{*}{\underset{G}{\Rightarrow}} w$.   ■

A grammar with lambda rules is not noncontracting. To build an equivalent noncontracting grammar, rules must be added to generate the strings whose derivations in the original grammar require the application of lambda rules. Assume that B is a nullable variable. There are two distinct roles that B can play in a derivation that is initiated by the application of the rule $A \rightarrow BAa$; it can derive a nonnull terminal string or it can derive the null string. In the latter case, the derivation has the form

$$A \Rightarrow BAa$$
$$\overset{*}{\Rightarrow} Aa$$
$$\overset{*}{\Rightarrow} u.$$

The string u can be derived without lambda rules by augmenting the grammar with the rule $A \rightarrow Aa$. Lemma 5.1.4 ensures that the addition of this rule does not affect the language of the grammar.

The rule $A \rightarrow BABa$ requires three additional rules to construct derivations without lambda rules. If both of the B's derive the null string, the rule $A \rightarrow Aa$ can be used in a noncontracting derivation. To account for all possible derivations of the null string from the two instances of the variable B, a noncontracting grammar requires the four rules

$$A \rightarrow BABa$$
$$A \rightarrow ABa$$
$$A \rightarrow BAa$$
$$A \rightarrow Aa.$$

Since the right-hand side of each of these rules is derivable from A, their addition to the rules of the grammar does not alter the language.

The previous technique constructs rules that can be added to a grammar G to derive strings in L(G) without the use of lambda rules. This process is used to construct a grammar without lambda rules that is equivalent to G. If L(G) contains the null string, there is no equivalent noncontracting grammar. All variables occurring in the derivation $S \overset{*}{\Rightarrow} \lambda$ must eventually disappear. To handle this special case, the rule $S \rightarrow \lambda$ is allowed in the new grammar but all other lambda rules are replaced. The derivations in the resulting grammar, with the exception of $S \Rightarrow \lambda$, are noncontracting. A grammar satisfying these conditions is called **essentially noncontracting.**

When constructing equivalent grammars, a subscript is used to indicate the restriction being imposed on the rules. The grammar obtained from G by removing lambda rules is denoted G_L.

Theorem 5.1.5
Let G = (V, Σ, P, S) be a context-free grammar. There is an algorithm to construct a context-free grammar $G_L = (V_L, \Sigma, P_L, S_L)$ that satisfies the following conditions:

i) $L(G_L) = L(G)$.

ii) S_L is not a recursive variable.

iii) $A \rightarrow \lambda$ is in P_L if and only if $\lambda \in L(G)$ and $A = S_L$.

Proof The start symbol can be made nonrecursive by the technique presented in Lemma 5.1.1. The set of variables V_L is simply V with a new start symbol added, if necessary. The productions of G_L are defined as follows:

i) If $\lambda \in L(G)$, then $S_L \to \lambda \in P_L$.

ii) Let $A \to w$ be a rule in P. If w can be written

$$w_1 A_1 w_2 A_2 \quad \ldots \quad w_k A_k w_{k+1}$$

where $A_1, A_2, \ldots, A_k$ are nullable variables of G, then

$$A \to w_1 w_2 \ldots w_k w_{k+1}$$

is a rule of P_L.

iii) $A \to \lambda \in P_L$ only if $\lambda \in L(G)$ and $A = S_L$.

The process of removing lambda rules creates a set of rules from each rule of the original grammar. A rule with n occurrences of nullable variables in the right-hand side produces 2^n rules. Condition iii) deletes all lambda rules other than $S \to \lambda$ from P_L.

Derivations in G_L utilize rules from G and those created by condition ii), each of which is derivable in G. Thus, $L(G_L) \subseteq L(G)$.

The opposite inclusion, that every string in $L(G)$ is also in $L(G_L)$, must also be established. We prove this by showing that every nonnull terminal string derivable from a variable of G is also derivable from that variable in G_L. Let $A \overset{n}{\underset{G}{\Rightarrow}} w$ be a derivation in G with $w \in \Sigma^+$. We prove that $A \overset{*}{\underset{G_L}{\Rightarrow}} w$ by induction on n, the length of the derivation of w in G. If $n = 1$, then $A \to w$ is a rule in P and, since $w \neq \lambda$, $A \to w$ is in P_L.

Assume that all terminal strings derivable from A by n or fewer rule applications can be derived from A in G_L. Note that this makes no claim concerning the length of the derivation in G_L. Let $A \overset{n+1}{\underset{G}{\Rightarrow}} w$ be a derivation of a terminal string. Explicitly specifying the first rule application, the derivation can be written

$$A \Rightarrow w_1 A_1 w_2 A_2 \ldots w_k A_k w_{k+1} \overset{n}{\underset{G}{\Rightarrow}} w$$

where $A_i \in V$ and $w_i \in \Sigma^*$. Since w is a terminal string, it can be written

$$w = w_1 p_1 w_2 p_2 \ldots w_k p_k w_{k+1}$$

with $p_i \in \Sigma^*$. By Lemma 3.1.5, each A_i derives p_i in G with a derivation of length n or less. For each $p_i \in \Sigma^+$, the inductive hypothesis ensures the existence of a derivation $A_i \overset{*}{\underset{G_L}{\Rightarrow}} p_i$. If $p_j = \lambda$, the variable A_j is nullable in G. Condition ii) generates a rule from

$$A \to w_1 A_1 w_2 A_2 \ldots w_k A_k w_{k+1}$$

in which each of the A_j's that derive the null string is deleted. A derivation of w in G_L can be constructed by first applying this rule and then deriving each $p_i \in \Sigma^+$ using the derivations provided by the inductive hypothesis. ∎

Example 5.1.4

Let G be the grammar given in Example 5.1.2. The nullable variables of G are $\{S, A, C\}$. The equivalent essentially noncontracting grammar G_L is given below.

$$G: S \rightarrow ACA \qquad\qquad G_L: S \rightarrow ACA \mid CA \mid AA \mid AC \mid A \mid C \mid \lambda$$
$$ A \rightarrow aAa \mid B \mid C \qquad\qquad\; A \rightarrow aAa \mid aa \mid B \mid C$$
$$ B \rightarrow bB \mid b \qquad\qquad\qquad\; B \rightarrow bB \mid b$$
$$ C \rightarrow cC \mid \lambda \qquad\qquad\qquad C \rightarrow cC \mid c$$

The rule $S \rightarrow A$ is obtained from $S \rightarrow ACA$ in two ways, deleting the leading A and C or the final A and C. All lambda rules, other than $S \rightarrow \lambda$, are discarded.   □

Although the grammar G_L is equivalent to G, the derivation of a string in these grammars may be quite different. The simplest example is the derivation of the null string. Six rule applications are required to derive the null string from the start symbol of the grammar G in Example 5.1.4, while the lambda rule in G_L generates it immediately. Leftmost derivations of the string *aba* are given in each of the grammars.

$$G: S \Rightarrow ACA \qquad\quad G_L: S \Rightarrow A$$
$$ \Rightarrow aAaCA \qquad\qquad\;\; \Rightarrow aAa$$
$$ \Rightarrow aBaCA \qquad\qquad\;\; \Rightarrow aBa$$
$$ \Rightarrow abaCA \qquad\qquad\;\; \Rightarrow aba$$
$$ \Rightarrow abaA$$
$$ \Rightarrow abaC$$
$$ \Rightarrow aba$$

The first rule application of the derivation in G_L generates only variables that eventually derive terminals. Thus, the application of lambda rules is averted.

5.2 Elimination of Chain Rules

The application of a rule $A \rightarrow B$ does not increase the length of the derived string nor does it produce additional terminal symbols; it simply renames a variable. Rules having this form are called **chain rules**. The removal of chain rules requires the addition of rules that allow the revised grammar to generate the same strings. The idea behind the removal process is realizing that a chain rule is nothing more than a renaming procedure. Consider the rules

$$A \rightarrow aA \mid a \mid B$$
$$B \rightarrow bB \mid b \mid C.$$

The chain rule $A \rightarrow B$ indicates that any string derivable from the variable B is also derivable from A. The extra step, the application of the chain rule, can be eliminated by adding A rules that directly generate the same strings as B. This can be accomplished by adding a rule $A \to w$ for each rule $B \to w$ and deleting the chain rule. The chain rule $A \to B$ can be replaced by three A rules.

$$A \to aA \mid a \mid bB \mid b \mid C$$
$$B \to bB \mid b \mid C$$

Unfortunately, another chain rule was created by this replacement. A derivation $A \overset{*}{\Rightarrow} C$ consisting solely of chain rules is called a **chain.** Algorithm 5.2.1 generates all variables that can be derived by chains from a variable A in an essentially noncontracting grammar. This set is denoted CHAIN(A). The set NEW contains the variables that were added to CHAIN(A) on the previous iteration.

Algorithm 5.2.1
Construction of the Set CHAIN(A)

input: essentially noncontracting context-free grammar $G = (V, \Sigma, P, S)$

1. CHAIN(A) := $\{A\}$
2. PREV := $\emptyset$.
3. **repeat**
     3.1. NEW := CHAIN(A) − PREV
     3.2. PREV := CHAIN(A)
     3.3. **for** each variable $B \in$ NEW **do**
             for each rule $B \to C$ **do**
                 CHAIN(A) := CHAIN(A) $\cup$ $\{C\}$
    until CHAIN(A) = PREV

Algorithm 5.2.1 is fundamentally different from the algorithm that generates the nullable variables. The difference is similar to the difference between bottom-up and top-down parsing strategies. The strategy for finding nullable variables begins by initializing the set with the variables that generate the null string with one rule application. The rules are then applied backward; if the right-hand side of a rule consists entirely of variables in NULL, then the left-hand side is added to the set being built.

The generation of CHAIN(A) follows a top-down approach. The repeat-until loop iteratively constructs all variables derivable from A using chain rules. Each iteration represents an additional rule application to the chains previously discovered. The proof that Algorithm 5.2.2 generates CHAIN(A) is left as an exercise.

Lemma 5.2.2

Let $G = (V, \Sigma, P, S)$ be an essentially noncontracting context-free grammar. Algorithm 5.2.1 generates the set of variables derivable from A using only chain rules.

The variables in CHAIN(A) determine the substitutions that must be made to remove the A chain rules. The grammar obtained by deleting the chain rules from G is denoted G_C.

Theorem 5.2.3

Let $G = (V, \Sigma, P, S)$ be an essentially noncontracting context-free grammar. There is an algorithm to construct a context-free grammar G_C that satisfies

i) $L(G_C) = L(G)$

ii) G_C has no chain rules.

Proof   The A rules of G_C are constructed from the set CHAIN(A) and the rules of G. The rule $A \rightarrow w$ is in P_C if there is a variable B and a string w that satisfy

i) $B \in$ CHAIN(A)

ii) $B \rightarrow w \in P$

iii) $w \notin V$.

Condition iii) ensures that P_C does not contain chain rules. The variables, alphabet, and start symbol of G_C are the same as those of G.

By Lemma 5.1.4, every string derivable in G_C is also derivable in G. Consequently, $L(G_C) \subseteq L(G)$. Now let $w \in L(G)$ and $A \overset{*}{\underset{G}{\Rightarrow}} B$ be a maximal sequence of chain rules used in the derivation of w. The derivation of w has the form

$$S \overset{*}{\underset{G}{\Rightarrow}} uAv \overset{*}{\underset{G}{\Rightarrow}} uBv \underset{G}{\Rightarrow} upv \overset{*}{\underset{G}{\Rightarrow}} w,$$

where $B \rightarrow p$ is a rule, but not a chain rule, in G. The rule $A \rightarrow p$ can be used to replace the sequence of chain rules in the derivation. This technique can be repeated to remove all chain rules in the derivation, producing a derivation of w in G_C.   ∎

Example 5.2.1

The grammar G_C is constructed from the grammar G_L in Example 5.1.4.

$$
\begin{aligned}
G_L: S &\rightarrow ACA \mid CA \mid AA \mid AC \mid A \mid C \mid \lambda \\
A &\rightarrow aAa \mid aa \mid B \mid C \\
B &\rightarrow bB \mid b \\
C &\rightarrow cC \mid c
\end{aligned}
$$

Since G_L is essentially noncontracting, Algorithm 5.2.1 generates the variables derivable using chain rules. The computations construct the sets

$$
\begin{aligned}
\text{CHAIN}(S) &= \{S, A, C, B\} \\
\text{CHAIN}(A) &= \{A, B, C\} \\
\text{CHAIN}(B) &= \{B\} \\
\text{CHAIN}(C) &= \{C\}.
\end{aligned}
$$

These sets are used to generate the rules of G_C.

$$P_C: S \rightarrow ACA \mid CA \mid AA \mid AC \mid aAa \mid aa \mid bB \mid b \mid cC \mid c \mid \lambda$$
$$A \rightarrow aAa \mid aa \mid bB \mid b \mid cC \mid c$$
$$B \rightarrow bB \mid b$$
$$C \rightarrow cC \mid c$$

□

The removal of chain rules increases the number of rules in the grammar but reduces the length of derivations. This is the same trade-off that accompanied the construction of an essentially noncontracting grammar. The restrictions require additional rules to generate the language but simplify the derivations.

Eliminating chain rules from an essentially noncontracting grammar preserves the noncontracting property. Let $A \rightarrow w$ be a rule created by the removal of chain rules. This implies that there is a rule $B \rightarrow w$ for some variable $B \in CHAIN(A)$. Since the original grammar was essentially noncontracting, the only lambda rule is $S \rightarrow \lambda$. The start symbol, being nonrecursive, is not a member of $CHAIN(A)$ for any $A \neq S$. It follows that no additional lambda rules are produced in the construction of P_C.

Each rule in an essentially noncontracting grammar without chain rules is of the form

i) $S \rightarrow \lambda$

ii) $A \rightarrow a$

iii) $A \rightarrow w$

where $w \in (V \cup \Sigma)^*$ is of length at least two. The rule $S \rightarrow \lambda$ is used only in the derivation of the empty string. The application of any other rule adds a terminal to the derived string or increases the length of the string.

5.3   Useless Symbols

A grammar is designed to generate a language. Each variable in the grammar should contribute to the generation of strings of the language. Variables are introduced to assist the string generation process. The construction of large grammars, making modifications to existing grammars, or sloppiness may produce variables that do not occur in derivations that generate terminal strings. Consider the grammar

$$G: S \rightarrow AC \mid BS \mid B$$
$$A \rightarrow aA \mid aF$$
$$B \rightarrow CF \mid b$$
$$C \rightarrow cC \mid D$$
$$D \rightarrow aD \mid BD \mid C$$
$$E \rightarrow aA \mid BSA$$
$$F \rightarrow bB \mid b.$$

What is L(G)? Are there variables that cannot possibly occur in the generation of terminal strings, and if so, why? Try to convince yourself that $L(G) = b^+$. To begin the process of identifying and removing useless symbols, we make the following definition.

Definition 5.3.1

Let G be a context-free grammar. A symbol $x \in (V \cup \Sigma)$ is **useful** if there is a derivation

$$S \overset{*}{\underset{G}{\Rightarrow}} uxv \overset{*}{\underset{G}{\Rightarrow}} w$$

where $u, v \in (V \cup \Sigma)^*$, and $w \in \Sigma^*$. A symbol that is not useful is said to be **useless**.

A variable is useful if it occurs in a derivation that begins with the start symbol and generates a terminal string. A terminal is useful if it occurs in a string in the language of G. For a variable to be useful, two conditions must be satisfied. The variable must occur in a sentential form of the grammar; that is, it must occur in a string derivable from S. Moreover, there must be a derivation of a terminal string (the null string is considered to be a terminal string) from the variable. A variable that occurs in a sentential form is said to be reachable from S. A two-part procedure to eliminate useless variables is presented. Each construction establishes one of the requirements of being useful.

Algorithm 5.3.2 builds a set, TERM, consisting of the variables that derive terminal strings. The strategy used in the algorithm is similar to that used to determine the set of nullable variables of a grammar. The proof that Algorithm 5.3.2 generates the desired set follows the techniques presented in the proof of Lemma 5.1.3 and is left as an exercise.

Algorithm 5.3.2
Construction of the Set of Variables That Derive Terminal Strings

input: context-free grammar $G = (V, \Sigma, P, S)$

1. TERM := $\{A \mid$ there is a rule $A \rightarrow w \in P$ with $w \in \Sigma^*\}$

2. **repeat**
      2.1. PREV := TERM.
      2.2. **for** each variable $A \in V$ **do**
               if there is an A rule $A \rightarrow w$ and $w \in (\text{PREV} \cup \Sigma)^*$ **then**
                  TERM := TERM $\cup \{A\}$.
   until PREV = TERM

Upon termination of the algorithm, TERM contains the variables of G that generate terminal strings. Variables not in TERM are useless; they cannot contribute to the generation of strings in L(G). This observation provides the motivation for the construction of a grammar G_T that is equivalent to G and contains only variables that derive terminal strings.

Theorem 5.3.3

Let $G = (V, \Sigma, P, S)$ be a context-free grammar. There is an algorithm to construct a context-free grammar $G_T = (V_T, \Sigma_T, P_T, S)$ that satisfies the following conditions:

i) $L(G_T) = L(G)$.

ii) Every variable in G_T derives a terminal string in G_T.

Proof P_T is obtained by deleting all rules containing variables of G that do not derive terminal strings, that is, all rules containing variables in $V - $ TERM.

$$V_T = \text{TERM}$$
$$P_T = \{A \rightarrow w \mid A \rightarrow w \text{ is a rule in } P, A \in \text{TERM and } w \in (\text{TERM} \cup \Sigma)^*\}$$
$$\Sigma_T = \{a \in \Sigma \mid a \text{ occurs in the right-hand side of a rule in } P_T\}$$

The set Σ_T consists of all the terminals occurring in the rules in P_T.

We must show that $L(G_T) = L(G)$. Since $P_T \subseteq P$, every derivation in G_T is also a derivation in G and $L(G_T) \subseteq L(G)$. To establish the opposite inclusion we must show that removing rules that contain variables in $V - $ TERM has no effect on the set of terminal strings generated. Let $S \overset{*}{\underset{G}{\Rightarrow}} w$ be a derivation of a string $w \in L(G)$. This is also a derivation in G_T. If not, a variable from $V - $ TERM must occur in an intermediate step in the derivation. A derivation from a sentential form containing a variable in $V - $ TERM cannot produce a terminal string. Consequently, all the rules in the derivation are in P_T and $w \in L(G_T)$.   ∎

Example 5.3.1

The grammar G_T is constructed for the grammar G introduced at the beginning of this section.

$$
\begin{aligned}
G: S &\rightarrow AC \mid BS \mid B \\
A &\rightarrow aA \mid aF \\
B &\rightarrow CF \mid b \\
C &\rightarrow cC \mid D \\
D &\rightarrow aD \mid BD \mid C \\
E &\rightarrow aA \mid BSA \\
F &\rightarrow bB \mid b
\end{aligned}
$$

Algorithm 5.3.2 is used to determine the variables of G that derive terminal strings.

Iteration	TERM	PREV
0	$\{B, F\}$	
1	$\{B, F, A, S\}$	$\{B, F\}$
2	$\{B, F, A, S, E\}$	$\{B, F, A, S\}$
3	$\{B, F, A, S, E\}$	$\{B, F, A, S, E\}$

Using the set TERM to build G_T produces

$$V_T = \{S, A, F, B, E\}$$
$$\Sigma_T = \{a, b\}$$
$$
\begin{aligned}
P_T: \quad & S \rightarrow BS \mid B \\
& A \rightarrow aA \mid aF \\
& B \rightarrow b \\
& E \rightarrow aA \mid BSA \\
& F \rightarrow bB \mid b.
\end{aligned}
$$

The indirectly recursive loops generated by the variables C and D, which can never be exited once entered, are discovered by the algorithm. All rules containing these variables are deleted.   □

The construction of G_T completes the first step in the removal of useless variables. All variables in G_T derive terminal strings. We must now remove the variables that do not occur in sentential forms of the grammar. A set REACH is built that contains all variables derivable from S.

Algorithm 5.3.4
Construction of the Set of Reachable Variables

input: context-free grammar $G = (V, \Sigma, P, S)$

1. REACH := $\{S\}$.

2. PREV := Ø.

3. **repeat**
    3.1. NEW := REACH − PREV.
    3.2. PREV := REACH.
    3.3. **for** each variable $A \in$ NEW **do**
        for each rule $A \rightarrow w$ **do** add all variables in w to REACH
   until REACH = PREV

Algorithm 5.3.4, like Algorithm 5.2.1, uses a top-down approach to construct the desired set of variables. The set REACH is initialized to S. Variables are added to REACH as they are discovered in derivations from S.

Lemma 5.3.5
Let $G = (V, \Sigma, P, S)$ be a context-free grammar. Algorithm 5.3.4 generates the set of variables reachable from S.

Proof First we show that every variable in REACH is derivable from S. The proof is by induction on the number of iterations of the algorithm.

The set REACH is initialized to S, which is clearly reachable. Assume that all variables in the set REACH after n iterations are reachable from S. Let B be a variable added to REACH in iteration $n + 1$. Then there is a rule $A \rightarrow uBv$ where A is in REACH after n iterations. By induction, there is a derivation $S \overset{*}{\Rightarrow} xAy$. Extending this derivation with the application of $A \rightarrow uBv$ establishes the reachability of B.

We now prove that every variable reachable from S is eventually added to the set REACH. If $S \overset{n}{\Rightarrow} uAv$, then A is added to REACH on or before iteration n. The proof is by induction on the length of the derivation from S.

The start symbol, the only variable reachable by a derivation of length zero, is added to REACH at step 1 of the algorithm. Assume that each variable reachable by a derivation of length n or less is inserted into REACH on or before iteration n.

Let $S \overset{n}{\Rightarrow} xAy \Rightarrow xuBvy$ be a derivation in G where the $n + 1$st rule applied is $A \rightarrow uBv$. By the inductive hypothesis, A has been added to REACH by iteration n. B is added to REACH on the succeeding iteration. ∎

Theorem 5.3.6

Let $G = (V, \Sigma, P, S)$ be a context-free grammar. There is an algorithm to construct a context-free grammar G_U that satisfies

i) $L(G_U) = L(G)$.

ii) G_U has no useless symbols.

Proof   The removal of useless symbols begins by building G_T from G. Algorithm 5.3.4 is used to generate the variables of G_T that are reachable from the start symbol. All rules of G_T that reference variables not reachable from S are deleted to obtain G_U.

$$V_U = \text{REACH}$$
$$P_U = \{A \rightarrow w \mid A \rightarrow w \in P_T, A \in \text{REACH and } w \in (\text{REACH} \cup \Sigma)^*\}$$
$$\Sigma_U = \{a \in \Sigma \mid a \text{ occurs in the right-hand side of a rule in } P_U\}$$

To establish the equality of $L(G_U)$ and $L(G_T)$ it is sufficient to show that every string derivable in G_T is also derivable in G_U. Let w be an element of $L(G_T)$. Every variable occurring in the derivation of w is reachable and each rule is in P_U. ∎

Example 5.3.2

The grammar G_U is constructed for the grammar G_T in Example 5.3.1. The set of reachable variables of G_T is constructed using Algorithm 5.3.4.

Iteration	REACH	PREV	NEW
0	$\{S\}$	$\varnothing$	
1	$\{S, B\}$	$\{S\}$	$\{S\}$
2	$\{S, B\}$	$\{S, B\}$	$\{B\}$

Removing all references to the variables A and F produces the grammar

$$G_U: S \rightarrow BS \mid B$$
$$B \rightarrow b.$$

The grammar G_U is equivalent to the grammar G given at the beginning of the section. Clearly, the language of these grammars is b^+. $\square$

Removing useless symbols consists of the two-part process outlined in Theorem 5.3.6. The first step is the removal of variables that do not generate terminal strings. The resulting grammar is then purged of variables that are not derivable from the start symbol. Applying these procedures in reverse order may not remove all the useless symbols, as shown in the next example.

Example 5.3.3

Let G be the grammar

$$G: S \rightarrow a \mid AB$$
$$A \rightarrow b.$$

The necessity of applying the transformations in the specified order is exhibited by applying the processes in both orders and comparing the results.

Remove variables that do not generate terminal strings:	Remove unreachable symbols:
$S \rightarrow a$	$S \rightarrow a \mid AB$
$A \rightarrow b$	$A \rightarrow b$

Remove unreachable symbols:	Remove variables that do not generate terminal strings:
$S \rightarrow a$	$S \rightarrow a$
	$A \rightarrow b$

The variable A and terminal b are useless, but they remain in the grammar obtained by reversing the order of the transformations. $\square$

The transformation of grammars to normal forms consists of a sequence of algorithmic steps, each of which preserves the previous ones. The removal of useless symbols will not undo any of the restrictions obtained by the construction of G_L or G_C. These transformations only remove rules; they do not alter any other feature of the grammar. However, useless symbols may be created by the process of transforming a grammar to an equivalent noncontracting grammar.

5.4   Chomsky Normal Form

A normal form is described by a set of conditions that each rule in the grammar must satisfy. The Chomsky normal form places restrictions on the length and the composition of the right-hand side of a rule.

Definition 5.4.1

A context-free grammar $G = (V, \Sigma, P, S)$ is in **Chomsky normal form** if each rule is of the form

  i) $A \rightarrow BC$

 ii) $A \rightarrow a$

iii) $S \rightarrow \lambda$

where $B, C \in V - \{S\}$.

The conversion of a grammar to Chomsky normal form continues the sequence of modifications presented in the previous sections.

Theorem 5.4.2

Let $G = (V, \Sigma, P, S)$ be a context-free grammar. There is an algorithm to construct a grammar $G' = (V, \Sigma, P', S)$ in Chomsky normal form that is equivalent to G.

Proof   We assume

  i) the start symbol of G is nonrecursive

 ii) G does not contain lambda rules other than $S \rightarrow \lambda$

iii) G does not contain chain rules

 iv) G does not contain useless symbols.

If these conditions are not satisfied by G, an equivalent grammar can be constructed that satisfies i) to iv). A rule in a grammar satisfying these conditions has the form $S \rightarrow \lambda$, $A \rightarrow a$, or $A \rightarrow w$, where $w \in ((V \cup \Sigma) - \{S\})^*$ and $length(w) > 1$. The set P' of rules of G' is built from the rules of G.

The only rule of G whose right-hand side has length zero is $S \rightarrow \lambda$. Since G does not contain chain rules, the right-hand side of a rule $A \rightarrow w$ is a single terminal whenever the length of w is one. In either case, the rules already satisfy the conditions of Chomsky normal form and are added to P'.

Let $A \rightarrow w$ be a rule with $length(w)$ greater than one. The string w may contain both variables and terminals. The first step is to remove the terminals from the right-hand side of all such rules. This is accomplished by adding new variables and rules that simply rename each terminal by a variable. The rule

$$A \rightarrow bDcF$$

can be replaced by the three rules

$$A \rightarrow B'DC'F$$
$$B' \rightarrow b$$
$$C' \rightarrow c.$$

After this transformation, the right-hand side of a rule consists of the null string, a terminal, or a string in V^+. Rules of the latter form must be broken into a sequence of rules each of whose right-hand side consists of two variables. The sequential application of these rules should generate the right-hand side of the original rule. Continuing with the previous example, the A rule is replaced by the rules

$$A \rightarrow B'T_1$$
$$T_1 \rightarrow DT_2$$
$$T_2 \rightarrow C'F.$$

The variables T_1 and T_2 are introduced to link the sequence of rules. Rewriting each rule whose right-hand side has length greater than two as a sequence of rules completes the transformation to Chomsky normal form. ∎

Example 5.4.1

Let G be the grammar

$$S \rightarrow aABC \mid a$$
$$A \rightarrow aA \mid a$$
$$B \rightarrow bcB \mid bc$$
$$C \rightarrow cC \mid c.$$

This grammar already satisfies the conditions placed on the start symbol and lambda rules and does not contain chain rules or useless symbols. The equivalent Chomsky normal form grammar is constructed by transforming the rules whose right-hand side has length greater than two.

$$
\begin{aligned}
G': S &\rightarrow A'T_1 \mid a \\
A' &\rightarrow a \\
T_1 &\rightarrow AT_2 \\
T_2 &\rightarrow BC \\
A &\rightarrow A'A \mid a \\
B &\rightarrow B'T_4 \mid B'C' \\
T_4 &\rightarrow C'B \\
C &\rightarrow C'C \mid c \\
B' &\rightarrow b \\
C' &\rightarrow c
\end{aligned}
$$

□

Example 5.4.2

The preceding techniques are used to transform the grammar AE to an equivalent grammar in Chomsky normal form. The start symbol of AE is nonrecursive and the grammar does not contain lambda rules. Removing the chain rules yields

$$S \rightarrow A + T \mid b \mid (A)$$
$$A \rightarrow A + T \mid b \mid (A)$$
$$T \rightarrow b \mid (A).$$

The transformation to Chomsky normal form requires the introduction of new variables. A brief description of the role of each new variable is given.

$S \rightarrow AY \mid b \mid LZ$	Y represents $+ T$
$Z \rightarrow AR$	Z represents $A)$
$A \rightarrow AY \mid b \mid LZ$	L represents $($
$T \rightarrow b \mid LZ$	R represents $)$
$Y \rightarrow PT$	P represents $+$
$P \rightarrow +$	
$L \rightarrow ($	
$R \rightarrow)$	

□

5.5 Removal of Direct Left Recursion

The halting conditions of the top-down parsing algorithms depend upon the generation of terminal prefixes to discover dead-ends. The directly left recursive rule $A \rightarrow A + T$ in the grammar AE introduced the possibility of unending computations in both the breadth-first and depth-first algorithms. Repeated applications of this rule fail to generate a prefix that can terminate the parse.

Consider derivations using the rules $A \rightarrow Aa \mid b$. Repeated applications of the directly left recursive rule $A \rightarrow Aa$ produce strings of the form Aa^i, $i \geq 0$. The derivation terminates with the application of the nonrecursive rule $A \rightarrow b$, generating ba^*. The derivation of $baaa$ has the form

$$A \Rightarrow Aa$$
$$\Rightarrow Aaa$$
$$\Rightarrow Aaaa$$
$$\Rightarrow baaa.$$

Applications of the directly left recursive rule generate a string of a's but do not increase the length of the terminal prefix. The prefix grows only when the nondirectly left recursive rule is applied.

To avoid the possibility of a nonterminating parse, directly left recursive rules must be removed from the grammar. Recursion itself cannot be removed; it is necessary to generate strings of arbitrary length. It is the left recursion that causes the problem, not recursion in general. The general technique for replacing these rules is illustrated by the following examples.

a) $A \rightarrow Aa \mid b$ b) $A \rightarrow Aa \mid Ab \mid b \mid c$ c) $A \rightarrow AB \mid BA \mid a$
                                                                            $B \rightarrow b \mid c$

The sets generated by these rules are ba^*, $(b \cup c)(a \cup b)^*$ and $(b \cup c)^*a(b \cup c)^*$, respectively. The direct left recursion builds a string to the right of the recursive variable. The recursive sequence is terminated by an A rule that is not directly left recursive. To build the string in a left-to-right manner, the nonrecursive rule is applied first and the remainder of the string is constructed by right recursion. The following rules generate the same strings as the previous examples without using direct left recursion.

a) $A \rightarrow bZ \mid b$ b) $A \rightarrow bZ \mid cZ \mid b \mid c$ c) $A \rightarrow BAZ \mid aZ \mid BA \mid a$
   $Z \rightarrow aZ \mid a$ $Z \rightarrow aZ \mid bZ \mid a \mid b$ $Z \rightarrow BZ \mid B$
                                                                            $B \rightarrow b \mid c$

The rules in a) generate ba^* with left recursion replaced by direct right recursion. With these rules, the derivation of $baaa$ increases the length of the terminal prefix with each rule application.

$$A \Rightarrow bZ$$
$$\Rightarrow baZ$$
$$\Rightarrow baaZ$$
$$\Rightarrow baaa$$

The removal of the direct left recursion requires the addition of a new variable to the grammar. This variable introduces a set of directly right recursive rules. Direct right recursion causes the recursive variable to occur as the rightmost symbol in the derived string.

   To remove direct left recursion, the A rules are divided into two categories: the directly left recursive rules

$$A \rightarrow Au_1 \mid Au_2 \mid \ldots \mid Au_j$$

and the rules

$$A \rightarrow v_1 \mid v_2 \mid \ldots \mid v_k$$

in which the first symbol of each v_i is not A. A derivation from these rules consists of applications of directly left recursive rules followed by the application of a rule $A \rightarrow v_i$, ending the direct recursion. Using the technique illustrated in the previous examples, new rules are constructed that initially generate v_i and then produce the remainder of the string using right recursion.

   The A rules initially place one of the v_i's on the left-hand side of the derived string.

$$A \rightarrow v_1 \mid \ldots \mid v_k \mid v_1 Z \mid \ldots \mid v_k Z$$

If the string contains a sequence of u_i's, these are generated by the Z rules

$$Z \rightarrow u_1 Z \mid \ldots \mid u_j Z \mid u_1 \mid \ldots \mid u_j$$

using right recursion.

Example 5.5.1

A set of rules without direct left recursion is constructed to generate the same strings as

$$A \rightarrow Aa \mid Aab \mid bb \mid b.$$

These rules generate $(b \cup bb)(a \cup ab)^*$. The left recursion in the original rules is terminated by applying $A \rightarrow b$ or $A \rightarrow bb$. To build these strings in a left-to-right manner, the A rules generate the leftmost symbol of the string.

$$A \rightarrow bb \mid b \mid bbZ \mid bZ$$

The Z rules generate $(a \cup ab)^+$ using right recursive rules.

$$Z \rightarrow aZ \mid abZ \mid a \mid ab \qquad \qquad \square$$

Lemma 5.5.1

Let $G = (V, \Sigma, P, S)$ be a context-free grammar and $A \in V$ a directly left recursive variable in G. There is an algorithm to construct an equivalent grammar $G' = (V', \Sigma, P', S')$ in which A is not directly left recursive.

Proof   We assume that the start symbol of G is nonrecursive and the only lambda rule is $S \rightarrow \lambda$. If this is not the case, G can be transformed to an equivalent grammar satisfying these conditions. The variables of G' are those of G augmented with one additional variable to generate the right recursive rules. P' is built from P using the technique outlined above.

The new A rules cannot be directly recursive since the first symbol of each of the v_i's is not A. The Z rules are also not directly left recursive. The variable Z does not occur in any of the v_i's and the v_i's are nonnull by the restriction on lambda rules in G. ■

This technique can be used repeatedly to remove all occurrences of directly left recursive rules while preserving the language of the grammar. Will this eliminate the possibility of unending computations in the top-down parsing algorithms? A derivation using the rules $A \rightarrow Bu$ and $B \rightarrow Av$ can generate the sentential forms

$$
\begin{aligned}
A &\Rightarrow Bu \\
&\Rightarrow Avu \\
&\Rightarrow Buvu \\
&\Rightarrow Avuvu \\
&\quad \vdots
\end{aligned}
$$

The difficulties associated with direct left recursion can also be caused by indirect left recursion. Additional transformations are required to remove all possible occurrences of left recursion.

5.6   Greibach Normal Form

The construction of terminal prefixes facilitates the discovery of dead-ends by the top-down parsing algorithms. A normal form, the Greibach normal form, is presented in which the application of every rule increases the length of the terminal prefix of the derived string. This ensures that left recursion, direct or indirect, cannot occur.

Definition 5.6.1

A context-free grammar $G = (V, \Sigma, P, S)$ is in **Greibach normal form** if each rule is of the form

 i) $A \rightarrow aA_1A_2 \ldots A_n$

 ii) $A \rightarrow a$

 iii) $S \rightarrow \lambda$

where $a \in \Sigma$, and $A_i \in V - \{S\}$ for $i = 1, 2, \ldots, n$.

There are several alternate definitions of the Greibach normal form. A common formulation requires a terminal symbol in the first position of the string but permits the remainder of the string to contain both variables and terminals.

Lemma 5.6.2 provides a schema for removing a rule while preserving the language generated by the grammar.

Lemma 5.6.2

Let $G = (V, \Sigma, P, S)$ be a context-free grammar. Let $A \rightarrow uBv$ be a rule in P and $B \rightarrow w_1 \mid w_2 \mid \ldots \mid w_n$ be the B rules of P. The grammar $G' = (V, \Sigma, P', S)$ where

$$P' = (P - \{A \rightarrow uBv\}) \cup \{A \rightarrow uw_1v \mid uw_2v \mid \ldots \mid uw_nv\}$$

is equivalent to G.

Proof   Since each rule $A \rightarrow uw_iv$ is derivable in G, the inclusion $L(G') \subseteq L(G)$ follows from Lemma 5.1.4.

The opposite inclusion is established by showing that every terminal string derivable in G using the rule $A \rightarrow uBv$ is also derivable in G'. The derivation of a terminal string that utilizes this rule has the form $S \overset{*}{\Rightarrow} pAq \Rightarrow puBvp \Rightarrow puw_ivp \overset{*}{\Rightarrow} w$. The same string can be generated in G' using the rule $A \rightarrow uw_iv$.   ∎

The conversion of a Chomsky normal form grammar to Greibach normal form uses two rule transformation techniques: the rule replacement scheme of Lemma 5.6.2 and the transformation that removes directly left recursive rules. The procedure begins by ordering the variables of the grammar. The start symbol is assigned the number one; the remaining variables may be numbered in any order. Different numberings change the transformations required to convert the grammar, but any ordering suffices.

The first step of the conversion is to construct a grammar in which every rule is of the form

i) $S \rightarrow \lambda$

ii) $A \rightarrow aw$

iii) $A \rightarrow Bw$

where $w \in V^*$ and the number assigned to B in the ordering of the variables is greater than the number of A. The rules are transformed to satisfy condition iii) according to the order in which the variables are numbered. The conversion of a Chomsky normal form grammar to Greibach normal form is illustrated by tracing the transformation of the rules of the grammar G.

$$G: S \rightarrow AB \mid \lambda$$
$$A \rightarrow AB \mid CB \mid a$$
$$B \rightarrow AB \mid b$$
$$C \rightarrow AC \mid c$$

The variables S, A, B, and C are numbered 1, 2, 3, and 4, respectively.

Since the start symbol of a Chomsky normal form grammar is nonrecursive, the S rules already satisfy the three conditions. The process continues by transforming the A rules into a set of rules in which the first symbol on the right-hand side is either a terminal or a variable assigned a number greater than two. The directly left recursive rule $A \rightarrow AB$ violates these restrictions. Lemma 5.5.1 can be used to remove the direct left recursion, yielding

$$S \rightarrow AB \mid \lambda$$
$$A \rightarrow CBR_1 \mid aR_1 \mid CB \mid a$$
$$B \rightarrow AB \mid b$$
$$C \rightarrow AC \mid c$$
$$R_1 \rightarrow BR_1 \mid B.$$

Now the B rules must be transformed to the appropriate form. The rule $B \rightarrow AB$ must be replaced since the number of B is three and A, which occurs as the first symbol on the right-hand side, is two. Lemma 5.6.2 permits the leading A in the right-hand side of the rule $B \rightarrow AB$ to be replaced by the right-hand side of the A rules, producing

$$S \rightarrow AB \mid \lambda$$
$$A \rightarrow CBR_1 \mid aR_1 \mid CB \mid a$$
$$B \rightarrow CBR_1B \mid aR_1B \mid CBB \mid aB \mid b$$
$$C \rightarrow AC \mid c$$
$$R_1 \rightarrow BR_1 \mid B.$$

Employing the replacement techniques of Lemma 5.6.2 to the C rules creates two directly left recursive rules.

$$S \rightarrow AB \mid \lambda$$
$$A \rightarrow CBR_1 \mid aR_1 \mid CB \mid a$$
$$B \rightarrow CBR_1B \mid aR_1B \mid CBB \mid aB \mid b$$
$$C \rightarrow CBR_1C \mid aR_1C \mid CBC \mid aC \mid c$$
$$R_1 \rightarrow BR_1 \mid B$$

The left recursion can be removed, introducing the new variable R_2.

$$S \rightarrow AB \mid \lambda$$
$$A \rightarrow CBR_1 \mid aR_1 \mid CB \mid a$$
$$B \rightarrow CBR_1B \mid aR_1B \mid CBB \mid aB \mid b$$
$$C \rightarrow aR_1C \mid aC \mid c \mid aR_1CR_2 \mid aCR_2 \mid cR_2$$
$$R_1 \rightarrow BR_1 \mid B$$
$$R_2 \rightarrow BR_1CR_2 \mid BCR_2 \mid BR_1C \mid BC$$

The original variables now satisfy the condition that the first symbol of the right-hand side of a rule is either a terminal or a variable whose number is greater than the number of the variable on the left-hand side. The variable with the highest number, in this case C, must have a terminal as the first symbol in each rule. The next variable, B, can have only C's or terminals as the first symbol. A B rule beginning with the variable C can then be replaced by a set of rules, each of which begins with a terminal, using the C rules and Lemma 5.6.2. Making this transformation, we obtain the rules

$$S \rightarrow AB \mid \lambda$$
$$A \rightarrow CBR_1 \mid aR_1 \mid CB \mid a$$
$$B \rightarrow aR_1B \mid aB \mid b$$
$$\rightarrow aR_1CBR_1B \mid aCBR_1B \mid cBR_1B \mid aR_1CR_2BR_1B \mid aCR_2BR_1B \mid cR_2BR_1B$$
$$\rightarrow aR_1CBB \mid aCBB \mid cBB \mid aR_1CR_2BB \mid aCR_2BB \mid cR_2BB$$
$$C \rightarrow aR_1C \mid aC \mid c \mid aR_1CR_2 \mid aCR_2 \mid cR_2$$
$$R_1 \rightarrow BR_1 \mid B$$
$$R_2 \rightarrow BR_1CR_2 \mid BCR_2 \mid BR_1C \mid BC$$

The second list of B rules is obtained by substituting for C in the rule $B \rightarrow CBR_1B$ and the third in the rule $B \rightarrow CBB$. The S and A rules must also be rewritten to remove variables from the initial position of the right-hand side of a rule. The substitutions in the A rules use the B and C rules, all of which now begin with a terminal. The A, B, and C rules can then be used to transform the S rules.

$$S \rightarrow \lambda$$
$$\rightarrow aR_1B \mid aB$$
$$\rightarrow aR_1CBR_1B \mid aCBR_1B \mid cBR_1B \mid aR_1CR_2BR_1B \mid aCR_2BR_1B \mid cR_2BR_1B$$
$$\rightarrow aR_1CBB \mid aCBB \mid cBB \mid aR_1CR_2BB \mid aCR_2BB \mid cR_2BB$$

$A \rightarrow aR_1 \mid a$
$\quad \rightarrow aR_1CBR_1 \mid aCBR_1 \mid cBR_1 \mid aR_1CR_2BR_1 \mid aCR_2BR_1 \mid cR_2BR_1$
$\quad \rightarrow aR_1CB \mid aCB \mid cB \mid aR_1CR_2B \mid aCR_2B \mid cR_2B$
$B \rightarrow aR_1B \mid aB \mid b$
$\quad \rightarrow aR_1CBR_1B \mid aCBR_1B \mid cBR_1B \mid aR_1CR_2BR_1B \mid aCR_2BR_1B \mid cR_2BR_1B$
$\quad \rightarrow aR_1CBB \mid aCBB \mid cBB \mid aR_1CR_2BB \mid aCR_2BB \mid cR_2BB$
$C \rightarrow aR_1C \mid aC \mid c \mid aR_1CR_2 \mid aCR_2 \mid cR_2$
$R_1 \rightarrow BR_1 \mid B$
$R_2 \rightarrow BR_1CR_2 \mid BCR_2 \mid BR_1C \mid BC$

Finally, the substitution process must be applied to each of the variables added in the removal of direct recursion. Rewriting these rules yields

$R_1 \rightarrow aR_1BR_1 \mid aBR_1 \mid bR_1$
$\quad \rightarrow aR_1CBR_1BR_1 \mid aCBR_1BR_1 \mid cBR_1BR_1 \mid aR_1CR_2BR_1BR_1 \mid aCR_2BR_1BR_1 \mid cR_2BR_1BR_1$
$\quad \rightarrow aR_1CBBR_1 \mid aCBBR_1 \mid cBBR_1 \mid aR_1CR_2BBR_1 \mid aCR_2BBR_1 \mid cR_2BBR_1$
$R_1 \rightarrow aR_1B \mid aB \mid b$
$\quad \rightarrow aR_1CBR_1B \mid aCBR_1B \mid cBR_1B \mid aR_1CR_2BR_1B \mid aCR_2BR_1B \mid cR_2BR_1B$
$\quad \rightarrow aR_1CBB \mid aCBB \mid cBB \mid aR_1CR_2BB \mid aCR_2BB \mid cR_2BB$
$R_2 \rightarrow aR_1BR_1CR_2 \mid aBR_1CR_2 \mid bR_1CR_2$
$\quad \rightarrow aR_1CBR_1BR_1CR_2 \mid aCBR_1BR_1CR_2 \mid cBR_1BR_1CR_2 \mid aR_1CR_2BR_1BR_1CR_2 \mid$
$\quad \quad aCR_2BR_1BR_1CR_2 \mid cR_2BR_1BR_1CR_2$
$\quad \rightarrow aR_1CBBR_1CR_2 \mid aCBBR_1CR_2 \mid cBBR_1CR_2 \mid aR_1CR_2BBR_1CR_2 \mid aCR_2BBR_1CR_2 \mid$
$\quad \quad cR_2BBR_1CR_2$
$R_2 \rightarrow aR_1BCR_2 \mid aBCR_2 \mid bCR_2$
$\quad \rightarrow aR_1CBR_1BCR_2 \mid aCBR_1BCR_2 \mid cBR_1BCR_2 \mid aR_1CR_2BR_1BCR_2 \mid aCR_2BR_1BCR_2 \mid$
$\quad \quad cR_2BR_1BCR_2$
$\quad \rightarrow aR_1CBBCR_2 \mid aCBBCR_2 \mid cBBCR_2 \mid aR_1CR_2BBCR_2 \mid aCR_2BBCR_2 \mid cR_2BBCR_2$
$R_2 \rightarrow aR_1BR_1C \mid aBR_1C \mid bR_1C$
$\quad \rightarrow aR_1CBR_1BR_1C \mid aCBR_1BR_1C \mid cBR_1BR_1C \mid aR_1CR_2BR_1BR_1C \mid aCR_2BR_1BR_1C \mid$
$\quad \quad cR_2BR_1BR_1C$
$\quad \rightarrow aR_1CBBR_1C \mid aCBBR_1C \mid cBBR_1C \mid aR_1CR_2BBR_1C \mid aCR_2BBR_1C \mid cR_2BBR_1C$
$R_2 \rightarrow aR_1BC \mid aBC \mid bC$
$\quad \rightarrow aR_1CBR_1BC \mid aCBR_1BC \mid cBR_1BC \mid aR_1CR_2BR_1BC \mid aCR_2BR_1BC \mid cR_2BR_1BC$
$\quad \rightarrow aR_1CBBC \mid aCBBC \mid cBBC \mid aR_1CR_2BBC \mid aCR_2BBC \mid cR_2BBC$

The resulting grammar in Greibach normal form has lost all the simplicity of the original grammar G. Designing a grammar in Greibach normal form is an almost impossible task. The construction of grammars should be done using simpler, intuitive rules. Like all the preceding transformations, the steps necessary to transform an arbitrary context-free grammar to Greibach normal form can be implemented on a computer. The input to such a program are the rules of a context-free grammar, and the result is an equivalent Greibach normal form grammar.

It should also be pointed out that useless symbols may be created by the rule replacements specified by Lemma 5.6.2. The variable A is a useful symbol of G, occurring in the derivation

$$S \Rightarrow AB \Rightarrow aB \Rightarrow ab.$$

In the conversion to Greibach normal form, the substitutions removed all occurrences of A from the right-hand side of rules. The string ab is generated by

$$S \Rightarrow aB \Rightarrow ab$$

in the equivalent Greibach normal form grammar.

Theorem 5.6.3

Let G be a context-free grammar. There is an algorithm to construct an equivalent context-free grammar in Greibach normal form.

Proof   The operations used in the construction of the Greibach normal form have previously been shown to generate equivalent grammars. All that remains is to show that the rules can always be transformed to satisfy the conditions necessary to perform the substitutions. These require that each rule has the form

$$A_k \rightarrow A_j w \text{ with } k < j$$

or

$$A_k \rightarrow aw$$

where the subscript represents the ordering of the variables.

The proof is by induction on the ordering of the variables. The basis is the start symbol, the variable numbered one. Since S is nonrecursive, this condition trivially holds. Now assume that all variables up to number k satisfy the condition. If there is a rule $A_k \rightarrow A_i w$ with $i < k$, the substitution can be applied to generate a set of rules each of which $A_k \rightarrow A_j w'$ where $j > i$. This process can be repeated, at most $k - i$ times, to yield a set of rules that are either directly left recursive or in the correct form. All directly left recursive variables can be transformed by using the technique of Lemma 5.5.1.   ∎

Example 5.6.1

The Chomsky and Greibach normal forms are constructed for the grammar

$$S \rightarrow SaB \mid aB$$
$$B \rightarrow bB \mid \lambda.$$

Adding a nonrecursive start symbol S' and removing lambda and chain rules yields

$$S' \rightarrow SaB \mid Sa \mid aB \mid a$$
$$S \; \rightarrow SaB \mid Sa \mid aB \mid a$$
$$B \; \rightarrow bB \mid b.$$

The Chomsky normal form is obtained by transforming the preceding rules. Variables A and C are used as aliases for a and b, respectively. T represents the string aB.

$$S' \rightarrow ST \mid SA \mid AB \mid a$$
$$S \rightarrow ST \mid SA \mid AB \mid a$$
$$B \rightarrow CB \mid b$$
$$T \rightarrow AB$$
$$A \rightarrow a$$
$$C \rightarrow b$$

The variables are ordered by S', S, B, T, A, C. Removing the direct left recursion produces the rules

$$S' \rightarrow ST \mid SA \mid AB \mid a$$
$$S \rightarrow ABZ \mid aZ \mid AB \mid a$$
$$B \rightarrow CB \mid b$$
$$T \rightarrow AB$$
$$A \rightarrow a$$
$$C \rightarrow b$$
$$Z \rightarrow TZ \mid AZ \mid T \mid A.$$

These rules satisfy the condition that requires the value of the variable on the left-hand side of a rule to be less than that of a leading variable on the right-hand side. Implementing the substitutions beginning with the A and C rules produces the Greibach normal form.

$$S' \rightarrow aBZT \mid aZT \mid aBT \mid aT \mid aBZA \mid aZA \mid aBA \mid aA \mid aB \mid a$$
$$S \rightarrow aBZ \mid aZ \mid aB \mid a$$
$$B \rightarrow bB \mid b$$
$$T \rightarrow aB$$
$$A \rightarrow a$$
$$C \rightarrow b$$
$$Z \rightarrow aBZ \mid aZ \mid aB \mid a$$

The derivation of the string $abaaba$ is given in each of the three equivalent grammars.

G	Chomsky Normal Form	Greibach Normal Form
$S \Rightarrow SaB$	$S' \Rightarrow SA$	$S' \Rightarrow aBZA$
$\Rightarrow SaBaB$	$\Rightarrow STA$	$\Rightarrow abZA$
$\Rightarrow SaBaBaB$	$\Rightarrow SATA$	$\Rightarrow abaZA$
$\Rightarrow aBaBaBaB$	$\Rightarrow ABATA$	$\Rightarrow abaaBA$
$\Rightarrow abBaBaBaB$	$\Rightarrow aBATA$	$\Rightarrow abaabA$
$\Rightarrow abaBaBaB$	$\Rightarrow abATA$	$\Rightarrow abaaba$
$\Rightarrow abaaBaB$	$\Rightarrow abaTA$	
$\Rightarrow abaabBaB$	$\Rightarrow abaABA$	
$\Rightarrow abaabaB$	$\Rightarrow abaaBA$	
$\Rightarrow abaaba$	$\Rightarrow abaabA$	
	$\Rightarrow abaaba$	

The derivation in the Chomsky normal form grammar generates six variables. Each of these is transformed to a terminal by a rule of the form $A \to a$. The Greibach normal form derivation generates a terminal with each rule application. The derivation is completed using only six rule applications.   □

The top-down parsing algorithms presented in Chapter 4 terminate for all input strings when using the rules of a grammar in Greibach normal form. The derivation of a string of length n, where n is greater than zero, requires exactly n rule applications. Each application adds one terminal symbol to the terminal prefix of the derived string. The construction of a path of length n in the graph of a grammar will either successfully terminate the parse or the derived string will be declared a dead-end.

Exercises

For Exercises 1–4, construct an equivalent essentially nondecreasing grammar G_L with a nonrecursive start symbol. Give a regular expression for the languages of each of the grammars.

1. G: $S \to aS \mid bS \mid B$
   $B \to bb \mid C \mid \lambda$
   $C \to cC \mid \lambda$

2. G: $S \to ABC \mid \lambda$
   $A \to aA \mid \lambda$
   $B \to bB \mid \lambda$
   $C \to cC \mid \lambda$

3. G: $S \to BSA \mid A$
   $A \to aA \mid \lambda$
   $B \to Bba \mid \lambda$

4. G: $S \to AB \mid BCS$
   $A \to aA \mid C$
   $B \to bbB \mid b$
   $C \to cC \mid \lambda$

5. Prove Lemma 5.2.2.

For Exercises 6 and 7, construct an equivalent grammar G_C that does not contain chain rules. Note that these grammars do not contain lambda rules.

6. G: $S \to AS \mid A$
   $A \to aA \mid bB \mid C$
   $B \to bB \mid b$
   $C \to cC \mid B$

7. G: $S \to A \mid B \mid C$
   $A \to aa \mid B$
   $B \to bb \mid C$
   $C \to cc \mid A$

8. Eliminate the chain rules from the grammar G_L of Exercise 1.

9. Eliminate the chain rules from the grammar G_L of Exercise 4.

10. Prove that Algorithm 5.3.2 generates the set of variables that derive terminal strings.

For Exercises 11–13, construct an equivalent grammar without useless symbols. Trace the generation of the sets of TERM and REACH used to construct G_T and G_U. Describe the language generated by the grammar.

11. G: $S \rightarrow AA \mid CD \mid bB$
    $A \rightarrow aA \mid a$
    $B \rightarrow bB \mid bC$
    $C \rightarrow cB$
    $D \rightarrow dD \mid d$

12. G: $S \rightarrow aA \mid BD$
    $A \rightarrow aA \mid aAB \mid aD$
    $B \rightarrow aB \mid aC \mid BF$
    $C \rightarrow Bb \mid aAC \mid E$
    $D \rightarrow bD \mid bC \mid b$
    $E \rightarrow aB \mid bC$
    $F \rightarrow aF \mid aG \mid a$
    $G \rightarrow a \mid b$

13. G: $S \rightarrow ACH \mid BB$
    $A \rightarrow aA \mid aF$
    $B \rightarrow CFH \mid b$
    $C \rightarrow aC \mid DH$
    $D \rightarrow aD \mid BD \mid Ca$
    $F \rightarrow bB \mid b$
    $H \rightarrow dH \mid d$

14. Show that all the symbols of G are useful. Construct an equivalent grammar G_C by removing the chain rules from G. Show that G_C contains useless symbols.

$$G: S \rightarrow A \mid CB$$
$$A \rightarrow C \mid D$$
$$B \rightarrow bB \mid b$$
$$C \rightarrow cC \mid c$$
$$D \rightarrow dD \mid d$$

15. Convert the grammar G to Chomsky normal form. G already satisfies the conditions on the start symbol S, lambda rules, useless symbols, and chain rules.

$$G: S \rightarrow aAbB \mid ABC \mid a$$
$$A \rightarrow aA \mid a$$
$$B \rightarrow bBcC \mid b$$
$$C \rightarrow abc$$

16. Convert the result of Exercise 8 to Chomsky normal form.

17. Convert the result of Exercise 9 to Chomsky normal form.

18. Convert the grammar

$$S \rightarrow A \mid ABa \mid AbA$$
$$A \rightarrow Aa \mid \lambda$$
$$B \rightarrow Bb \mid BC$$
$$C \rightarrow CB \mid CA \mid bB$$

   to Chomsky normal form.

19. Let G be a grammar in Chomsky normal form.

   a) What is the length of a derivation of a string of length n in L(G)?

   b) What is the maximum depth of a derivation tree for a string of length n in L(G)?

   c) What is the minimum depth of a derivation tree for a string of length n in L(G)?

20. Construct a grammar G' that contains no directly left recursive rules and is equivalent to G.

$$G: S \rightarrow A \mid C$$
$$A \rightarrow AaB \mid AaC \mid B \mid a$$
$$B \rightarrow Bb \mid Cb$$
$$C \rightarrow cC \mid c$$

   Give a leftmost derivation of the string *aaccacb* in the grammars G and G'.

21. Construct a Greibach normal form grammar equivalent to

$$S \rightarrow aAb \mid a$$
$$A \rightarrow SS \mid b.$$

22. Convert the Chomsky normal form grammar

$$S \rightarrow AB \mid BC$$
$$A \rightarrow AB \mid a$$
$$B \rightarrow AA \mid CB \mid b$$
$$C \rightarrow a \mid b$$

   to Greibach normal form. Process the variables according to the order S, A, B, C.

23. Convert the Chomsky normal form grammar

$$S \rightarrow AB$$
$$A \rightarrow BB \mid CC$$
$$B \rightarrow AD \mid CA$$
$$C \rightarrow a$$
$$D \rightarrow b$$

   to Greibach normal form. Process the variables according to the order S, A, B, C, D.

24. Use the Chomsky normal form of the grammar AE given in Example 5.4.2 to construct the Greibach normal form. Use the ordering S, Z, A, T, Y, P, L, R. Remove all useless symbols that are created by the transformation to Greibach normal form.

25. Use the breadth-first top-down parsing algorithm and the grammar from Exercise 24 to construct a derivation of $(b + b)$. Compare this with the parse given in Fig. 4.3.

26. Use the depth-first top-down parsing algorithm and the grammar from Exercise 24 to construct a derivation of $(b) + b$. Compare this with the parse given in Example 4.4.2.

27. Prove that every context-free language is generated by a grammar in which each of the rules is of the form

   i) $S \rightarrow \lambda$

   ii) $A \rightarrow a$

   iii) $A \rightarrow aB$

   iv) $A \rightarrow aBC$

   where $A, B, C \in V$, and $a \in \Sigma$.

Bibliographic Notes

The constructions for removing lambda rules and chain rules were presented in Bar-Hillel, Perles, and Shamir [1961]. Chomsky normal form was introduced in Chomsky [1959]. Greibach normal form is from Greibach [1965]. A grammar whose rules satisfy the conditions of Exercise 27 is said to be in 2-normal form. A proof that 2-normal form grammars generate the entire set of context-free languages can be found in Hopcroft and Ullman [1969] and Harrison [1978]. Additional normal forms for context-free grammars are given in Harrison [1978].

PART III

Automata
and Languages

CHAPTER 6

Finite Automata

An effective procedure that determines whether an input string is in a language is called a language acceptor or recognizer. When parsing with a grammar in Greibach normal form, the top-down parsers of Chapter 4 can be thought of as acceptors of context-free languages. The generation of prefixes guarantees that the computation of the parser produces an answer for every input string. The objective of this chapter is to define a class of abstract machines whose computations, like those of a parser, determine the acceptability of an input string.

Properties common to all machines include the processing of input and the generation of output. A vending machine takes coins as input and returns food or beverages as output. A combination lock expects a sequence of numbers and opens the lock if the input sequence is correct. The input to the machines introduced in this chapter consists of a string over an alphabet. The result of the computation indicates whether the input string is acceptable.

The previous examples exhibit a property that we take for granted in mechanical computation, determinism. When the appropriate amount of money is inserted into a vending machine, we are upset if nothing is forthcoming. Similarly, we expect the combination to open the lock and all other sequences to fail. Initially, we require machines to be deterministic. This condition will be relaxed to examine the effects of nondeterminism on the capabilities of computation.

6.1   A Finite-State Machine

A formal definition of a machine is not concerned with the hardware involved in the operation of the machine but rather with a description of the internal operations as the machine processes the input. A vending machine may be built with levers, a combination lock with tumblers, and a parser is a program that is run on a computer. What sort of description encompasses the features of each of these seemingly different types of mechanical computation?

A simple newspaper vending machine, similar to those found on many street corners, is used to illustrate the components of a finite-state machine. The input to the machine consists of nickels, dimes, and quarters. When 30 cents is inserted, the cover of the machine may be opened and a paper removed. If the total of the coins exceeds 30 cents, the machine graciously accepts the overpayment and does not give change.

The newspaper machine on the street corner has no memory, at least not as we usually conceive of memory in a computing machine. However, the machine "knows" that an additional 5 cents will unlatch the cover when 25 cents has previously been inserted. This knowledge is acquired by the machine altering its internal state whenever input is received and processed.

A machine state represents the status of an ongoing computation. The internal operation of the vending machine can be described by the interactions of the following seven states. The names of the states, given in italics, indicate the progress made toward opening the cover.

- *needs 30 cents*—the state of the machine before any coins are inserted.
- *needs 25 cents*—the state after a nickel has been input.
- *needs 20 cents*—the state after two nickels or a dime have been input.
- *needs 15 cents*—the state after three nickels or a dime and a nickel have been input.
- *needs 10 cents*—the state after four nickels, a dime and two nickels, or two dimes have been input.
- *needs 5 cents*—the state after a quarter, five nickels, two dimes and a nickel, or one dime and three nickels have been input.
- *needs 0 cents*—the state that represents having at least 30 cents input.

The insertion of a coin causes the machine to alter its state. When 30 cents or more are input, the state *needs 0 cents* is entered and the latch is opened. Such a state is called accepting since it indicates the correctness of the input.

The design of the machine must represent each of the components symbolically. Rather than a sequence of coins, the input to the abstract machine is a string of symbols. A labeled directed graph known as a **state diagram** is often used to represent the transformations of the internal state of the machine. The nodes of the state diagram are the states described above. The *needs m cents* node is represented simply by *m* in the state

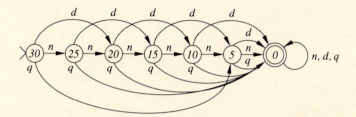

FIGURE 6.1   State diagram of newspaper vending machine.

diagram. The state of the machine at the beginning of a computation is designated ⟩○. The initial state for the newspaper vending machine is the node *30*.

The arcs are labeled *n*, *d*, or *q*, representing the input of a nickel, dime, or quarter. An arc from node *x* to node *y* labeled *v* specifies that processing input *v* when the machine is in state *x* causes the machine to enter state *y*. Figure 6.1 gives the state diagram for the newspaper vending machine. The arc labeled *d* from node *15* to *5* represents the change of state of the machine when *15* cents has previously been processed and a dime is input. The cycles of length one from node *0* to itself indicate that any input that increases the total past *30* cents leaves the latch unlocked.

Input to the machine consists of strings from $\{n, d, q\}^*$. The sequence of states entered during the processing of an input string can be traced by following the arcs in the state diagram. The machine is in its initial state at the beginning of a computation. The arc labeled by the first input symbol is traversed, specifying the subsequent machine state. The next symbol of the input string is processed by traversing the appropriate arc from the current node, the node reached by traversal of the previous arc. This procedure is repeated until the entire input string has been processed. The string is accepted if the computation terminates in the accepting state. The string *dndn* is accepted by the vending machine while the string *nndn* is not accepted since the computation terminates in state *5*.

6.2   Deterministic Finite Automata

The analysis of the vending machine required separating the fundamentals of the design from the implementational details. The implementation-independent description is often referred to as an abstract machine. We now introduce a class of abstract machines whose computations can be used to determine the acceptability of input strings.

Definition 6.2.1

A **deterministic finite automaton** (DFA) is a quintuple $M = (Q, \Sigma, \delta, q_0, F)$ where Q is a finite set of states, Σ a finite set called the alphabet, $q_0 \in Q$ a distinguished state known as the start state, F a subset of Q called the final or accepting states, and δ a total function from $Q \times \Sigma$ to Q known as the transition function.

We have referred to a deterministic finite automaton as an abstract machine. To reveal its mechanical nature, the operation of a DFA is described in terms of components that are present in many familiar computing machines. An automaton can be thought of as a machine consisting of five components: a single internal register, a set of values for the register, a tape, a tape reader, and an instruction set.

The states in a DFA represent the internal status of the machine and are often denoted $q_0, q_1, q_2, \ldots, q_n$. The register of the machine, also called the finite control, contains one of the states as its value. At the beginning of a computation the value of the register is q_0, the start state of the DFA.

The input is a finite sequence of elements from the alphabet Σ. The tape stores the input until needed by the computation. The tape is divided into squares, each square capable of holding one element from the alphabet. Since there is no upper bound to the length of an input string, the tape must be of unbounded length. The input to a computation of the automaton is placed on an initial segment of the tape.

The tape head reads a single square of the input tape. The body of the machine consists of the tape head and the register. The position of the tape head is indicated by placing the body of the machine under the tape square being scanned. The current state of the automaton is specified by the value on the register. The initial configuration of a computation with input *baba* is depicted

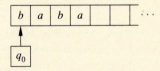

A computation of an automaton consists of the execution of a sequence of instructions. The execution of an instruction alters the state of the machine and moves the tape head one square to the right. The instruction set is constructed from the transition function of the DFA. The machine state and the symbol scanned determine the instruction to be executed. The action of a machine in state q_i scanning an *a* is to reset the state to $\delta(q_i, a)$. Since δ is a total function, there is exactly one instruction specified for every combination of state and input symbol, hence the deterministic in DFA.

A computation of an automaton determines the acceptability of the input string. A computation begins with the tape head scanning the leftmost square of the tape and the register containing the state q_0. The state and symbol are used to select the instruction. The machine then alters its state as prescribed by the instruction and the tape head moves to the right. The transformation of the machine by the execution of an instruction cycle is exhibited in Fig. 6.2. The instruction cycle is repeated until the tape head scans a blank square, at which time the computation terminates. An input string is **accepted** if the

$$M: Q = \{q_0, q_1\} \qquad \delta(q_0, a) = q_1$$
$$\Sigma = \{a, b\} \qquad \delta(q_0, b) = q_0$$
$$F = \{q_1\} \qquad \delta(q_1, a) = q_1$$
$$\delta(q_1, b) = q_0$$

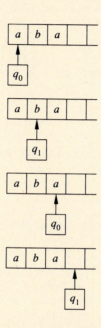

FIGURE 6.2 Computation in a DFA.

computation terminates in an accepting state; otherwise it is rejected. The computation in Fig. 6.2 exhibits the acceptance of the string *aba*.

Definition 6.2.2

Let $M = (Q, \Sigma, \delta, q_0, F)$ be a DFA. The **language** of M, denoted $L(M)$, is the set of strings in Σ^* accepted by M.

A DFA can be considered to be a language acceptor; the language recognized by the machine is simply the set of strings that are accepted by its computations. The language of the machine in Fig. 6.2 is the set of all strings over $\{a, b\}$ that end in *a*. Two machines that accept the same language are said to be **equivalent**.

A DFA reads the input in a left-to-right manner; once an input symbol has been processed, it has no further effect on the computation. At any point during the computation, the result depends only on the current state and the unprocessed input. This combination is called an **instantaneous machine configuration** and is represented by the ordered pair $[q_i, w]$, where $w \in \Sigma^*$. The instruction cycle of a DFA transforms one machine configuration to another. The notation $[q_i, aw] \vdash_M [q_j, w]$ indicates that configuration $[q_j, w]$ is obtained from $[q_i, aw]$ by the execution of one instruction cycle of the machine M. The symbol $\vdash_M$, read "yields," defines a function from $Q \times \Sigma^+$ to $Q \times \Sigma^*$ that can be used to trace computations of the DFA. The M is omitted when there is no possible ambiguity.

Definition 6.2.3
The function $\vdash_M$ on $Q \times \Sigma^+$ is defined by

$$[q_i, aw] \vdash_M [\delta(q_i, a), w]$$

for $a \in \Sigma$ and $w \in \Sigma^*$, where δ is the transition function of the DFA M.

The notation $[q_i, u] \vdash^* [q_j, v]$ is used to indicate that configuration $[q_j, v]$ can be obtained from $[q_i, u]$ by zero or more transitions.

Example 6.2.1

The DFA M accepts the set of strings over $\{a, b\}$ that contain the substring bb. That is, $L(M) = (a \cup b)^* bb(a \cup b)^*$.

$$M: Q = \{q_0, q_1, q_2\}$$
$$\Sigma = \{a, b\}$$
$$F = \{q_2\}$$

The transition function δ is given in a tabular form called the transition table. The states are listed vertically and the alphabet horizontally. The action of the automaton in state q_i with input a can be determined by finding the intersection of the row corresponding to q_i and column corresponding to a.

δ	a	b
q_0	q_0	q_1
q_1	q_0	q_2
q_2	q_2	q_2

The computations of M for input strings *abba* and *abab* are traced using the function $\vdash$. The string *abba* is accepted since the computation halts in state q_2.

$[q_0, abba]$	$[q_0, abab]$
$\vdash [q_0, bba]$	$\vdash [q_0, bab]$
$\vdash [q_1, ba]$	$\vdash [q_1, ab]$
$\vdash [q_2, a]$	$\vdash [q_0, b]$
$\vdash [q_2, \lambda]$	$\vdash [q_1, \lambda]$
accepts	rejects

□

Example 6.2.2

The newspaper vending machine from the previous section can be represented by a DFA with the following states, alphabet, and transition function. The start state is the state 30.

$$Q = \{0, 5, 10, 15, 20, 25, 30\}$$
$$\Sigma = \{n, d, q\}$$
$$F = \{0\}$$

δ	n	d	q
0	0	0	0
5	0	0	0
10	5	0	0
15	10	5	0
20	15	10	0
25	20	15	0
30	25	20	5

The language of the vending machine consists of all strings that represent a sum of 30 cents or more. Construct a regular expression that defines the language of this machine. □

The transition function specifies the action of the machine for a given state and element from the alphabet. This function can be extended to a function $\hat{\delta}$ whose input consists of a state and a string over the alphabet. The function $\hat{\delta}$ is constructed by recursively extending the domain from elements of Σ to strings of arbitrary length.

Definition 6.2.4

The **extended transition function** $\hat{\delta}$ of a DFA with transition function δ is a function from $Q \times \Sigma^*$ to Q defined by recursion on the length of the input string.

i) Basis: $length(w) = 0$. Then $w = \lambda$ and $\hat{\delta}(q_i, \lambda) = q_i$.
  $length(w) = 1$. Then $w = a$, for some $a \in \Sigma$, and $\hat{\delta}(q_i, a) = \delta(q_i, a)$.

ii) Recursive step: Let w be a string of length $n > 1$. Then $w = ua$ and $\hat{\delta}(q_i, ua) = \delta(\hat{\delta}(q_i, u), a)$.

The computation of a machine in state q_i with string w halts in state $\hat{\delta}(q_i, w)$. The evaluation of the function $\hat{\delta}(q_0, w)$ simulates the repeated applications of the transition function required to process the string w. A string w is accepted if $\hat{\delta}(q_0, w) \in F$. Using this notation, the language of a DFA M is the set $L(M) = \{w \mid \hat{\delta}(q_0, w) \in F\}$.

6.3   State Diagrams and Examples

The state diagram of a DFA is a labeled directed graph in which the nodes represent the states of the machine and the arcs are obtained from the transition function.

Definition 6.3.1

The state diagram of a DFA $(Q, \Sigma, \delta, q_0, F)$ is a labeled directed graph G defined by the following conditions:

 i) The nodes of G are the elements of Q.

 ii) The labels on the arcs of G are elements of Σ.

 iii) q_0 is the initial node, depicted $\times\!\bigcirc$.

 iv) F is the set of accepting nodes; each accepting node is depicted $\bigcirc\!\!\!\bigcirc$.

 v) There is an arc from node q_i to q_j labeled a if $\delta(q_i, a) = q_j$.

 vi) For every node q_i and symbol a, there is exactly one arc labeled a leaving q_i.

The graph in Fig. 6.1 is the state diagram for the newspaper vending machine DFA. Because of the intuitive nature of the graphic representation, we will often present the state diagram rather than the sets and transition function that comprise the formal definition of a DFA.

A transition of a DFA is represented by an arc in the state diagram. Tracing the computation of a DFA in the corresponding state diagram constructs a path that begins at node q_0 and "spells" the input string. Let $\mathbf{p}_w$ be a path beginning at q_0 that spells w and let q_w be the terminal node of $\mathbf{p}_w$. Theorem 6.3.2 proves that there is only one such path for every string $w \in \Sigma^*$. Moreover, q_w is the state of the DFA upon completion of the processing of w.

Theorem 6.3.2

Let $M = (Q, \Sigma, \delta, q_0, F)$ be a DFA and let $w \in \Sigma^*$. Then w determines a unique path $\mathbf{p}_w$ in the state diagram of M and $\hat{\delta}(q_0, w) = q_w$.

Proof   The proof is by induction on the length of the string. If the length of w is zero, then $\hat{\delta}(q_0, \lambda) = q_0$. The corresponding path is the null path that begins and terminates with q_0.

Assume that the result holds for all strings of length n or less. Let $w = ua$ be a string of length $n + 1$. By the inductive hypothesis, there is a unique path $\mathbf{p}_u$ that spells u and $\hat{\delta}(q_0, u) = q_u$. The path $\mathbf{p}_w$ is constructed by following the arc labeled a from q_u. This is the only path from q_0 that spells w. If $\mathbf{p}_w$ were not unique, deleting the final arc of the distinct paths that spell w would produce distinct paths spelling u. But this contradicts the inductive hypothesis. The terminal state of the path $\mathbf{p}_w$ is given by the transition $\delta(q_u, a)$. From the definition of the extended transition function $\hat{\delta}(q_0, w) = \delta(\hat{\delta}(q_0, u), a)$. By the inductive hypothesis $\hat{\delta}(q_0, u) = q_u$ and $q_w = \delta(q_u, a)$ as desired.   ∎

Example 6.3.1

The state diagram of the DFA in Example 6.2.1 is

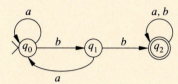

The states are used to record the number of consecutive b's processed. The state q_2 is entered when a substring bb is encountered. Once the machine enters q_2 the remainder of the input is processed, leaving the state unchanged. The computation of the DFA with input $ababb$ and the corresponding path in the state diagram are

Computation	Path
$[q_0, ababb]$	$q_0,$
$\vdash [q_0, babb]$	$q_0,$
$\vdash [q_1, abb]$	$q_1,$
$\vdash [q_0, bb]$	$q_0,$
$\vdash [q_1, b]$	$q_1,$
$\vdash [q_2, \lambda]$	q_2

The string $ababb$ is accepted since the halting state of the machine, which is also the terminal state of the path that spells $ababb$, is the accepting state q_2.   □

Example 6.3.2

The DFA

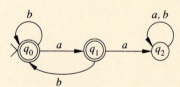

accepts $(b \cup ab)^*(a \cup \lambda)$, the set of strings over $\{a, b\}$ that do not contain the substring aa.   □

Example 6.3.3

Strings over $\{a, b\}$ that contain the substring bb or do not contain the substring aa are accepted by the DFA depicted below. This language is the union of the languages of the previous examples.

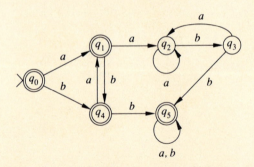

The state diagrams for machines that accept the strings with substring *bb* or without substring *aa* seem simple compared with the machine that accepts the union of those two sets. There does not appear to be an intuitive way to combine the state diagrams of the constituent machines to create the desired composite machine. The next two examples show that this is not the case for machines that accept complementary sets of strings. The state diagram for a DFA can easily be transformed into the state diagram for another machine that accepts all and only the strings rejected by the original DFA.

Example 6.3.4

The DFA M accepts the language consisting of all strings over $\{a, b\}$ that contain an even number of a's and an odd number of b's.

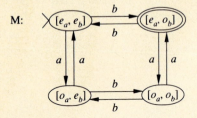

At any step of the computation, there are four possibilities for the parities of the input symbols processed: even number of a's and even number of b's, even number of a's and odd number of b's, odd number of a's and even number of b's, odd number of a's and odd number of b's. These four states are represented by ordered pairs. Processing a symbol changes one of the parities, designating the appropriate transition.   □

Example 6.3.5

Let M be the DFA constructed in Example 6.3.4. A DFA M′ is constructed that accepts all strings over $\{a, b\}$ that do not contain an even number of a's and an odd number of b's. In other words, $L(M') = \{a, b\}^* - L(M)$. Any string rejected by M is accepted by

M' and vice versa. A state diagram for the machine M' can be obtained from that of M by interchanging the accepting and nonaccepting states.

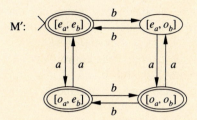

The preceding example shows the relationship between machines that accept complementary sets of strings. This relationship is formalized by the following result.

Theorem 6.3.3

Let M = (Q, Σ, δ, q_0, F) be a DFA. Then M' = (Q, Σ, δ, q_0, Q − F) is a DFA with L(M') = $\Sigma^* $ − L(M).

Proof   Let $w \in \Sigma^*$ and $\hat{\delta}$ be the extended transition function constructed from δ. For each $w \in$ L(M), $\hat{\delta}(q_0, w) \in$ F. Hence, $w \notin$ L(M'). Conversely, if $w \notin$ L(M), then $\hat{\delta}(q_0, w) \in$ Q − F and $w \in$ L(M'). ∎

Example 6.3.6

Let Σ = {0, 1, 2, 3}. A string in Σ^* is a sequence of integers from Σ. The DFA M determines whether the sum of elements of a string is divisible by 4. The strings *1 2 3 0 2* and *0 1 3 0* should be accepted and *0 1 1 1* rejected. The states represent the value of the sum of the processed input modulo 4.

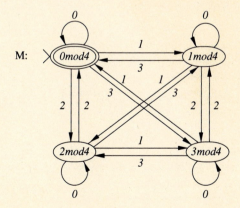

Our definition of DFA allowed only two possible outputs, accept or reject. The definition of output can be extended to have a value associated with each state. The result of a computation is the value associated with the state in which the computation terminates. A machine of this type is called a Moore machine after E. F. Moore, who introduced this type of finite-state computation. Associating the value i with the state $i \bmod 4$, the machine in Example 6.3.6 acts as a modulo 4 adder.

By definition, a DFA must process the entire input even if the result has already been established. Example 6.3.7 exhibits a type of determinism, sometimes referred to as incomplete determinism; each configuration has at most one action specified. The transitions of such a machine are defined by a partial function from $Q \times \Sigma$ to Q. As soon as it is possible to determine that a string is not acceptable, the computation halts. A computation that halts before processing the entire input string rejects the input.

Example 6.3.7

The state diagram below defines an incompletely specified DFA that accepts $(ab)^*c$. A computation terminates unsuccessfully as soon as the input varies from the desired pattern.

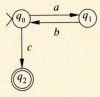

An incompletely specified DFA can easily be transformed into an equivalent DFA. The transformation requires the addition of a nonaccepting "error" state. This state is entered whenever the incompletely specified machine enters a configuration for which no action is indicated. Upon entering the error state, the computation of the DFA reads the remainder of the string and halts.

Example 6.3.8

The DFA

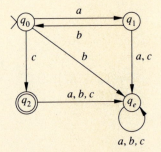

accepts the same language as the incompletely specified DFA in Example 6.3.7. The state q_e is the error state that ensures the processing of the entire string.   □

6.4   **Nondeterministic Finite Automata**

We now alter our definition of machine to allow nondeterministic computation. In a nondeterministic automaton there may be several instructions that can be executed from a given machine configuration. Although this property may seem unnatural for computing machines, the flexibility of nondeterminism often facilitates the design of language acceptors.

A transition in a nondeterministic finite automaton (NFA) has the same effect as one in a DFA, to change the state of the machine based on the current state and symbol. The transition function must specify all possible states that the machine may enter from a given machine configuration. This is accomplished by having the value of the transition function be a set of states. The graphic representation of state diagrams is used to illustrate the alternatives that can occur in nondeterministic computation. Any finite number of transitions may be specified for a given state q_n and symbol a. The value of the nondeterministic transition function is given below the corresponding diagram.

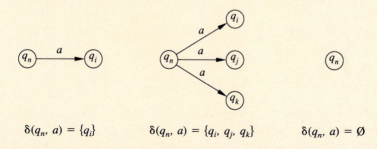

$$\delta(q_n, a) = \{q_i\} \qquad \delta(q_n, a) = \{q_i, q_j, q_k\} \qquad \delta(q_n, a) = \varnothing$$

With the exception of the transition function, the components of an NFA are identical to those of a DFA.

Definition 6.4.1

A **nondeterministic finite automaton** is a quintuple $M = (Q, \Sigma, \delta, q_0, F)$ where Q is a finite set of states, Σ a finite set called the alphabet, $q_0 \in Q$ a distinguished state known as the start state, F a subset of Q called the final or accepting states, and δ a total function from $Q \times \Sigma$ to $\mathscr{P}(Q)$ known as the transition function.

The relationship between DFAs and NFAs can be summarized by the seemingly paradoxical phrase "every deterministic finite automaton is nondeterministic." The transition function of a DFA specifies exactly one state that may be entered from a given state and input symbol while an NFA allows zero, one, or more states.

A string input to an NFA may generate several distinct computations. The notion of halting and string acceptance must be revised to conform to the flexibility of nondeterministic computation. Computations in an NFA are traced using the $\vdash$ notation introduced in the previous section.

Example 6.4.1

An NFA M is given along with three distinct computations for the string *ababb*.

$$M: Q = \{q_0, q_1, q_2\}$$
$$\Sigma = \{a, b\}$$
$$F = \{q_2\}$$

δ	a	b
q_0	$\{q_0\}$	$\{q_0, q_1\}$
q_1	$\emptyset$	$\{q_2\}$
q_2	$\emptyset$	$\emptyset$

$[q_0, ababb]$	$[q_0, ababb]$	$[q_0, ababb]$
$\vdash [q_0, babb]$	$\vdash [q_0, babb]$	$\vdash [q_0, babb]$
$\vdash [q_0, abb]$	$\vdash [q_1, abb]$	$\vdash [q_0, abb]$
$\vdash [q_0, bb]$		$\vdash [q_0, bb]$
$\vdash [q_0, b]$		$\vdash [q_1, b]$
$\vdash [q_0, \lambda]$		$\vdash [q_2, \lambda]$

The second computation of the machine M halts after the execution of three instructions since no action is specified when the machine is in state q_1 scanning an a. The first computation processes the entire input and halts in a rejecting state while the final computation halts in an accepting state.   □

An input string is accepted if there is a computation that processes the entire string and halts in an accepting state. A string is in the language of a nondeterministic machine if there is one computation that accepts it; the existence of other computations that do not accept the string is irrelevant. The third computation given in Example 6.4.1 demonstrates that *ababb* is in the language of machine M.

Definition 6.4.2

The **language** of an NFA M, denoted L(M), is the set of strings accepted by the M. That is, $L(M) = \{w \mid \text{there is a computation } [q_0, w] \overset{*}{\vdash} [q_i, \lambda] \text{ with } q_i \in F\}$.

Definition 6.4.3

The state diagram of an NFA $M = (Q, \Sigma, \delta, q_0, F)$ is a labeled directed graph G defined by the following conditions:

i) The nodes of G are the elements of Q.

ii) The labels of the arcs of G are elements of Σ.

iii) q_0 is the initial node.

iv) F is the set of accepting nodes.

v) There is an arc from node q_i to q_j labeled a if $q_j \in \delta(q_i, a)$.

The relationship between DFAs and NFAs is clearly exhibited by comparing the properties of the corresponding state diagrams. Definition 6.4.3 is obtained from Definition 6.3.1 by omitting condition vi), which translates the deterministic property of the DFA transition function into its graphic representation.

Example 6.4.2

The state diagram for the NFA M from Example 6.4.1 is

Pictorially, it is clear that the language accepted by M is $(a \cup b)^*bb$. ☐

Example 6.4.3

The state diagrams M_1 and M_2 define finite automata that accept $(a \cup b)^*bb(a \cup b)^*$.

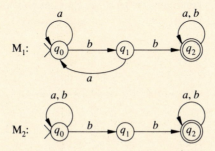

M_1 is the DFA from Example 6.3.1. The path exhibiting the acceptance of strings by M_1 enters q_2 when the first substring bb is encountered. M_2 can enter the accepting state upon processing any occurrence of bb. ☐

Example 6.4.4

An NFA that accepts strings over $\{a, b\}$ with the substring aa or bb can be constructed by combining a machine that accepts strings with bb (Example 6.4.3) with a similar machine that accepts strings with aa.

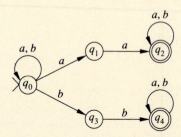

A path exhibiting the acceptance of a string reads the input in state q_0 until an occurrence of the substring aa or bb is encountered. At this point, the path branches to either q_1 or q_3, depending upon the substring. There are three distinct paths that exhibit the acceptance of the string $abaaabb$.   □

The flexibility permitted by the use of nondeterminism does not always simplify the problem of constructing a machine that accepts $L(M_1) \cup L(M_2)$ from the machines M_1 and M_2. This can be seen by attempting to construct an NFA that accepts the language of the DFA in Example 6.3.3.

Example 6.4.5

The strings over $\{a, b\}$ containing the substring $abba$ are accepted by the machines M_1 and M_2. The states record the progress made in obtaining the desired substring. The DFA M_1 must back up when the current substring is discovered not to have the desired form. If a b is scanned when the machine is in state q_3, q_0 is entered since the last four symbols processed, $abbb$, indicate no progress has been made toward recognizing $abba$.

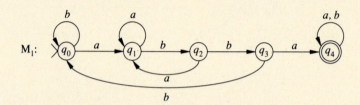

The halting conditions of an NFA can be used to avoid the necessity of backing up when the current substring is discovered not to have the desired form. M_2 uses these techniques to accept the same language as M_1.

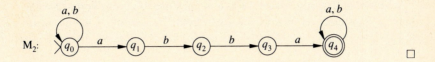

Example 6.4.6

The NFA defined by the state diagram given below accepts the set $\{a^i b^i \mid i \le n\}$, for an arbitrary but fixed integer n. The states a_k count the number of a's, and then the b_k's ensure an equal number of b's.

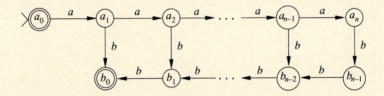

This technique cannot be extended to accept $\{a^i b^i \mid i \ge 0\}$ since an infinite number of states would be needed. In the next chapter we will show that this language is not accepted by any finite automaton.   □

6.5   Lambda Transitions

The transitions from state to state, in both deterministic and nondeterministic automata, were initiated by the processing of an input symbol. The definition of NFA is relaxed to allow state transitions without requiring input to be processed. A transition of this form is called a **lambda transition**. The class of nondeterministic machines that utilize lambda transitions is denoted NFA-λ.

Definition 6.5.1

A nondeterministic finite automaton with lambda transitions is a quintuple M = (Q, Σ, δ, q_0, F) where Q, δ, q_0, and F are the same as in an NFA. The transition function is a function from Q × (Σ ∪ {λ}) to $\mathcal{P}$(Q).

The definition of halting must be extended to include the possibility of the computation continuing with lambda transitions after the input string has been completely processed. Following the definition of acceptance in an NFA, the input is accepted if there is a computation that processes the entire string and halts in an accepting state. As before, the language of an NFA-λ is denoted L(M).

The state diagram for an NFA-λ is constructed according to Definition 6.4.3 with lambda transitions represented by arcs labeled by lambda. Lambda moves can be used to construct complex machines from simpler machines. Let M_1 and M_2 be the machines

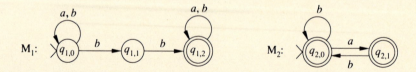

that accept $(a \cup b)^* bb(a \cup b)^*$ and $(b \cup ab)^*(a \cup \lambda)$, respectively. Composite machines are built by appropriately combining the state diagrams of M_1 and M_2.

Example 6.5.1

The language of the NFA-λ M is $L(M_1) \cup L(M_2)$.

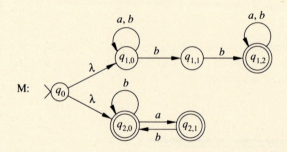

A computation in the composite machine M begins by following a lambda arc to the start state of either M_1 or M_2. If the path **p** exhibits the acceptance of a string by machine M_i, then that string is accepted by the path in M consisting of the lambda arc from q_0 to $q_{i,0}$ followed by **p** in the copy of the machine M_i. Since the initial move in each computation does not process an input symbol, the language of M is $L(M_1) \cup L(M_2)$. Compare the simplicity of the machine obtained by this construction to that of the deterministic state diagram in Example 6.3.3.   □

Example 6.5.2

An NFA-λ that accepts $L(M_1)L(M_2)$, the concatenation of the languages of M_1 and M_2, is constructed by joining the two machines with a lambda arc.

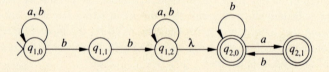

An input string is accepted only if it consists of a string from $L(M_1)$ concatenated with one from $L(M_2)$. The lambda transition allows the computation to enter M_2 whenever a prefix of the input string is accepted by M_1.   □

Example 6.5.3

Lambda transitions are used to construct an NFA-λ that accepts all strings of even length over $\{a, b\}$. First we build the state diagram for a machine that accepts strings of length two.

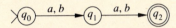

To accept the null string, a lambda arc is added from q_0 to q_2. Strings of any positive, even length are accepted by following the lambda arc from q_2 to q_0 to repeat the sequence q_0, q_1, q_2.

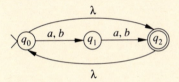

                                                                                           □

The constructions presented in Examples 6.5.1 and 6.5.2 can be generalized to constructing machines that accept the union, concatenation, and Kleene star of languages accepted by existing machines. We begin by transforming an NFA-λ into a form amenable to these constructions.

Lemma 6.5.2

Let $M = (Q, \Sigma, \delta, q_0, F)$ be an NFA-λ. There is an equivalent NFA-λ $M' = (Q \cup \{q_0', q_f\},$ $\Sigma, \delta', q_0', \{q_f\})$ that satisfies the following conditions:

i) The in-degree of q_0' is zero.

ii) The only accepting state of M' is q_f.

iii) The out-degree of the q_f is zero.

Proof   The transition function of M' is constructed from that of M by adding the lambda transitions

$$\delta(q_0', \lambda) = \{q_0\}$$
$$\delta(q_i, \lambda) = \{q_f\} \text{ for every } q_i \in F$$

for the new states q_0' and q_f. The lambda transition from q_0' to q_0 permits the computation to proceed to the original machine M without affecting the input. A computation of M'

that accepts an input string is identical to that of M followed by a lambda transition from the accepting state of M to the accepting state q_f of M'. ∎

Theorem 6.5.3

Let M_1 and M_2 be two NFA-λ's. There are NFA-λ's that accept $L(M_1) \cup L(M_2)$, $L(M_1)L(M_2)$, and $L(M_1)^*$.

Proof   We assume, without loss of generality, that M_1 and M_2 satisfy the conditions of Lemma 6.5.2. Because of the restrictions on the start and final states, the machines M and M_2 are depicted

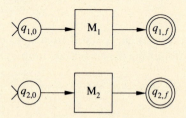

The languages $L(M_1) \cup L(M_2)$, $L(M_1)L(M_2)$, and $L(M_1)^*$ are accepted by the composite machines

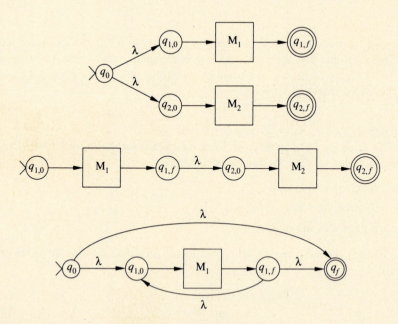

respectively. ∎

6.6   Removing Nondeterminism

Three classes of finite automata have been introduced in the previous sections, each class being a generalization of its predecessor. By relaxing the deterministic restriction, have we created a more powerful class of machines? More precisely, is there a language accepted by an NFA that is not accepted by any DFA? We will show that this is not the case. Moreover, an algorithm is presented that converts an NFA-λ to an equivalent DFA.

The state transitions in DFAs and NFAs accompanied the processing of an input symbol. To relate the transitions in an NFA-λ to the processing of input, we build a modified transition function t, called the input transition function, whose value is the set of states that can be entered by processing a single input symbol from a given state. The value of $t(q_1, a)$ for the diagram in Fig. 6.3 is the set $\{q_2, q_3, q_5, q_6\}$. State q_4 is omitted since the transition from state q_1 does not process an input symbol.

The function t is defined in terms of the transition function δ and the paths in the state diagram that spell the null string. The node q_j is said to be in the lambda closure of q_i if there is a path from q_i to q_j that spells the null string.

Definition 6.6.1

The **lambda closure** of a state q_i, denoted λ-*closure*(q_i), is defined recursively by

  i) Basis: $q_i \in$ λ-*closure*(q_i).

  ii) Recursive step: Let q_j be an element of λ-*closure*(q_i). If $q_k \in$ δ$(q_j, λ)$, then $q_k \in$ λ-*closure*(q_i).

  iii) Closure: q_j is in λ-*closure*(q_i) only if it can be obtained from q_i by a finite number of applications of operations in ii).

The set λ-*closure*(q_i) can be constructed following the techniques presented in Algorithm 4.2.1, which determines the chains in a context-free grammar. The input transition function is defined using the lambda closure.

Path	String Processed
q_1, q_2	a
q_1, q_2, q_3	a
q_1, q_4	λ
q_1, q_4, q_5	a
q_1, q_4, q_5, q_6	a

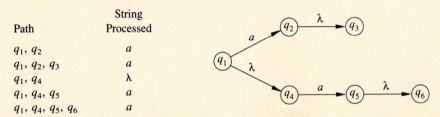

FIGURE 6.3   Paths with lambda transitions.

Definition 6.6.2

The **input transition function** t of an NFA-λ M is a function from $Q \times \Sigma$ to $\mathscr{P}(Q)$ defined by

$$t(q_i, a) = \bigcup_{q_j \in \lambda\text{-}closure(q_i)} \lambda\text{-}closure(\delta(q_j, a))$$

where δ is the transition function of M.

For an NFA without lambda transitions, the input transition function t is identical to the transition function δ of the automaton.

Example 6.6.1

Transition tables are given for the transition function δ and the input transition function t of the NFA-λ with state diagram M. The language of M is $a^+c^*b^*$.

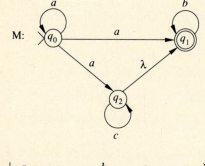

δ	a	b	c	λ
q_0	$\{q_0, q_1, q_2\}$	$\emptyset$	$\emptyset$	$\emptyset$
q_1	$\emptyset$	$\{q_1\}$	$\emptyset$	$\emptyset$
q_2	$\emptyset$	$\emptyset$	$\{q_2\}$	$\{q_1\}$

t	a	b	c
q_0	$\{q_0, q_1, q_2\}$	$\emptyset$	$\emptyset$
q_1	$\emptyset$	$\{q_1\}$	$\emptyset$
q_2	$\emptyset$	$\{q_1\}$	$\{q_1, q_2\}$

$\square$

The input transition function of a nondeterministic automaton is used to construct an equivalent deterministic automaton. The procedure uses the state diagram of the NFA-λ to construct the state diagram of the equivalent DFA. Acceptance in a nondeterministic machine is determined by the existence of a computation that processes the entire string and halts in a terminal state. There may be several paths in the state diagram of an NFA-λ that represent the processing of an input string while the state diagram of a DFA contains exactly one such path. To remove the nondeterminism, the DFA simulates the simultaneous exploration of all possible computations in the NFA-λ.

The nodes of the DFA are sets of nodes from the NFA-λ. The key to the algorithm is step 2.1.1, which generates the nodes of the equivalent DFA. The set Y consists of all the states that can be entered by processing the symbol a from any state in the set X. This relationship is represented in the state diagram of the deterministic equivalent by an arc from X to Y labeled a. The paths in the state diagram of an NFA-λ M are used to construct the state diagram of an equivalent DFA DM (deterministic equivalent of M).

The nodes of DM are generated in the set Q'. The start node is lambda closure of the start node of the original NFA-λ.

Algorithm 6.6.3
Construction of DM, a DFA Equivalent to NFA-λ M

input: an NFA-λ $M = (Q, \Sigma, \delta, q_0, F)$
     input transition function t of M

1. initialize Q' to λ-*closure*(q_0)

2. **repeat**
    2.1. **if** there is a node $X \in Q'$ and a symbol a with no arc leaving X labeled a **then**
        2.1.1. let $Y = \bigcup_{q_i \in X} t(q_i, a)$
        2.1.2. **if** $Y \notin Q'$ **then** set $Q' := Q' \cup \{Y\}$
        2.1.3. add an arc from X to Y labeled a
      else done := *true*
    until done

3. the set of accepting states of DM is $F' = \{X \in Q' \mid X \text{ contains an element } q_i \in F\}$

The NFA-λ from Example 6.6.1 is used to illustrate the construction of nodes for the equivalent DFA. The start node of DM is the singleton set containing the start node of M. A transition from q_0 processing an a can terminate in q_0, q_1, or q_2. We construct a node $\{q_0, q_1, q_2\}$ for the DFA and connect it to $\{q_0\}$ by an arc labeled a. The path from $\{q_0\}$ to $\{q_0, q_1, q_2\}$ in DM represents the three possible ways of processing the symbol a from state q_0 in M.

Since DM is to be deterministic, the node $\{q_0\}$ must have arcs labeled b and c leaving it. Arcs from q_0 to Ø labeled b and c are added to indicate that there is no action specified by the NFA-λ when the machine is in state q_0 scanning these symbols.

The node $\{q_0\}$ has the deterministic form; there is exactly one arc leaving it for every member of the alphabet. Figure 6.4(a) shows DM at this stage of its construction. Two additional nodes, $\{q_0, q_1, q_2\}$ and Ø, have been created. Both of these must be made deterministic.

An arc leaving node $\{q_0, q_1, q_2\}$ terminates in a node consisting of all the states that can be reached by processing the input symbol from the states q_0, q_1, or q_2 in M. The input transition function $t(q_i, a)$ specifies the states reachable by processing an a from q_i. The arc from $\{q_0, q_1, q_2\}$ labeled a terminates in the set consisting of the union of the $t(q_0, a)$, $t(q_1, a)$, and $t(q_2, a)$. The set obtained from this union is again $\{q_0, q_1, q_2\}$. An arc from $\{q_0, q_1, q_2\}$ to itself is added to the diagram designating this transition.

Figure 6.4(b) gives the completed deterministic equivalent of the M. Computations of the nondeterministic machine with input aaa can terminate in state q_0, q_1, or q_2. The acceptance of the string is exhibited by the path that terminates in q_1. Processing aaa in DM terminates in state $\{q_0, q_1, q_2\}$. This state is accepting in DM since it contains the accepting state q_1 of M.

The algorithm for constructing the deterministic state diagram consists of repeatedly adding arcs to make the nodes in the diagram deterministic. While constructing arcs, new nodes may be created and added to the diagram. The procedure terminates when all the nodes are deterministic. Since each node is a subset of Q, at most $card(\mathcal{P}(Q))$ nodes can be constructed. Algorithm 6.6.3 always terminates since $card(\mathcal{P}(Q))card(\Sigma)$ is an upper bound on the number of iterations of the repeat-until loop. Theorem 6.6.4 establishes the equivalence of M and DM.

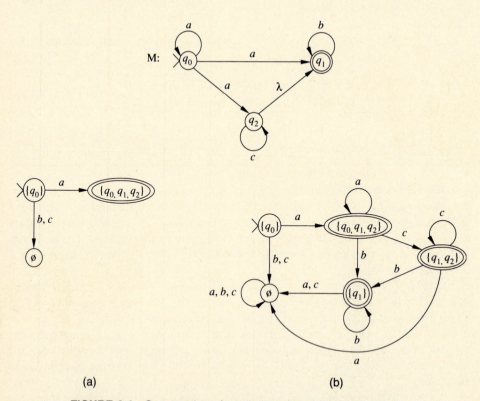

(a)   (b)

FIGURE 6.4   Construction of equivalent deterministic automaton.

Theorem 6.6.4

Let $w \in \Sigma^*$ and $Q_w = \{q_{w_1}, q_{w_2}, \ldots, q_{w_j}\}$ be the set of states entered upon the completion of the processing of the string w in M. Processing w in DM terminates in state Q_w.

Proof   The proof is by induction on the length of the string w. A computation of M that processes the empty string terminates at a node in λ-*closure*(q_0). This set is the start state of DM.

Assume the property holds for all strings of length n and let $w = ua$ be a string of length $n + 1$. Let $Q_u = \{q_{u_1}, q_{u_2}, \ldots, q_{u_k}\}$ be the terminal states reached by processing the entire string u in M. By the inductive hypothesis, processing u in DM terminates in Q_u. Computations processing ua in M terminate in states that can be reached by processing an a from a state in Q_u. This set, Q_w, can be defined using the input transition function.

$$Q_w = \bigcup_{i=1}^{k} t(q_{u_i}, a)$$

This completes the proof since Q_w is the state entered by processing a from state Q_u of DM.   ∎

The acceptance of a string in a nondeterministic automaton depends upon the existence of one computation that processes the string and terminates in an accepting state. The node Q_w contains the terminal states of all the paths generated by computations in M that process w. If w is accepted by M, then Q_w contains an accepting state of M. The presence of an accepting node makes Q_w an accepting state of DM and, by the previous theorem, w is accepted by DM.

Conversely, let w be a string accepted by DM. Then Q_w contains an accepting state of M. The construction of Q_w guarantees the existence of a computation in M that processes w and terminates in that accepting state. These observations provide the justification for Corollary 6.6.5.

Corollary 6.6.5

The finite automata M and DM are equivalent.

Example 6.6.2

The NFA M accepts the language a^+b^+. Algorithm 6.6.3 is used to construct an equivalent DFA.

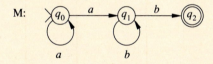

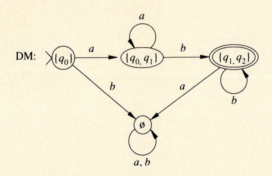

DM:

Algorithm 6.6.3 completes the following cycle describing the relationships between the classes of finite automata.

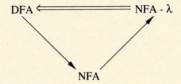

The arrows represent inclusion; every DFA can be reformulated as an NFA which is, in turn, an NFA-λ. The double arrow from NFA-λ to DFA indicates the existence of an equivalent deterministic machine.

6.7   Finite Automata and Regular Sets

Every finite automaton with alphabet Σ accepts a language over Σ. We will show that the set of languages accepted by automata consists of precisely the regular sets over Σ.

First we show that every regular set is accepted by some NFA-λ. The proof follows the recursive definition of the regular sets (Definition 2.3.1). The regular sets are built from the basis elements $\varnothing$, λ, and singleton sets containing elements from the alphabet. State diagrams for machines that accept these sets are

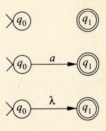

The regular sets are constructed from the basis elements using union, concatenation, and the Kleene star operation. Note that each of these machines satisfies the restrictions described in Lemma 6.5.2. That is, the machines contain a single accepting state. Moreover, there are no arcs entering the start state or leaving the accepting state.

Lambda transitions can be used to combine existing machines to construct more complex composite machines. Let M_1 and M_2 be two finite automata whose start and final states satisfy the prescribed criteria. Composite machines that accept $L(M_1) \cup L(M_2)$, $L(M_1)L(M_2)$, and $L(M_1)^*$ are constructed from M_1 and M_2. The techniques used are similar to those presented in Theorem 6.5.3. Like the machines that accept the basis elements, the composite machines will also have a start state with in-degree zero and a single accepting state with out-degree zero. Using repeated applications of these constructions, an automaton can be constructed to accept any regular set. Let S_{M_1}, F_{M_1} and S_{M_2}, F_{M_2} be the start and accepting states of M_1 and M_2, respectively. The start state and final state of the composite machine are denoted S and F.

The language $L(M_1) \cup L(M_2)$ is accepted by the machine

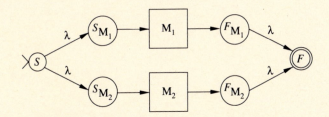

A string is processed by following a lambda arc to M_1 or M_2. If the string is accepted by either of these machines, the lambda arc can be traversed to reach the accepting state of the composite machine. This construction may be thought of as building a machine that runs M_1 and M_2 in parallel. The input is accepted if either of the machines successfully terminates.

Concatenation can be obtained by operating the component machines sequentially. The start state of the composite machine is S_{M_1} and the accepting state is F_{M_2}. The machines are joined by adding a lambda arc from the final state of M_1 to the start state of M_2. When a prefix of the input string is accepted by M_1, the lambda arc transfers the processing to M_2. If the remainder of the string is accepted by M_2, the processing terminates in F_{M_2}, the accepting state of the composite machine.

A machine that accepts $L(M_1)^*$ must be able to cycle through M_1 any number of times. The lambda arc from F_{M_1} to S_{M_1} permits the necessary cycling. Another lambda arc is added from S to F to accept the null string.

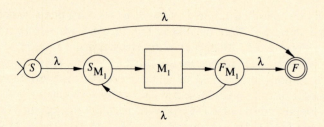

Example 6.7.1

The techniques presented above are used to construct an NFA-λ that accepts $(a \cup b)^*ba$. The machine is built following the recursive definition of the regular expression. The language accepted by each intermediate machine is indicated by the expression above the state diagram.

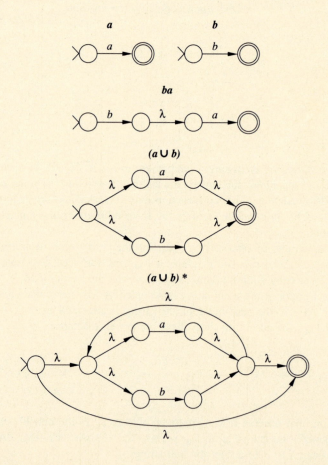

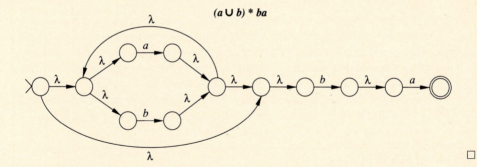

$(a \cup b) * ba$

6.8 Expression Graphs

The constructions in the previous section demonstrate that every regular set is recognized by a finite automaton. We will now show that every language accepted by an automaton is regular. To accomplish this, we extend the notion of a state diagram.

Definition 6.8.1

An **expression graph** is a labeled directed graph in which the arcs are labeled by regular expressions. An expression graph, like a state diagram, contains a distinguished start node and a set of accepting nodes.

The state diagram of an automaton with alphabet Σ can be considered an expression graph. The labels consist of lambda and expressions corresponding to the elements of Σ. Arcs in an expression graph can also be labeled by $\emptyset$. Paths in expression graphs generate regular expressions. The language of an expression graph is the union of the sets represented by the accepted regular expressions. The graphs

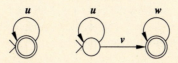

accept the regular expressions u^* and u^*vw^*.

Because of the simplicity of the graphs, the expressions accepted by the previous examples are obvious. A procedure is developed to reduce an arbitrary expression graph to one of two simple forms. This reduction is accomplished by repeatedly removing nodes from the graph in a manner that produces the expression accepted by the graph.

The state diagram of a finite automaton may have any number of accepting states. Each of these states exhibits the acceptance of a set of strings, the strings whose processing successfully terminates in the state. The language of the machine is the union of these sets. To determine the language of an automaton, the previous observation allows us to consider the accepting states separately. The algorithm to construct a regular expression from a state diagram does exactly this; it builds an expression for the set of strings accepted by each individual accepting state.

The nodes of the NFA-λ in Algorithm 6.8.2 are assumed to be numbered. The label of an arc from node i to node j is denoted $w_{i,j}$. If there is no arc from node i to j, $w_{i,j} = \emptyset$.

Algorithm 6.8.2
Construction of Regular Expression from a Finite Automaton

input: state diagram G of a finite automaton
       the nodes of G are numbered 1, 2, . . . , n

1. Make m copies of G, each of which has one accepting state. Call these graphs $G_1, G_2, \ldots, G_m$. Each accepting node of G is the accepting node of G_t, for some $t = 1, 2, \ldots, m$

2. **for** each G_t **do**
    2.1. **repeat**
          2.1.1. choose a node i in G_t that is neither the start nor the accepting node of G_t
          2.1.2. delete the node i from G_t according to the following procedure:
                for every j, k not equal to i (this includes $j = k$) **do**
                  i) **if** $w_{j,i} \neq \emptyset$, $w_{i,k} \neq \emptyset$, and $w_{i,i} = \emptyset$ **then** add an arc from node j to node k labeled $w_{j,i}w_{i,k}$
                  ii) **if** $w_{j,i} \neq \emptyset$, $w_{i,k} \neq \emptyset$, and $w_{i,i} \neq \emptyset$ **then** add an arc from node j to node k labeled $w_{j,i}(w_{i,i})^* w_{i,k}$
                  iii) **if** nodes j and k have arcs labeled $w_1, w_2, \ldots, w_s$ connecting them **then** replace them by a single arc labeled $w_1 \cup w_2 \cup \cdots \cup w_s$
                  iv) remove the node i and all arcs incident to it in G_t
        until the only nodes in G_t are the start node and the single accepting node
    2.2. determine the expression accepted by G_t
    end for

3. The regular expression accepted by G is obtained by joining the expressions for each G_t with $\cup$.

The deletion of node i is accomplished by finding all paths j, i, k of length two that have i as the intermediate node. An arc from j to k is added bypassing the node i. If there is no arc from i to itself, the new arc is labeled by the concatenation of the expressions on each of the component arcs. If $w_{i,i} \neq \emptyset$, then the arc $w_{i,i}$ can be traversed any number of times before following the arc from i to k. The label for the new arc is $w_{j,i}(w_{i,i})^* w_{i,k}$. These graph transformations are illustrated below.

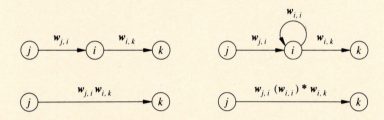

Step 2.2 in the algorithm may appear to be begging the question; the objective of the entire algorithm is to determine the expression accepted by G_t's. After the node-deletion process is completed, the regular expression can easily be obtained from the resulting graph. The reduced graph has at most two nodes, the start node and an accepting node. If these are the same node, the reduced graph has the form

accepting w^*. A graph with distinct start and accepting nodes reduces to

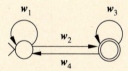

and accepts the expression $w_1^* w_2(w_3 \cup w_4(w_1)^* w_2)^*$. This expression may be simplified if any of the arcs in the graph are labeled $\emptyset$.

Example 6.8.1

The reduction technique of Algorithm 6.8.2 is used to generate a regular expression for the language of the NFA with state diagram G.

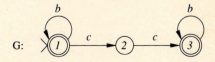

Two expression graphs, each with a single accepting node, are constructed from G.

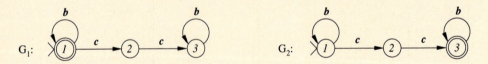

Reducing G_1 consists of deleting nodes 2 and 3.

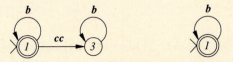

The expression accepted by G_1 is b^*. The removal of node 2 produces the reduction of G_2, yielding b^*ccb^*.

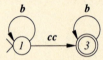

The expression accepted by G, built from the expressions accepted by G_1 and G_2, is $b^* \cup b^*ccb^*$.   □

The results of the previous two sections yield a characterization of the regular sets originally established by Kleene. The technique presented in Section 6.7 can be used to build an NFA-λ to accept any regular set. Conversely, Algorithm 6.8.2 constructs a regular expression for the language accepted by a finite automaton. Using the equivalence of deterministic and nondeterministic machines, Kleene's theorem can be expressed in terms of languages accepted by deterministic finite automata.

Theorem 6.8.3 (Kleene)

A language L is accepted by a DFA with alphabet Σ if, and only if, L is a regular set over Σ.

6.9   Effective Computation

A computation or procedure is called **discrete** if it consists of a sequence of indivisible actions. The fundamental properties of discrete computation will be discussed using the computations of a DFA and the generation of strings in a context-free grammar as examples. The transitions of a computation in a DFA comprise a sequence of discrete actions. The application of a rule is the indivisible action in the generation of a string. A derivation consists of a sequence of rule applications that transforms the start symbol of the grammar into a terminal string.

The process of walking down a flight of stairs and rolling a ball down a hill illustrates the difference between discrete and nondiscrete processes. Descending the stairs consists of a discrete sequence of actions, taking each step in order. A ball rolling down a hill is a continuous process. The descent cannot be naturally decomposed into a sequence of indivisible actions. Machines that record or compute with continuous data are called analog devices.

A computation is deterministic if there is precisely one action specified for every possible set of circumstances. The functionality of the transitions in a DFA assures deterministic computation. A desirable effect of determinism is that repetition of a computation will always produce the same outcome.

The generation of derivations in a context-free grammar is a nondeterministic process. If A is the leftmost variable in a string, any A rule can be applied. When the order of the application of the rules is specified, as with the backtracking parsing algorithms, the procedure is deterministic. Algorithm 4.4.1 requires that the rules be applied in a sequence determined by their numerical ordering. A deterministic computation need not terminate, as exhibited by Example 4.4.2.

The term **effective procedure** is used to describe processes we intuitively understand as computable. An effective procedure consists of a finite set of instructions defining the operation of the procedure. The execution of an instruction is mechanical; it requires no cleverness or ingenuity on the part of the machine or person doing the computation. The operation of an effective procedure consists of sequentially executing a finite number of instructions and terminating. These properties can be summarized as follows: An effective procedure is a deterministic discrete process that halts for all possible input values. Computation in a DFA is clearly effective.

The preceding discussion of effectiveness is not a definition, just a compilation of properties attributed to algorithmic computation. Computability will be defined precisely in terms of the computations of another class of finite-state machines, the Turing machines. A mathematical characterization of functions that can be effectively computed is given in Chapter 13.

A **decision procedure** is an effective procedure that determines whether the input satisfies a desired property. More succinctly, a decision procedure is a discrete, deterministic process that halts with output yes or no for every possible input. A question for which there is no decision procedure is called **undecidable.** To show that a property is undecidable, it is necessary to establish that no effective procedure can precisely identify the elements that satisfy the property. The existence of undecidable problems will be established in Chapter 11.

Exercises

1. Let M be the deterministic finite automaton

$$Q = \{q_0, q_1, q_2\}$$
$$\Sigma = \{a, b\}$$
$$F = \{q_2\}$$

δ	a	b
q_0	q_0	q_1
q_1	q_2	q_1
q_2	q_2	q_0

a) Give the state diagram of M.

b) Trace the computations of M that process the strings
   i) *abaa*.   ii) *bbbabb*.
   iii) *bababa*.   iv) *bbbaa*.

c) Which of the strings from b) are accepted by M?

d) Give a regular expression for L(M).

2. Let M be the DFA whose state diagram is given below.

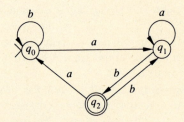

a) Construct the transition table of M.

b) Which of the strings *baba, baab, abab, abaaab* are accepted by M?

c) Give a regular expression for L(M).

3–10 (**4, 9**). Build the state diagram of a deterministic finite automaton that accepts the strings described in Exercises 2.6, 2.9, 2.11–2.13, 2.19, 2.24, and 2.25.

11. Give the state diagram of a DFA that accepts the following languages:

a) $(ab)^* ba$ b) $(ab)^* (ba)^*$ c) $aa(a \cup b)^+ bb$

d) $((aa)^+ bb)^*$ e) $(ab^* a)^*$

12. Let M be the nondeterministic finite automaton whose state diagram is given below.

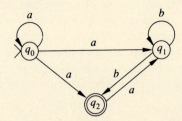

a) Construct the transition table of M.

b) Trace all computations of the string *aaabb* in M.

c) Is *aaabb* in L(M)?

d) Give a regular expression for L(M).

13. Construct the state diagram of an NFA that accepts the following languages:

   a) $(ab)^* \cup a^*$ b) $(abc)^* a^*$

   c) $(ba \cup bb)^* \cup (ab \cup aa)^*$ d) $(ab^+ a)^+$

For Exercises 14–20 give the state diagram of an NFA that accepts the given language.

14. The set of strings over $\{1, 2, 3\}$ the sum of whose elements is divisible by six.

15. The set of strings over $\{a, b, c\}$ in which the number of a's plus the number of b's plus twice the number of c's is divisible by six.

16. The set of strings over $\{a, b\}$ in which every substring of length four has at least one b.

17. The set of strings over $\{a, b, c\}$ in which every substring of length four has exactly one b.

18. The set of strings over $\{a, b\}$ whose third to the last symbol is b.

19. The set of strings over $\{a, b\}$ that contain an even number of substrings *ba*.

20. The set of strings over $\{a, b\}$ that have both or neither *aa* and *bb* as substrings.

21. Construct the state diagram of a DFA that accepts the strings over $\{a, b\}$ ending with the substring *abba*. Give the state diagram of an NFA with six arcs that accepts the same language.

22. Let M be the NFA-λ

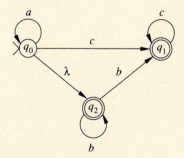

a) Give a regular expression for L(M).

b) Compute λ-*closure*(q_i) for $i = 0, 1, 2$.

c) Give the input transition function t for M.

d) Use Algorithm 6.6.3 to construct a state diagram of a DFA that is equivalent to M.

23. Use Algorithm 6.6.3 to construct the state diagram of a DFA equivalent to the NFA in Example 6.5.2.

24. Use Algorithm 6.6.3 to construct the state diagram of a DFA equivalent to the NFA in Exercise 12.

25. Give a recursive definition of the extended transition function $\hat{\delta}$ of an NFA-λ. The value $\hat{\delta}(q_i, w)$ is the set of states that can be reached by computations that begin at node q_i and completely process the string w.

26. For each of the following diagrams, use Algorithm 6.8.2 to construct a regular expression for the language accepted by the automaton.

a)

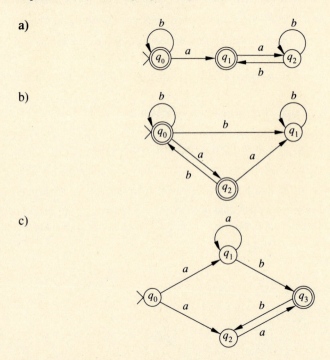

b)

c)

27. For each of the state diagrams in Exercise 26, use Algorithm 6.6.3 to construct the state diagram of a DFA that accepts the same language.

28. Use the technique from Section 6.7 to build the state diagram of an NFA-λ that accepts the language $(ab)^*ba$. Compare this with the DFA constructed in Excercise 11a).

Bibliographic Notes

The equivalence of regular expressions and languages accepted by finite automata was established by Kleene [1956]. The proof given in Section 6.8 is modeled after that of

McNaughton and Yamada [1960]. An algorithm for minimalizing the number of states in a DFA was presented in Nerode [1958]. The algorithm of Hopcroft [1971] increases the efficiency of the minimalization technique.

Nondeterministic finite automata were introduced by Rabin and Scott [1959]. A two-way automaton allows the tape head to move in both directions. A proof that two-way and one-way automata accept the same languages can be found in Rabin and Scott [1959] and Shepardson [1959]. Alternative interpretations of the result of finite-state computations were studied in Mealy [1955] and Moore [1956]. Transitions in Mealy machines are accompanied by the generation of output. The theory and applications of finite automata are developed in the books by Minsky [1967]; Salomaa [1973]; Denning, Dennis, and Qualitz [1978]; and Bavel [1983].

CHAPTER 7

Regular Languages and Sets

Grammars were introduced as language generators and finite automata as language acceptors. Kleene's theorem established that finite automata accept precisely the regular sets. This chapter develops the relationship between the generation and the acceptance of regular sets.

7.1 Regular Grammars and Finite Automata

A context-free grammar is called regular (Section 3.3) if each rule is of the form $A \rightarrow aB$, $A \rightarrow a$, or $A \rightarrow \lambda$. A string derivable in a regular grammar contains at most one variable which, if present, occurs as the rightmost symbol. A derivation is terminated by the application of a rule of the form $A \rightarrow a$ or $A \rightarrow \lambda$. A language generated by a regular grammar is called regular.

The language a^+b^+ is generated by the grammar G and accepted by the NFA M. The states of M have been named S, A, and Z to facilitate the comparison of computation and generation. The computation of M that accepts $aabb$ is given along with the derivation that generates the string in G.

$$G: S \rightarrow aS \mid aA$$
$$A \rightarrow bA \mid b$$

M:

169

Derivation	Computation	String Processed
$S \Rightarrow aS$	$[S, aabb] \vdash [S, abb]$	a
$\Rightarrow aaA$	$\vdash [A, bb]$	aa
$\Rightarrow aabA$	$\vdash [A, b]$	aab
$\Rightarrow aabb$	$\vdash [Z, \lambda]$	$aabb$

A computation in an automaton begins with the input string, sequentially processes the leftmost symbol, and halts when the entire string has been analyzed. Generation, on the other hand, begins with the start symbol of the grammar and adds terminal symbols to the prefix of the derived sentential form. The derivation terminates with the application of a lambda rule or a rule whose right-hand side is a single terminal.

The example illustrates the correspondence between the generation of a terminal string in a grammar and processing the string by a computation of an automaton. The state of the automaton is identical to the variable in the derived string. The final rule application of the derivation removes the variable from the derived string. A computation terminates when the entire string has been processed, and the result is designated by the final state. The accepting state Z, which does not correspond to a variable in the grammar, is added to M to represent the completion of the derivation of G.

The state diagram of an NFA M can be constructed directly from the rules of a grammar G. The states of the automaton consist of the variables of the grammar and, possibly, an additional accepting state. In the previous example, transitions $\delta(S, a) = S$, $\delta(S, a) = A$, and $\delta(A, b) = A$ of M correspond to the rules $S \rightarrow aS$, $S \rightarrow aA$, and $A \rightarrow bA$ of G. The left-hand side of the rule represents the current state of the machine. The terminal on the right-hand side is the input symbol. The state corresponding to the variable on the right-hand side of the rule is entered as a result of the transition.

Since the rule terminating a derivation does not add a variable to the string, the consequences of an application of a lambda rule or a rule of the form $A \rightarrow a$ must be incorporated into the construction of the corresponding automaton.

Theorem 7.1.1

Let $G = (V, \Sigma, P, S)$ be a regular grammar. Define the NFA $M = (Q, \Sigma, \delta, S, F)$ as follows:

i) $Q = \begin{cases} V \cup \{Z\} & \text{where } Z \notin V, \text{ if P contains a rule } A \rightarrow a \\ V & \text{otherwise.} \end{cases}$

ii) $\delta(A, a) = B$ whenever $A \rightarrow aB \in P$
   $\delta(A, a) = Z$ whenever $A \rightarrow a \in P$.

iii) $F = \begin{cases} \{A \mid A \rightarrow \lambda \in P\} \cup \{Z\} & \text{if } Z \in Q \\ \{A \mid A \rightarrow \lambda \in P\} & \text{otherwise.} \end{cases}$

Then $L(M) = L(G)$.

Proof The construction of the machine transitions from the rules of the grammar allows every derivation of G to be traced by a computation in M. The derivation of a terminal string has the form $S \Rightarrow \lambda$, $S \overset{*}{\Rightarrow} wC \Rightarrow wa$ or $S \overset{*}{\Rightarrow} wC \Rightarrow w$ where the derivation $S \overset{*}{\Rightarrow} wC$ consists of the application of rules of the form $A \rightarrow aB$. If L(G) contains the null string, then S is an accepting state of M and $\lambda \in L(M)$. Induction can be used to establish the existence of a computation in M that processes the string w and terminates in state C whenever wC is a sentential form of G.

The derivation of a nonnull string is terminated by the application of a rule $C \rightarrow a$ or $C \rightarrow \lambda$. In a derivation of the form $S \overset{*}{\Rightarrow} wC \Rightarrow wa$, the final rule application corresponds to the transition $\delta(C, a) = Z$, causing the machine to halt in the accepting state Z. A derivation of the form $S \overset{*}{\Rightarrow} wC \Rightarrow w$ is terminated by the application of a lambda rule. Since $C \rightarrow \lambda$ is a rule of G, the state C is accepting in M. The acceptance of w in M is exhibited by the computation that corresponds to the derivation $S \overset{*}{\Rightarrow} wC$.

Conversely, let $w = ua$ be a string accepted by M. A computation accepting w has the form

$$[S, w] \overset{*}{\vdash} [B, \lambda] \quad \text{where } B \neq Z$$

or

$$[S, w] \overset{*}{\vdash} [A, a] \vdash [Z, \lambda].$$

In the former case, B is the right-hand side of a lambda rule of G. The string wB can be derived by applying the rules that correspond to transitions in the computation. The generation of w is completed by the application of the lambda rule. Similarly, a derivation of uA can be constructed from the transitions in the computation $[S, w] \overset{*}{\vdash} [A, a]$. The string w is obtained by terminating this derivation with the rule $A \rightarrow a$. Thus every string accepted by M is in the language of G. ■

Example 7.1.1

The grammar G generates and the NFA M accepts the language $a^*(a \cup b^+)$.

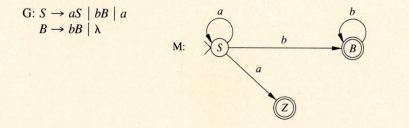

The preceding transformation can be reversed to construct a regular grammar from an NFA. The transition $\delta(A, a) = B$ produces the rule $A \rightarrow aB$. Since every transition results in a new machine state, no rules of the form $A \rightarrow a$ are produced. These rules generate derivations of the form $S \overset{*}{\Rightarrow} wC$ that mimic computations in the automaton. Rules must be added to terminate the derivations. When C is an accepting state, a computation that terminates in state C exhibits the acceptance of w. Completing the derivation $S \overset{*}{\Rightarrow} wC$ with the application of a rule $C \rightarrow \lambda$ generates w in G. The grammar is completed by adding lambda rules for all accepting states of the automaton.

These constructions can be applied sequentially to shift from automaton to grammar and back again. A grammar G constructed from an NFA M using the previous techniques can be transformed into an equivalent automaton M' using the construction presented in Theorem 7.1.1.

$$ M \longrightarrow G \longrightarrow M' $$

Since G contains only rules of the form $A \rightarrow aB$ or $A \rightarrow \lambda$, the NFA M' is identical to M.

A regular grammar G can be converted to an NFA that, in turn, can be reconverted into a grammar G'.

$$ G \longrightarrow M \longrightarrow G' $$

G', the grammar that results from these conversions, can be obtained directly from G by adding a single new variable, call it Z, to the grammar and the rule $Z \rightarrow \lambda$. All rules $A \rightarrow a$ are then replaced by $A \rightarrow aZ$.

Example 7.1.2

A regular grammar that accepts L(M) is constructed from the automaton M from Example 7.1.1.

$$ G': S \rightarrow aS \mid bB \mid aZ $$
$$ B \rightarrow bB \mid \lambda $$
$$ Z \rightarrow \lambda $$

The transitions provide the S rules and the first B rule. The lambda rules are added since B and Z are accepting states.   □

The two conversion techniques allow us to conclude that the languages generated by regular grammars are precisely those accepted by finite automata. It follows from Theorems 6.8.3 and 7.1.1 that the language generated by a regular grammar is a regular set. The conversion from automaton to regular grammar guarantees that every regular set is generated by some regular grammar. This yields another categorization of the regular sets: the languages generated by regular grammars.

Example 7.1.3

The language of the regular grammar from Example 3.2.8 is the set of strings over $\{a, b, c\}$ that do not contain the substring abc. Theorem 7.1.1 is used to construct an

NFA that accepts this language.

$$S \rightarrow bS \mid cS \mid aB \mid \lambda$$
$$B \rightarrow aB \mid cS \mid bC \mid \lambda$$
$$C \rightarrow aB \mid bS \mid \lambda$$

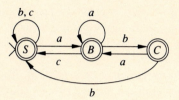

Example 7.1.4

A regular grammar with alphabet $\{a, b\}$ that generates strings with an even number of a's and an odd number of b's can be constructed from the DFA in Example 6.3.4. This machine is reproduced below with the states $[e_a, e_b]$, $[o_a, e_b]$, $[e_a, o_b]$ and $[o_a, o_b]$ renamed S, A, B, and C, respectively.

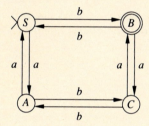

The associated grammar is

$$S \rightarrow aA \mid bB$$
$$A \rightarrow aS \mid bC$$
$$B \rightarrow bS \mid aC \mid \lambda$$
$$C \rightarrow aB \mid bA.$$

7.2 A Nonregular Language

The incompletely specified DFA

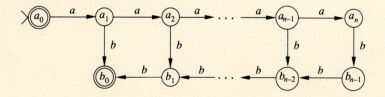

accepts the language $\{a^i b^i \mid i \leqslant n\}$. The states a_i count the number of leading a's in the input string. Upon processing the first b, the machine enters the sequence of states b_i. The accepting state b_0 is entered when an equal number of b's are processed. We will prove that any deterministic automaton built to accept the language $L = \{a^i b^i \mid i \geqslant 0\}$ must have an infinite sequence of states that have the same role as the a_i's in the previous diagram.

Assume L is accepted by a DFA M. The extended transition function $\hat{\delta}$ is used to show that the automaton M must have an infinite number of states. Let a_i be the state of the machine entered upon processing the string a^i; that is, $\hat{\delta}(q_0, a^i) = a_i$. For all $i, j \geqslant 0$ with $i \neq j$, $a^i b^i \in L$ and $a^j b^i \notin L$. Hence, $\hat{\delta}(q_0, a^i b^i) \neq \hat{\delta}(q_0, a^j b^i)$ since the former is an accepting state and the latter rejecting. Now $\hat{\delta}(q_0, a^i b^i) = \hat{\delta}(\hat{\delta}(q_0, a^i), b^i) = \hat{\delta}(a_i, b^i)$ and $\hat{\delta}(q_0, a^j b^i) = \hat{\delta}(\hat{\delta}(q_0, a^j), b^i) = \hat{\delta}(a_j, b^i)$. We conclude that $a_i \neq a_j$ since $\hat{\delta}(a_i, b^i) \neq \hat{\delta}(a_j, b^i)$.

We have shown that states a_i and a_j are distinct for all values of $i \neq j$. Any deterministic finite-state machine that accepts L must contain an infinite sequence of states corresponding to the a_i's. This violates the restriction that limits a DFA to a finite number of states. Consequently there is no DFA that accepts L, or equivalently, L is not regular. The preceding argument establishes Theorem 7.2.1.

Theorem 7.2.1

The language $\{a^i b^i \mid i \geqslant 0\}$ is not regular.

The argument establishing Theorem 7.2.1 is an example of a nonexistence proof. We have shown that no DFA can be constructed, no matter how clever the designer, to accept the language $\{a^i b^i \mid i \geqslant 0\}$. Proofs of existence and nonexistence have an essentially different flavor. A language can be shown to be regular by constructing an automaton that accepts it. A proof of nonregularity requires proving that no machine can accept the language.

Theorem 7.2.1 can be generalized to establish the nonregularity of a number of languages.

Corollary 7.2.2 (to the proof of Theorem 7.2.1)

Let L be a language containing strings u_i and v_i, $i \geqslant 0$, with $u_i v_i \in L$ and $u_i v_j \notin L$ for all $i, j \geqslant 0$ and $i \neq j$. Then L is not a regular language.

The proof is identical to Theorem 7.2.1 with u_i replacing a^i and v_i replacing b^i.

Example 7.2.1

The set L consisting of the palindromes over $\{a, b\}$ is not regular. By Corollary 7.2.2, it is sufficient to discover two sequences of strings u_i and v_i that satisfy $u_i v_i \in L$ and

$u_i v_j \notin L$ for all $i \neq j$. The strings

$$u_i = a^i b$$
$$v_i = a^i$$

fulfill these requirements.   □

Example 7.2.2

Grammars were introduced as a formal structure to facilitate the definition of languages. Corollary 7.2.2 can be used to show that regular grammars are not a powerful enough tool to define programming languages containing arithmetic or Boolean expressions in infix form. The grammar AE (Section 4.3), which generates infix additive expressions, demonstrates the nonregularity of these languages.

$$AE: S \rightarrow A$$
$$A \rightarrow T \mid A + T$$
$$T \rightarrow b \mid (A)$$

Infix notation permits, in fact requires, the nesting of parentheses. The grammar generates strings containing an equal number of left and right parentheses surrounding a correctly formed expression. The derivation

$$S \Rightarrow T$$
$$\Rightarrow (A)$$
$$\Rightarrow (T)$$
$$\Rightarrow (b)$$

exhibits the generation of the string (b) in AE. Repeated applications of the sequence of rules $T \Rightarrow (A) \Rightarrow (T)$ before terminating the derivation with the application of the rule $T \rightarrow b$ generates the strings (b), $((b))$, $(((b)))$, ... The strings $(^i b$ and $)^i$ satisfy the requirements of the sequences u_i and v_i of Corollary 7.2.2. Thus the language defined by the grammar AE is not regular. A similar argument can be used to show that programming languages such as Pascal, PL/I, and ALGOL, among others, are not regular.   □

7.3   The Pumping Lemma for Regular Languages

The existence of nonregular sets was established in the previous section. The proof consisted of demonstrating the impossibility of constructing a DFA that accepts the language. In this section a more general criterion for establishing nonregularity is developed. The main result, the pumping lemma for regular languages, requires strings in a regular language to admit decompositions satisfying certain repetition properties.

Pumping a string refers to constructing new strings by repeating (pumping) substrings in the original string. Acceptance in the state diagram of a DFA illustrates pumping strings.

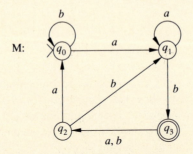

M:

Consider the string $z = ababbaaab$ in L(M). This string can be decomposed into substrings u, v, and w where $z = uvw$, $u = a$, $v = bab$, and $w = baaab$. The strings $a(bab)^i baaab$ are obtained by pumping the substring bab in $ababbaaab$.

As usual, processing z in the DFA M corresponds to generating a path in the state diagram of M. The decomposition of z into u, v, and w breaks the path in the state diagram into three subpaths. The subpaths generated by the computation of substrings $u = a$ and $w = baaab$ are q_0, q_1 and $q_1, q_3, q_2, q_0, q_1, q_3$. Processing the second component of the decomposition generates the cycle q_1, q_3, q_2, q_1. The pumped strings $uv^i w$ are also accepted by the DFA since the repetition of the substring simply adds additional trips around the cycle q_1, q_3, q_2, q_1 before the processing of w terminates the computation in state q_3.

The pumping lemma requires the existence of such a decomposition for all sufficiently long strings in the language of a DFA. Two lemmas are presented establishing conditions guaranteeing the existence of cycles in paths in the state diagram of a DFA. The proofs utilize a simple counting argument known as the **pigeonhole principle**. This principle is based on the observation that when there are a number of boxes and a greater number of items to be distributed among them, one of the boxes must receive more than one item.

Lemma 7.3.1

Let G be the state diagram of a DFA with k states. Any path of length k in G contains a cycle.

Proof   A path of length k contains $k + 1$ nodes. Since there are only k nodes in G, there must be a node, call it q_i, that occurs in at least two positions in the path. The subpath from the first occurrence of q_i to the second produces the desired cycle.   ■

Paths with length greater than k can be divided into an initial subpath of length k and the remainder of the path. Lemma 7.3.1 guarantees the existence of a cycle in the initial subpath. The preceding remarks are formalized in Corollary 7.3.2.

Corollary 7.3.2

Let G be the state diagram of a DFA with k states and let **p** be a path of length k or more. The path **p** can be decomposed into subpaths **q**, **r**, and **s** where **p** = **qrs**, the length of **qr** is less than or equal to k, and **r** is a cycle.

Theorem 7.3.3 (Pumping Lemma for Regular Languages)

Let L be a regular language that is accepted by a DFA M with k states. Let z be any string in L with $length(z) \geq k$. Then z can be written uvw with $length(uv) \leq k$, $length(v) > 0$, and $uv^iw \in L$ for all $i \geq 0$.

Proof   Let $z \in L$ be a string with length $n \geq k$. Processing z in M generates a path of length n in the state diagram of M. By Corollary 7.3.2, this path can be broken into subpaths **q**, **r**, and **s** where **r** is a cycle in the state diagram. The decomposition of z into u, v, and w consists of the strings spelled by the paths **q**, **r**, and **s**.   ∎

Properties of the particular DFA that accepts the language L are not specifically mentioned in the proof of the pumping lemma. The argument holds for all such DFAs, including the DFA with the minimal number of states. The statement of the theorem could be altered to specify k as the number of states in the minimal DFA accepting L.

The pumping lemma is a powerful tool for proving that languages are not regular. Every string of length k or more in a regular language, where k is the value specified by the pumping lemma, must have an appropriate decomposition. To show that a language is not regular it suffices to find one string that does not satisfy the conditions of the pumping lemma. The use of the pumping lemma to establish nonregularity is illustrated in the following examples. The technique consists of choosing a string z in L and showing that there is no decomposition uvw of z in which uv^iw is in L for all $i \geq 0$.

Example 7.3.1

Let $L = \{z \in \{a, b\}^* \mid length(z)$ is a perfect square$\}$. Assume that L is regular. This implies that L is accepted by some DFA. Let k be the number of states of the DFA. By the pumping lemma, every string $z \in L$ of length k or more can be decomposed into substrings u, v, and w such that $length(uv) \leq k$, $v \neq \lambda$, and $uv^iw \in L$ for all $i \geq 0$.

Consider any string z of length k^2. The pumping lemma requires a decomposition of z into substrings u, v, and w with $0 < length(v) \leq k$. This observation can be used to place an upper bound on the length of uv^2w.

$$
\begin{aligned}
length(uv^2w) &= length(uvw) + length(v) \\
&= k^2 + length(v) \\
&\leq k^2 + k \\
&< k^2 + 2k + 1 \\
&= (k + 1)^2
\end{aligned}
$$

The length of uv^2w is greater than k^2 and less than $(k + 1)^2$ and therefore is not a perfect square. We have shown that there is no possible decomposition of z that satisfies the conditions of the pumping lemma. The assumption that L is regular leads to a contradiction, establishing the nonregularity of L.   □

Example 7.3.2

The language $L = \{a^i \mid i \text{ is prime}\}$ is not regular. Assume that a DFA with k states accepts L. Let n be a prime greater than k. If L is regular, the pumping lemma implies that a^n can be decomposed into substrings uvw, $v \neq \lambda$, such that uv^iw is in L for all $i \geq 0$. Assume such a decomposition exists.

The length of $z = uv^{n+1}w$ must be prime if z is in L. But

$$
\begin{aligned}
length(uv^{n+1}w) &= length(uvwv^n) \\
&= length(uvw) + length(v^n) \\
&= n + n(length(v)) \\
&= n(1 + length(v)).
\end{aligned}
$$

Since its length is not prime, $uv^{n+1}w$ is not in L. Thus there is no division of a^n that satisfies the pumping lemma and L is not regular.   □

The pumping lemma can be used to determine the size of the language accepted by a DFA. Pumping a string generates an infinite sequence of strings that are accepted by the DFA. To determine whether a regular language is finite or infinite it is necessary only to determine if it contains a "pumpable" string.

Theorem 7.3.4

Let M be a DFA with k states.

i) L(M) is not empty if, and only if, M accepts a string z with $length(z) < k$.

ii) L(M) has an infinite number of members if, and only if, M accepts a string z where $k \leq length(z) < 2k$.

Proof

i) L(M) is clearly not empty if a string of length less than k is accepted by M.

Now let M be a machine whose language is not empty and let z be the smallest string in L(M). Assume that the length of z is greater than $k - 1$. By the pumping lemma, z can be written uvw where $uv^iw \in L$. In particular, $uv^0w = uw$ is a string smaller than z in L. This contradicts the assumption of the minimality of the length of z. Therefore, $length(z) < k$.

ii) If M accepts a string z with $k \leq length(z) < 2k$, then z can be decomposed into uvw satisfying the conditions of the pumping lemma. This implies that the strings uv^iw are in L for all $i \geq 0$.

Assume that L(M) is infinite. We must show that there is a string whose length is between k and $2k - 1$ in L(M). Since there are only finitely many strings over a finite alphabet with length less than k, L(M) must contain strings of length greater than $k - 1$.

Choose a string $z \in$ L(M) whose length is as small as possible but greater than $k - 1$. If $k \leqslant length(z) < 2k$, there is nothing left to show. Assume that $length(z) \geqslant 2k$. By the pumping lemma, $z = uvw$, $length(v) \leqslant k$, and $uv^0w = uw \in$ L(M). But this is a contradiction since uw is a string whose length is greater than $k - 1$ but strictly smaller than the length of z.   ∎

The preceding result establishes a decision procedure for determining the cardinality of the language of a DFA. If k is the number of states and j the size of the alphabet of the automaton, there are $(j^k - 1)/(j - 1)$ strings having length less than k. By Theorem 7.3.4, testing each of these determines whether the language is empty. Testing all strings with length between k and $2k - 1$ resolves the question of finite or infinite. This, of course, is an extremely inefficient procedure. Nevertheless, it is effective, yielding the following corollary.

Corollary 7.3.5

Let M be a DFA. There is a decision procedure to determine whether

i) L(M) is empty

ii) L(M) is finite

iii) L(M) is infinite.

7.4   Closure Properties of Regular Languages

Regular languages have been defined, generated, and accepted. A language over an alphabet Σ is regular if it is

i) a regular set (expression) over Σ

ii) accepted by DFA, NFA, or NFA-λ

iii) generated by a regular grammar.

A set of languages is closed under an operation if the application of the operation to members of the set results in a member of the set. Each of the equivalent formulations of regularity will be used in determining the closure properties of the set of regular languages.

The recursive definition of regular sets establishes closure for the unary operation Kleene star and the binary operations union and concatenation. This was also proved in Theorem 6.5.3 using acceptance by finite-state machines.

Theorem 7.4.1

Let L_1 and L_2 be two regular languages. The languages L_1L_2, $L_1 \cup L_2$, and L_1^* are regular languages.

The regular languages are also closed under complementation. If L is regular over the alphabet Σ, then so is $\bar{L} = \Sigma^* - L$, the set containing all strings in Σ^* that are not in L. Theorem 6.3.3 uses the properties of DFAs to construct a machine that accepts $\bar{L}$ from one that accepts L.

Theorem 7.4.2

Let L be a regular language over Σ. The language $\bar{L}$ is regular.

Theorems 7.4.3 and 7.4.4 establish closure results for the operation intersection. The first result is positive; the intersection of two regular languages produces a regular language. The latter result is negative; the intersection of a regular language with a context-free language need not be regular.

Theorem 7.4.3

Let L_1 and L_2 be regular languages over Σ. The language $L_1 \cap L_2$ is regular.

Proof   By DeMorgan's law

$$L_1 \cap L_2 = (\overline{\bar{L}_1 \cup \bar{L}_2}).$$

The right-hand side of the equality is regular since it is built from L_1 and L_2 using union and complementation.   ∎

Theorem 7.4.4

Let L_1 be a regular language and L_2 be a context-free language. The language $L_1 \cap L_2$ is not necessarily regular.

Proof   Let $L_1 = a^*b^*$ and $L_2 = \{a^i b^i \mid i \geq 0\}$. L_2 is context-free since it is generated by the grammar $S \to aSb \mid \lambda$. The intersection of L_1 and L_2 is L_2, which is not regular by Theorem 7.2.1.   ∎

Closure properties provide additional tools for establishing the regularity or nonregularity of languages. The operations of complementation and intersection, as well as union, concatenation, and Kleene star, can be used to combine regular languages.

Example 7.4.1

Let L be the language over $\{a, b\}$ consisting of all strings that contain the substring aa but do not contain bb. The regular languages $L_1 = (a \cup b)^* aa(a \cup b)^*$ and $L_2 = (a \cup b)^* bb(a \cup b)^*$ accept strings containing substrings aa and bb, respectively. Hence, $L = L_1 \cap \bar{L}_2$ is regular.   □

Example 7.4.2

The language $L = \{a^i b^j \mid i, j \geq 0$ and $i \neq j\}$ is not regular. If L is regular then, by Theorems 7.4.2 and 7.4.3, so is $\bar{L} \cap a^*b^*$. But $\bar{L} \cap a^*b^* = \{a^i b^i \mid i \geq 0\}$, which we know is not regular.   □

The closure results can be combined with Corollary 7.3.5 to develop a decision procedure that determines whether two DFAs accept the same language.

Corollary 7.4.5

Let M_1 and M_2 be two DFAs. There is a decision procedure to determine whether M_1 and M_2 are equivalent.

Proof Let L_1 and L_2 be the languages accepted by M_1 and M_2. By Theorems 7.4.1, 7.4.2, and 7.4.3, the language

$$L = (L_1 \cap \bar{L}_2) \cup (\bar{L}_1 \cap L_2)$$

is regular. L is empty if, and only if, L_1 and L_2 are identical. By Corollary 7.3.5, there is a decision procedure to determine whether L is empty, or equivalently, whether M_1 and M_2 accept the same language. ∎

Exercises

1. Let G be the grammar

$$G: S \rightarrow aS \mid bA \mid a$$
$$A \rightarrow aS \mid bA \mid b.$$

   a) Use Theorem 7.1.1 to build an NFA M that accepts L(G).

   b) Using the result of a), build a DFA M' that accepts L(G).

   c) Construct a regular grammar from M that generates L(M).

   d) Construct a regular grammar from M' that generates L(M').

   e) Give a regular expression for L(G).

2. Use Corollary 7.2.2 to show that each of the following sets is not regular.

   a) The set of strings over $\{a, b\}$ with the same number of a's and b's.

   b) The set of palindromes of even length over $\{a, b\}$.

   c) The set of strings over $\{(,)\}$ in which the parentheses are paired. Examples include λ, (), () (), (()) ().

   d) The language $\{a^i(ab)^j(ca)^{2i} \mid i, j > 0\}$.

3. Use the pumping lemma to show that each of the following sets is not regular.

   a) The set of palindromes over $\{a, b\}$.

   b) $\{a^n b^m \mid n < m\}$.

   c) $\{ww \mid w \in \{a, b\}^*\}$.

   d) The set of initial sequences of the infinite string

$$abaabaaabaaaab \ldots ba^n ba^{n+1} b \ldots .$$

   e) The set of strings over $\{a, b\}$ in which the number of a's is a perfect cube.

4. Prove that the set of nonpalindromes over $\{a, b\}$ is not a regular language.

5. Let L be a regular language over $\{a, b, c\}$. Show that each of the following sets is regular.

   a) $\{w \mid w \in L \text{ and } w \text{ contains an } a\}$.

   b) $\{w \mid w \in L \text{ or } w \text{ contains an } a\}$.

   c) $\{w \mid w \notin L \text{ and } w \text{ does not contain an } a\}$.

6. Let L_1 be a nonregular language and L_2 an arbitrary finite language.

   a) Prove that $L_1 \cup L_2$ is nonregular.

   b) Prove that $L_1 - L_2$ is nonregular.

   c) Show that the conclusions of parts a) and b) are not true if L_2 is not assumed to be finite.

7. Let L be a regular language. Show that the following languages are regular.

   a) The set $P = \{u \mid uv \in L\}$ of prefixes of L.

   b) The set $S = \{v \mid uv \in L\}$ of suffixes of L.

   c) The set $L^R = \{w^R \mid w \in L\}$ of reversals of L.

   d) The set $E = \{uv \mid v \in L\}$ of strings that have a suffix in L.

8. Let L be a regular language containing only strings of even length. Let L' be the language $\{u \mid uv \in L \text{ and } length(u) = length(v)\}$. L' is the set of all strings that contain the first half of strings from L. Prove that L' is regular.

9. Let Σ_1 and Σ_2 be two alphabets. A **homomorphism** is a total function h from Σ_1^* to Σ_2^* that preserves concatenation. That is, h satisfies

   i) $h(\lambda) = \lambda$

   ii) $h(uv) = h(u)h(v)$.

   a) Let $L_1 \subseteq \Sigma_1^*$ be a regular language. Show that the set $\{h(w) \mid w \in L_1\}$ is regular over Σ_2. This set is called the **homomorphic image** of L_1 under h.

   b) Let $L_2 \subseteq \Sigma_2^*$ be a regular language. Show that the set $\{w \in \Sigma_1^* \mid h(w) \in L_2\}$ is regular. This set is called the **inverse image** of L_2 under h.

10. A context-free grammar $G = (V, \Sigma, P, S)$ is called **right-linear** if each rule is of the form

    i) $A \rightarrow u$

    ii) $A \rightarrow uB$

    where $A, B \in V$, and $u \in \Sigma^*$. Show that the right-linear grammars generate precisely the regular sets.

11. A context-free grammar $G = (V, \Sigma, P, S)$ is called **left-regular** if each rule is of the form

    i) $A \rightarrow \lambda$

    ii) $A \rightarrow a$

    iii) $A \rightarrow Ba$

where $A, B \in V$, and $a \in \Sigma$.

a) Design an algorithm to construct an NFA that accepts the language of a left-regular grammar.

b) Show that the left-regular grammars generate precisely the regular sets.

12. A context-free grammar $G = (V, \Sigma, P, S)$ is called **left-linear** if each rule is of the form

   i) $A \rightarrow u$

   ii) $A \rightarrow Bu$

where $A, B \in V$, and $u \in \Sigma^*$. Show that the left-linear grammars generate precisely the regular sets.

Bibliographic Notes

Chomsky and Miller [1958] established the equivalence of the languages generated by regular grammars and accepted by finite automata. The pumping lemma for regular languages is from Bar-Hillel, Perles, and Shamir [1961]. Closure under homomorphisms (Exercise 9) is from Ginsburg and Rose [1963b]. The closure of regular sets under reversal was noted by Rabin and Scott [1959]. Additional closure results for regular sets can be found in Bar-Hillel, Perles, and Shamir [1961], Ginsburg and Rose [1963b], and Ginsburg [1966].

CHAPTER 8

Pushdown Automata and Context-Free Languages

Regular languages have been characterized as the languages generated by regular grammars and accepted by finite automata. This chapter presents a class of machines, the pushdown automata, that accepts the context-free languages. A pushdown automaton is a finite-state machine augmented with external memory. The addition of a stack to a finite-state machine provides the pushdown automaton with a first-in, last-out memory management capability.

8.1 Pushdown Automata

Theorem 7.2.1 established that the language $\{a^i b^i \mid i \geq 0\}$ is not accepted by any finite automaton. The restriction of having finitely many states does not allow the automaton to "remember" the number of a's in the input string. To recognize this language, a machine needs the ability to record the processing of any finite number of a's. A new type of automaton is constructed that augments the state-input transitions of a finite automaton with the ability to utilize unlimited memory.

A pushdown stack, or simply a stack, is added to a finite automaton to construct a new machine known as a pushdown automaton (PDA). Stack operations affect only the top item of the stack; a push places an element on the stack and a pop removes the top element. Definition 8.1.1 formalizes the concept of a pushdown automaton. The components Q, Σ, q_0, and F of a PDA are the same as in a finite automaton.

Definition 8.1.1

A **pushdown automaton** is a sextuple $(Q, \Sigma, \Gamma, \delta, q_0, F)$ where Q is a set of states, Σ a finite set called the input alphabet, Γ a finite set called the stack alphabet, q_0 the initial state, $F \subseteq Q$ a set of final states, and δ a transition function from $Q \times (\Sigma \cup \{\lambda\}) \times (\Gamma \cup \{\lambda\})$ to subsets of $Q \times (\Gamma \cup \{\lambda\})$.

A PDA has two alphabets: an input alphabet Σ from which the input strings are built and a stack alphabet Γ whose elements may be stored on the stack. Elements of the stack alphabet are denoted by capital letters. A stack is represented as a string of stack elements; the element on the top of the stack is the leftmost symbol in the string. Greek letters represent strings of stack symbols. The notation $A\alpha$ represents a stack with A as the top element. An empty stack is denoted λ.

A PDA consults the current state, input symbol, and the symbol on the top of the stack to determine the machine transition. The transition function δ lists all possible transitions for a given state, symbol, and stack top combination. The value of the transition function

$$\delta(q_i, a, A) = \{[q_j, B], [q_k, C]\}$$

indicates that two transitions are possible when the automaton is in state q_i scanning an a with A on the top of the stack. The transition

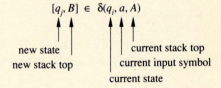

causes the machine to

i) change the state from q_i to q_j
ii) process the symbol a (advance the tape head)
iii) remove A from the top of the stack (pop the stack)
iv) push B onto the stack.

The domain of the transition function permits lambda in the input symbol and stack top positions. A lambda argument specifies that the value of the component should be neither consulted nor acted upon by the transition. The applicability of the transition is completely determined by the positions that do not contain lambda.

If the input position is lambda, the transition does not process an input symbol. Transition i) pops and ii) pushes the stack symbol A without altering the state or the input.

i) $[q_i, \lambda] \in \delta(q_i, \lambda, A)$

ii) $[q_i, A] \in \delta(q_i, \lambda, \lambda)$

iii) $[q_i, \lambda] \in \delta(q_j, a, \lambda)$

Transition iii) is the PDA equivalent of a finite automaton transition. The applicability is determined only by the state and input symbol; the transition does not affect the stack.

A PDA configuration is represented by the triple $[q_i, w, \alpha]$ where q_i is the machine state, w the unprocessed input, and α the stack. The notation $[q_i, w, \alpha] \mid_{\overline{M}} [q_j, v, \beta]$ indicates that configuration $[q_j, v, \beta]$ can be obtained from $[q_i, w, \alpha]$ by a single transition of the PDA M. As before, $\mid_{\overline{M}}^*$ represents the result of a sequence of transitions. When there is no possibility of confusion, the subscript M is omitted. A computation of a PDA is a sequence of transitions beginning with the machine in the initial state with an empty stack.

We are now ready to construct a PDA M to recognize the language $\{a^i b^i \mid i \geqslant 0\}$. Processing input symbol a causes A to be pushed onto the stack. Processing b pops the stack, matching the number of a's to the number of b's. The computation generated by the input string $aabb$ illustrates the actions of M.

$$
\begin{aligned}
\text{M: } Q &= \{q_0, q_1\} \\
\Sigma &= \{a, b\} \\
\Gamma &= \{A\} \\
F &= \{q_0, q_1\} \\
\delta(q_0, a, \lambda) &= \{[q_0, A]\} \\
\delta(q_0, b, A) &= \{[q_1, \lambda]\} \\
\delta(q_1, b, A) &= \{[q_1, \lambda]\}
\end{aligned}
\qquad
\begin{aligned}
&[q_0, aabb, \lambda] \\
&\vdash [q_0, abb, A] \\
&\vdash [q_0, bb, AA] \\
&\vdash [q_1, b, A] \\
&\vdash [q_1, \lambda, \lambda]
\end{aligned}
$$

The computation of M processes the entire input string and halts in an accepting state with an empty stack. These conditions become our criteria for acceptance.

Definition 8.1.2

Let $M = (Q, \Sigma, \Gamma, \delta, q_0, F)$ be a PDA. A string $w \in \Sigma^*$ is **accepted** by M if there is a computation

$$[q_0, w, \lambda] \mid^* [q_i, \lambda, \lambda]$$

where $q_i \in F$. The **language** of M, denoted L(M), is the set of strings accepted by M.

A computation that accepts a string is called successful. A computation that processes the entire input string and halts in a nonaccepting configuration is said to be unsuccessful. Because of the nondeterministic nature of the transition function, there may be computations that cannot complete the processing of the input string. Such computations are also called unsuccessful.

Example 8.1.1

The PDA M accepts the language $\{wcw^R \mid w \in \{a, b\}^*\}$. The stack is used to record the string w as it is processed. Stack symbols A and B represent input a and b, respectively.

$$M: Q = \{q_0, q_1\} \qquad \delta(q_0, a, \lambda) = \{[q_0, A]\}$$
$$\Sigma = \{a, b, c\} \qquad \delta(q_0, b, \lambda) = \{[q_0, B]\}$$
$$\Gamma = \{A, B\} \qquad \delta(q_0, c, \lambda) = \{[q_1, \lambda]\}$$
$$F = \{q_1\} \qquad \delta(q_1, a, A) = \{[q_1, \lambda]\}$$
$$\delta(q_1, b, B) = \{[q_1, \lambda]\}$$

A successful computation records the string w on the stack as it is processed. Once the c is encountered, the accepting state q_1 is entered and the stack contains a string representing w^R. The computation of M with input $abcba$ is given below.

$$[q_0, abcba, \lambda]$$
$$\vdash [q_0, bcba, A]$$
$$\vdash [q_0, cba, BA]$$
$$\vdash [q_1, ba, BA]$$
$$\vdash [q_1, a, A]$$
$$\vdash [q_1, \lambda, \lambda] \qquad\qquad \square$$

A PDA is **deterministic** if there is at most one transition that is applicable for each combination of state, input symbol, and stack top. Two transitions $[q_j, B] \in \delta(q_i, u, A)$, $[q_k, C] \in \delta(q_i, v, B)$ are called **compatible** if any of the following conditions are satisfied:

i) $u = v$ and $A = B$.

ii) $u = v$ and $A = \lambda$ or $B = \lambda$.

iii) $A = B$ and $u = \lambda$ or $v = \lambda$.

iv) $u = \lambda$ or $v = \lambda$ and $A = \lambda$ or $B = \lambda$.

Compatible transitions can be applied to the same machine configurations. A PDA is deterministic if it does not contain distinct compatible transitions. Both the PDA in Example 8.1.1 and the machine constructed to accept $\{a^i b^i \mid i \geq 0\}$ are deterministic.

Example 8.1.2

The language $L = \{a^i \mid i \geq 0\} \cup \{a^i b^i \mid i \geq 0\}$ contains strings consisting solely of a's or an equal number of a's and b's. The stack maintains a record of the number of a's processed until a b is encountered or the computation is completed.

$$Q = \{q_0, q_1, q_2\} \qquad \delta(q_0, a, \lambda) = \{[q_0, A]\}$$
$$\Sigma = \{a, b\} \qquad \delta(q_0, \lambda, \lambda) = \{[q_2, \lambda]\}$$
$$\Gamma = \{A\} \qquad \delta(q_0, b, A) = \{[q_1, \lambda]\}$$
$$F = \{q_1, q_2\} \qquad \delta(q_1, b, A) = \{[q_1, \lambda]\}$$
$$\delta(q_2, \lambda, A) = \{[q_2, \lambda]\}$$

When scanning an a in state q_0, there are two transitions that are applicable. A string of the form $a^i b^i$, $i > 0$, is accepted by a computation that remains in states q_0 and q_1. If a transition to state q_2 follows the processing of the final a in a string a^i, the stack is emptied and the input is accepted. Entering q_2 in any other manner results in an unsuccessful computation. □

Example 8.1.3

The even-length palindromes over $\{a, b\}$ are accepted by the PDA M.

$$
\begin{aligned}
\text{M: } Q &= \{q_0, q_1\} & \delta(q_0, a, \lambda) &= \{[q_0, A]\} \\
\Sigma &= \{a, b\} & \delta(q_0, b, \lambda) &= \{[q_0, B]\} \\
\Gamma &= \{A, B\} & \delta(q_0, \lambda, \lambda) &= \{[q_1, \lambda]\} \\
F &= \{q_1\} & \delta(q_1, a, A) &= \{[q_1, \lambda]\} \\
& & \delta(q_1, b, B) &= \{[q_1, \lambda]\}
\end{aligned}
$$

That is, $L(M) = \{ww^R \mid w \in \{a, b\}^*\}$. A successful computation remains in state q_0 while processing the string w and enters state q_1 upon reading the first symbol in w^R. Unlike the strings in Example 8.1.1, the strings in L do not contain a middle marker that induces the change from state q_0 to q_1. Nondeterminism allows the machine to "guess" when the middle of the string has been reached. Transitions to q_1 that do not occur immediately after processing the last element of w result in unsuccessful computations. □

8.2 Variations on the PDA Theme

Pushdown automata are often defined in a manner that differs slightly from Definition 8.1.1. In this section we examine several alterations to our definition that preserve the set of accepted languages.

Along with changing the state, a transition in a PDA is accompanied by three actions: popping the stack, pushing a stack element, and processing an input symbol. A PDA is called **atomic** if each transition causes only one of the three actions to occur. Transitions in an atomic PDA have the form

$$
\begin{aligned}
[q_j, \lambda] &\in \delta(q_i, a, \lambda) \\
[q_j, \lambda] &\in \delta(q_i, \lambda, A) \\
[q_j, A] &\in \delta(q_i, \lambda, \lambda).
\end{aligned}
$$

Theorem 8.2.1 shows that the languages accepted by atomic PDAs are the same as those accepted by PDAs. Moreover, it outlines a method to construct an equivalent atomic PDA from an arbitrary PDA.

Theorem 8.2.1

Let M be a PDA. Then there is an atomic PDA M′ with $L(M') = L(M)$.

Proof To construct M′, the nonatomic transitions of M are replaced by a sequence of atomic transitions. Let $[q_j, B] \in \delta(q_i, a, A)$ be a transition of M. The atomic equivalent requires two new states, p_1 and p_2, and the transitions

$$[p_1, \lambda] \in \delta(q_i, a, \lambda)$$
$$\delta(p_1, \lambda, A) = \{[p_2, \lambda]\}$$
$$\delta(p_2, \lambda, \lambda) = \{[q_j, B]\}.$$

In a similar manner, a transition that consists of changing the state and performing two additional actions can be replaced with a sequence of two atomic transitions. Removing all nonatomic transitions produces an equivalent atomic PDA.   ∎

An extended transition is an operation on a PDA that pushes a string of elements, rather than just a single element, onto the stack. The transition $[q_j, BCD] \in \delta(q_i, u, A)$ pushes BCD onto the stack with B becoming the new stack top. The apparent generalization does not increase the set of languages accepted by pushdown automata. A PDA containing extended transitions is called an **extended** PDA. Each extended PDA can be converted into an equivalent PDA in the sense of Definition 8.1.1.

To construct a PDA from an extended PDA, extended transitions are converted to a sequence of transitions each of which pushes a single stack element. A transition that pushes k elements requires $k - 1$ additional states to push the elements in the correct order. The sequence of transitions

$$[p_1, D] \in \delta(q_i, u, A)$$
$$\delta(p_1, \lambda, \lambda) = \{[p_2, C]\}$$
$$\delta(p_2, \lambda, \lambda) = \{[q_j, B]\}$$

pushes the string BCD onto the stack and leaves the machine in state q_j. This produces the same result as the single extended transition $[q_j, BCD] \in \delta(q_i, u, A)$. The preceding argument yields Theorem 8.2.2.

Theorem 8.2.2
Let M be an extended PDA. Then there is a PDA M' such that L(M') = L(M).

Example 8.2.1
Let $L = \{a^i b^{2i} \mid i \geq 1\}$. A PDA, an atomic PDA, and an extended PDA are constructed to accept L. The input alphabet $\{a, b\}$, stack alphabet $\{A\}$, and accepting state q_1 are the same for each automaton.

PDA	Atomic PDA	Extended PDA
$Q = \{q_0, q_1, q_2\}$	$Q = \{q_0, q_1, q_2, q_3, q_4\}$	$Q = \{q_0, q_1\}$
$\delta(q_0, a, \lambda) = \{[q_2, A]\}$	$\delta(q_0, a, \lambda) = \{[q_3, \lambda]\}$	$\delta(q_0, a, \lambda) = \{[q_0, AA]\}$
$\delta(q_2, \lambda, \lambda) = \{[q_0, A]\}$	$\delta(q_3, \lambda, \lambda) = \{[q_2, A]\}$	$\delta(q_0, b, A) = \{[q_1, \lambda]\}$
$\delta(q_0, b, A) = \{[q_1, \lambda]\}$	$\delta(q_2, \lambda, \lambda) = \{[q_0, A]\}$	$\delta(q_1, b, A) = \{[q_1, \lambda]\}$
$\delta(q_1, b, A) = \{[q_1, \lambda]\}$	$\delta(q_0, b, \lambda) = \{[q_4, \lambda]\}$	
	$\delta(q_4, \lambda, A) = \{[q_1, \lambda]\}$	
	$\delta(q_1, b, \lambda) = \{[q_4, \lambda]\}$	

□

By Definition 8.1.2, input is accepted if there is a computation that processes the entire string and terminates in an accepting state with an empty stack. This type of acceptance is referred to as acceptance by final state and empty stack. We will show that defining acceptance in terms of the final state or the configuration of the stack alone does not change the set of languages recognized by pushdown automata.

A string w is accepted by **final state** if there is a computation $[q_0, w, \lambda] \vdash^* [q_i, \lambda, \alpha]$ where q_i is an accepting state and $\alpha \in \Gamma^*$, that is, a computation that processes the input and terminates in an accepting state. A language accepted by final state is denoted L_F.

Lemma 8.2.3

Let L be a language accepted by a PDA M $= (Q, \Sigma, \Gamma, \delta, q_0, F)$ with acceptance defined by final state. Then there is a PDA that accepts L by final state and empty stack.

Proof   A PDA M$' = (Q \cup \{q_f\}, \Sigma, \Gamma, \delta', q_0, \{q_f\})$ is constructed from M by adding a state q_f and transitions for q_f. Intuitively, a computation in M$'$ that accepts a string should be identical to one in M except for the addition of transitions that empty the stack. The transition function δ' is constructed by augmenting δ with the transitions

$$\delta'(q_i, \lambda, \lambda) = \{[q_f, \lambda]\} \quad \text{for all } q_i \in F$$
$$\delta'(q_f, \lambda, A) = \{[q_f, \lambda]\} \quad \text{for all } A \in \Gamma.$$

Let $[q_0, w, \lambda] \vdash^*_M [q_i, \lambda, \alpha]$ be a computation accepting w by final state. In M$'$, this computation is completed by entering the accepting state q_f and emptying the stack.

$$[q_0, w, \lambda]$$
$$\vdash^*_{M'} [q_i, \lambda, \alpha]$$
$$\vdash_{M'} [q_f, \lambda, \alpha]$$
$$\vdash^*_{M'} [q_f, \lambda, \lambda]$$

We must also guarantee that the new transitions do not cause M$'$ to accept strings that are not in L(M). The only accepting state of M$'$ is q_f, which can be entered from any accepting state of M. The transitions for q_f pop the stack but do not process input. Entering q_f with unprocessed input results in an unsuccessful computation.   □

A string w is said to be accepted by **empty stack** if there is a computation $[q_0, w, \lambda] \vdash^* [q_i, \lambda, \lambda]$. No restriction is imposed on the halting state q_i. The language accepted by a PDA M by empty stack is denoted $L_E(M)$.

Lemma 8.2.4

Let L be a language accepted by a PDA M $= (Q, \Sigma, \Gamma, \delta, q_0, F)$ with acceptance defined by empty stack. Then there is a PDA that accepts L by final state and empty stack.

Proof   Define M$' = (Q, \Sigma, \Gamma, \delta, q_0, Q)$ to be identical to M except that all the states of M$'$ are final states. Every computation of M that terminates in an empty stack also terminates in a final state in M$'$. Hence $L_E(M) = L(M')$.   ■

Lemmas 8.2.3 and 8.2.4 show that every language accepted by final state or empty stack is also accepted by final state and empty stack. Clearly, any language accepted by final state and empty stack is accepted by a pushdown automaton using the less restrictive forms of acceptance. These observations yield the following theorem.

Theorem 8.2.5

The following three conditions are equivalent:

i) The language L is accepted by some PDA.

ii) There is a PDA M_1 with $L_F(M_1) = L$.

iii) There is a PDA M_2 with $L_E(M_2) = L$.

8.3   Pushdown Automata and Context-Free Languages

The variations of the pushdown automaton illustrate the robustness of acceptance using a stack memory. The characterization of pushdown automata as acceptors of context-free languages is established by developing a correspondence between computations in a PDA and derivations in a context-free grammar.

First we prove that every context-free language is accepted by an extended PDA. To accomplish this, the rules of the grammar are used to generate the transitions of an equivalent PDA. Let L be a context-free language and G a grammar in Greibach normal form with L(G) = L. The rules of G, except for $S \rightarrow \lambda$, have the form $A \rightarrow aA_1A_2 \ldots A_n$. In a leftmost derivation, the variables A_i must be processed in a left-to-right manner. Pushing $A_1A_2 \ldots A_n$ onto the stack stores the variables in the order required by the derivation.

The Greibach normal form grammar G that accepts $\{a^ib^i \mid i > 0\}$ is used to illustrate the construction of an equivalent PDA.

$$G: S \rightarrow aAB \mid aB$$
$$A \rightarrow aAB \mid aB$$
$$B \rightarrow b$$

The PDA has two states: a start state q_0 and an accepting state q_1. An S rule of the form $S \rightarrow aA_1A_2 \ldots A_n$ generates a transition that processes the terminal symbol a, pushes the variables $A_1A_2 \ldots A_n$ onto the stack, and enters state q_1. The remainder of the computation uses the input symbol and the stack top to determine the appropriate transition. The transition function of the PDA is defined directly from the rules of G.

$$\delta(q_0, a, \lambda) = \{[q_1, AB], [q_1, B]\}$$
$$\delta(q_1, a, A) = \{[q_1, AB], [q_1, B]\}$$
$$\delta(q_1, b, B) = \{[q_1, \lambda]\}$$

The computation obtained by processing *aaabbb* exhibits the correspondence between derivations in the Greibach normal form grammar and computations in the associated PDA.

$$
\begin{array}{ll}
S \Rightarrow aAB & [q_0, aaabbb, \lambda] \vdash [q_1, aabbb, AB] \\
 \Rightarrow aaABB & \vdash [q_1, abbb, ABB] \\
 \Rightarrow aaaBBB & \vdash [q_1, bbb, BBB] \\
 \Rightarrow aaabBB & \vdash [q_1, bb, BB] \\
 \Rightarrow aaabbB & \vdash [q_1, b, B] \\
 \Rightarrow aaabbb & \vdash [q_1, \lambda, \lambda]
\end{array}
$$

The derivation generates a string consisting of a prefix of terminals followed by a suffix of variables. Processing an input symbol corresponds to its generation in the derivation. The stack of the PDA contains the variables in the derived string.

Theorem 8.3.1

Let L be a context-free language. Then there is a PDA that accepts L.

Proof   Let $G = (V, \Sigma, P, S)$ be a grammar in Greibach normal form that generates L. An extended PDA M with start state q_0 is defined by

$$
\begin{aligned}
Q_M &= \{q_0, q_1\} \\
\Sigma_M &= \Sigma \\
\Gamma_M &= V - \{S\} \\
F_M &= \{q_1\}
\end{aligned}
$$

with transitions

$$
\begin{aligned}
\delta(q_0, a, \lambda) &= \{[q_1, w] \mid S \to aw \in P\} \\
\delta(q_1, a, A) &= \{[q_1, w] \mid A \to aw \in P \text{ and } A \in V - \{S\}\} \\
\delta(q_0, \lambda, \lambda) &= \{[q_1, \lambda]\} \text{ if } S \to \lambda \in P.
\end{aligned}
$$

We first show that $L \subseteq L(M)$. Let $S \overset{*}{\Rightarrow} uw$ be a derivation with $u \in \Sigma^+$ and $w \in V^*$. We will prove that there is a computation

$$
[q_0, u, \lambda] \overset{*}{\vdash} [q_1, \lambda, w]
$$

in M. The proof is by induction on the length of the derivation and utilizes the correspondence between derivations in G and computations in M.

The basis consists of derivations $S \Rightarrow aw$ of length one. The transition generated by the rule $S \to aw$ yields the desired computation. Assume that for all strings uw generated by derivations $S \overset{n}{\Rightarrow} uw$ there is a computation

$$
[q_0, u, \lambda] \overset{*}{\vdash} [q_1, \lambda, w] \text{ in M.}
$$

Now let $S \overset{n+1}{\Longrightarrow} uw$ be a derivation with $u = va \in \Sigma^+$ and $w \in V^*$. This derivation can be written

$$
S \overset{n}{\Rightarrow} vAw_2 \Rightarrow uw
$$

where $w = w_1 w_2$ and $A \to a w_1$ is a rule in P. The inductive hypothesis and the transition $[q_1, w_1] \in \delta(q_1, a, A)$ combine to produce the computation

$$[q_0, va, \lambda] \overset{*}{\vdash} [q_1, a, A w_2]$$
$$\vdash [q_1, \lambda, w_1 w_2].$$

For every string u in L of positive length, the acceptance of u is exhibited by the computation in M corresponding to the derivation $S \overset{*}{\Rightarrow} u$. If $\lambda \in$ L, then $S \to \lambda$ is a rule of G and the computation $[q_0, \lambda, \lambda] \vdash [q_1, \lambda, \lambda]$ accepts the null string.

The opposite inclusion, $L(M) \subseteq L$, is established by showing that for every computation $[q_0, u, \lambda] \overset{*}{\vdash} [q_1, \lambda, w]$ there is a corresponding derivation $S \overset{*}{\Rightarrow} uw$ in G. The proof is also by induction and is left as an exercise.   ∎

To complete the categorization of context-free languages as precisely those accepted by pushdown automata, we must show that every language accepted by a PDA is context-free. The rules of a grammar are constructed from the transitions of the automaton. The grammar is designed so that the application of a rule corresponds to a transition in the PDA. Let $M = (Q, \Sigma, \Gamma, \delta, q_0, F)$ be a PDA. An extended PDA M' with transition function δ' is constructed from M by augmenting δ with the transitions

i) $\delta'(q_i, u, A) = \{[q_j, A] \mid A \in \Gamma\}$ whenever $[q_j, \lambda] \in \delta(q_i, u, \lambda)$

ii) $\delta'(q_i, u, A) = \{[q_j, BA] \mid A \in \Gamma\}$ whenever $[q_j, B] \in \delta(q_i, u, \lambda)$.

The interpretation of these transitions is that a transition of M that does not remove an element from the stack can be considered to initially pop the stack and later replace the stack top. Any string accepted by a computation that utilizes a new transition can also be obtained by applying the original transition; hence, $L(M) = L(M')$.

A grammar $G = (V, \Sigma, P, S)$ is constructed from the transitions of M'. The alphabet of G is the input alphabet of M'. The variables of G consist of a start symbol S and objects of the form $\langle q_i, A, q_j \rangle$ where the q's are states of M' and $A \in \Gamma \cup \{\lambda\}$. The variable $\langle q_i, A, q_j \rangle$ represents a computation that begins in state q_i, ends in q_j, and removes the symbol A from the stack. The rules of G are constructed as follows:

1. $S \to \langle q_0, \lambda, q_j \rangle$ for each $q_j \in F$.

2. Each transition $[q_j, B] \in \delta(q_i, x, A)$, where $A \in \Gamma \cup \{\lambda\}$, generates the set of rules

$$\{\langle q_i, A, q_k \rangle \to x \langle q_j, B, q_k \rangle \mid q_k \in Q\}.$$

3. Each transition $[q_j, BA] \in \delta(q_i, x, A)$, where $A \in \Gamma$, generates the set of rules

$$\{\langle q_i, A, q_k \rangle \to x \langle q_j, B, q_n \rangle \langle q_n, A, q_k \rangle \mid q_k, q_n \in Q\}.$$

4. For each state $q_k \in Q$,

$$\langle q_k, \lambda, q_k \rangle \to \lambda.$$

A derivation begins with a rule of type 1 whose right-hand side represents a computation that begins in state q_0, ends in a final state, and terminates with an empty stack, in other words, a successful computation in M'. Rules of types 2 and 3 trace the action of the machine. Rules of type 3 correspond to the extended transitions of M'. In a computation, these transitions increase the size of the stack. The effect of the corresponding rule is to introduce an additional variable into the derivation.

Rules of type 4 are used to terminate derivations. The rule $\langle q_k, \lambda, q_k \rangle \rightarrow \lambda$ represents a computation from a state q_k to itself that does not alter the stack, that is, the null computation.

Example 8.3.1

A grammar G is constructed from the PDA M. The language of M is the set $\{a^n cb^n \mid n \geq 0\}$.

$$M: Q = \{q_0, q_1\} \qquad \delta(q_0, a, \lambda) = \{[q_0, A]\}$$
$$\Sigma = \{a, b, c\} \qquad \delta(q_0, c, \lambda) = \{[q_1, \lambda]\}$$
$$\Gamma = \{A\} \qquad \delta(q_1, b, A) = \{[q_1, \lambda]\}$$
$$F = \{q_1\}$$

The transitions $\delta(q_0, a, A) = \{[q_0, AA]\}$ and $\delta(q_0, c, A) = \{[q_1, A]\}$ are added to M to construct M'. The rules of the grammar G are given below, preceded by the transition from which they were constructed.

Transition	Rule
	$S \rightarrow \langle q_0, \lambda, q_1 \rangle$
$\delta(q_0, a, \lambda) = \{[q_0, A]\}$	$\langle q_0, \lambda, q_0 \rangle \rightarrow a \langle q_0, A, q_0 \rangle$
	$\langle q_0, \lambda, q_1 \rangle \rightarrow a \langle q_0, A, q_1 \rangle$
$\delta(q_0, a, A) = \{[q_0, AA]\}$	$\langle q_0, A, q_0 \rangle \rightarrow a \langle q_0, A, q_0 \rangle \langle q_0, A, q_0 \rangle$
	$\langle q_0, A, q_1 \rangle \rightarrow a \langle q_0, A, q_0 \rangle \langle q_0, A, q_1 \rangle$
	$\langle q_0, A, q_0 \rangle \rightarrow a \langle q_0, A, q_1 \rangle \langle q_1, A, q_0 \rangle$
	$\langle q_0, A, q_1 \rangle \rightarrow a \langle q_0, A, q_1 \rangle \langle q_1, A, q_1 \rangle$
$\delta(q_0, c, \lambda) = \{[q_1, \lambda]\}$	$\langle q_0, \lambda, q_0 \rangle \rightarrow c \langle q_1, \lambda, q_0 \rangle$
	$\langle q_0, \lambda, q_1 \rangle \rightarrow c \langle q_1, \lambda, q_1 \rangle$
$\delta(q_0, c, A) = \{[q_1, A]\}$	$\langle q_0, A, q_0 \rangle \rightarrow c \langle q_1, A, q_0 \rangle$
	$\langle q_0, A, q_1 \rangle \rightarrow c \langle q_1, A, q_1 \rangle$
$\delta(q_1, b, A) = \{[q_1, \lambda]\}$	$\langle q_1, A, q_0 \rangle \rightarrow b \langle q_1, \lambda, q_0 \rangle$
	$\langle q_1, A, q_1 \rangle \rightarrow b \langle q_1, \lambda, q_1 \rangle$
	$\langle q_0, \lambda, q_0 \rangle \rightarrow \lambda$
	$\langle q_1, \lambda, q_1 \rangle \rightarrow \lambda$

The relationship between computations in a PDA and derivations in the associated grammar are demonstrated using the grammar and PDA of Example 8.3.1. The derivation begins with the application of an S rule; the remaining steps correspond to the processing of an input symbol in M'. The first component of the leftmost variable contains the state of the computation. The third component of the rightmost variable contains the accepting state in which the computation will terminate. The stack can be retrieved from the second component of the variables.

$$
\begin{array}{ll}
[q_0, aacbb, \lambda] & S \Rightarrow \langle q_0, \lambda, q_1 \rangle \\
\vdash [q_0, acbb, A] & \Rightarrow a \langle q_0, A, q_1 \rangle \\
\vdash [q_0, cbb, AA] & \Rightarrow aa \langle q_0, A, q_1 \rangle \langle q_1, A, q_1 \rangle \\
\vdash [q_1, bb, AA] & \Rightarrow aac \langle q_1, A, q_1 \rangle \langle q_1, A, q_1 \rangle \\
\vdash [q_1, b, A] & \Rightarrow aacb \langle q_1, \lambda, q_1 \rangle \langle q_1, A, q_1 \rangle \\
& \Rightarrow aacb \langle q_1, A, q_1 \rangle \\
\vdash [q_1, \lambda, \lambda] & \Rightarrow aacbb \langle q_1, \lambda, q_1 \rangle \\
& \Rightarrow aacbb
\end{array}
$$

The variable $\langle q_0, \lambda, q_1 \rangle$, obtained by the application of the S rule, indicates that a computation from state q_0 to state q_1 that does not alter the stack is required. The result of subsequent rule application signals the need for a computation from q_0 to q_1 that removes an A from the top of the stack. The fourth rule application demonstrates the necessity for augmenting the transitions of M when δ contains transitions that do not remove a symbol from the stack. The application of the rule $\langle q_0, A, q_1 \rangle \rightarrow c \langle q_1, A, q_1 \rangle$ represents a computation that processes c without removing the A from the top of the stack.

Theorem 8.3.2
Let M be a PDA. Then there is a context-free grammar G with L(G) = L(M).

The grammar G is constructed as outlined above from the extended PDA M'. We must show that there is a derivation $S \overset{*}{\Rightarrow} w$ if, and only if, $[q_0, w, \lambda] \overset{*}{\vdash} [q_j, \lambda, \lambda]$ for some $q_j \in F$. This follows from Lemmas 8.3.3 and 8.3.4, which establish the correspondence of derivations in G to computations in M'.

Lemma 8.3.3
If $\langle q_i, A, q_j \rangle \overset{*}{\Rightarrow} w$ where $w \in \Sigma^*$ and $A \in \Gamma \cup \{\lambda\}$, then $[q_i, w, A] \overset{*}{\vdash} [q_j, \lambda, \lambda]$.

Proof   The proof is by induction on the length of derivations of terminal strings from variables of the form $\langle q_i, A, q_j \rangle$. The basis consists of derivations of strings consisting of a single rule application. The null string is the only terminal string derivable with one rule application. The derivation has the form $\langle q_i, \lambda, q_i \rangle \Rightarrow \lambda$ utilizing a rule of type 4. The null computation in state q_i yields $[q_i, \lambda, \lambda] \overset{*}{\vdash} [q_i, \lambda, \lambda]$ as desired.

Assume that there is a computation $[q_i, v, A] \overset{*}{\vdash} [q_j, \lambda, \lambda]$ whenever $\langle q_i, A, q_j \rangle \overset{n}{\Rightarrow} v$. Let w be a terminal string derivable from $\langle q_i, A, q_j \rangle$ by a derivation of length $n + 1$. The first step of the derivation consists of the application of a rule of type 2 or 3. A derivation initiated by a rule of type 2 can be written

$$\langle q_i, A, q_j \rangle \Rightarrow u \langle q_k, B, q_j \rangle$$
$$\overset{n}{\Rightarrow} uv = w$$

where $\langle q_i, A, q_j \rangle \to u \langle q_k, B, q_j \rangle$ is a rule of G. By the inductive hypothesis, there is a computation $[q_k, v, B] \overset{*}{\vdash} [q_j, \lambda, \lambda]$ corresponding to the derivation $\langle q_k, B, q_j \rangle \overset{n}{\Rightarrow} v$.

The rule $\langle q_i, A, q_j \rangle \to u \langle q_k, B, q_j \rangle$ in G is generated by a transition $[q_k, B] \in \delta(q_i, u, A)$. Combining this transition with the computation established by the inductive hypothesis yields

$$[q_i, uv, A] \vdash [q_k, v, B]$$
$$\overset{*}{\vdash} [q_j, \lambda, \lambda].$$

If the first step of the derivation is a rule of type 3, the derivation can be written

$$\langle q_i, A, q_j \rangle \Rightarrow u \langle q_k, B, q_n \rangle \langle q_n, A, q_j \rangle$$
$$\overset{n}{\Rightarrow} w.$$

The corresponding computation is constructed from the transition $[q_k, BA] \in \delta(q_i, u, A)$ and two invocations of the inductive hypothesis.   ∎

Lemma 8.3.4
If $[q_i, w, A] \overset{*}{\vdash} [q_j, \lambda, \lambda]$ where $A \in \Gamma \cup \{\lambda\}$, then there is a derivation $\langle q_i, A, q_j \rangle \overset{*}{\Rightarrow} w$.

Proof   The null computation from configuration $[q_i, \lambda, \lambda]$ is the only computation of M that uses no transitions. The corresponding derivation consists of a single application of the rule $\langle q_i, \lambda, q_i \rangle \to \lambda$.

Assume that every computation $[q_i, v, A] \overset{n}{\vdash} [q_j, \lambda, \lambda]$ has a corresponding derivation $\langle q_i, A, q_j \rangle \overset{*}{\Rightarrow} v$ in G. Consider a computation of length $n + 1$. A computation beginning with a nonextended transition can be written

$$[q_i, w, A]$$
$$\vdash [q_k, v, B]$$
$$\overset{n}{\vdash} [q_j, \lambda, \lambda]$$

where $w = uv$ and $[q_k, B] \in \delta(q_i, u, A)$. By the inductive hypothesis there is a derivation $\langle q_k, B, q_j \rangle \overset{*}{\Rightarrow} v$. The first transition generates the rule $\langle q_i, A, q_j \rangle \to u \langle q_k, B, q_j \rangle$ in G. Hence a derivation of w from $\langle q_i, A, q_j \rangle$ can be obtained by

$$\langle q_i, A, q_j \rangle \Rightarrow u \langle q_k, B, q_j \rangle$$
$$\overset{*}{\Rightarrow} uv.$$

A computation in M′ beginning with an extended transition $[q_j, BA] \in \delta(q_i, u, A)$ has the form

$$[q_i, w, A]$$
$$\vdash [q_k, v, BA]$$
$$\overset{*}{\vdash} [q_m, y, A]$$
$$\overset{*}{\vdash} [q_j, \lambda, \lambda].$$

where $w = uv$ and $v = xy$. The rule $\langle q_i, A, q_j \rangle \rightarrow u \langle q_k, B, q_m \rangle \langle q_m, A, q_j \rangle$ is generated by the first transition of the computation. By the inductive hypothesis, G contains derivations

$$\langle q_k, B, q_m \rangle \overset{*}{\Rightarrow} x$$
$$\langle q_m, A, q_j \rangle \overset{*}{\Rightarrow} y.$$

Combining these derivations with the preceding rule produces a derivation of w from $\langle q_i, A, q_j \rangle$.   ∎

Proof of Theorem 8.3.2   Let w be any string in L(G) with derivation $S \Rightarrow \langle q_0, \lambda, q_j \rangle \overset{*}{\Rightarrow} w$. By Lemma 8.3.2, there is a computation $[q_0, w, \lambda] \overset{*}{\underset{M'}{\vdash}} [q_j, \lambda, \lambda]$ exhibiting the acceptance of w by M'.

Conversely, if $w \in L(M) = L(M')$ then there is a computation $[q_0, w, \lambda] \overset{*}{\vdash} [q_j, \lambda, \lambda]$ that accepts w. Lemma 8.3.3 establishes the existence of a corresponding derivation $\langle q_0, \lambda, q_j \rangle \overset{*}{\Rightarrow} w$ in G. Since q_j is an accepting state, G contains a rule $S \rightarrow \langle q_0, \lambda, q_j \rangle$. Initiating the previous derivation with this rule generates w in the grammar G.   ∎

8.4   The Pumping Lemma for Context-Free Languages

The pumping lemma establishes a periodicity property for strings in context-free languages. Recursive derivations in a context-free grammar have the form $A \overset{*}{\Rightarrow} uAv$. Derivation trees are used to establish conditions that ensure the presence of recursive subderivations in derivations of sufficiently long strings. Throughout this section the grammars are assumed to be in Chomsky normal form. With this assumption, the derivation of every string in the language can be represented as a binary tree.

Lemma 8.4.1
Let G be a context-free grammar in Chomsky normal form and $A \overset{*}{\Rightarrow} w$ a derivation of $w \in \Sigma^*$ with derivation tree T. If the depth of T is n, then $length(w) \leq 2^{n-1}$.

Proof   The proof is by induction on the depth of the derivation tree. Since G is in Chomsky normal form, a derivation tree of depth one that represents the generation of a terminal string must have one of the following two forms.

In either case, the length of the derived string is less than or equal to 2^0 as required.

Assume that the property holds of all derivation trees of depth n or less. Let $A \overset{*}{\Rightarrow} w$ be a derivation with tree T of depth $n + 1$. The derivation can be written $A \Rightarrow BC \overset{*}{\Rightarrow} uv$

where $B \overset{*}{\Rightarrow} u$, $C \overset{*}{\Rightarrow} v$, and $w = uv$. The derivation tree of $A \overset{*}{\Rightarrow} w$ is constructed from T_B and T_C, the derivation trees $B \overset{*}{\Rightarrow} u$ and $C \overset{*}{\Rightarrow} v$.

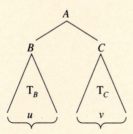

The trees T_B and T_C both have depth n or less. By the inductive hypothesis, $length(u) \leqslant 2^{n-1}$ and $length(v) \leqslant 2^{n-1}$. Therefore, $length(w) = length(uv) \leqslant 2^n$. ∎

Corollary 8.4.2
Let $G = (V, \Sigma, P, S)$ be a context-free grammar in Chomsky normal form and $S \overset{*}{\Rightarrow} w$ a derivation of $w \in L(G)$. If $length(w) \geqslant 2^n$, then the derivation tree has depth at least $n+1$.

Theorem 8.4.3 (Pumping Lemma for Context-Free Languages)
Let L be a context-free language. There is a number k, depending on L, such that any string $z \in L$ with $length(z) > k$ can be written $z = uvwxy$ where

i) $length(vwx) \leqslant k$

ii) $length(v) + length(x) > 0$

iii) $uv^iwx^iy \in L$, for $i \geqslant 0$.

Proof Let $G = (V, \Sigma, P, S)$ be a Chomsky normal form grammar that generates L and let $n = card(V)$. We show that all strings in L with length 2^n or greater can be decomposed to satisfy the conditions of the pumping lemma. Let $z \in L(G)$ be such a string and $S \overset{*}{\Rightarrow} z$ a derivation in G. By the corollary, there is a path of length at least $n+1 = card(V) + 1$ in the derivation tree. Since this path consists of $n+2$ nodes, only one of which is a terminal symbol, the pigeonhole principle guarantees that some variable A must occur twice in this path. The derivation tree can be divided into subtrees as follows:

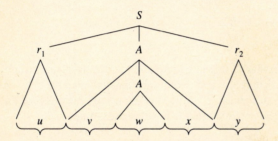

The derivation of z consists of the subderivations

1. $S \overset{*}{\Rightarrow} r_1 A r_2$
2. $r_1 \overset{*}{\Rightarrow} u$
3. $A \overset{*}{\Rightarrow} vAx$
4. $A \overset{*}{\Rightarrow} w$
5. $r_2 \overset{*}{\Rightarrow} y$.

Subderivation 3 may be omitted or be repeated any number of times before applying subderivation 4. The resulting derivations generate the strings $uv^i wx^i y \in L(G) = L$. ∎

Like its counterpart for regular languages, the pumping lemma provides a tool for demonstrating that languages are not context-free.

Example 8.4.1

The language $L = \{a^i b^i c^i \mid i \geq 0\}$ is not context-free. Assume L is context-free. By Theorem 8.4.1, the string $w = a^k b^k c^k$, where k is the number specified by the pumping lemma, can be decomposed into substrings $uvwxy$ that satisfy the repetition properties. Consider the possibilities for the substrings v and x. If either of these contains more than one type of terminal symbol then $uv^2 wx^2 y$ contains a b preceding an a or a c preceding a b. In either case, the resulting string is not in L.

By the previous observation, v and x must be substrings of one of a^k, b^k, or c^k. Since at most one of the strings v and x is null, $uv^2 wx^2 y$ increases the number of at least one, maybe two, but not all three types of terminal symbols. This implies that $uv^2 wx^2 y \notin L$. Thus there is no decomposition of $a^k b^k c^k$ satisfying the conditions of the pumping lemma; consequently, L is not context-free. □

Example 8.4.2

The language $L = \{a^i b^j a^i b^j \mid i, j \geq 0\}$ is not context-free. Let k be the number specified by the pumping lemma and $z = a^k b^k a^k b^k$. Assume there is a decomposition $uvwxy$ of z that satisfies the conditions of the pumping lemma. Condition ii) requires the length of vwx to be at most k. This implies that vwx is a string containing only one type of terminal or the concatenation of two such strings. That is,

i) $vwx \in a^*$ or $vwx \in b^*$
ii) $vwx \in a^* b^*$ or $vwx \in b^* a^*$.

By an argument similar to that in Example 8.4.1, the substrings v and x contain only one type of terminal. Pumping v and x increases the number of a's or b's in only one of the substrings in z. Since there is no decomposition of z satisfying the conditions of the pumping lemma, we conclude that L is not context-free. □

Example 8.4.3

The language $L = \{w \in a^* \mid length(w)$ is prime$\}$ is not context-free. Assume L is context-free and n a prime greater than k, the constant of Theorem 8.4.3. The string a^n must have a decomposition $uvwxy$ that satisfies the conditions of the pumping lemma. Let $m = length(u) + length(w) + length(y)$. The length of $uv^iwx^iy = m + i(n - m)$.

In particular, $length(uv^mwx^my) = m + m(n - m) = m(1 + n - m)$. Since the length of uv^mwx^my is not prime, the string is not in L. Thus, L is not context-free.   □

8.5   Closure Properties of Context-Free Languages

The flexibility of the rules of context-free grammars is used to establish closure results for the set of context-free languages. Operations that preserve context-free languages provide another tool for proving that languages are context-free. These operations, combined with the pumping lemma, can also be used to show that certain languages are not context-free.

Theorem 8.5.1
The set of context-free languages is closed under the operations union, concatenation, and Kleene star.

Proof   Let L_1 and L_2 be two context-free languages generated by $G_1 = (V_1, \Sigma_1, P_1, S_1)$ and $G_2 = (V_2, \Sigma_2, P_2, S_2)$, respectively. The sets V_1 and V_2 of variables are assumed to be disjoint. Since we may rename variables, this assumption imposes no restriction on the grammars.

A context-free grammar will be constructed from G_1 and G_2 which establishes the desired closure property.

i) Union: Define $G = (V_1 \cup V_2 \cup \{S\}, \Sigma_1 \cup \Sigma_2, P_1 \cup P_2 \cup \{S \to S_1 \mid S_2\}, S)$. A string w is in L(G) if, and only if, there is a derivation $S \Rightarrow S_i \overset{*}{\underset{G_i}{\Rightarrow}} w$ for $i = 1$ or 2. Thus w is in L_1 or L_2. On the other hand, any derivation $S_i \overset{*}{\underset{G_i}{\Rightarrow}} w$ can be initialized with the rule $S \to S_i$ to generate w in G.

ii) Concatenation: Define $G = (V_1 \cup V_2 \cup \{S\}, \Sigma_1 \cup \Sigma_2, P_1 \cup P_2 \cup \{S \to S_1S_2\}, S)$. The start symbol initiates derivations in both G_1 and G_2. A leftmost derivation of a terminal string in G has the form $S \Rightarrow S_1S_2 \overset{*}{\Rightarrow} uS_2 \overset{*}{\Rightarrow} uv$ where $u \in L_1$ and $v \in L_2$. The derivation of u uses only rules from P_1 and v rules from P_2. Hence $L(G) \subseteq L_1L_2$. The opposite inclusion is established by observing that every string w in L_1L_2 can be written uv with $u \in L_1$ and $v \in L_2$. The derivations $S_1 \overset{*}{\underset{G_1}{\Rightarrow}} u$ and $S_2 \overset{*}{\underset{G_2}{\Rightarrow}} v$ along with the S rule of G generate w in G.

iii) Kleene star: Define $G = (V_1, \Sigma_1, P_1 \cup \{S \to S_1S \mid \lambda\}, S)$. The S rule of G generates any number of copies of S_1. Each of these, in turn, initiates the derivation of a string in L_1. The concatenation of any number of strings from L_1 yields L_1^*.   ∎

Theorem 8.5.1 presented positive closure results for the set of context-free languages. A simple example is given to show that the context-free languages are not closed under intersection. Finally, we combine the closure properties of union and intersection to obtain a similar negative result for complementation.

Theorem 8.5.2

The set of context-free languages is not closed under intersection or complementation.

Proof

i) Intersection: Let $L_1 = \{a^i b^i c^j \mid i, j \geq 0\}$ and $L_1 = \{a^j b^i c^i \mid i, j \geq 0\}$. L_1 and L_2 are both context-free, since they are generated by G_1 and G_2, respectively.

$$G_1: S \rightarrow BC \qquad\qquad G_2: S \rightarrow AB$$
$$B \rightarrow aBb \mid \lambda \qquad\qquad A \rightarrow aA \mid \lambda$$
$$C \rightarrow cC \mid \lambda \qquad\qquad B \rightarrow bBc \mid \lambda$$

The intersection of L_1 and L_2 is the set $\{a^i b^i c^i \mid i \geq 0\}$, which, by Example 8.4.1, is not context-free.

ii) Complementation: Let L_1 and L_2 be any two context-free languages. If the context-free languages are closed under complementation, then, using Theorem 8.5.1, the language

$$L = \overline{\overline{L_1} \cup \overline{L_2}}$$

is context-free. By DeMorgan's law, $L = L_1 \cap L_2$. This implies that the context-free languages are closed under intersection, contradicting the result of part i).   ∎

Theorem 7.4.4 demonstrated that the intersection of a regular and context-free language need not be regular. The correspondence between languages and automata is used to establish a positive closure property for the intersection of regular and context-free languages.

Let R be a regular language accepted by a DFA N and L a context-free language accepted by PDA M. We show that $R \cap L$ is context-free by constructing a single PDA that simulates the operation of both N and M. The states of this composite machine are ordered pairs consisting of a state from M and one from N.

Theorem 8.5.3

Let R be a regular language and L a context-free language. Then the language $R \cap L$ is context-free.

Proof   Let $N = (Q_N, \Sigma_N, \delta_N, q_0, F_N)$ be a DFA that accepts R and $M = (Q_M, \Sigma_M, \Gamma, \delta_M, p_0, F_M)$ a PDA that accepts L. The machines N and M are combined to construct a PDA

$$M' = (Q_M \times Q_N, \Sigma_M \cup \Sigma_N, \Gamma, \delta, [p_0, q_0], F_M \times F_N)$$

that accepts $R \cap L$. The transition function of M' is defined to "run the machines M and N in parallel." The first component of the ordered pair traces the sequence of states entered by the machine M and the second component by N. The transition function of M' is defined by

i) $\delta([p, q], a, A) = \{[[p', q'], B] \mid [p', B] \in \delta_M(p, a, A) \text{ and } \delta_N(q, a) = q'\}$

ii) $\delta([p, q], \lambda, A) = \{[[p', q], B] \mid [p', B] \in \delta_M(p, \lambda, A)\}.$

Every transition of a DFA processes an input symbol while a PDA may contain transitions that do not process input. The transitions introduced by condition ii) simulate the action of a PDA transition that does not process an input symbol.

A string w is accepted by M' if there is a computation

$$[[p_0, q_0], w, \lambda] \vdash^* [[p_i, q_j], \lambda, \lambda]$$

where p_i and q_j are final states of M and N, respectively.

The inclusion $L(N) \cap L(M) \subseteq L(M')$ is established by showing that there is a computation

$$[[p_0, q_0], w, \lambda] \vdash^*_{M'} [[p_i, q_j], u, \alpha]$$

whenever

$$[p_0, w, \lambda] \vdash^*_M [p_i, u, \alpha] \qquad \text{and} \qquad [q_0, w] \vdash^*_N [q_j, u]$$

are computations in M and N. The proof is by induction on the number of transitions in the PDA M.

The basis consists of the null computation in M. This computation terminates with $p_i = p_0$, $u = w$, and M containing an empty stack. The only computation in N that terminates with the original string is the null computation; thus, $q_j = q_0$. The corresponding computation in the composite machine is the null computation in M'.

Assume the result holds for all computations of M having length n. Let

$$[p_0, w, \lambda] \vdash^{n+1}_M [p_i, u, \alpha] \qquad \text{and} \qquad [q_0, w] \vdash^*_N [q_j, u]$$

be computations in the PDA and DFA, respectively. The computation in M can be written

$$
\begin{aligned}
&[p_0, w, \lambda] \\
\vdash^n\ &[p_k, v, \beta] \\
\vdash\ &[p_i, u, \alpha]
\end{aligned}
$$

where either $v = u$ or $v = au$. We consider each of the possibilities for v separately.

Case 1: $v = u$. In this case, the final transition of the computation in M does not process an input symbol. The computation in M is completed by a transition of the form $[p_i, B] \in \delta_M(p_k, \lambda, A)$. This transition generates $[[p_i, q_j], B] \in \delta([p_k, q_j], \lambda, A)$ in M'. The computation

$$
\begin{aligned}
&[[p_0, q_0], w, \lambda] \vdash^n_{M'} [[p_k, q_j], v, \beta] \\
& \vdash_{M'} [[p_i, q_j], v, \alpha]
\end{aligned}
$$

is obtained from the inductive hypothesis and the preceding transition of M'.

Case 2: $v = au$. The computation in N that reduces w to u can be written

$$[q_0, w]$$
$$\vdash_N^* [q_m, v]$$
$$\vdash_N [q_j, u]$$

where the final step utilizes a transition $\delta_N(q_m, a) = q_j$. The DFA and PDA transitions for input symbol a combine to generate the transition $[[p_i, q_j], B] \in \delta([p_k, q_m], a, A)$ in M'. Applying this transition to the result of the computation established by the inductive hypothesis produces

$$[[p_0, q_0], w, \lambda] \vdash_{M'}^n [[p_k, q_m], v, \beta]$$
$$\vdash_{M'} [[p_i, q_j], u, \alpha].$$

The opposite inclusion, $L(M') \subseteq L(N) \cap L(M)$, is proved using induction on the length of computations in M'. The proof is left as an exercise. ∎

Example 8.5.1

Let L be the language $\{ww \mid w \in \{a, b\}^*\}$. L is not context-free but $\overline{L}$ is.

i) Assume L is context-free. Then, by Theorem 8.5.2,

$$L \cap a^*b^*a^*b^* = \{a^ib^ja^ib^j \mid i, j \geq 0\}$$

is context-free. However, this language was shown not to be context-free in Example 8.4.2, contradicting our assumption.

ii) To show that $\overline{L}$ is context-free, we construct two context-free grammars G_1 and G_2 with $L(G_1) \cup L(G_2) = \overline{L}$.

$$G_1: S \rightarrow aA \mid bA \mid a \mid b \qquad\qquad G_2: S \rightarrow AB \mid BA$$
$$A \rightarrow aS \mid bS \qquad\qquad\qquad\qquad A \rightarrow ZAZ \mid a$$
$$B \rightarrow ZBZ \mid b$$
$$Z \rightarrow a \mid b$$

The grammar G_1 generates the strings of odd length over $\{a, b\}$, all of which are in $\overline{L}$. G_2 generates the set of even-length strings in $\overline{L}$. Such a string may be written $u_1xv_1u_2yv_2$ where $x, y \in \Sigma$ and $x \neq y$; $u_1, u_2, v_1, v_2 \in \Sigma^*$ with $length(u_1) = length(u_2)$ and $length(v_1) = length(v_2)$. Since the u's and v's are arbitrary strings in Σ^*, this characterization can be rewritten u_1xpqyv_2 where $length(p) = length(u_1)$ and $length(q) = length(v_2)$. The recursive variables of G_2 generate precisely this set of strings. □

8.6   A Two-Stack Automaton

Finite automata accept regular languages. Pushdown automata accept context-free languages. The increase in the set of languages accepted was due to the addition of a stack memory. Are two stacks, like two heads, better than one? In this section the notion of pushdown automata is extended to include machines with two stacks.

Definition 8.6.1
A **two-stack** PDA is structure $(Q, \Sigma, \Gamma, \delta, q_0, F)$. Q, Σ, Γ, q_0, and F are the same as in a one-stack PDA. The transition function maps $Q \times (\Sigma \cup \{\lambda\}) \times (\Gamma \cup \{\lambda\}) \times (\Gamma \cup \{\lambda\})$ to subsets of $Q \times (\Gamma \cup \{\lambda\}) \times (\Gamma \cup \{\lambda\})$.

A transition consults the state, the input symbol, and both stack tops. The action of a transition may alter any or all of these components. Unlike the alterations to PDAs proposed in Section 8.2, an additional stack enlarges the set of languages accepted. The interplay between the stacks allows the machine to retain a copy of the stack while using the other stack to process the input.

Example 8.6.1
The two-stack PDA defined below accepts the language $L = \{a^i b^i c^i \mid i \geq 0\}$. The first stack is used to match the a's and b's and the second the b's and c's.

$$Q = \{q_0, q_1, q_2\} \qquad \delta(q_0, \lambda, \lambda, \lambda) = \{[q_2, \lambda, \lambda]\}$$
$$\Sigma = \{a, b, c\} \qquad \delta(q_0, a, \lambda, \lambda) = \{[q_0, A, \lambda]\}$$
$$\Gamma = \{A\} \qquad \delta(q_0, b, A, \lambda) = \{[q_1, \lambda, A]\}$$
$$F = \{q_2\} \qquad \delta(q_1, b, A, \lambda) = \{[q_1, \lambda, A]\}$$
$$\delta(q_1, c, \lambda, A) = \{[q_2, \lambda, \lambda]\}$$
$$\delta(q_2, c, \lambda, A) = \{[q_2, \lambda, \lambda]\} \qquad \square$$

Clearly, every context-free language is accepted by a two-stack automaton. The acceptance of $\{a^i b^i c^i \mid i \geq 0\}$ by a two-stack automaton shows that the context-free languages comprise a proper subset of the languages accepted by two-stack PDAs.

Regular grammars recognize the strings a^i, pushdown automata $a^i b^i$, and two-stack pushdown automata $a^i b^i c^i$. Is yet another stack necessary to accept $a^i b^i c^i d^i$? Example 8.6.2 illustrates a technique by which two-stack automata can be used to recognize strings consisting of any number of substrings of equal length.

Example 8.6.2
The two-stack PDA M accepts the language $L = \{a^i b^i c^i d^i \mid i \geq 0\}$. The computations of M process the strings of L in the following manner:

i) Processing a pushes A onto stack one.

ii) Processing b pops A and pushes B onto stack two.

iii) Processing c pops B and pushes C onto stack one.

iv) Processing d pops C.

$$M: Q = \{q_0, q_1, q_2, q_3\}$$

$$\delta(q_0, \lambda, \lambda, \lambda) = \{[q_3, \lambda, \lambda]\}$$

$$\Sigma = \{a, b, c, d\} \qquad \delta(q_0, a, \lambda, \lambda) = \{[q_0, A, \lambda]\}$$

$$\Gamma = \{A, B, C\} \qquad \delta(q_0, b, A, \lambda) = \{[q_1, \lambda, B]\}$$

$$F = \{q_3\} \qquad \delta(q_1, b, A, \lambda) = \{[q_1, \lambda, B]\}$$

$$\delta(q_1, c, \lambda, B) = \{[q_2, C, \lambda]\}$$

$$\delta(q_2, c, \lambda, B) = \{[q_2, C, \lambda]\}$$

$$\delta(q_2, d, C, \lambda) = \{[q_3, \lambda, \lambda]\}$$

$$\delta(q_3, d, C, \lambda) = \{[q_3, \lambda, \lambda]\} \qquad \square$$

The languages accepted by two-stack automata include, but are not limited to, the context-free languages. Techniques developed in Chapter 9 will allow us to categorize the languages accepted by two-stack PDAs.

Exercises

1. Let M be the PDA

$$Q = \{q_0, q_1, q_2\} \qquad \delta(q_0, a, \lambda) = \{[q_0, A]\}$$

$$\Sigma = \{a, b\} \qquad \delta(q_0, \lambda, \lambda) = \{[q_1, \lambda]\}$$

$$\Gamma = \{A\} \qquad \delta(q_0, b, A) = \{[q_2, \lambda]\}$$

$$F = \{q_1, q_2\} \qquad \delta(q_1, \lambda, A) = \{[q_1, \lambda]\}$$

$$\delta(q_2, b, A) = \{[q_2, \lambda]\}$$

$$\delta(q_2, \lambda, A) = \{[q_2, \lambda]\}.$$

   a) Describe the language accepted by M.

   b) Trace all computations of the strings *aab, abb, aba* in M.

   c) Show that *aabb, aaab* $\in$ L(M).

2. Let M be the PDA in Example 8.1.3.

   a) Trace all computations of the strings *ab, abb, abbb* in M.

   b) Show that *aaaa, baab* $\in$ L(M).

   c) Show that *aaa, ab* $\notin$ L(M).

3. Construct a PDA that accepts each of the following languages.

   a) $\{a^i b^j \mid i \leqslant j\}$

   b) $\{a^i c^j b^i \mid i, j \geqslant 0\}$

   c) $\{a^i b^j c^k \mid i + k = j\}$

   d) $\{w \mid w \in \{a, b\}^* \text{ and } w \text{ has the same number of } a\text{'s and } b\text{'s}\}$

   e) $\{w \mid w \in \{a, b\}^* \text{ and } w \text{ has twice as many } a\text{'s as } b\text{'s}\}$

   f) $\{a^i b^i \mid i \geqslant 0\} \cup a^* \cup b^*$

g) $\{a^i b^j c^k \mid i = j \text{ or } j = k\}$

h) $\{a^i b^j \mid i \neq j\}$

i) $\{a^i b^j \mid i \leqslant j \leqslant 2i\}$

j) $\{a^{i+j} b^i c^j \mid i, j > 0\}$

k) the set of palindromes over $\{a, b\}$

4. Construct a PDA with only two stack elements that accepts the language

$$\{wdw^R \mid w \in \{a, b, c\}^*\}.$$

5. Use the technique of Theorem 8.3.1 to construct a PDA that accepts the language of the Greibach normal form grammar

$$S \rightarrow aABA \mid aBB$$
$$A \rightarrow bA \mid b$$
$$B \rightarrow cB \mid c.$$

6. Let M be the PDA

$$Q = \{q_0, q_1, q_2\} \qquad \delta(q_0, a, \lambda) = \{[q_0, A]\}$$
$$\Sigma = \{a, b\} \qquad \delta(q_0, b, A) = \{[q_1, \lambda]\}$$
$$\Gamma = \{A\} \qquad \delta(q_1, b, \lambda) = \{[q_2, \lambda]\}$$
$$F = \{q_2\} \qquad \delta(q_2, b, A) = \{[q_1, \lambda]\}.$$

a) Describe the language accepted by M.

b) Using the technique from Theorem 8.3.2, build a context-free grammar G that generates L(M).

c) Trace the computation of *aabbbb* in M.

d) Give the derivation of *aabbbb* in G.

7. Let G be a grammar in Greibach normal form and M the PDA constructed from G. Prove that if $[q_0, u, \lambda] \overset{*}{\vdash} [q_1, \lambda, w]$, then there is a derivation $S \overset{*}{\Rightarrow} uw$ in G. This completes the proof of Theorem 8.3.1.

8. Let $L = \{a^{2i} b^i \mid i \geqslant 0\}$.

a) Construct a PDA M_1 with $L(M_1) = L$.

b) Construct an atomic PDA M_2 with $L(M_2) = L$.

c) Construct an extended PDA M_3 with $L(M_3) = L$.

d) Trace the computation that accepts the string *aab* in each of the automata constructed in parts a), b), and c).

9. Let $L = \{a^{2i} b^{3i} \mid i \geqslant 0\}$.

a) Construct a PDA M_1 with $L(M_1) = L$.

b) Construct an atomic PDA M_2 with $L(M_2) = L$.

c) Construct an extended PDA M_3 with $L(M_3) = L$.

d) Trace the computation that accepts the string *aabbb* in each of the automata constructed in parts a), b), and c).

10. Let L be the language $\{w \in \{a, b\}^* \mid w$ has a prefix containing more *b*'s than *a*'s$\}$. For example, *baa, abba, abbaaa* $\in$ L but *aab, aabbab* $\notin$ L.

   a) Construct a PDA that accepts L by final state.

   b) Construct a PDA that accepts L by empty stack.

11. Theorem 8.3.2 presented a technique for constructing an equivalent grammar from an extended PDA. The transitions of the PDA pushed at most two variables onto the stack. Generalize this construction to build equivalent grammars from arbitrary extended PDAs. Prove that the resulting grammar generates the language of the PDA.

12. Use the pumping lemma to prove that each of the languages is not context-free.

   a) $\{a^k \mid k$ is a perfect square$\}$

   b) $\{a^i b^j c^i d^j \mid i, j \geq 0\}$

   c) $\{a^i b^{2i} a^i \mid i \geq 0\}$

   d) $\{a^i b^j c^k \mid i < j < k\}$

   e) $\{ww^R w \mid w \in \{a, b\}^*\}$

   f) The set of finite-length prefixes of the infinite string

   $$abaabaaabaaaab \ldots ba^n ba^{n+1} b \ldots$$

13. a) Prove that the language $L_1 = \{a^i b^{2i} c^j \mid i, j \geq 0\}$ is context-free.

   b) Prove that the language $L_2 = \{a^j b^i c^{2i} \mid i, j \geq 0\}$ is context-free.

   c) Prove that $L_1 \cap L_2$ is not context-free.

14. a) Prove that the language $L_1 = \{a^i b^i c^j d^j \mid i, j \geq 0\}$ is context-free.

   b) Prove that the language $L_2 = \{a^j b^i c^i d^k \mid i, j, k \geq 0\}$ is context-free.

   c) Prove that $L_1 \cap L_2$ is not context-free.

15. Let M be the PDA in Example 8.1.1.

   a) Trace the computation in M that accepts *bbcbb*.

   b) Use the technique from Theorem 8.3.2 to construct a grammar G that accepts L(M).

   c) Give the derivation of *bbcbb* in G.

16. a) Construct a DFA N that accepts all strings in $\{a, b\}^*$ with an odd number of *a*'s.

   b) Construct a PDA M that accepts $\{a^{3i} b^i \mid i \geq 0\}$.

   c) Use the technique from Theorem 8.5.3 to construct a PDA M' that accepts L(N) $\cap$ L(M).

   d) Trace the computations that accept *aaab* in N, M, and M'.

17. Let $G = (V, \Sigma, P, S)$ be a context-free grammar. Define an extended PDA M as follows:

$$Q = \{q_0\}$$
$$\Sigma = \Sigma_G$$
$$\Gamma = \Sigma_G \cup V$$
$$F = \{q_0\}$$
$$\delta(q_0, \lambda, A) = \{[q_0, w] \mid A \rightarrow w \in P\}$$
$$\delta(q_0, a, a) = \{[q_0, \lambda] \mid a \in \Sigma\}.$$

   Prove that $L(M) = L(G)$.

18. Complete the proof of Theorem 8.5.3.

19. Let L be a context-free language over Σ and $a \in \Sigma$. Define $er_a(L)$ to be the set obtained by removing all occurrences of a from strings of L. $er_a(L)$ is the language L with a erased. For example, if $abab$, $bacb$, $aa \in L$, then bb, bcb, and $\lambda \in er_a(L)$. Prove that $er_a(L)$ is context-free. Hint: Convert the grammar that generates L to one that generates $er_a(L)$.

20. The notion of a string homomorphism was introduced in Exercise 7.9. Let L be a context-free language over Σ and $h: \Sigma^* \rightarrow \Sigma^*$ a homomorphism.

   a) Prove that $h(L) = \{h(w) \mid w \in L\}$ is context-free, that is, that the context-free languages are closed under homomorphisms.

   b) Use the result of part a) to show that $er_a(L)$ is context-free.

   c) Give an example to show that the homomorphic image of a non-context-free language may be context-free.

21. Let $h: \Sigma^* \rightarrow \Sigma^*$ be a homomorphism and L a context-free language over Σ. Prove that $\{w \mid h(w) \in L\}$ is context-free. In other words, the set of context-free languages is closed under inverse homomorphic images.

22. Use closure under homomorphic images and inverse images to show that the following languages are not context-free.

   a) $\{a^i b^j c^i d^j \mid i, j \geqslant 0\}$

   b) $\{a^i b^{2i} c^{3i} \mid i \geqslant 0\}$

   c) $\{(ab)^i (bc)^i (ca)^i \mid i \geqslant 0\}$

23. Prove that the set of context-free languages is closed under reversal.

24. Construct a two-stack PDA that accepts the following languages.

   a) $\{a^i b^{2i} a^i \mid i \geqslant 0\}$

   b) $\{a^i b^j a^i b^j \mid i, j \geqslant 0\}$

   c) $\{ww \mid w \in \{a, b\}^*\}$

Bibliographic Notes

Pushdown automata were introduced in Oettinger [1961]. The relationship between context-free languages and pushdown automata was discovered by Chomsky [1962], Evey [1963], and Schutzenberger [1963]. Closure properties for context-free languages presented in Section 8.5 are from Bar-Hillel, Perles, and Shamir [1961] and Scheinberg [1960]. A solution to Exercises 20 and 21 can be found in Ginsburg and Rose [1963b].

The pumping lemma for context-free languages is from Bar-Hillel, Perles, and Shamir [1961]. A stronger version of the pumping lemma is given in Ogden [1968]. Parikh's theorem [1966] provides another tool for establishing that languages are not context-free.

CHAPTER 9

Turing Machines

The Turing machine, introduced by Alan Turing, exhibits many of the features commonly associated with a modern computer. This is no accident; the Turing machine predated the stored program computer and provided a model for its design and development. Utilizing a sequence of elementary operations, a Turing machine may access and alter any memory position. A Turing machine, unlike a computer, has no limitation on the amount of time or memory available for a computation. The Turing machine is another step in the development of finite-state computing machines. In a sense to be made precise in Chapters 11 and 13, this class of machine represents the culmination of the progression of increasingly powerful machines.

9.1 The Standard Turing Machine

A Turing machine is a finite-state machine in which a transition prints a symbol on the tape. The tape head may move in either direction, allowing the machine to read and manipulate the input as many times as desired. The structure of a Turing machine is similar to that of a finite automaton with the transition function incorporating these additional features.

Definition 9.1.1
A **Turing machine** is a quintuple $M = (Q, \Sigma, \Gamma, \delta, q_0)$ where Q is a finite set of states, Γ is a finite set called the tape alphabet, Γ contains a special symbol B that represents a

blank, Σ is a subset of $\Gamma - \{B\}$ called the input alphabet, δ is a partial function from $Q \times \Gamma$ to $Q \times \Gamma \times \{L, R\}$, and $q_0 \in Q$ is a distinguished state called the start state.

The tape of a Turing machine extends indefinitely in one direction. The tape positions are numbered by the natural numbers with the leftmost position numbered zero.

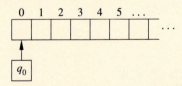

A computation begins with the tape head in state q_0 scanning the leftmost position. The input, a string from Σ^*, is written on the tape beginning at position one. Position zero and the remainder of the tape are assumed to be blank. The tape alphabet provides additional symbols that may be used during a computation.

A transition consists of three actions: changing the state, writing a symbol on the square scanned by the tape head, and moving the tape head. The direction of the movement is specified by the final component of the transition. An L indicates a move of one tape position to the left and R one position to the right. The machine configuration

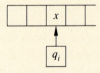

and transition $\delta(q_i, x) = [q_j, y, L]$ combine to produce the new configuration

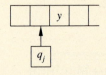

The transition changed the state from q_i to q_j, replaced the tape symbol x with y, and moved the tape head one square to the left. The ability of the machine to move in both directions and process blanks introduces the possibility of a computation continuing indefinitely.

A Turing machine **halts** when it encounters a state, symbol pair for which no transition is defined. A transition from tape position zero may specify a move to the left of the boundary of the tape. When this occurs, the computation is said to **terminate abnormally**. When we say that a computation halts, we mean that it terminates in a normal fashion.

Turing machines are designed to perform computations on strings from the input alphabet. A computation begins with the tape head scanning the leftmost tape square with the input string beginning at position one. All tape squares to the right of the input string are assumed to be blank. The Turing machine defined in Definition 9.1.1, with initial conditions as described above, is referred to as the **standard Turing machine.**

Example 9.1.1

The transition function of a standard Turing machine with input alphabet $\{a, b\}$ is given below. The transition from state q_0 moves the tape head to position one to read the input. The transitions in state q_1 read the input string and interchange the symbols a and b. The transitions in q_2 return the machine to the initial position.

δ	B	a	b
q_0	q_1, B, R		
q_1	q_2, B, L	q_1, b, R	q_1, a, R
q_2		q_2, a, L	q_2, b, L

A Turing machine can be graphically represented by a state diagram. The transition $\delta(q_i, x) = [q_j, y, d]$, $d \in \{L, R\}$, is depicted by an arc from q_i to q_j labeled $x/y\ d$. The state diagram

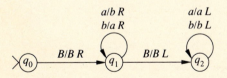

represents the Turing machine defined above.   □

A machine configuration consists of the state, the tape, and the position of the tape head. At any step in a computation of a standard Turing machine, only a finite segment of the tape is nonblank. A configuration is denoted $uq_i vB$ where uv is the string spelled by the symbols on the tape from the left-hand boundary to the rightmost nonblank symbol. Recall that B represents a blank tape position. The notation $uq_i vB$ indicates that the machine is in state q_i scanning the first symbol of v.

This representation of machine configurations can be used to trace the computations of a Turing machine. The notation $uq_i vB \vdash_M xq_j yB$ indicates that the configuration $xq_j yB$ is obtained from $uq_i vB$ by a single transition of M. Following the standard conventions, $uq_i vB \vdash_M^* xq_j yB$ signifies that $xq_j yB$ can be obtained from $uq_i vB$ by a finite number, possibly zero, of transitions. The reference to the machine is omitted when there is no possible ambiguity.

The Turing machine in Example 9.1.1 interchanges the a's and b's in the input string. Tracing the computation generated by the input string *abab* yields

$$q_0BababB$$
$$\vdash Bq_1ababB$$
$$\vdash Bbq_1babB$$
$$\vdash Bbaq_1abB$$
$$\vdash Bbabq_1bB$$
$$\vdash Bbabaq_1B$$
$$\vdash Bbabq_2aB$$
$$\vdash Bbaq_2baB$$
$$\vdash Bbq_2abaB$$
$$\vdash Bq_2babaB$$
$$\vdash q_2BbabaB.$$

Example 9.1.2

The Turing machine COPY with input alphabet $\{a, b\}$ produces a copy of the input string. That is, a computation with input BuB terminates with the tape $BuBuB$.

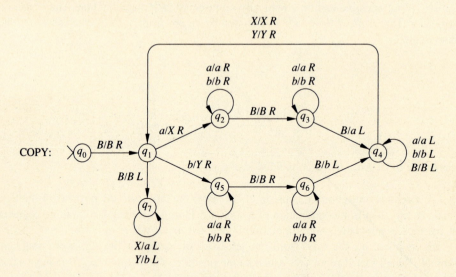

The computation copies the input string one symbol at a time beginning with the leftmost symbol in the input. Tape symbols X and Y record the portion of the input that has been copied. The first unmarked symbol in the string specifies the arc to be taken from state q_1. The cycle q_1, q_2, q_3, q_4, q_1 replaces an a with an X and adds an a to the string being constructed. Similarly, the lower branch copies a b using Y to mark the input string. After the entire string has been copied, the X's and Y's are returned to a's and b's in state q_7.   □

9.2   Turing Machines as Language Acceptors

Turing machines have been introduced as a paradigm for effective computation. A Turing machine computation is comprised of a sequence of elementary operations. The machines constructed in the previous section were designed to illustrate the features of Turing machine computations. The computations read and manipulated the symbols on the tape; no interpretation was given to the result of a computation. Turing machines can be designed to recognize languages and to compute functions. The result of a computation can be defined in terms of the state in which computation terminates or the configuration of the tape at the end of the computation.

Turing machines may be used as language acceptors; a computation accepts or rejects the input string. Initially, acceptance is defined by the final state of the computation. This is similar to the technique used by finite and pushdown automata to accept strings. Unlike finite and pushdown automata, a Turing machine need not read the entire input to accept the string. A Turing machine augmented with final states is a sextuple $(Q, \Sigma, \Gamma, \delta, q_0, F)$ where $F \subseteq Q$ is the set of final states.

Definition 9.2.1

Let $M = (Q, \Sigma, \Gamma, \delta, q_0, F)$ be a Turing machine. A string $u \in \Sigma^*$ is **accepted by final state** if the computation of M with input u halts in a final state. A computation that terminates abnormally rejects the input regardless of the final state of the machine. The language of M, L(M), is the set of all strings accepted by M.

A language accepted by a Turing machine is called a **recursively enumerable language.** If the Turing machine halts for all input strings, the language is said to be **recursive.** The computations of a Turing machine provide a decision procedure for membership in a recursive language. The state of the machine in which the computation terminates determines whether the input string is in the language. The terminology recursive and recursively enumerable has its origin in the functional interpretation of Turing computability that will be presented in Chapter 13.

Example 9.2.1

The Turing machine

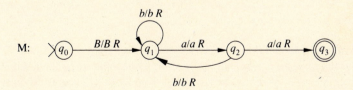

accepts the language $(a \cup b)^* aa(a \cup b)^*$. The computation

$$q_0BaabbB$$
$$\vdash Bq_1aabbB$$
$$\vdash Baq_2abbB$$
$$\vdash Baaq_3bbB$$

examines only the first half of the input before accepting the string $aabb$. The language $(a \cup b)^* aa(a \cup b)^*$ is recursive; the computations of M halt for every input string. A successful computation terminates when a substring aa is encountered. All other computations halt upon reading the first blank following the input.   □

Example 9.2.2

The language $\{a^i b^i c^i \mid i \geq 0\}$ is accepted by the Turing machine

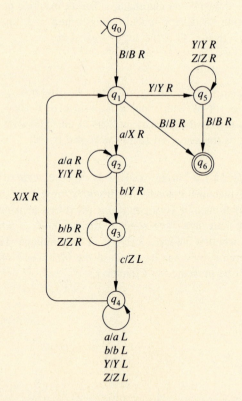

The tape symbols X, Y, and Z mark the a's, b's, and c's as they are matched. The computation successfully terminates when all the symbols in the input string have been transformed to the appropriate tape symbol. The transition from q_1 to q_6 accepts the null string.   □

Languages can be recognized by Turing machines without requiring the addition of final states. This alternative approach accepts a string if computation generated by the string causes the Turing machine to halt. When acceptance is defined by halting, the machine is defined by the quintuple $(Q, \Sigma, \Gamma, \delta, q_0)$ introduced in Definition 9.1.1. The final states are omitted since they play no role in the determination of the language of the machine.

Definition 9.2.2

Let $M = (Q, \Sigma, \Gamma, \delta, q_0)$ be a Turing machine. A string $u \in \Sigma^*$ is **accepted by halting** if the computation of M with input u halts.

Theorem 9.2.3

The following statements are equivalent:

i) The language L is accepted by a Turing machine by final state.

ii) The language L is accepted by a Turing machine by halting.

Proof   Let $M = (Q, \Sigma, \Gamma, \delta, q_0)$ be a Turing machine that accepts L by halting. The machine $M' = (Q, \Sigma, \Gamma, \delta, q_0, Q)$, in which every state is a final state, accepts L by final state.

Conversely, let $M = (Q, \Sigma, \Gamma, \delta, q_0, F)$ be a Turing machine with language L. Define the machine $M' = (Q \cup \{q_f\}, \Sigma, \Gamma, \delta', q_0)$ that accepts by halting as follows:

i) If $\delta(q_i, x)$ is defined, then $\delta'(q_i, x) = \delta(q_i, x)$.

ii) For each state $q_i \in Q - F$, if $\delta(q_i, x)$ is undefined, then $\delta'(q_i, x) = [q_f, x, R]$.

iii) For each $x \in \Gamma$, $\delta'(q_f, x) = [q_f, x, R]$.

Computations that accept strings in M and M' are identical. An unsuccessful computation in M may halt in a rejecting state or fail to terminate. When an unsuccessful computation in M terminates, the computation in M' enters the state q_f. Upon entering q_f, the machine moves indefinitely to the right. The only computations that terminate in M' are those that are generated by computations of M that halt in an accepting state. Thus $L(M') = L(M)$.   ∎

Example 9.2.3

The Turing machine from Example 9.2.1 is altered to accept $(a \cup b)^* aa(a \cup b)^*$ by halting. The machine below is constructed as specified by Theorem 9.2.3. A computation enters q_f only when the entire input string has been read. The machine obtained by deleting the arcs from q_0 to q_f and from q_f to q_f labeled $a/a\ R$ and $b/b\ R$ also accepts $(a \cup b)^* aa(a \cup b)^*$ by halting.

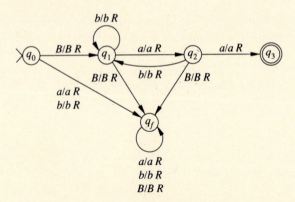

Unless noted otherwise, Turing machines will accept by final state. The definition of a Turing machine dictates the method of acceptance for computations of the machine.

9.3 Multitrack Machines

The remainder of the chapter is dedicated to examining variations of the standard Turing machine model. Each of the variations appears to increase the capability of the machine. We prove that the languages accepted by these generalized machines are precisely those accepted by the standard Turing machines.

A multitrack tape is one in which the tape is divided into tracks. A tape position in an n-track tape contains n symbols from the tape alphabet. The diagram depicts a two-track tape with the tape head scanning the second position.

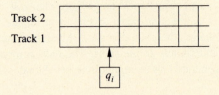

The machine reads an entire tape position. Multiple tracks increase the amount of information that can be considered when determining the appropriate transition. A tape position in a two-track machine is represented by the ordered pair $[x, y]$ where x is the symbol in track 1 and y in track 2.

The states, input alphabet, tape alphabet, initial state, and final states of a two-track machine are the same as in the standard Turing machine. A two-track transition reads and rewrites the entire tape position. A transition of a two-track machine is written $\delta(q_i, [x, y]) = [q_j, [z, w], d]$ where $d \in \{L, R\}$.

The input to a two-track machine is placed in the standard input position in track 1. All the positions in track 2 are initially blank. Acceptance in multitrack machines is defined by final state.

We will show that the languages accepted by two-track machines are precisely the recursively enumerable languages. The argument easily generalizes to n-track machines.

Theorem 9.3.1

A language L is accepted by a two-track Turing machine if, and only if, it is accepted by a standard Turing machine.

Proof   Clearly, if L is accepted by a standard Turing machine it is accepted by a two-track machine. The equivalent two-track machine simply ignores the presence of the second track.

Let $M = (Q, \Sigma, \Gamma, \delta, q_0, F)$ be a two-track machine. A one-track machine will be constructed in which a single tape square contains the same information as a tape position in the two-track tape. The representation of a two-track tape position as an ordered pair indicates how this can be accomplished. The tape alphabet of the equivalent one-track machine M′ consists of ordered pairs of tape elements of M. The input to the two-track machine consists of ordered pairs whose second component is blank. The one-track machine

$$M' = (Q, \Sigma \times \{B\}, \Gamma \times \Gamma, \delta', q_0, F)$$

with transition function

$$\delta'(q_i, [x, y]) = \delta(q_i, [x, y])$$

accepts L(M).   ∎

9.4   Two-Way Tape

A Turing machine with a two-way tape is identical to the standard model except that the tape extends indefinitely in both directions. Since a two-way tape has no left boundary, the input can be placed anywhere on the tape. All other tape positions are assumed to be blank. The tape head is initially positioned on the blank to the immediate left of the input string.

A machine with a two-way tape can be constructed to simulate the actions of a standard machine by placing a special symbol on the tape to represent the left-hand boundary of the one-way tape. The symbol #, which is assumed not to be an element of the tape alphabet of the standard machine, is used to simulate the boundary of the tape. A computation in the equivalent machine with two-way tape begins by writing # to the immediate left of the initial tape head position. The remainder of a computation in the two-way machine is identical to that of the one-way machine except when the computation of the one-way machine terminates abnormally. When the one-way computation attempts to move to the left of the tape boundary, the two-way machine reads the symbol # and enters a nonaccepting state that terminates the computation.

The standard Turing machine M accepts strings over $\{a, b\}$ in which the first b, if present, is preceded by at least three a's.

All the states of M other than q_0 are accepting. When the first b is encountered, the tape head moves four positions to the left, if possible. Acceptance is completely determined by the boundary of the tape. A string is rejected by M whenever the tape head attempts to cross the left-hand boundary. All computations that remain within the bounds of the tape accept the input.

The transitions from states q_s and q_t insert the simulated end marker to the left of the initial position of the tape head of M′, the two-way machine that accepts L(M). After writing the simulated boundary, the computation enters a copy of the one-way machine M. The failure state q_f is entered in M′ when a computation in M attempts to move to the left of the tape boundary.

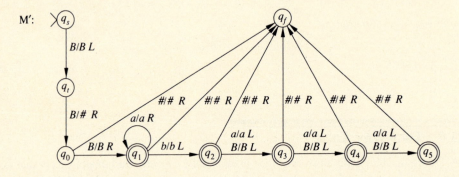

We will now show that a language accepted by a machine with a two-way tape is accepted by a standard Turing machine. The argument utilizes Theorem 9.3.1, which establishes the interdefinability of two-track and standard machines. The tape positions of the two-way tape can be numbered by the complete set of integers. The initial position of the tape head is numbered zero, and the input begins at position one.

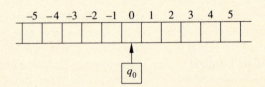

Imagine taking the two-way infinite tape and folding it so that position $-i$ sits directly above position i. Adding an unnumbered tape square over position zero produces a two-track tape. The symbol in tape position i of the two-way tape is stored in the corresponding position of the one-way, two-track tape. A computation on a two-way infinite tape can be simulated on this one-way, two-track tape.

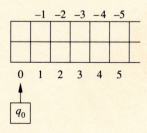

Let $M = (Q, \Sigma, \Gamma, \delta, q_0, F)$ be a Turing machine with a two-way tape. Using the correspondence between a two-way tape and two-track tape, a Turing machine M' with one-way, two-track tape is constructed to accept $L(M)$. A transition of M is specified by the state and the symbol scanned. M', scanning a two-track tape, reads two symbols at each tape position. The symbols U (up) and D (down) are introduced to designate which of the two tracks should be used to determine the transition. This information is maintained by the states of the two-track machine.

The components of M' are constructed from those of M and the symbols U and D.

$$Q' = (Q \cup \{q_s, q_t\}) \times \{U, D\}$$
$$\Sigma' = \Sigma$$
$$\Gamma' = \Gamma \cup \{\#\}$$
$$F' = \{[q_i, U], [q_i, D] \mid q_i \in F\}.$$

The initial state of M' is a pair $[q_s, D]$. The transition from this state writes the marker $\#$ on the upper track in the leftmost tape position. A transition from $[q_t, D]$ returns the tape head to its original position to begin the simulation of a computation of M. The transitions of M' are defined as follows:

1. $\delta'([q_s, D], [B, B]) = [[q_t, D], [B, \#], R]$.

2. For every $x \in \Gamma$, $\delta'([q_t, D], [x, B]) = [[q_0, D], [x, B], L]$.

3. For every $z \in \Gamma - \{\#\}$ and $d \in \{L, R\}$, $\delta'([q_i, D], [x, z]) = [[q_j, D], [y, z], d]$ whenever $\delta(q_i, x) = [q_j, y, d]$ is a transition of M.

4. For every $x \in \Gamma - \{\#\}$ and $d \in \{L, R)$, $\delta'([q_i, U], [z, x]) = [[q_j, U], [z, y], d']$ whenever $\delta(q_i, x) = [q_j, y, d]$ is a transition of M where d' is the opposite direction of d.

5. $\delta'([q_i, D], [x, \#]) = [[q_j, U], [y, \#], R]$ whenever $\delta(q_i, x) = [q_j, y, L]$ is a transition of M.

6. $\delta'([q_i, D], [x, \#]) = [[q_j, D], [y, \#], R]$ whenever $\delta(q_i, x) = [q_j, y, R]$ is a transition of M.

7. $\delta'([q_i, U], [x, \#]) = [[q_j, D], [y, \#], R]$ whenever $\delta(q_i, x) = [q_j, y, R]$ is a transition of M.

8. $\delta'([q_i, U], [x, \#]) = [[q_j, U], [y, \#], R]$ whenever $\delta(q_i, x) = [q_j, y, L]$ is a transition of M.

A transition generated by schema 3 simulates a transition of M in which the tape head begins and ends in positions labeled with nonnegative values. In the simulation, this is represented by writing on the lower track of the tape. Transitions defined in 4 use only the upper track of the two-track tape. These correspond to transitions of M that occur to the left of position zero on the two-way infinite tape.

The remaining transitions simulate the transitions of M from position zero on the two-way tape. Regardless of the U or D in the state, transitions from position zero are determined by the tape symbol on track 1. When the track is specified by D, the transition is defined by schema 5 or 6. Transitions defined in 7 and 8 are applied when the state is $[q_i, U]$.

The preceding informal arguments outline the proof of the equivalence of one-way and two-way Turing machines.

Theorem 9.4.1
A language L is accepted by a Turing machine with a two-way tape if, and only if, it is accepted by a standard Turing machine.

9.5   Multitape Machines

A k-tape machine consists of k tapes and k independent tape heads. The states and alphabets of a multitape machine are the same as in a standard Turing machine. The machine reads the tapes simultaneously but has only one state. This is depicted by connecting each of the independent tape heads to a single control indicating the current state.

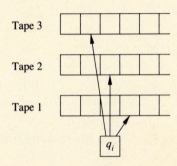

A transition is determined by the state and the symbols scanned by each of the tape heads. A transition in a multitape machine may

  i) change the state

 ii) write a symbol on each of the tapes

iii) independently reposition each of the tape heads.

The repositioning consists of moving the tape head one square to the left or one square to the right or leaving it at its current position. A transition of a two-tape machine scanning x_1 on tape 1 and x_2 on tape 2 is written $\delta(q_i, x_1, x_2) = [q_j; y_1, d_1; y_2, d_2]$ where $x_i, y_i \in \Gamma$ and $d_i \in \{L, R, S\}$. This transition causes the machine to write y_i on tape i. The symbol d_i specifies the direction of the movement of tape head i: L signifies a move to the left, R a move to the right, and S means the head remains stationary.

The input to a multitape machine is placed in the standard position on tape 1. All the other tapes are assumed to be blank. The tape heads originally scan the leftmost position of each tape. Any tape head attempting to move to the left of the boundary of its tape terminates the computation unsuccessfully.

A standard Turing machine is a multitape Turing machine with a single tape. Consequently every recursively enumerable language is accepted by a multitape machine. A computation in a two-tape machine can be simulated by a computation in a five-track machine. The argument can be generalized to show that any language accepted by a k-tape machine is accepted by a $2k+1$-track machine.

Theorem 9.5.1

A language L is accepted by a multitape Turing machine if, and only if, it is accepted by a standard Turing machine.

Let $M = (Q, \Sigma, \Gamma, \delta, q_0, F)$ be a two-tape machine. The tape heads of a multitape machine are independently positioned on the two tapes.

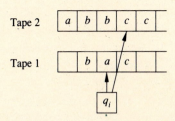

The single tape head of a multitrack machine reads all the tracks of a fixed position. The five-track machine M' is constructed to simulate the computations of M. Tracks 1 and 3 maintain the information stored on tapes 1 and 2 of the two-tape machine. Tracks 2 and 4 have a single nonblank square indicating the position of the tape heads of the multitape machines.

Track 5	#					
Track 4				X		
Track 3	a	b	b	c	c	
Track 2			X			
Track 1		b	a	c		

The initial action of the simulation in the multitrack machine is to write # in the leftmost position of track 5 and X in the leftmost positions of tracks 2 and 4. The remainder of the computation of the multitrack machine consists of a sequence of actions that simulate the transitions of the two-tape machine.

A transition of the two-tape machine is determined by the two symbols being scanned and the machine state. The simulation in the five-track machine records the symbols marked by each of the X's. The states are 8-tuples of the form $[s, q_i, x_1, x_2, y_1, y_2, d_1, d_2]$ where $q_i \in Q$; $x_i, y_i \in \Sigma \cup \{U\}$; and $d_i \in \{L, R, S, U\}$. The element s represents the status of the simulation of the transition. The symbol U, added to the tape alphabet and the set of directions, indicates that this item is unknown.

Let $\delta(q_i, x_1, x_2) = [q_j; y_1, d_1; y_2, d_2]$ be a two-tape transition. M' begins the simulation of a transition of M in the state $[f1, q_i, U, U, U, U, U, U]$. The following five actions simulate a transition of M in the multitrack machine.

1. $f1$ (find first symbol): M' moves to the right until it reads the X on track 2. State $[f1, q_i, x_1, U, U, U, U, U]$ is entered, where x_1 is the symbol in track 1 under the X. After recording the symbol on track 1 in the state, M' returns to the initial position. The # on track 5 is used to reposition the tape head.

2. $f2$ (find second symbol): The same sequence of actions records the symbol beneath the X on track 4. M' enters state $[f2, q_i, x_1, x_2, U, U, U, U]$ where x_2 is the symbol in track 3 under the X. The tape head is then returned to the initial position.

3. M' enters the state $[p1, q_j, x_1, x_2, y_1, y_2, d_1, d_2]$. This state contains the information needed to simulate the transition of the M.

4. $p1$ (print first symbol): M' moves to the right to the X in track 2 and writes the symbol y_1 on track 1. The X on track 2 is moved in the direction designated by d_1. The machine then returns to the initial position.

5. $p2$ (print second symbol): M' moves to the right to the X in track 4 and writes the symbol y_2 on track 3. The X on track 4 is moved in the direction designated by d_2. The simulation cycle terminates by returning the tape head to the initial position.

If $\delta(q_i, x_1, x_2)$ is undefined in the two-tape machine, the simulation halts after returning to the initial position following step 2. A state $[f2, q_i, x_1, y_1, U, U, U, U]$ is a final state of the multitrack machine M' whenever q_i is a final state of M.

Example 9.5.1

The set $\{a^k \mid k \text{ is a perfect square}\}$ is a recursively enumerable language. The design of a three-tape machine that accepts this language is presented. Tape 1 contains the input string. The input is compared with a string of X's on tape 2 whose length is a perfect square. Tape 3 holds a string whose length is the square root of the string on tape 2. The initial configuration for a computation with input $aaaaa$ is

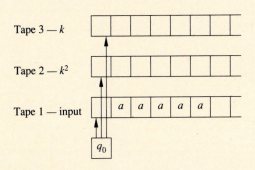

The values of k and k^2 are incremented until the length of the string on tape 2 is greater than or equal to the length of the input. A machine to perform these comparisons consists of the following actions:

1. If the input is the null string, the computation halts in an accepting state. If not, tapes 2 and 3 are initialized by writing X in position one. The three tape heads are then moved to position one.

2. Tape 3 contains a sequence of k X's and tape 2 k^2 X's. Simultaneously, the heads on tapes 1 and 2 move to the right while both heads scan nonblank squares. The head reading tape 3 remains at position one.

   a) If both heads simultaneously read a blank, the computation halts and the string is accepted.

   b) If tape head 1 reads a blank and tape head 2 an X, the computation halts and the string is rejected.

3. The tapes are reconfigured for comparison with the next perfect square.

   a) An X is added to the right end of the string of X's on tape 2.

   b) Two copies of the string on tape 3 are concatenated to the right end of the string on tape 2. This constructs a sequence of $(k+1)^2$ X's on tape 2.

   c) An X is added to the right end of the string of X's on tape 3. This constructs a sequence of $k+1$ X's on tape 3.

   d) The tape heads are then repositioned at position one of their respective tapes.

4. Steps 2–4 are repeated.

Tracing the computation for the input string *aaaaa*, step 1 produces the configuration

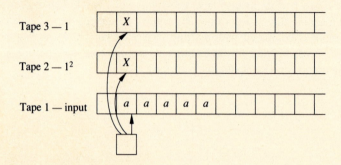

The simultaneous left-to-right movement of tape heads 1 and 2 halts when tape head 2 scans the blank in position two.

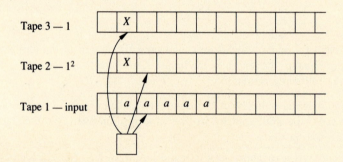

Part c) of step 3 reformats tapes 2 and 3 so that the input string can be compared with the next perfect square.

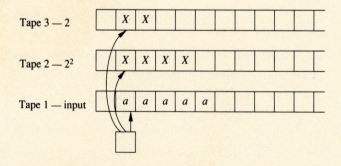

Another iteration of step 2 halts and rejects the input.

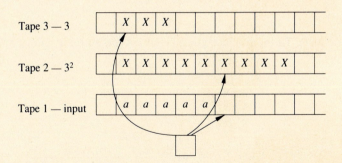

Tape 3 — 3

Tape 2 — 3^2

Tape 1 — input

The machine outlined above is defined by the following transitions:

$\delta(q_0, B, B, B) = [q_1; B, R; B, R; B, R]$ 'initialize the tape'
$\delta(q_1, a, B, B) = [q_2; a, S; X, S; X, S]$

$\delta(q_2, a, X, X) = [q_2; a, R; X, R; X, S]$ 'compare strings on tapes 1 and 2'
$\delta(q_2, B, B, X) = [q_3; B, S; B, S; X, S]$ 'accept'
$\delta(q_2, a, B, X) = [q_4; a, S; X, R; X, S]$

$\delta(q_4, a, B, X) = [q_5; a, S; X, R; X, S]$ 'rewrite tapes 2 and 3'
$\delta(q_4, a, B, B) = [q_6; a, L; B, L; X, L]$
$\delta(q_5, a, B, X) = [q_4; a, S; X, R; X, R]$

$\delta(q_6, a, X, X) = [q_6; a, L; X, L; X, L]$ 'reposition tape heads'
$\delta(q_6, a, X, B) = [q_6; a, L; X, L; B, S]$
$\delta(q_6, a, B, B) = [q_6; a, L; B, L; B, S]$
$\delta(q_6, B, X, B) = [q_6; B, S; X, L; B, S]$
$\delta(q_6, B, B, B) = [q_2; B, R; B, R; B, R]$ 'repeat comparison cycle'

The accepting states are q_1 and q_3. The null string is accepted in q_1. Strings a^k, where k is a perfect square greater than 0, are accepted in q_3.   □

9.6   Nondeterministic Turing Machines

A nondeterministic Turing machine may specify any finite number of transitions for a given configuration. The components of a nondeterministic machine, with the exception of the transition function, are identical to those of the standard Turing machine. Transitions in a nondeterministic machine are defined by a partial function from $Q \times \Gamma$ to subsets of $Q \times \Gamma \times \{L, R\}$.

Whenever the transition function indicates that more than one action is possible, a computation arbitrarily chooses one of the transitions. An input string is accepted by a nondeterministic machine if there is a computation that terminates in an accepting state.

Example 9.6.1

The nondeterministic Turing machine given below accepts strings containing a c preceded or followed by ab.

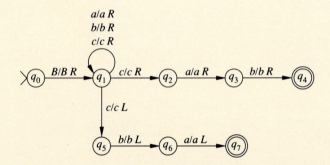

The machine processes the input in state q_1 until a c is encountered. When this occurs, the computation may continue in state q_1, enter state q_2 to determine if the c is followed by ab, or enter q_5 to determine if the c is preceded by ab. In the language of nondeterminism, the computation chooses a c and then chooses one of the conditions to check.   □

A nondeterministic Turing machine may produce several computations for a single input string. The computations can be enumerated by ordering the alternative transitions for a state, symbol pair. Let n be the maximum number of transitions defined for any combination of state and tape symbol. The numbering assumes that $\delta(q_i, x)$ defines n, not necessarily distinct, transitions for every state q_i and tape symbol x with $\delta(q_i, x) \neq \emptyset$. If the transition function defines fewer than n transitions, one transition is assigned several numbers to complete the ordering.

A sequence $(m_1, m_2, \ldots, m_k)$ of values from 1 to n defines a computation in the nondeterministic machine. The computation associated with this sequence consists of k or fewer transitions. The jth transition is determined by the state, tape symbol scanned and m_j, the jth number in the sequence. Assume the $j-1$st transition leaves the machine in state q_i scanning x. If $\delta(q_i, x) = \emptyset$, the computation halts. Otherwise, the machine executes the transition in $\delta(q_i, x)$ numbered m_j.

The transitions of the nondeterministic machine in Example 9.6.1 can be ordered as follows:

State	Symbol	Transition	State	Symbol	Transition
q_0	B	1 q_1, B, R	q_2	a	1 q_3, a, R
		2 q_1, B, R			2 q_3, a, R
		3 q_1, B, R			3 q_3, a, R

State	Symbol	Transition	State	Symbol	Transition
q_1	a	1 q_1, a, R	q_3	b	1 q_4, b, R
		2 q_1, a, R			2 q_4, b, R
		3 q_1, a, R			3 q_4, b, R
q_1	b	1 q_1, b, R	q_5	b	1 q_6, b, L
		2 q_1, b, R			2 q_6, b, L
		3 q_1, b, R			3 q_6, b, L
q_1	c	1 q_1, c, R	q_6	a	1 q_7, a, L
		2 q_2, c, R			2 q_7, a, L
		3 q_5, c, L			3 q_7, a, L

The computations defined by the input string $acab$ and the sequences $(1, 1, 1, 1, 1)$, $(1, 1, 2, 1, 1)$, and $(2, 2, 3, 3, 1)$ are

$q_0BacabB$ 1	$q_0BacabB$ 1	$q_0BacabB$ 2
$\vdash Bq_1acabB$ 1	$\vdash Bq_1acabB$ 1	$\vdash Bq_1acabB$ 2
$\vdash Baq_1cabB$ 1	$\vdash Baq_1cabB$ 2	$\vdash Baq_1cabB$ 3
$\vdash Bacq_1abB$ 1	$\vdash Bacq_2abB$ 1	$\vdash Bq_5acabB$
$\vdash Bacaq_1bB$ 1	$\vdash Bacaq_3bB$ 1	
$\vdash Bacabq_1B$	$\vdash Bacabq_4B$	

The number on the right designates the transition used to obtain the subsequent configuration. The third computation terminates prematurely since no transition is defined when the machine is in state q_5 scanning an a. The string $acab$ is accepted since the computation defined by $(1, 1, 2, 1, 1)$ terminates in state q_4.

The machine constructed in Example 9.6.1 accepts strings by final state. As with standard machines, acceptance in nondeterministic Turing machines can be defined by final state or by halting alone. Exercise 9.21 establishes that these alternative approaches recognize the same languages.

Nondeterminism does not increase the capabilities of Turing computation; the languages accepted by nondeterministic machines are precisely those accepted by deterministic machines. Let $M = (Q, \Sigma, \Gamma, \delta, q_0)$ be a nondeterministic machine that accepts strings by halting. Assume that the transitions of M have been numbered according to the previous scheme with n the maximum number of transitions for a state, symbol pair. A deterministic three-tape machine M' is constructed to accept the language of M. Acceptance in M' is also defined by halting.

The computations of M are simulated in M'. The correspondence between a sequence $(m_1, \ldots, m_k)$ and a computation of M' ensures that all possible computations of length k are examined. A computation in M' consists of the actions:

1. A sequence of integers from 1 to n is written on tape 3.
2. The input string on tape 1 is copied to the standard position on tape 2.

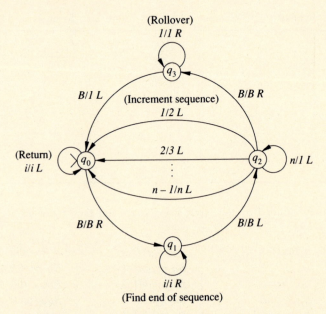

FIGURE 9.1 Turing machine generating $\{1, 2, \ldots, n\}^*$.

3. The computation of M defined by the sequence on tape 3 is simulated on tape 2.

4. If the simulation halts, the computation of M' halts and input is accepted.

5. A new sequence is generated on tape 3 and steps 2–5 are repeated.

We will examine the actions that affect tapes 2 and 3 of M'. The simulation is guided by the sequence of values on tape 3. The deterministic standard Turing machine in Fig. 9.1 generates all sequences of integers from 1 to n. Sequences of length one are generated in numeric order, followed by sequences of length two, and so on. A computation begins in state q_0 at position zero. When the tape head returns to position zero the tape contains the next sequence of values. The notation i/i abbreviates $1/1, 2/2, \ldots, n/n$.

Consider a nondeterministic machine M in which the computation defined by the sequence $(1, 3, 2, 1, 1)$ and input string $abcd$ is

$$q_0 BabcdB \quad 1$$
$$\vdash Bq_1 abcdB \quad 3$$
$$\vdash Bdq_2 bcdB \quad 2$$
$$\vdash Bq_3 dacdB.$$

The sequence $(1, 3, 2, 1, 1)$ that defines the computation of M is written on tape 3 of M'. The configuration of the three-tape machine M' prior to the execution of the third transition of M is

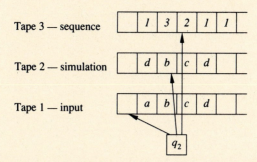

Transition 2 from state q_2 with M scanning b causes the machine to print a, enter state q_3, and move to the left. This transition is simulated in M' by the transition $\delta'(q_2, B, b, 2) = [q_3; B, S; a, L; 2, R]$. The transition of M' alters tape 2 as prescribed by the transition of M and moves the head on tape 3 to indicate the subsequent transition.

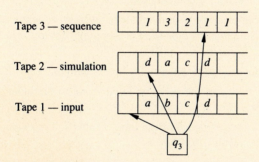

The machine M' is constructed by interweaving the enumeration of the sequences on tape 3 with the simulation on tape 2. The computation in M' sequentially simulates computations of the nondeterministic machine. M' halts when the sequence on tape 3 defines a computation that halts in M. Since acceptance was defined by halting, L(M') = L(M).

A nondeterministic Turing machine can be defined with a multiple-track tape, two-way tape, or multiple tapes. Machines defined using these alternative configurations can also be shown to accept precisely the recursively enumerable languages.

Exercises

1. Let M be the Turing machine defined by

δ	B	a	b	c
q_0	q_1, B, R			
q_1	q_2, B, L	q_1, a, R	q_1, c, R	q_1, c, R
q_2		q_2, c, L		q_2, b, L

a) Trace the computation for the input string *aabca*.

b) Trace the computation for the input string *bcbc*.

c) Give the state diagram of M.

d) Describe the result of a computation in M.

2. Let M be the Turing machine defined by

δ	B	a	b	c
q_0	q_1, B, R			
q_1	q_1, B, R	q_1, a, R	q_1, b, R	q_2, c, L
q_2		q_2, b, L	q_2, a, L	

a) Trace the computation for the input string *abcab*.

b) Trace the first six transitions of the computation for the input string *abab*.

c) Give the state diagram of M.

d) Describe the result of a computation in M.

3. Construct a Turing machine with input alphabet $\{a, b\}$ to perform each of the following operations. Note that the tape head is scanning position zero in state q_f whenever a computation terminates.

a) Move the input one space to the right. Input configuration q_0BuB, result q_fBBuB.

b) Concatenate a copy of the reversed input string to the input. Input configuration q_0BuB, result q_fBuu^RB.

c) Insert a blank between each of the input symbols. For example: input configuration q_0BabaB, result $q_fBaBbBaB$.

d) Erase the *b*'s from the input. For example: input configuration $q_0BbabaababB$, result $q_fBaaaaB$.

4. Construct a Turing machine with two-way tape and input alphabet $\{a\}$ that halts if the tape contains a nonblank square. The symbol *a* may be anywhere on the tape, not necessarily to the immediate right of the tape head.

5. A two-dimensional Turing machine is one in which the tape consists of a two-dimensional array of tape squares.

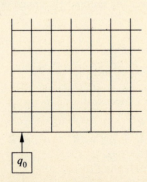

A transition consists of rewriting a square and moving the head to any one of the four adjacent squares. A computation begins with the tape head reading the corner position. The transitions of the two-dimensional machine are written $\delta(q_i, x) = [q_j, y, d]$ where d is U (up), D (down), L (left), or R (right). Design a two-dimensional Turing machine with input alphabet $\{a\}$ that halts if the tape contains a nonblank square.

6. Construct a Turing machine with input alphabet $\{a, b\}$ that accepts the following languages by final state:

    a) $\{a^i b^i \mid i \geqslant 0\}$

    b) $\{a^i b^j a^i b^j \mid i, j > 0\}$

    c) strings with the same number of a's and b's

    d) $\{ww^R \mid w \in \{a, b\}^*\}$

7. Construct a Turing machine with input alphabet $\{a, b, c\}$ that accepts strings in which the first c is preceded by the substring aaa. A string must contain a c to be accepted by the machine.

8. The transitions of a Turing machine may be defined by a partial function from $Q \times \Gamma$ to $Q \times \Gamma \times \{L, R, S\}$ where S indicates that the tape head remains stationary. Prove that machines defined in this manner recognize precisely the recursively enumerable languages.

9. An **atomic** Turing machine is one in which every transition consists of a change of state and one other action. The transition may write on the tape or move the tape head, but not both. Prove that the atomic Turing machines recognize precisely the recursively enumerable languages.

10. A **context-sensitive** Turing machine is one in which the applicability of a transition is determined not only by the symbol scanned but also by the symbol in the tape square to the right of the tape head. A transition has the form

$$\delta(q_i, xy) = [q_j, z, d] \quad x, y, z \in \Gamma; d \in \{L, R\}.$$

When the machine is in state q_i scanning an x, the transition may be applied only when the tape position to the immediate right of the tape head contains a y. In this case, the x is replaced by z, the machine enters state q_j, and the tape head moves in direction d.

    a) Let M be a standard Turing machine. Define a context-sensitive Turing machine M′ that accepts L(M). Hint: Define the transition function of M′ from that of M.

    b) Let $\delta(q_i, xy) = [q_j, z, d]$ be a context-sensitive transition. Show that the result of the application of this transition can be obtained by a sequence of standard Turing machine transitions. You must consider both of the cases when transition $\delta(q_i, xy)$ is applicable and when it isn't.

    c) Use parts a) and b) to conclude that context-sensitive machines accept precisely the recursively enumerable languages.

11. Prove that every recursively enumerable language is accepted by a Turing machine with a single accepting state.

12. An alternative method of acceptance by final state can be defined as follows: a string u is accepted by a Turing machine M if the computation of M with input u enters (but does not necessarily terminate in) a final state. With this definition, a string may be accepted even though the computation of the machine does not terminate. Prove that the languages accepted by this definition are precisely the recursively enumerable languages.

13. Let L be the set of palindromes over $\{a, b\}$.

    a) Build a standard Turing machine that accepts L.

    b) Build a two-tape machine that accepts L.

14. Construct a two-tape Turing machine that accepts strings in which each a is followed by an increasing number of b's, that is, the strings are of the form

$$ab^{n_1}ab^{n_2} \ldots ab^{n_k}, k > 0 \quad \text{where } n_1 < n_2 < \cdots < n_k.$$

15. Construct a nondeterministic Turing machine whose language is the set of strings over $\{a, b\}$ that contain a substring u satisfying the following two properties:

    i) $length(u) \geq 3$.

    ii) u contains the same number of a's and b's.

16. Construct a two-tape nondeterministic Turing machine that accepts the strings of odd length over $\{a, b, c\}$ with a c in the middle position. Every computation with input w should halt after at most $length(w) + 1$ transitions.

17. Construct a two-tape nondeterministic Turing machine that accepts $\{uu \mid u \in \{a, b\}^*\}$. Every computation with input w should terminate after at most $2(length(w)) + 2$ transitions.

18. Prove that a language L is recursive if, and only if, L and $\bar{L}$ are recursively enumerable.

19. Prove that the recursive languages are closed under union, intersection, and complement.

20. Let L be a language accepted by a nondeterministic Turing machine in which every computation terminates. Prove that L is recursive.

21. Prove the equivalent of Theorem 9.2.3 for nondeterministic Turing machines.

22. A machine that generates all sequences consisting of integers from 1 to n was given in Fig. 9.1. Trace the first seven cycles of the machine for $n = 3$. A cycle consists of the tape head returning to the initial position in state q_0.

23. Construct a Turing machine that generates the set $L = \{a^i \mid i \text{ is divisible by 3}\}$. L is generated by a machine M under the following conditions:

    i) Whenever the machine is in state q_0 scanning the leftmost square, an element of L is on the tape.

    ii) All elements of L are eventually generated.

24. Construct a Turing machine that generates the set $\{a^i b^i \mid i \geq 0\}$.

25. Prove that the two-stack automata introduced in Section 8.6 recognize precisely the recursively enumerable languages.

26. Define a nondeterministic two-track Turing machine. Prove that these machines accept precisely the recursively enumerable languages.

27. Prove that every context-free language is recursive. Hint: Construct a nondeterministic two-tape Turing machine that simulates the computation of a pushdown automaton.

Bibliographic Notes

The Turing machine was introduced by Turing [1936] as a model for algorithmic computation. Turing's original machine was deterministic, consisting of a two-way tape and a single tape head. Independently, Post [1936] introduced a family of abstract machines with the same computational capabilities as Turing machines.

The capabilities and limitations of Turing machines as language acceptors are examined in Chapter 11. The use of Turing machines for the computation of functions is presented in Chapters 12 and 13. The books by Minsky [1967], Brainerd and Landweber [1974], and Hennie [1977] give an introduction to computability and Turing machines.

CHAPTER 10

The Chomsky Hierarchy

Phrase-structure grammars provide a formal system for generating strings over an alphabet. The productions or rules of a grammar specify permissible string transformations. Families of grammars are categorized by the form of the productions. The regular and context-free grammars introduced in Chapter 3 are two important families of phrase-structure grammars. In this chapter, two additional families of grammars, the unrestricted grammars and context-sensitive grammars, are presented. These four families comprise the Chomsky hierarchy, named after Noam Chomsky, who proposed them as syntactic models of natural language.

Automata were designed to mechanically recognize the regular and context-free languages. The relationship between grammatical generation and mechanical acceptance is extended to the new families of grammars. Turing machines are shown to recognize the languages generated by unrestricted grammars. A class of machines, the linear-bounded automata, obtained by limiting the memory available to a Turing machine accepts the languages generated by context-sensitive grammars.

10.1   Unrestricted Grammars

The unrestricted grammars are the largest class of phrase-structure grammars. A production $u \rightarrow v$ indicates that an occurrence of a substring u in a string may be replaced with the string v. A derivation is a sequence of permissible replacements. The only constraint on a production of an unrestricted grammar is that the left-hand side cannot be null. These general string rewriting systems are also called type 0 grammars.

Definition 10.1.1

An **unrestricted grammar** is a quadruple (V, Σ, P, S) where V is a finite set of variables, Σ (the alphabet) is a finite set of terminal symbols, P is a set of productions, and S is a distinguished element of V. A production of an unrestricted grammar has the form $u \rightarrow v$ where $u \in (V \cup \Sigma)^+$ and $v \in (V \cup \Sigma)^*$. The sets V and Σ are assumed to be disjoint.

The previously defined families of grammars are subsets of the more general class of unrestricted grammars. A context-free grammar is a phrase-structure grammar in which the left-hand side of every rule is single variable. The productions of a regular grammar are required to have the form

i) $A \rightarrow aB$

ii) $A \rightarrow a$

iii) $A \rightarrow \lambda$

where $A, B \in V$, and $a \in \Sigma$.

The notational conventions introduced in Chapter 3 for context-free grammars are used for arbitrary phrase-structure grammars. The application of the rule $u \rightarrow v$ to the string xuy, written $xuy \Rightarrow xvy$, produces the string xvy. A string q is **derivable** from p, $p \overset{*}{\Rightarrow} q$, if there is a sequence of rule applications that transforms p to q. The **language** of G, denoted L(G), is the set of terminal strings derivable from the start symbol S. Symbolically, $L(G) = \{w \in \Sigma^* \mid S \overset{*}{\Rightarrow} w\}$.

Example 10.1.1

The unrestricted grammar

$$
\begin{aligned}
V &= \{S, A, C\} \\
\Sigma &= \{a, b, c\} \\
S &\rightarrow aAbc \mid \lambda \\
A &\rightarrow aAbC \mid \lambda \\
Cb &\rightarrow bC \\
Cc &\rightarrow cc
\end{aligned}
$$

with start symbol S generates the language $\{a^i b^i c^i \mid i \geq 0\}$. The string $a^i b^i c^i$, $i > 0$, is generated by a derivation that begins

$$
\begin{aligned}
S &\Longrightarrow aAbc \\
&\overset{i-1}{\Longrightarrow} a^i A(bC)^{i-1}bc \\
&\Longrightarrow a^i(bC)^{i-1}bc.
\end{aligned}
$$

The rule $Cb \rightarrow bC$ allows the final C to pass through the b's that separate it from the c's at the end of the string. Upon reaching the first c, the variable C is replaced with c. □

Example 10.1.2

The unrestricted grammar with terminal alphabet $\{a, b, [,]\}$ defined by the productions

$$
\begin{aligned}
S &\rightarrow aT[a] \mid bT[b] \mid [\;] \\
T[&\rightarrow aT[A \mid bT[B \mid [\\
Aa &\rightarrow aA \\
Ab &\rightarrow bA \\
Ba &\rightarrow aB \\
Bb &\rightarrow bB \\
A] &\rightarrow a] \\
B] &\rightarrow b]
\end{aligned}
$$

generates the language $\{u[u] \mid u \in \{a, b\}^*\}$.

The addition of a terminal to the first string is accompanied by the generation of the variable A or B. Using the rules that interchange the position of a variable and a terminal, the derivation progresses by passing the variable through the copy of the string enclosed in the brackets. When the variable is adjacent to the symbol], the appropriate terminal is added to the second string. The entire process may be repeated to generate additional terminal symbols or terminated by the application of the rule $T[\rightarrow [$. The derivation

$$
\begin{aligned}
S &\Rightarrow aT[a] \\
&\Rightarrow aaT[Aa] \\
&\Rightarrow aaT[aA] \\
&\Rightarrow aaT[aa] \\
&\Rightarrow aabT[Baa] \\
&\Rightarrow aabT[aBa] \\
&\Rightarrow aabT[aaB] \\
&\Rightarrow aabT[aab] \\
&\Rightarrow aab[aab]
\end{aligned}
$$

exhibits the roles of the variables in a derivation. □

In the preceding grammars, the left-hand side of each rule contained a variable. This is not required by the definition of unrestricted grammar. However, the imposition of the restriction that the left-hand side of a rule must contain a variable does not reduce the set of languages that can be generated (Exercise 3).

Theorem 10.1.2

Let $G = (V, \Sigma, P, S)$ be an unrestricted grammar. Then $L(G)$ is a recursively enumerable language.

Proof We will sketch the design of a three-tape nondeterministic Turing machine M that accepts $L(G)$. Tape 1 holds the input and tape 2 a representation of the rules of G. A rule $u \rightarrow v$ is represented on tape 2 by the string $u\#v$ where # is a tape symbol reserved for this purpose. Rules are separated by two consecutive #'s. The derivations of G are simulated on tape 3.

A computation of the machine M that accepts L(G) consists of the following actions:

1. S is written on position one of tape 3.
2. The rules of G are written on tape 2.
3. A rule $u\#v$ is chosen from tape 2.
4. An instance of the string u is chosen on tape 3, if one exists. Otherwise, the computation halts in a rejecting state.
5. The string u is replaced by v on tape 3.
6. If the strings on tape 3 and tape 1 match, the computation halts in an accepting state.
7. To apply another rule, steps 3–7 are repeated.

Since the length of u and v may differ, the simulation of a rule application $xuy \Rightarrow xvy$ may require shifting the position of the string y.

For any string $p \in L(G)$, there is a sequence of rule applications that derives p. This derivation will be examined by one of the nondeterministic computations of the machine M. Conversely, the actions of M on tape 3 generate precisely the strings derivable from S in G. The only strings accepted by M are terminal strings in L(G). Thus, $L(M) = L(G)$. ∎

Example 10.1.3

The language $L = \{a^i b^i c^i \mid i \geqslant 0\}$ is generated by the rules

$$
\begin{aligned}
S &\rightarrow aAbc \mid \lambda \\
A &\rightarrow aAbC \mid \lambda \\
Cb &\rightarrow bC \\
Cc &\rightarrow cc.
\end{aligned}
$$

Computations of the machine that accepts L simulate derivations of the grammar. The rules of the grammar are represented on tape 2 by

$$BS\#aAbc\#\#S\#\#\#A\#aAbC\#A\#\#\#Cb\#bC\#\#Cc\#cc\#\#B.$$

The rule $S \rightarrow \lambda$ is represented by the string $S\#\#\#$. The first # separates the left-hand side of the rule from the right-hand side. The right-hand side of the rule, the null string in this case, is followed by the string $\#\#$. □

Theorem 10.1.3

Let L be a recursively enumerable language. Then there is an unrestricted grammar G with $L(G) = L$.

Proof Since L is recursively enumerable, it is accepted by a deterministic Turing machine $M = (Q, \Sigma, \Gamma, \delta, q_0, F)$. An unrestricted grammar $G = (V, \Sigma, P, S)$ is designed whose derivations simulate the computations of M. Considering the nonblank segment of the tape as a string over Γ^*, the effect of a Turing machine transition $\delta(q_i, x) = [q_j, y, R]$ on the configuration uq_ixvB can be represented by the string transformation $uq_ixvB \Rightarrow uyq_jvB$.

The derivation of a terminal string in G consists of three distinct subderivations:

i) the generation of a string $u[q_0Bu]$ where $u \in \Sigma^*$

ii) the simulation of a computation of M on the string $[q_0Bu]$

iii) the removal of the simulation substring.

The grammar G contains a variable A_i for each terminal symbol $a_i \in \Sigma$. These variables, along with S, T, [, and], are used in the generation of the strings $u[q_0Bu]$. The simulation of a computation uses variables corresponding to the states of M. The variables E_R and E_L are used in the third phase of a derivation. The set of terminals of G is the input alphabet of M.

$$\Sigma = \{a_1, a_2, \ldots, a_n\}$$
$$V = \{S, T, E_R, E_L, [,], A_1, A_2, \ldots, A_n\} \cup Q$$

The rules for each of the three parts of a derivation are given separately. A derivation begins by generating $u[q_0Bu]$ where u is an arbitrary string in Σ^*. The strategy used for generating strings of this form was presented in Example 10.1.2.

1. $S \rightarrow a_iT[a_i] \mid [q_0B]$ for $1 \leqslant i \leqslant n$
2. $A_ia_j \rightarrow a_jA_i$ for $1 \leqslant i, j \leqslant n$
3. $A_i] \rightarrow a_i]$ for $1 \leqslant i \leqslant n$
4. $T[\rightarrow a_iT[A_i \mid [q_0B$

The computation of the Turing machine with input u is simulated on the string $[q_0Bu]$. The rules are obtained by rewriting of the transitions of M as string transformations.

5. $q_ixy \rightarrow zq_jy$ whenever $\delta(q_i, x) = [q_j, z, R]$ and $y \in \Gamma$
6. $q_ix] \rightarrow zq_jB]$ whenever $\delta(q_i, x) = [q_j, z, R]$
7. $yq_ix \rightarrow q_jyz$ whenever $\delta(q_i, x) = [q_j, z, L]$ and $y \in \Gamma$

If the computation halts in an accepting state, the derivation erases the string within the brackets. The variable E_R erases the string to the right of the halting position of the tape head. Upon reaching the end marker], the variable E_L (erase left) is generated.

8. $q_ix \rightarrow E_R$ whenever $\delta(q_i, x)$ is undefined and $q_i \in F$
9. $E_Rx \rightarrow E_R$ for $x \in \Gamma$
10. $E_R] \rightarrow E_L$
11. $xE_L \rightarrow E_L$ for $x \in \Gamma$
12. $[E_L \rightarrow \lambda$

The derivation that begins by generating $u[q_0Bu]$ terminates with u whenever $u \in L(M)$. If $u \notin L(M)$, the brackets enclosing the simulation of the computation are never erased and the derivation does not produce a terminal string.   ∎

Properties of unrestricted grammars can be used to establish closure results for recursively enumerable languages. The proofs, similar to those presented in Theorem 8.5.1 for context-free languages, are left as exercises.

Theorem 10.1.4
The set of recursively enumerable languages is closed under union, concatenation, and Kleene star.

10.2   Context-Sensitive Grammars

The context-sensitive grammars represent an intermediate step between the context-free and the unrestricted grammars. No restrictions are placed on the left-hand side of a production, but the length of the right-hand side is required to be at least that of the left.

Definition 10.2.1
A phrase-structure grammar $G = (V, \Sigma, P, S)$ is called **context-sensitive** if each production has the form $u \to v$ where $u \in (V \cup \Sigma)^+$, $v \in (V \cup \Sigma)^+$, and $length(u) \leqslant length(v)$.

These grammars are also called monotonic or noncontracting since the length of the derived string remains the same or increases with each rule application. A rule that satisfies the conditions of Definition 10.2.1 is called **monotonic**. The language generated by a context-sensitive grammar is called, not surprisingly, a context-sensitive language.

Context-sensitive grammars were originally defined as phrase-structure grammars in which each production is of the form $uAv \to uwv$ where $A \in V$, $w \in (V \cup \Sigma)^+$ and $u, v \in (V \cup \Sigma)^*$. The preceding rule indicates that variable A can be transformed to w only when it appears in the context of being preceded by u and followed by v. Clearly, every grammar defined in this manner is monotonic. On the other hand, a transformation defined by a monotonic rule can be generated by a set of rules of the form $uAv \to uwv$ (Exercises 12 and 13).

The monotonic property of the rules guarantees that the null string is not an element of a context-sensitive language. Removing the rule $S \to \lambda$ from the grammar in Example 10.1.1, we obtain the unrestricted grammar

$$
\begin{aligned}
S &\to aAbc \\
A &\to aAbC \mid \lambda \\
Cb &\to bC \\
Cc &\to cc
\end{aligned}
$$

that generates the language $\{a^i b^i c^i \mid i > 0\}$. The lambda rule violates the monotonicity of rules. Replacing the S and A rules with

$$S \rightarrow aAbc \mid abc$$
$$A \rightarrow aAbC \mid abC$$

produces an equivalent context-sensitive grammar.

A nondeterministic Turing machine, similar to the machine in Theorem 10.1.2, is designed to accept a context-sensitive language. The noncontracting nature of the rules permits the length of the input string to be used to terminate the simulation of an unsuccessful derivation. When the length of the derived string surpasses that of the input, the computation halts and rejects the string.

Theorem 10.2.2

Every context-sensitive language is recursive.

Proof   Following the approach developed in Theorem 10.1.2, derivations of the context-sensitive grammar are simulated on a three-tape nondeterministic Turing machine M. The entire derivation, rather than just the result, is recorded on tape 3. When a rule $u \rightarrow v$ is applied to the string xuy on tape 3, the string xvy is written on the tape following $xuy\#$. The symbol $\#$ is used to separate the derived strings.

A computation of M with input string p performs the following sequence of actions:

1. $S\#$ is written beginning at position one of tape 3.
2. The rules of G are written on tape 2.
3. A rule $u\#v$ is chosen from tape 2.
4. Let $q\#$ be the most recent string written on tape 3.
   a) An instance of the string u in q is chosen, if one exists. In this case, q can be written xuy.
   b) Otherwise, the computation halts in a rejecting state.
5. $xvy\#$ is written on tape 3 immediately following $q\#$.
6. a) If $xvy = p$, the computation halts in an accepting state.
   b) If xvy occurs at another position on tape 3, the computation halts in a rejecting state.
   c) If $length(xvy) > length(p)$, the computation halts in a rejecting state.
7. Steps 3–7 are repeated.

There are only a finite number of strings in $(V \cup \Sigma)^*$ with length less than or equal to $length(p)$. This implies that every derivation eventually halts, enters a cycle, or derives a string of length greater than $length(p)$. A computation halts at step 4 when the rule that has been selected cannot be applied to the current string. Cyclic derivations, $S \overset{*}{\Rightarrow} w \overset{+}{\Rightarrow} w$, are terminated in step 6b). The length bound is used in step 6c) to terminate all other unsuccessful derivations.

Every string in L(G) is generated by a noncyclic derivation. The simulation of such a derivation causes M to accept the string. Since every computation of M halts, L(G) is recursive (Exercise 9.20).   ∎

10.3   Linear-Bounded Automata

We have examined several alterations to the standard Turing machine that do not alter the set of languages recognized by the machines. Restricting the amount of the tape available for a computation decreases the capabilities of a Turing machine computation. A linear-bounded automaton is a Turing machine in which the amount of available tape is determined by the length of the input string. The input alphabet contains two symbols, $\langle$ and $\rangle$, that designate the left and right boundaries of the tape.

Definition 10.3.1

A **linear-bounded automaton** (LBA) is a structure $M = (Q, \Sigma, \Gamma, \delta, q_0, \langle, \rangle, F)$ where $Q, \Sigma, \Gamma, \delta, q_0$, and F are the same as for a nondeterministic Turing machine. The symbols $\langle$ and $\rangle$ are distinguished elements of Γ.

The initial configuration of a computation is $q_0\langle w\rangle$, requiring $length(w) + 2$ tape positions. The endmarkers $\langle$ and $\rangle$ are written on the tape but not considered part of the input. A computation remains within the boundaries specified by $\langle$ and $\rangle$. The endmarkers may be read by the machine but cannot be erased. Transitions scanning $\langle$ must designate a move to the right and those reading $\rangle$ to the left. A string $w \in (\Gamma - \{\langle, \rangle\})^*$ is accepted by an LBA if a computation with input $\langle w\rangle$ halts in an accepting state.

We will show that every context-sensitive language is accepted by a linear-bounded automaton. An LBA is constructed to simulate the derivations of the context-sensitive grammar. The Turing machine constructed to simulate the derivations of an unrestricted grammar begins by writing the rules of the grammar on one of the tapes. The restriction on the amount of tape available to an LBA prohibits this approach. Instead, states and transitions of the LBA are used to encode the rules.

Consider a context-sensitive grammar with variables $\{S, A\}$ and terminal alphabet $\{a\}$. The application of a rule $Sa \rightarrow aAS$ can be simulated by a sequence of transitions in an LBA (Fig. 10.1). The first two transitions verify that the string on the tape beginning at the position of the tape head matches the left-hand side of the rule.

The application of the rule generates a string transformation $uSav \Rightarrow uaASv$. Before Sa is replaced with aAS, the string v is traversed to determine whether the derived string fits on the segment of the tape available to the computation. If the $\rangle$ is read, the computation terminates. Otherwise, the string v is shifted one position to the right and Sa is replaced by aAS.

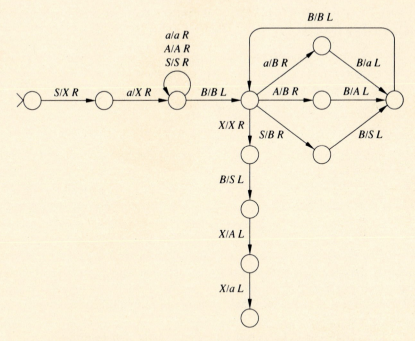

FIGURE 10.1   LBA simulation of application of $Sa \rightarrow aAS$.

Theorem 10.3.2

Let L be a context-sensitive language. Then there is a linear-bounded automaton M with L(M) = L.

Proof   Since L is a context-sensitive language, L = L(G) for some context-sensitive grammar $G = (V, \Sigma, P, S)$. An LBA M with a two-track tape is constructed to simulate the derivations of G. The first track contains the input, including the endmarkers. The second track holds the string generated by the simulated derivation.

Each rule of G is encoded in a submachine of M. A computation of M with input $\langle p \rangle$ consists of the following sequence of actions:

1. S is written on track 2 in position one.

2. The tape head is moved into a position in which it scans a symbol of the string on track 2.

3. A rule $u \rightarrow v$ is selected, and the computation attempts to apply the rule.

4. a) If a substring on track 2 beginning at the position of the tape head does not match u, the computation halts in a rejecting state.

   b) If the tape head is scanning u but the string obtained by replacing u by v is greater than $length(p)$, then the computation halts in a rejecting state.

   c) Otherwise, u is replaced by v on track 2.

5. If track 2 contains the string p, the computation halts in an accepting state.

6. Steps 2–6 are repeated.

Every string in L is generated by a derivation of G. The simulation of the derivation causes M to accept the string. Conversely, a computation of M with input $\langle p \rangle$ that halts in an accepting state consists of a sequence of string transformations generated by steps 2 and 3. These transformations define a derivation of p in G.   ∎

Theorem 10.3.3

Let L be a language accepted by a linear-bounded automaton. Then $L - \{\lambda\}$ is a context-sensitive language.

Proof   Let $M = (Q, \Sigma_M, \Gamma, \delta, q_0, \langle, \rangle, F)$ be an LBA that accepts L. A context-sensitive grammar G is designed to generate L(M). Following the approach presented in Theorem 10.1.3, a computation of M that accepts the input string p is simulated by a derivation of p in G. The techniques used to construct an unrestricted grammar that simulates a Turing machine computation cannot be employed since the rules that erase the simulation do not satisfy the monotonicity restrictions of a context-sensitive grammar. The inability to erase symbols in a derivation of context-sensitive grammar restricts the length of a derived string to that of the input. The simulation is accomplished by using composite objects as variables.

The terminal alphabet of G is obtained from the input alphabet of M by deleting the endmarkers. Ordered pairs are used as variables. The first component of an ordered pair is a terminal symbol. The second is a string consisting of a combination of an input symbol and possibly a state and endmarker(s).

$$\Sigma_G = \Sigma_M - \{\langle, \rangle\} = \{a_1, a_2, \ldots, a_n\}$$
$$V = \{S, A, [a_i, a_j], [a_i, \langle a_j], [a_i, a_j)], [a_i, \langle a_j \rangle], [a_i, q_k a_j], [a_i, q_k \langle a_j], [a_i, \langle q_k a_j],$$
$$[a_i, q_k a_j)], [a_i, a_j q_k)], [a_i, q_k \langle a_j)], [a_i, \langle q_k a_j)], [a_i, \langle a_j q_k)]\}$$
where $a_i, a_j \in \Sigma_G$ and $q_k \in Q$

The S and A rules generate ordered pairs whose components represent the input string and the initial configuration of a computation of M.

1. $S \rightarrow [a_i, q_0 \langle a_i] A$
   $\rightarrow [a_i, q_0 \langle a_i)]$
   for every $a_i \in \Sigma_G$
2. $A \rightarrow [a_i, a_i] A$
   $\rightarrow [a_i, a_i)]$
   for every $a_i \in \Sigma_G$

Derivations using the S and A rules generate sequences of ordered pairs of the form

$$[a_i, q_0 \langle a_i)]$$
$$[a_i, q_0 \langle a_{i_1}] [a_{i_2}, a_{i_2}] \ldots [a_{i_n}, a_{i_n})].$$

The string obtained by concatenating the elements in the first component of the ordered pairs, $a_{i_1} a_{i_2} \ldots a_{i_n}$, represents the input string to a computation of M. The second components produce $q_0 \langle a_{i_1} a_{i_2} \ldots a_{i_n} \rangle$, the initial configuration of the LBA.

The rules that simulate a computation are obtained by rewriting the transitions of M as transformations that alter the second components of the ordered pairs. Note that the second components do not produce the string $q_0 \langle \; \rangle$; the computation with the null string as input is not simulated by the grammar. The techniques presented in Theorem 10.1.3 can be modified to produce the rules needed to simulate the computations of M. The details are left as an exercise.

Upon the completion of a successful computation, the derivation must generate the original input string. When an accepting configuration is generated, the variable with the accepting state in the second component of the ordered pair is transformed into the terminal symbol contained in the first component.

3. $[a_i,\ q_k \langle a_j] \rightarrow a_i$ $[a_i,\ q_k \langle a_j \rangle] \rightarrow a_i$
   $[a_i,\ \langle q_k a_j] \rightarrow a_i$ $[a_i,\ \langle q_k a_j \rangle] \rightarrow a_i$
   $[a_i,\ q_k a_j] \rightarrow a_i$ $[a_i,\ \langle a_j q_k \rangle] \rightarrow a_i$
   $[a_i,\ q_k a_j \rangle] \rightarrow a_i$
   $[a_i,\ a_j q_k \rangle] \rightarrow a_i$
   whenever $\delta(q_k, a_j) = \emptyset$ and $q_k \in F$

The derivation is completed by transforming the remaining variables to the terminal contained in the first component.

4. $[a_i,\ u] a_j \rightarrow a_i a_j$
   $a_j [a_i,\ u] \rightarrow a_j a_i$
   for every $a_j \in \Sigma_G$ and $[a_i,\ u] \in V$ ∎

10.4 The Chomsky Hierarchy

Chomsky numbered the four families of grammars (and languages) that comprise the hierarchy. Unrestricted, context-sensitive, context-free, and regular grammars are referred to as type 0, type 1, type 2, and type 3 grammars, respectively. The restrictions placed on the rules increase with the number of the grammar. The nesting of families of grammars that comprise the Chomsky hierarchy induces a nesting of the corresponding languages. Every context-free language containing the null string is generated by a context-free grammar in which $S \rightarrow \lambda$ is the only lambda rule (Theorem 5.1.5). Removing this single lambda rule produces a context-sensitive grammar that generates $L - \{\lambda\}$. Thus, the language $L - \{\lambda\}$ is context-sensitive whenever L is context-free. Ignoring the complications presented by the null string in context-sensitive languages, every type i language is also type $(i - 1)$.

The preceding inclusions are proper. The set $\{a^i b^i \mid i \geq 0\}$ is context-free but not regular (Theorem 7.2.1). Similarly, $\{a^i b^i c^i \mid i > 0\}$ is context-sensitive but not context-free (Example 8.4.1). In Chapter 11, a language L_H is constructed that is recursively enumerable but not recursive. Combining this with Theorem 10.2.2 establishes the proper inclusion of context-sensitive languages in the set of recursively enumerable languages.

Each class of languages in the Chomsky hierarchy has been characterized as the languages generated by a family of grammars and accepted by a type of machine. The relationships developed between generation and recognition are summarized in the following table.

Grammars	Languages	Accepting Machines
Type 0 grammars, phrase-structure grammars, unrestricted grammars	Recursively enumerable languages	Turing machine, nondeterministic Turing machine
Type 1 grammars, context-sensitive grammars, monotonic grammars	Context-sensitive languages	Linear-bounded automata
Type 2 grammars, context-free grammars	Context-free languages	Pushdown automata
Type 3 grammars, regular grammars, left-linear grammars, right-linear grammars	Regular languages	Deterministic finite automata, nondeterministic finite automata

Exercises

1. Design unrestricted grammars to generate the following languages:

   a) $\{a^i b^j a^i b^j \mid i, j \geq 0\}$

   b) $\{a^i b^i c^i d^i \mid i \geq 0\}$

   c) $\{www \mid w \in \{a, b\}^*\}$

2. Prove that every terminal string generated by the grammar

$$
\begin{aligned}
S &\rightarrow aAbc \mid \lambda \\
A &\rightarrow aAbC \mid \lambda \\
Cb &\rightarrow bC \\
Cc &\rightarrow cc
\end{aligned}
$$

   has the form $a^i b^i c^i$ for some $i \geq 0$.

3. Prove that every recursively enumerable language is generated by a grammar in which each rule has the form $u \rightarrow v$ where $u \in V^+$ and $v \in (V \cup \Sigma)^*$.

4. Prove that the recursively enumerable languages are closed under the following operations:

   a) union

   b) intersection

   c) concatenation

   d) Kleene star

   e) homomorphic images

5. Let M be an LBA with alphabet Σ. Outline a general approach to construct monotonic rules that simulate the computation of M. The rules of the grammar should consist of variables in the set

   $$\{[a_i, a_j], [a_i, \langle a_j], [a_i, a_j)], [a_i, \langle a_j)], [a_i, q_k a_j], [a_i, q_k\langle a_j], [a_i, \langle q_k a_j], [a_i, q_k a_j)],$$
   $$[a_i, a_j q_k)], [a_i, q_k\langle a_j)], [a_i, \langle q_k a_j)], [a_i, \langle a_j q_k)]\}$$

   where $a_i, a_j \in \Sigma$. This completes the construction of the grammar in Theorem 10.3.3.

6. Prove that the context-sensitive languages are not closed under arbitrary homomorphisms. A homomorphism is λ-free if $h(u) = \lambda$ implies $u = \lambda$. Prove that the context-sensitive grammars are closed under λ-free homomorphisms.

7. Let L be a recursively enumerable language over Σ and c a terminal symbol not in Σ. Show that there is a context-sensitive language L' over $\Sigma \cup \{c\}$ such that, for every $w \in \Sigma^*$, $w \in$ L if, and only if, $wc^i \in$ L' for some $i \geqslant 0$.

8. Prove that every recursively enumerable language is the homomorphic image of a context-sensitive language. Hint: Use Exercise 7.

9. A grammar is said to be context-sensitive with erasing if every rule has the form $uAv \rightarrow uwv$ where $A \in$ V and $u, v, w \in (V \cup \Sigma)^*$. Prove that this family of grammars generates the recursively enumerable languages.

10. A linear-bounded automaton is deterministic if at most one transition is specified for each state and tape symbol. Prove that every context-free language is accepted by a deterministic LBA.

11. Let L be a context-sensitive language that is accepted by a deterministic LBA. Prove that $\bar{\text{L}}$ is context-sensitive. Note that a computation in an arbitrary deterministic LBA need not halt.

12. Let $u \rightarrow v$ be a monotonic rule. Construct a sequence of monotonic rules, each of whose right-hand side has length two or less, that defines the same transformation as $u \rightarrow v$.

13. Construct a sequence of context-sensitive rules $uAv \rightarrow uwv$ that define the same transformation as the monotonic rule $AB \rightarrow CD$. Hint: A sequence of three rules, each of whose left-hand side and right-hand side is of length two, suffices.

14. Use the results from Exercises 12 and 13 to prove that every context-sensitive language is generated by a grammar in which each rule has the form $uAv \rightarrow uwv$ where $w \in \Sigma^+$ and $u, v \in (V \cup \Sigma)^*$.

15. Let G be the monotonic grammar

$$G: S \rightarrow SBA \mid a$$
$$BA \rightarrow AB$$
$$aA \rightarrow aaB$$
$$B \rightarrow b.$$

   a) Give a derivation of *aaabbbb*.

   b) What is L(G)?

   c) Construct a context-free grammar that generates L(G).

Bibliographic Notes

The Chomsky hierarchy was introduced by Chomsky [1959]. This paper includes the proof that the unrestricted grammars generate precisely recursively enumerable languages. Linear-bounded automata were presented in Myhill [1960]. The relationship between linear-bounded automata and context-sensitive languages was developed by Landweber [1963] and Kuroda [1964]. Solutions to Exercises 10 to 12, which exhibit the relationship between monotonic and context-sensitive grammars, can be found in Kuroda [1964].

PART IV

Decidability
and Computability

CHAPTER 11

Decidability

A decision problem is a set of questions whose answers are either yes or no. A solution to a decision problem is an effective procedure that determines the answer for each question in the set. A decision problem is undecidable if there is no algorithm that solves the problem. The ability of Turing machines to return affirmative and negative responses makes them an appropriate mathematical system for constructing solutions to decision problems. The Church-Turing thesis asserts that a Turing machine can be designed to solve any decision problem that is solvable by any effective procedure. Techniques are developed to establish the undecidability of several important questions concerning the capabilities of algorithmic computation.

11.1 Decision Problems

A **decision problem P** is a set of questions each of which has a yes or no answer. The single question, "Is 8 a perfect square?" is an example of the type of question that comprises a decision problem. A decision problem usually consists of an infinite number of related questions. For example, the problem P_{SQ} of determining whether an arbitrary natural number is a perfect square consists of the following questions:

p_0: Is 0 a perfect square?
p_1: Is 1 a perfect square?
p_2: Is 2 a perfect square?
$\vdots$

A solution to a decision problem **P** is an algorithm that determines the appropriate answer to every question **p** ∈ **P**.

Since a solution to a decision problem is an algorithm, a review of our intuitive notion of algorithmic computation may be beneficial. We have not, and probably cannot, precisely define algorithm. This notion falls into the category of "I can't describe it but I know one when I see one." We can, however, list several properties that seem fundamental to the concept of algorithm. An algorithm that solves a decision problem should be

- complete—it produces an answer, either positive or negative, to each question in the problem domain
- mechanistic—it consists of a finite sequence of instructions each of which can be carried out without requiring insight, ingenuity, or guesswork
- deterministic—when presented with identical input, it always produces the same result.

A procedure that satisfies the preceding properties is often called **effective.**

The computations of a standard Turing machine are clearly mechanistic and deterministic. A Turing machine that halts for every input string is also complete. Because of the intuitive effectiveness of their computations, Turing machines provide a formal framework that can be used to construct solutions to decision problems. A problem is answered affirmatively if the input is accepted by a Turing machine and negatively if it is rejected.

Recall the newspaper vending machine described at the beginning of Chapter 6. Thirty cents in nickels, dimes, and quarters is required to open the latch. If more than 30 cents is inserted, the machine keeps the entire amount. Consider the problem of a miser who wants to buy a newspaper but refuses to pay more than the minimum. A solution to this problem is a procedure that determines whether a set of coins contains a combination that totals exactly 30 cents.

The transformation of a decision problem from its natural domain to an equivalent problem that can be answered by a Turing machine is known as constructing a representation of the problem. To solve the correct-change problem with a Turing machine, the problem must be formulated as a question of accepting strings. The miser's change can be represented as an element of $\{n, d, q\}^*$ where n, d, and q designate a nickel, a dime, and a quarter, respectively. Note that a representation is not unique; there are six strings that represent the set of coins consisting of a nickel, a dime, and a quarter.

The Turing machine in Fig. 11.1 solves the correct-change problem. The sequences in the start state represent the five distinct combinations of coins that provide an affirmative answer to the question. For example, the solution consisting of one dime and four nickels is represented by $(d, 4n)$. The sequences in the state entered as the result of a transition specify the coins that, when combined with the previously processed coins, produce a combination that totals exactly 30 cents.

We have chosen the standard model of the Turing machine as a formal system in which solutions to decision problems are formulated. The completeness property of effective

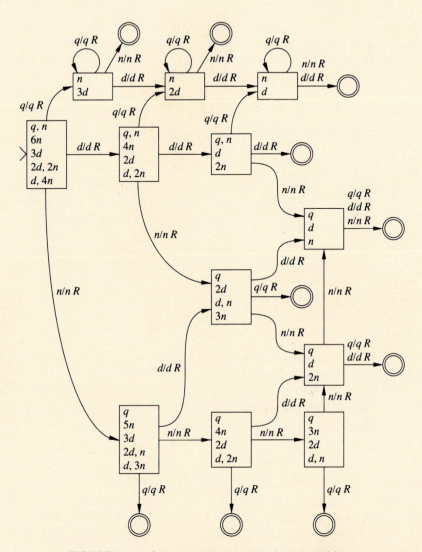

FIGURE 11.1   Solution to the correct-change problem.

computation requires the computation of the machine to terminate for every input string. Thus the language accepted by a Turing machine that solves a decision problem is recursive. Conversely, every deterministic Turing machine M that recognizes a recursive language can be considered a solution to a decision problem. The machine M solves the problem consisting of questions of the form, "Is the string $w \in \Sigma^*$ in L(M)?"

The duality between solvable decision problems and recursive languages can be exploited to broaden the techniques available for establishing the decidability of a decision problem. A problem is decidable if it has a representation in which the accepted input comprises a recursive language. Since computations of deterministic multitrack and multi-tape machines can be simulated on a standard Turing machine, solutions using these machines also establish the decidability of a problem.

Example 11.1.1

The decision problem P_{SQ} is decidable. The three-tape Turing machine from Example 9.5.1 solves P_{SQ}.   □

Determinism is one of the fundamental properties of algorithms. However, it is often much easier to design a nondeterministic Turing machine to solve a decision problem. In Section 9.6 it was shown that every language accepted by a nondeterministic Turing machine is also accepted by a deterministic one. A solution to a decision problem requires more than a machine that accepts the appropriate strings; it also demands that all computations terminate. A nondeterministic machine in which every computation terminates can be used to establish the existence of a decision procedure. The languages of such machines are recursive (Exercise 9.20), ensuring the existence of a deterministic solution.

Example 11.1.2

The problem of determining whether there is a path from a node x to a node y in a directed graph is decidable. A directed graph consists of a finite set of nodes N and arcs $A \subseteq N \times N$. An arc $[a, b]$ is represented by the string ab. The symbol # is used to separate arcs. The input to the machine consists of a representation of the graph followed by the nodes x and y. Two #'s separate x and y from the representation of the graph. The directed graph

$$N = \{a, b, c\}$$
$$A = \{[a, b], [a, a], [b, c], [c, b]\}$$

is represented by the string $ab\#aa\#bc\#cb$. A computation to determine whether there is a path from c to a in this graph begins with the input $ab\#aa\#bc\#cb\#\#ca$.

A nondeterministic two-tape Turing machine M is designed to solve the path problem. The actions of M are summarized below.

1. The input is checked to determine if its format is that of a representation of a directed graph followed by two nodes. If not, M halts and rejects the string.

2. The input is now assumed to have form $R\#\#xy$, where R is the representation of a directed graph. If x and y are identical, M halts in an accepting state.

3. The node x is written on tape 2 in the leftmost position.

4. Let u be the rightmost nonblank symbol on tape 2. An arc uv, where v is not already on tape 2, is nondeterministically chosen from R. If no such arc exists, M halts in a rejecting state.

5. If $v = y$, M halts in an accepting state. Otherwise, v is written at the end of the string on tape 2 and steps 4 and 5 are repeated.

Steps 4 and 5 generate paths beginning with node x on tape 2. Every computation of M terminates after at most n iterations, where n is the number of nodes in the graph, since step 4 guarantees that only noncyclic paths are examined. It follows that L(M) is recursive and the problem is decidable.   □

11.2   The Church-Turing Thesis

The concept of an abstract machine was introduced to provide a formalization of algorithmic computation. Turing machines have been used to recognize languages and solve decision problems. These computations are restricted to returning a yes or no answer. The Church-Turing thesis asserts that every solvable decision problem can be transformed into an equivalent Turing machine problem.

By defining the result of a computation by the symbols on the tape when the machine halts, Turing machines can be used to compute functions. Chapters 12 and 13 examine capabilities and limitations of evaluating functions using Turing machine computations. A more general and concise form of the Church-Turing thesis in terms of effectively computable functions is presented in Chapter 13. Since our attention has been focused on yes/no problems, the Church-Turing thesis is presented and its implications discussed for this class of problems.

A solution to a decision problem requires the computation to return an answer for every instance of the problem. Relaxing this restriction, we obtain the notion of a partial solution. A partial solution to a decision problem **P** is a, not necessarily complete, effective procedure that returns an affirmative response for every $\mathbf{p} \in \mathbf{P}$ whose answer is yes. If the answer to **p** is negative, however, the procedure may return no or fail to produce an answer.

Just as a solution to a decision problem can be formulated as a question of membership in a recursive language, a partial solution to a decision problem is equivalent to the question of membership in a recursively enumerable language.

The Church-Turing thesis for decision problems   There is an effective procedure to solve a decision problem if, and only if, there is a Turing machine accepting a recursive language that solves the problem.

The extended Church-Turing thesis for decision problems   A decision problem **P** is partially solvable if, and only if, there is a Turing machine that accepts precisely the elements of **P** whose answer is yes.

To appreciate the content of the Church-Turing thesis, it is necessary to understand the nature of the assertion. The Church-Turing thesis is not a mathematical theorem; it cannot be proved. This would require a formal definition of the intuitive notion of an effective procedure. The claim could, however, be disproved. This could be accomplished by discovering an effective procedure that cannot be computed by a Turing machine. There is an impressive pool of evidence that suggests that such a procedure will not be found. More about that later.

The Church-Turing thesis may be considered to provide a definition of algorithmic computation. This is an extremely limiting viewpoint. There are many systems that satisfy our intuitive notion of an effective algorithm, for example, the machines designed by Post [1936], recursive functions [Kleene, 1936], and the lambda calculus of Church [1941]. These are but a few of the systems designed to perform effective computations. Moreover, who can predict the formalisms and techniques that will be developed in the future? The Church-Turing thesis does not claim that these other systems do not perform algorithmic computation. It does, however, assert that a computation performed in any such system can be accomplished by a suitably designed Turing machine. Perhaps the strongest evidence supporting the Church-Turing thesis is that all known effective procedures have been able to be transformed into equivalent Turing machines.

The robustness of the standard Turing machine offers additional support for the Church-Turing thesis. Adding multiple tracks, multiple tapes, and nondeterministic computation does not increase the set of recognizable languages. Other approaches to computation, developed independently of formalization of Turing machines, have been shown to recognize the same languages. In Chapter 10 we demonstrated that the recursively enumerable languages are precisely those generated by unrestricted grammars.

A proof by the Church-Turing thesis is a shortcut often taken in establishing the existence of a decision algorithm. Rather than constructing a Turing machine solution to a decision problem, the solution is described as a procedure that is intuitively effective. The Church-Turing thesis guarantees that a Turing machine can be designed to solve the problem. We have tacitly been using the Church-Turing thesis in this manner throughout the presentation of Turing computability. For complicated machines, we simply gave an effective description of the actions of a computation of the machine. We assumed that the complete machine could then be explicitly constructed, if desired.

The Church-Turing thesis asserts that a decision problem **P** has a solution if, and only if, there is a Turing machine that determines the answer for every $\mathbf{p} \in \mathbf{P}$. If no such Turing machine exists, the problem is said to be **undecidable.** A Turing machine computation is not encumbered by the restrictions that are inherent in any "real" computing device. The existence of a Turing machine solution to a decision problem depends entirely on the nature of the problem itself and not on the availability of memory or central processor time. The universality of Turing machine computations also has consequences for undecidability. If a problem cannot be solved by a Turing machine, it clearly cannot be solved by a resource-limited machine. The remainder of this chapter is dedicated to demonstrating the undecidability of several important problems from computability theory and formal language theory.

11.3 The Halting Problem for Turing Machines

The most famous of the undecidable problems is concerned with the properties of Turing machines themselves. The halting problem may be formulated as follows: Given an arbitrary Turing machine M with input alphabet Σ and a string $w \in \Sigma^*$, will the computation of M with input w halt? We will show that there is no algorithm that decides the halting problem. The undecidability of the halting problem is one of the fundamental results in the theory of computer science.

It is important to understand the statement of the problem. We may be able to determine that a particular Turing machine will halt for a given string. In fact, the exact set of strings for which a particular Turing machine halts may be known. For example, the machine in Example 9.2.3 halts for all and only the strings containing the substring *aa*. A solution to the halting problem, however, requires a general algorithm that answers the halting question for *every* possible combination of Turing machine and input string.

A solution to the halting problem requires the Turing machine M and the string w to be represented as an input string. We will consider the halting problem for Turing machines with fixed input and tape alphabets. For the remainder of this section we assume that all Turing machines have input alphabet $\{0, 1\}$ and tape alphabet $\{0, 1, B\}$. The states are denoted $\{q_0, q_1, \ldots, q_n\}$ with q_0 the start state.

A Turing machine is completely defined by its transition function. A transition of a deterministic Turing machine has the form $\delta(q_i, x) = [q_j, y, d]$ where $q_i, q_j \in Q; x, y \in \Gamma$; and $d \in \{L, R\}$. We encode the elements of M using strings of *1*'s.

Symbol	Encoding
0	*1*
1	*11*
B	*111*
q_0	*1*
q_1	*11*
.	.
.	.
.	.
q_i	1^{i+1}
L	*1*
R	*11*

Let *en(x)* denote the encoding of a symbol *x*. A transition $\delta(q_i, x) = [q_j, y, d]$ is encoded by the string

$$en(q_i)0en(x)0en(q_j)0en(y)0en(d).$$

The *0*'s separate the components of the transition. A representation of the machine is constructed from the encoded transitions. Two consecutive *0*'s are used to separate transitions. The beginning and end of the representation are designated by three *0*'s.

Example 11.3.1

The Turing machine

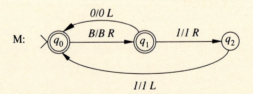

M:

0/0 L

B/B R   1/1 R

1/1 L

accepts the null string and strings of length two or more beginning with *0* or *11*. The encoded transitions of M are given in the table below.

Transition	Encoding
$\delta(q_0, B) = [q_1, B, R]$	*101110110111011*
$\delta(q_1, 0) = [q_0, 0, L]$	*1101010101*
$\delta(q_1, 1) = [q_2, 1, R]$	*110110111011011*
$\delta(q_2, 1) = [q_0, 1, L]$	*1110110101101*

The machine M is represented by the string

00010111011011101100110101010100110110111011011001110110101101000.   □

A Turing machine can be constructed to determine whether an arbitrary string $u \in \{0, 1\}^*$ is the encoding of a deterministic Turing machine. The computation examines u to see if it consists of a prefix *000* followed by a finite sequence of encoded transitions separated by *00*'s followed by *000*. A string that satisfies these conditions is the representation of some Turing machine M. The machine M is deterministic if the combination of the state and input symbol in every encoded transition is distinct.

Utilizing the encoding scheme, the representation of a Turing machine with input alphabet $\{0, 1\}$ is itself a string over $\{0, 1\}$. The proof of Theorem 11.3.1 does not depend upon the features of this particular encoding. The argument is valid for any representation that encodes a Turing machine as a string over its input alphabet. The representation of the M is denoted $R(M)$.

Theorem 11.3.1

The halting problem for Turing machines is undecidable.

Proof   The proof is by contradiction. Assume that there is a Turing machine H that solves the halting problem. A string is accepted by H if

i) the input consists of the representation of a Turing machine M followed by a string w

ii) the computation of M with input w halts.

Otherwise, H rejects the input. The operation of the machine H is depicted by the diagram

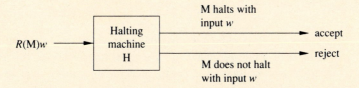

The machine H is modified to construct a Turing machine H′. The computations of H′ are the same as H except H′ loops indefinitely whenever H terminates in an accepting state, that is, whenever M halts on input w. The transition function of H′ is constructed from that of H by adding transitions that cause H′ to move indefinitely to the right upon entering a terminating configuration of H.

H′ is combined with a copy machine to construct another Turing machine D. The input to D is a Turing machine representation $R(M)$. A computation of D begins by creating the string $R(M)R(M)$ from the input $R(M)$. The computation continues by running H′ on $R(M)R(M)$.

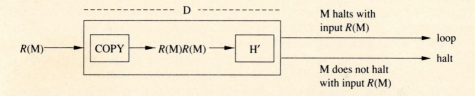

The input to the machine D may be the representation of any Turing machine with alphabet $\{0, 1, B\}$. In particular, D is such a machine. Consider a computation of D with input $R(D)$. Rewriting the previous diagram with M replaced by D and $R(M)$ by $R(D)$, we get

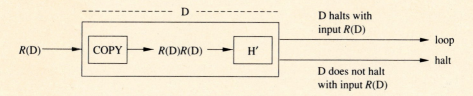

Examining the preceding computation, we see that D halts with input $R(D)$ if, and only if, D does not halt for input $R(D)$. This is obviously a contradiction. However, the machine D can be constructed directly from a machine H that solves the halting problem. The assumption that the halting problem is decidable produces the preceding contradiction. Therefore, we conclude that the halting problem is undecidable. ∎

Corollary 11.3.2

The language $L_H = \{R(M)w \mid R(M)$ is the representation of a Turing machine M and M halts with input $w\}$ over $\{0, 1\}^*$ is not recursive.

A similar argument can be used to establish the undecidability of the halting problem for Turing machines with arbitrary alphabets. The essential feature of this approach is the ability to encode the transitions of a Turing machine as a string over its own input alphabet. Two tape symbols are sufficient to construct such an encoding.

11.4   A Universal Machine

The halting problem provides a negative result concerning the ability to determine the outcome of a Turing machine computation from a description of the machine. The undecidability of the halting problem establishes that the language L_H, consisting of all strings $R(M)w$ for which machine M halts with input w, is not recursive. We will exhibit a single machine U that accepts the input $R(M)w$ whenever the computation of M halts with input w. Note that this machine does not solve the halting problem since U is not guaranteed to reject strings for which M does not halt. In fact, a computation of U with input $R(M)w$ will continue indefinitely whenever M does not halt with input w.

The Turing machines in this section are assumed to be deterministic with tape alphabet $\{0, 1, B\}$. The machine U is called a **universal Turing machine** since the outcome of any computation of a machine M with input w can be obtained by the computation of U with input $R(M)w$. The universal machine alone is sufficient to obtain the results of the computations of the entire family of machines.

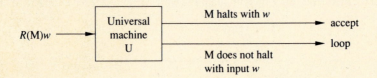

Theorem 11.4.1

The language L_H is recursively enumerable.

Proof   A deterministic three-tape machine U is designed to accept L_H. A computation of U begins with the input on tape 1. The encoding scheme presented in Section 11.3 is used to represent the input Turing machine. If the input string has the form $R(M)w$, the computation of M with input w is simulated on tape 3. The universal machine uses the information encoded in the representation $R(M)$ to simulate the transitions of M. A computation of U consists of the following actions:

1. If the input string does not have the form $R(M)w$ for a deterministic Turing machine M and string w, U moves indefinitely to the right.

2. The string w is written on tape 3 beginning at position one. The tape head is then repositioned at the leftmost square of the tape. The configuration of tape 3 is the initial configuration of a computation of M with input w.

3. A single 1, the encoding of state q_0, is written on tape 2.

4. A transition of M is simulated on tape 3. The transition of M is determined by the symbol scanned on tape 3 and the state encoded on tape 2. Let x be the symbol from tape 3 and q_i the state encoded on tape 2.

   a) Tape 1 is scanned for a transition whose first two components match $en(q_i)$ and $en(x)$. If there is no such transition, U halts and accepts the input.

   b) Assume tape 1 contains the encoded transition $en(q_i)0en(x)0en(q_j)0en(y)0en(d)$. Then

      i) $en(q_i)$ is replaced by $en(q_j)$ on tape 2.
      ii) The symbol y is written on tape 3.
      iii) The tape head of tape 3 is moved in the direction specified by d.

5. The next transition of M is simulated by repeating steps 4 and 5.

The simulations of the universal machine U accept the strings in L_H. The computations of U loop indefinitely for strings in $\{0, 1\}^* - L_H$. Since $L_H = L(U)$, L_H is recursively enumerable.   ∎

The undecidability of the halting problem established that L_H is not recursive. Combining this with Corollary 11.3.2, we obtain Corollary 11.4.2.

Corollary 11.4.2
The recursive languages are a proper subset of the recursively enumerable languages.

The computation of the universal machine U with input $R(M)$ and w simulates the computation M with input w. The ability to obtain the results of one machine via the computations of another facilitates the design of complicated Turing machines. When we say that a Turing machine M' "runs machine M with input w" we mean that M' is supplied with input $R(M)w$ and simulates the computation of M.

11.5   Reducibility

A decision problem **P** is Turing reducible to a problem **P**′ if there is a Turing machine that takes any problem $p_i \in P$ as input and produces an associated problem $p_i' \in P'$ where the answer to the original problem p_i can be obtained from the answer to p_i'. If a

Input $p_i \in$ **P**

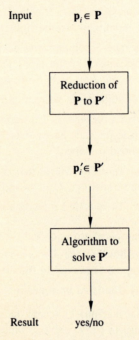

Result   yes/no

FIGURE 11.2 Solution of p_i using reduction to p_i'.

decision problem **P**′ is decidable and **P** is reducible to **P**′ then **P** is also decidable. A solution to **P** can be obtained by combining the reduction with the algorithm that solves **P**′ (Fig. 11.2).

Reduction is a technique commonly employed in problem solving. When faced with a new problem, we often try to translate it into a problem that has previously been solved. This is precisely the strategy employed by the reduction of decision problems.

Example 11.5.1

Consider the problem **P** of recognizing strings in the language $L = \{uu \mid u = a^i b^i c^i$ for some $i \geq 0\}$. The machine M in Example 9.2.2 accepts the language $\{a^i b^i c^i \mid i \geq 0\}$. We will reduce the problem **P** to that of recognizing a single instance of $a^i b^i c^i$. The original problem can then be solved using the reduction and the machine M. The reduction is obtained as follows:

1. The input string w is copied.
2. The copy of w is used to determine whether $w = uu$ for some string $u \in \{a, b, c\}^*$.

3. If $w \neq uu$, then the tape is erased and a single a is written in the input position.

4. If $w = uu$, then the tape is erased, leaving u in the input position.

If the input string w has the form uu, then $w \in L$ if, and only if, $u = a^i b^i c^i$ for some i. The machine M has been designed to answer precisely this question. On the other hand, if $w \neq uu$ the reduction produces the string a. This string is subsequently rejected by M, indicating that the input $w \notin L$. $\qquad\square$

Reduction has important implications for undecidability as well as decidability. Assume that **P** is undecidable and that **P** is reducible to a problem **P′**. Then **P′** is also undecidable. If **P′** were decidable, the algorithm that solves **P′** could be used to construct a decision procedure for **P**.

The **blank tape problem** is the problem of deciding whether a Turing machine halts when a computation is initiated with a blank tape. The blank tape problem is a special case of the halting problem since it is concerned only with the question of halting when the input is the null string. We will show that the halting problem is reducible to the blank tape problem.

Theorem 11.5.1

There is no algorithm that determines whether an arbitrary Turing machine halts when a computation is initiated with a blank tape.

Proof   Assume that there is a machine B that solves the blank tape problem. Such a machine can be represented

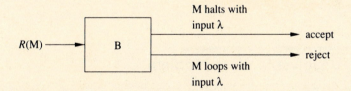

A new machine is constructed by adding a preprocessor N to B. The input to N is the representation of a Turing machine M followed by an input string w. The result of a computation of N is the representation of a machine M′ that

1. writes w on a blank tape

2. returns the tape head to the initial position with the machine in the initial state of M

3. runs M.

$R(M′)$ is obtained by adding encoded transitions to $R(M)$ and suitably renaming the start state of M. The machine M′ has been constructed so that it halts when run with a blank tape if, and only if, M halts with input w.

Sequentially running the machines N and B produces the composite machine

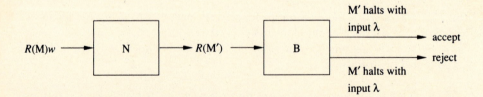

Tracing a computation, we see that the composite machine solves the halting problem. The preprocessor N reduces the halting problem to the blank tape problem. It follows that the blank tape problem is undecidable.   ∎

The relationship between Turing machines and unrestricted grammars developed in Section 10.1 can be used to transfer the undecidability results from the domain of machines to the domain of grammars. Consider the problem of deciding whether a string w is generated by a grammar G. We can reduce the halting problem to the question of generation in an unrestricted grammar. Let M be a Turing machine and w an input string for M. First construct a Turing machine M' that accepts every string for which M halts (make every state of M an accepting state). In M', halting and accepting are synonymous.

Using Theorem 10.1.3, a grammar $G_{M'}$ can be constructed with $L(G_{M'}) = L(M')$. An algorithm that decides whether $w \in L(G_{M'})$ also determines whether the computation of M' (and M) halts.

11.6   An Unsolvable Word Problem

A semi-Thue system is a special type of grammar consisting of a single alphabet Σ and a set P of rules. A rule has the form $u \to v$ where $u \in \Sigma^+$ and $v \in \Sigma^*$. There is no division of the symbols into variables and terminals nor is there a designated start symbol. As before, $u \overset{*}{\Rightarrow} v$ signifies that u is derivable from v by a finite number of rule applications.

The word problem for semi-Thue systems is the problem of determining, for an arbitrary semi-Thue system $S = (\Sigma, P)$ and strings $u, v \in \Sigma^*$, whether v is derivable from u in S. We will show that the halting problem is reducible to the word problem for semi-Thue systems. The reduction is obtained by developing a relationship between semi-Thue systems and Turing machines.

Let $M = (Q, \Sigma, \Gamma, \delta, q_0, F)$ be a deterministic Turing machine. Modifying the construction presented in Theorem 10.1.3, a semi-Thue system $S_M = (\Sigma_{M'}, P_M)$ is constructed whose derivations simulate the computations of M. The alphabet of S_M is the set $Q \cup \Gamma \cup \{[,], q_f, q_R, q_L\}$. The set P_M of rules of S_M is defined by

1. $q_i xy \rightarrow zq_j y$ whenever $\delta(q_i, x) = [q_j, z, R]$ and $y \in \Gamma$
2. $q_i x] \rightarrow zq_j B]$ whenever $\delta(q_i, x) = [q_j, z, R]$
3. $yq_i x \rightarrow q_j yz$ whenever $\delta(q_i, x) = [q_j, z, L]$ and $y \in \Gamma$
4. $q_i x \rightarrow q_R$ if $\delta(q_i, x)$ is undefined
5. $q_R x \rightarrow q_R$ for $x \in \Gamma$
6. $q_R] \rightarrow q_L]$
7. $xq_L \rightarrow q_L$ for $x \in \Gamma$
8. $[q_L \rightarrow [q_f.$

The rules that generate the string $[q_0 Bw]$ in Theorem 10.1.3 are omitted since the word problem for a semi-Thue system is concerned with derivability of a string v from another string u, not from a distinguished start symbol. The erasing rules (5–8) have been modified to generate the string $[q_f]$ whenever the computation of M with input w halts.

The simulation of a computation of M in S_M manipulates strings of the form $[uqv]$. Lemma 11.6.1 lists several important properties of derivations of S_M that simulate a computation of M.

Lemma 11.6.1

Let M be a deterministic Turing machine, S_M the semi-Thue system constructed from M, and let $w = [uqv]$ be a string with $u, v \in \Gamma^*$, and $q \in Q \cup \{q_f, q_R, q_L\}$.

i) There is at most one string z such that $w \underset{S_M}{\Rightarrow} z$.

ii) If there is such a z, then z also has the form $[u'q'v']$ with $u', v' \in \Gamma^*$, and $q' \in Q \cup \{q_f, q_R, q_L\}$.

Proof The application of a rule replaces one instance of an element of $Q \cup \{q_f, q_R, q_L\}$ with another. The determinism of M guarantees that there is at most one rule in P_M that can be applied to $[uqv]$ whenever $q \in Q$. If $q = q_R$ there is a unique rule that can be applied to $[uq_R v]$. This rule is determined by the first symbol of $v]$. Similarly, there is only one rule that can be applied to $[uq_L]$. Finally, there are no rules in P_M that can be applied to a string containing q_f.

Condition ii) follows immediately from the form of the rules of P_M. ∎

A computation of M that halts with input w produces a derivation $[q_0 Bw] \underset{S_M}{\overset{*}{\Rightarrow}} [uq_R v]$. The erasure rules transform this string to $[q_f]$. These properties are combined to yield Lemma 11.6.2.

Lemma 11.6.2

A deterministic Turing machine M halts with input w if, and only if, $[q_0 Bw] \underset{S_M}{\overset{*}{\Rightarrow}} [q_f]$.

Example 11.6.1

The language of the Turing machine

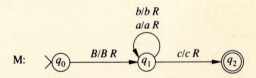

is $(a \cup b)^* c(a \cup b \cup c)^*$. The computation that accepts ac is given with the corresponding derivation of $[q_f]$ from $[q_0BacB]$ in the semi-Thue system S_M.

$$
\begin{array}{ll}
q_0BacB & [q_0BacB] \\
\vdash Bq_1acB & \Rightarrow [Bq_1acB] \\
\vdash Baq_1cB & \Rightarrow [Baq_1cB] \\
\vdash Bacq_2B & \Rightarrow [Bacq_2B] \\
& \Rightarrow [Bacq_RB] \\
& \Rightarrow [Bacq_R] \\
& \Rightarrow [Bacq_L] \\
& \Rightarrow [Baq_L] \\
& \Rightarrow [Bq_L] \\
& \Rightarrow [q_L] \\
& \Rightarrow [q_f]
\end{array}
$$

$\square$

Theorem 11.6.3

The word problem for semi-Thue systems is undecidable.

Proof   The preceding lemmas sketch the reduction of the halting problem to the word problem for semi-Thue systems. For a Turing machine M and corresponding semi-Thue system S_M, the computation of M with input w halting is equivalent to the derivability of $[q_f]$ from $[q_0Bw]$ in S_M. An algorithm that solves the word problem could also be used to solve the halting problem.   ∎

By Theorem 11.6.3, there is no algorithm that solves the word problem for an arbitrary semi-Thue system $S = (\Sigma, P)$ and pair of strings in Σ^*. The relationships developed in Lemma 11.6.2 can be used to prove that there are particular semi-Thue systems whose word problems are undecidable.

Theorem 11.6.4

Let M be a deterministic Turing machine that accepts a nonrecursive language. The word problem for the semi-Thue system S_M is undecidable.

Proof   Since M recognizes a nonrecursive language, the halting problem for M is undecidable (Exercise 8). The correspondence between computations of M and derivations of S_M yields the undecidability of the word problem for this system.   ∎

11.7   The Post Correspondence Problem

The undecidable problems presented in the preceding sections have been concerned with the properties of Turing machines or mathematical systems that simulate Turing machines. The Post correspondence problem is a combinatorial question that can be described as a simple game of manipulating dominoes. A domino consists of two strings from a fixed alphabet, one on the top half of the domino and the other on the bottom.

The game begins when one of the dominoes is placed on a table. Another domino is then placed to the immediate right of the domino on the table. This process is repeated, constructing a sequence of adjacent dominoes. A Post correspondence system can be thought of as defining a finite set of dominoes. We assume that there are an unlimited number of each type of domino. Playing a domino does not limit the number of future moves.

A string is obtained by concatenating the strings in the top halves of a sequence of dominoes. We refer to this as the top string. Similarly, a sequence of dominoes defines a bottom string. The game is successfully completed by constructing a finite sequence of dominoes in which the top and bottom strings are identical. Consider the Post correspondence system defined by dominoes

a	c	ba	acb
ac	ba	a	b

The sequence

a	c	ba	a	acb
ac	ba	a	ac	b

is a solution to this Post correspondence system.

Formally, a **Post correspondence system** consists of an alphabet Σ and a finite set of ordered pairs $[u_i, v_i]$, $i = 1, 2, \ldots, n$ where $u_i, v_i \in \Sigma^+$. A solution to a Post correspondence system is a sequence $i_1, i_2, \ldots, i_k$ such that

$$u_{i_1} u_{i_2} \ldots u_{i_k} = v_{i_1} v_{i_2} \ldots v_{i_k}.$$

The problem of determining whether a Post correspondence system has a solution is the **Post correspondence problem.**

Example 11.7.1

The Post correspondence system with alphabet $\{a,\ b\}$ and ordered pairs [*aaa, aa*], [*baa, abaaa*] has a solution

aaa	baa	aaa
aa	abaaa	aa

☐

Example 11.7.2

Consider the Post correspondence system with alphabet $\{a,\ b\}$ and ordered pairs [*ab, aba*], [*bba, aa*], [*aba, bab*]. A solution must begin with the domino

since this is the only pair in which the first symbols agree. The string in the top half of the next domino must begin with *a*. There are two possibilities:

ab	ab
aba	aba

i)

ab	aba
aba	bab

ii)

The fourth elements of the strings in i) do not match. The only possible way of constructing a solution is to extend ii). Employing the same reasoning as before, the first element in the top of the next domino must be *b*. This lone possibility produces

ab	aba	bba
aba	bab	aa

which cannot be the initial subsequence of a solution since the seventh elements in the top and bottom differ. We have shown that there is no way of "playing the dominoes" in which the top and bottom strings are identical. Hence, this Post correspondence system has no solution.   □

Theorem 11.7.1

There is no algorithm that determines whether an arbitrary Post correspondence system has a solution.

Proof   Let $S = (\Sigma, P)$ be a semi-Thue system with alphabet $\{0, 1\}$ whose word problem is unsolvable. The existence of such a system is assured by Corollary 11.4.2 and Theorem 11.6.4.

For each pair of strings $u, v \in \Sigma^*$, we will construct a Post correspondence system $C_{u,v}$ that has a solution if, and only if, $u \underset{S}{\overset{*}{\Rightarrow}} v$. Since the latter problem is undecidable, there can be no general algorithm that solves the Post correspondence problem.

We begin by augmenting the set of productions of S with the rules $0 \rightarrow 0$ and $1 \rightarrow 1$. Derivations in the resulting system are identical to those in S except for the possible addition of rule applications that do not transform the string. The application of such a rule, however, guarantees that whenever $u \underset{S}{\overset{*}{\Rightarrow}} v$, v may be obtained from u by a derivation of even length. By abuse of notation, the augmented system is also denoted S.

Now let u and v be strings over $\{0, 1\}^*$. A Post correspondence system $C_{u,v}$ is constructed from u, v, and S. The alphabet of $C_{u,v}$ consists of $0, \bar{0}, 1, \bar{1}, [,], *$, and $\bar{*}$. A string w consisting entirely of "barred" symbols is denoted $\bar{w}$.

Each production $x_i \rightarrow y_i$, $i = 1, 2, \ldots, n$, of S (including $0 \rightarrow 0$ and $1 \rightarrow 1$) defines two dominoes

$\bar{y}_i$	y_i
x_i	$\bar{x}_i$

The system is completed by the dominoes

$[u*$	$*$	$\bar{*}$	$]$
$[$	$\bar{*}$	$*$	$\bar{*}v]$

The dominoes

0	$\bar{0}$	1	$\bar{1}$
$\bar{0}$	0	$\bar{1}$	1

can be combined to form sequences dominoes that spell

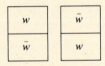

for any string $w \in \{0, 1\}^*$. We will feel free to use these composite dominoes when constructing a solution to a Post correspondence system $C_{u,v}$.

First we show that $C_{u,v}$ has a solution whenever $u \overset{*}{\underset{S}{\Rightarrow}} v$. Let

$$u = u_0 \Rightarrow u_1 \Rightarrow \cdots \Rightarrow u_k \Rightarrow v$$

be a derivation of even length. The rules $0 \to 0$ and $1 \to 1$ ensure that there is derivation of even length whenever the v is derivable from u. The ith step of the derivation can be written

$$u_{i-1} = p_{i-1}x_{j_{i-1}}q_{i-1} \Rightarrow p_{i-1}y_{j_{i-1}}q_{i-1} = u_i$$

where u_i is obtained from u_{i-1} by an application of the rule $x_{j_{i-1}} \to y_{j_{i-1}}$. The string

$$[u_0 * \bar{u}_1 * u_2 * \cdots * \bar{u}_{k-1} * u_k]$$

is a solution to $C_{u,v}$. This solution can be constructed as follows:

1. Initially play

2. To obtain a match, dominoes spelling the string $u = u_0$ on the bottom are played, producing

$[u*$	$\bar{p}_0$	$\bar{y}_{j_0}$	$\bar{q}_0$	$\bar{*}$
$[$	p_0	x_{j_0}	q_0	$*$

The dominoes spelling p_0 and q_0 are composite dominoes. The middle domino is generated by the rule $x_{j_0} \to y_{j_0}$.

3. Since $p_0 y_{j_0} q_0 = u_1$, the top string can be written $[u_0 * \bar{u}_1$ and the bottom $[u_0$. Following the strategy employed above, dominoes must be played to spell $\bar{u}_1$ on the bottom.

$[u*$	$\bar{p}_0$	$\bar{y}_{j_0}$	$\bar{q}_0$	$*$	p_1	y_{j_1}	q_1	$*$
$[$	p_0	x_{j_0}	q_0	$*$	$\bar{p}_1$	$\bar{x}_{j_1}$	$\bar{q}_1$	$\bar{*}$

4. This process is continued for steps 2, 3, ..., $k-1$ of the derivation.

$[u*$	$\bar{p}_0$	$\bar{y}_{j_0}$	$\bar{q}_0$	$*$	p_1	y_{j_1}	q_1	$*$	$\cdots$	p_{k-1}	$y_{j_{k-1}}$	q_{k-1}
$[$	p_0	x_{j_0}	q_0	$*$	$\bar{p}_1$	$\bar{x}_{j_1}$	$\bar{q}_1$	$\bar{*}$	$\cdots$	$\bar{p}_{k-1}$	$\bar{x}_{j_{k-1}}$	$\bar{q}_{k-1}$

5. Completing the sequence with the domino

produces the string $[u_0*\bar{u}_1\bar{*}u_2* \cdots *\bar{u}_{k-1}\bar{*}u_k]$ in both the top and the bottom, solving the correspondence system.

We will now show that a derivation $u \overset{*}{\Rightarrow} w$ can be constructed from a solution to the Post correspondence system $C_{u,v}$. A solution to $C_{u,v}$ must begin with

since this is the only domino whose strings begin with the same symbol. By the same argument, a solution must end with

Thus the string spelled by a solution has the form $[u*w\bar{*}v]$. If w contains $]$, then the solution can be written $[u*x\bar{*}v]y\bar{*}v]$. Since $]$ occurs in only one domino and is the rightmost symbol on both the top and the bottom of that domino, the string $[u*x\bar{*}v]$ is also a solution of $C_{u,v}$.

In light of the previous observation, let $[u* \cdots \bar{*}v]$ be a string that is a solution of the Post correspondence system $C_{u,v}$ in which] occurs only as the rightmost symbol. The information provided by the dominoes at the ends of a solution determines the structure of the entire solution. The solution begins with

A sequence of dominoes that spell u on the bottom must be played in order to match the string already generated on the top. Let $u = x_{i_1} x_{i_2} \ldots x_{i_k}$ be bottom strings in the dominoes that spell u in the solution. Then the solution has the form

$[u*$	$\bar{y}_{i_1}$	$\bar{y}_{i_2}$	$\bar{y}_{i_3}$	$\ldots$	$\bar{y}_{i_k}$	$\bar{*}$
$[$	x_{i_1}	x_{i_2}	x_{i_3}	$\ldots$	x_{i_k}	$*$

Since each domino represents a derivation $x_{i_j} \Rightarrow y_{i_j}$, we combine these to obtain the derivation $u \overset{*}{\Rightarrow} u_1$, where $u_1 = y_{i_1} y_{i_2} \ldots y_{i_k}$. The prefix of the top string of the dominoes that comprise the solution has the form $[u*\bar{u}_1\bar{*}$, and the prefix of the bottom string is $[u*$. Repeating this process, we see that a solution defines a sequence of strings

$$[u*\bar{u}_1\bar{*}u_2* \ldots \bar{*}v]$$
$$[u*\bar{u}_1\bar{*}u_2*\bar{u}_3\bar{*} \ldots \bar{*}v]$$
$$[u*\bar{u}_1\bar{*}u_2*\bar{u}_3\bar{*}u_4* \ldots \bar{*}v]$$
$$\vdots$$
$$[u*\bar{u}_1\bar{*}u_2*\bar{u}_3\bar{*}u_4* \ldots \bar{u}_{k-1}\bar{*}v]$$

where $u_i \overset{*}{\Rightarrow} u_{i+1}$ with $u_0 = u$ and $u_k = v$. Combining these produces a derivation $u \overset{*}{\Rightarrow} v$.

The preceding two arguments comprise a reduction of the word problem for the semi-Thue system S to the Post correspondence problem. It follows that the Post correspondence problem is undecidable. ∎

11.8   Undecidable Problems in Context-Free Grammars

Context-free grammars provide an important tool for defining the syntax of programming languages. The undecidability of the Post correspondence problem can be used to establish the undecidability of several important questions concerning the languages generated by context-free grammars.

Let $C = (\Sigma_C, \{[u_1, v_1], [u_2, v_2], \ldots, [u_n, v_n]\})$ be a Post correspondence system. Two context-free grammars G_U and G_V are constructed from the ordered pairs of C.

$$G_U: V_U = \{S_U\}$$
$$\Sigma_U = \Sigma_C \cup \{1, 2, \ldots, n\}$$
$$P_U = \{S_U \rightarrow u_i S_U i, S_U \rightarrow u_i i \mid i = 1, 2, \ldots, n\}$$

$$G_V: V_V = \{S_V\}$$
$$\Sigma_V = \Sigma_C \cup \{1, 2, \ldots, n\}$$
$$P_V = \{S_V \rightarrow v_i S_V i, S_V \rightarrow v_i i \mid i = 1, 2, \ldots, n\}$$

Determining whether a Post correspondence system C has a solution reduces to deciding the answers to certain questions concerning derivability in corresponding grammars G_U and G_V. The grammar G_U generates the strings that can appear in the top half of a sequence of dominoes. The digits in the rule record the sequence of dominoes that generate the string. Similarly, G_V generates the strings that can be obtained from the bottom half of a sequence of dominoes.

The Post correspondence system C has a solution if there is a sequence $i_1 i_2 \ldots i_{k-1} i_k$ such that

$$u_{i_1} u_{i_2} \ldots u_{i_{k-1}} u_{i_k} = v_{i_1} v_{i_2} \ldots v_{i_{k-1}} v_{i_k}.$$

In this case, G_U and G_V contain derivations

$$S_U \underset{G_U}{\overset{*}{\Rightarrow}} u_{i_1} u_{i_2} \ldots u_{i_{k-1}} u_{i_k} i_k i_{k-1} \ldots i_2 i_1$$
$$S_V \underset{G_V}{\overset{*}{\Rightarrow}} v_{i_1} v_{i_2} \ldots v_{i_{k-1}} v_{i_k} i_k i_{k-1} \ldots i_2 i_1.$$

where $u_{i_1} u_{i_2} \ldots u_{i_{k-1}} u_{i_k} i_k i_{k-1} \ldots i_2 i_1 = v_{i_1} v_{i_2} \ldots v_{i_{k-1}} v_{i_k} i_k i_{k-1} \ldots i_2 i_1$. Hence, the intersection of L(G) and $L(G_V)$ is not empty.

Conversely, assume that $w \in L(G_U) \cap L(G_V)$. Then w consists of a string $w' \in \Sigma_C^+$ followed by a sequence $i_k i_{k-1} \ldots i_2 i_1$. The string $w' = u_{i_1} u_{i_2} \ldots u_{i_{k-1}} u_{i_k} = v_{i_1} v_{i_2} \ldots v_{i_{k-1}} v_{i_k}$ is a solution to C.

Theorem 11.8.1

There is no algorithm that determines whether the languages of two context-free grammars are disjoint.

Proof   Assume there is such an algorithm. Then the Post correspondence problem could be solved as follows:

1. For an arbitrary Post correspondence system C, construct the grammars G_U and G_V from the ordered pairs of C.

2. Use the algorithm to determine whether $L(G_U)$ and $L(G_V)$ are disjoint.

3. Then C has a solution if, and only if, $L(G_U) \cap L(G_V)$ is nonempty.

Step 1 comprises a reduction of the Post correspondence problem to that of determining whether two context-free languages are disjoint. Since the Post correspondence problem has already been shown to be undecidable, we conclude that the question of the intersection of context-free languages is also undecidable.   ∎

The set of context-free languages is not closed under complementation. However, for an arbitrary Post correspondence system C, the languages $\overline{L(G_U)}$ and $\overline{L(G_V)}$ are context-free. The task of constructing context-free grammars that generate these languages is left as an exercise.

Theorem 11.8.2

There is no algorithm that determines whether the language of a context-free grammar $G = (V, \Sigma, P, S)$ is Σ^*.

Proof   First, note that $L = \Sigma^*$ is equivalent to $\overline{L} = \emptyset$. We use this observation and show that there is no algorithm that determines whether $\overline{L(G)}$ is empty.

Again, let C be a Post correspondence system. Since $\overline{L(G_U)}$ and $\overline{L(G_V)}$ are context-free, so is $L = \overline{L(G_U)} \cup \overline{L(G_V)}$. Now $\overline{L} = L(G_U) \cap L(G_V)$. An algorithm that determines whether $\overline{L} = \emptyset$ can also be used to determine whether $L(G_U)$ and $L(G_V)$ are disjoint.   ∎

Theorem 11.8.3

There is no algorithm that determines whether an arbitrary context-free grammar is ambiguous.

Proof   A grammar is ambiguous if it contains a string that can be generated by two distinct leftmost derivations. As before, we begin with an arbitrary Post correspondence system C and construct G_U and G_V. These grammars are combined to obtain the grammar

$$G: V = \{S, S_U, S_V\}$$
$$\Sigma = \Sigma_C$$
$$P = P_U \cup P_V \cup \{S \to S_U, S \to S_V\}$$

with start symbol S.

Clearly all derivations of G are leftmost; every sentential form contains at most one variable. A derivation of G consists of the application of an S rule followed by a derivation of G_U or G_V. The grammars G_U and G_V are unambiguous; distinct derivations generate distinct suffixes of integers. This implies that G is ambiguous if, and only if, $L(G_U) \cap L(G_V) \neq \emptyset$. But this condition is equivalent to the existence of a solution to the original Post correspondence system C. Since the Post correspondence problem is reducible to the problem of determining whether a context-free grammar is ambiguous, the latter problem is also undecidable.   ∎

Exercises

In Exercises 1–4, describe a Turing machine that solves the specified decision problem. Use Example 11.1.2 as a model for defining the actions of a computation of the machine. You need not explicitly construct the transition function.

1. Design a two-tape Turing machine that determines whether two strings u and v over $\{a, b\}$ are identical. A computation should require no more than $3(length(u) + 1)$ transitions.

2. Design a Turing machine whose computations decide whether a natural number is prime. Represent the natural number n by a sequence of $n + 1$ 1's.

3. Let $G = (V, \Sigma, P, S)$ be a regular grammar.
   a) Construct a representation for the grammar G.
   b) Design a Turing machine that decides whether a string w is in L(G). The use of nondeterminism facilitates the construction of the desired machine.

4. A tour in a directed graph is a path $p_0, p_1, \ldots, p_n$ in which
   i) $p_0 = p_n$.
   ii) for $0 < i, j \leqslant n$, $i \neq j$ implies $p_i \neq p_j$.
   iii) every node in the graph occurs in the path.

   Design a Turing machine that decides whether a directed graph contains a tour.

5. Let M be the Turing machine

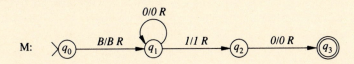

   a) What is L(M)?
   b) Give the representation of M using the encoding from Section 11.3.

6. Construct a Turing machine that determines whether a string over $\{0, 1\}^*$ is the encoding of a nondeterministic Turing machine.

7. Given an arbitrary Turing machine M and input string w, will the computation of M with input w halt in fewer than 100 transitions? Describe a Turing machine that solves this decision problem.

8. Let M be a deterministic Turing machine that accepts a nonrecursive language. Prove that the halting problem for M is undecidable. That is, there is no machine that takes input w and determines whether the computation of M halts with input w.

9. Prove that there is no algorithm that determines whether an arbitrary Turing machine halts for any input. That is, $R(M)$ is accepted if M halts for some string w. Otherwise, $R(M)$ is rejected.

10. Prove that there is no algorithm that determines whether an arbitrary Turing machine halts for all input strings.

11. Prove that there is no algorithm with input a Turing machine $M = (Q, \Sigma, \Gamma, \delta, q_0, F)$, state $q_i \in Q$, and string $w \in \Sigma^*$ that determines whether the computation of M with input w enters state q_i.

12. Prove that there is no algorithm with input a Turing machine $M = (Q, \Sigma, \Gamma, \delta, q_0, F)$, tape symbol x, and string $w \in \Sigma^*$ that determines whether the computation of M with input w prints the symbol x.

13. Find a solution for each of the following Post correspondence systems.

    a) $[a, aa], [bb, b], [a, bb]$

    b) $[a, aaa], [aab, b], [abaa, ab]$

    c) $[aa, aab], [bb, ba], [abb, b]$

14. Show that the following Post correspondence systems have no solutions.

    a) $[ab, a], [ba, bab], [b, aa], [ba, ab]$

    b) $[ab, aba], [baa, aa], [aba, baa]$

    c) $[ab, bb], [aa, ba], [ab, abb], [bb, bab]$

15. Prove that the Post correspondence problem for systems with a one-symbol alphabet is decidable.

16. Let C be a Post correspondence system. Construct a context-free grammar that generates $\overline{L(G_U)}$.

17. Prove that there is no algorithm that determines whether the intersection of the languages of two context-free grammars contains infinitely many elements.

18. Prove that there is no algorithm that determines whether the complement of the language of a context-free grammar contains infinitely many elements.

Bibliographic Notes

Turing [1936] envisioned the theoretical computing machine he designed to be capable of performing all effective computations. This viewpoint, now known as the Church-Turing thesis, was formalized by Church [1936]. Turing's original paper also included the undecidability of the halting problem and the design of a universal machine. The proof of the undecidability of the halting problem presented in Section 11.3 is from Minsky [1967].

The string transformation systems of Thue were introduced in Thue [1914]. The undecidability of the word problem for semi-Thue systems was established by Post [1947].

The undecidability of the Post correspondence problem was presented in Post [1946]. The proof of Theorem 11.7.1, based on the technique of Floyd [1964], is from Davis and Weyuker [1983]. Undecidability results for context-free languages, including Theorem 11.8.1, can be found in Bar-Hillel, Perles, and Shamir [1961]. The undecidability of ambiguity of context-free languages was established by Cantor [1962], Floyd [1962], and Chomsky and Schutzenberger [1963]. The question of inherent ambiguity is shown to be unsolvable by Ginsburg and Ullian [1966a].

CHAPTER 12

Numeric Computation

Turing machines have been used as a computational framework for constructing solutions to decision problems and for recognizing languages. The result of a computation was determined by final state or by halting. In either case there are only two possible outcomes: accept or reject. The result of a Turing machine computation can also be defined in terms of the symbols written on the tape when the computation terminates. Defining the result in terms of the halting configuration permits an infinite number of possible outcomes. This technique will be used to construct Turing machines that compute number theoretic functions.

12.1 Computation of Functions

A function $f: X \rightarrow Y$ can be thought of as a mapping that assigns at most one value of the range Y to each element of the domain X. Adopting a computational viewpoint, the variables of f are referred to as the input of the function. The definition of a function does not specify how to obtain $f(x)$, the value assigned to x by the function f, from the input x. Turing machines will be designed to compute the values of functions. The domain and range of a function computed by a Turing machine consist of strings over the input alphabet of the machine. Recall that the term function refers to both partial and total functions.

Definition 12.1.1

A deterministic one-tape Turing machine $M = (Q, \Sigma, \Gamma, \delta, q_0, q_f)$ computes the unary function $f: \Sigma^* \to \Sigma^*$ if

i) there is only one transition from the state q_0 and it has the form $\delta(q_0, B) = [q_i, B, R]$

ii) there are no transitions of the form $\delta(q_i, x) = [q_0, x, d]$ for any $q_i \in Q$, $x \in \Gamma$ and $d \in \{L, R\}$

iii) there are no transitions of the form $\delta(q_f, B)$

iv) the computation with input u halts in the configuration $q_f B v B$ whenever $f(u) = v$

v) the computation continues indefinitely whenever $f(u)\uparrow$.

A function is said to be **Turing computable** if there is a Turing machine that computes it. A Turing machine that computes a function has two distinguished states: the initial state q_0 and the final state q_f. A computation begins with a transition from state q_0 that positions the tape head at the beginning of the input string. The state q_0 is never reentered; its sole purpose is to initiate the computation. All computations that terminate do so in state q_f. Upon termination, the value of the function is written on the tape beginning at position one. The remainder of the tape is blank.

An arbitrary function need not have the same domain and range. Turing machines can be designed to compute functions from Σ^* to a specific set R by designating an input alphabet Σ and a range R. Condition iv) is then interpreted as requiring the string v to be an element of R.

To highlight the distinguished states q_0 and q_f, a Turing machine M that computes a function is depicted by the diagram

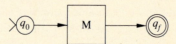

Intuitively, the computation remains inside the box labeled M until termination. This diagram is somewhat simplistic since Definition 12.1.1 permits transitions from state q_f. However, condition iii) ensures that there are no transitions from q_f when the machine is scanning a blank. When this occurs, the computation terminates with the result written on the tape.

Example 12.1.1

The Turing machine M computes the function f from $\{a, b\}^*$ to $\{a, b\}^*$ defined by

$$f(u) = \begin{cases} \lambda & \text{if } u \text{ contains an } a \\ \uparrow & \text{otherwise.} \end{cases}$$

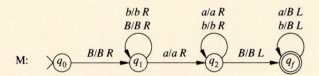

The function f is undefined if the input does not contain an a. In this case, the machine moves indefinitely to the right in state q_1. When an a is encountered, the machine enters state q_2 and reads the remainder of the input. The computation is completed by erasing the input while returning to the initial position. A computation that terminates produces the configuration $q_f BB$ designating the null string as the result.   □

The machine M was designed to compute the unary function f. It should be neither surprising nor alarming that computations of M do not satisfy the requirements of Definition 12.1.1 when the input does not have the anticipated form. A computation of M initiated with input $BbBbBaB$ terminates in the configuration $BbBbq_f B$. In this halting configuration, the tape does not contain a single value and the tape head is not in the correct position. This is just another manifestation of the time-honored "garbage in, garbage out" principle of computer science.

Functions with more than one argument are computed in a similar manner. The input is placed on the tape with the arguments separated by blanks. The initial configuration of a computation of a ternary function f with input aba, bbb, and bab is

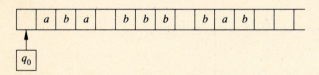

If $f(aba, bbb, bab)$ is defined, the computation terminates with the configuration $q_f Bf(aba, bbb, bab)B$. The initial configuration for $f(aa, \lambda, bb)$ is

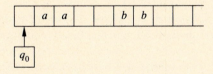

The consecutive blanks in tape positions three and four indicate that the second argument is the null string.

Example 12.1.2

The Turing machine given below computes the binary function of concatenation of strings over $\{a, b\}$. The initial configuration of a computation with input strings u and v has the form $q_0 BuBvB$. Either or both of the input strings may be null.

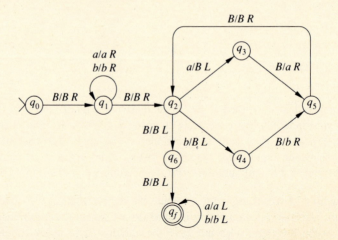

The initial string is read in state q_1. The cycle formed by states q_2, q_3, q_5, q_2 translates an a one position to the left. Similarly, q_2, q_4, q_5, q_2 shift a b to the left. These cycles are repeated until the entire second argument has been translated left, producing the configuration $q_f BuvB$.   □

12.2   Numeric Computation

We have seen that Turing machines can be used to compute the values of functions whose domain and range consist of strings over the input alphabet. In this section we turn our attention to numeric computation, in particular the computation of number theoretic functions. A **number theoretic function** is a function of the form $f: \mathbf{N} \times \mathbf{N} \times \cdots \times \mathbf{N} \to \mathbf{N}$. The domain consists of natural numbers or n-tuples of natural numbers. The function $sq: \mathbf{N} \to \mathbf{N}$ defined by $sq(n) = n^2$ is a unary number theoretic function. The standard operations of addition and multiplication define binary number theoretic functions.

The transition from symbolic to numeric computation requires only a change of perspective since numbers are represented by strings of symbols. The input alphabet of the Turing machine is determined by the representation of the natural numbers used in the computation. We will represent the natural number n by the string 1^{n+1}. The number zero is represented by the string 1, the number one by 11, and so on. This notational scheme is known as the unary representation of the natural numbers. The unary representation of a natural number n is denoted $\bar{n}$. Using the unary representation, the input alphabet for a machine that computes a number theoretic function is the singleton set $\{1\}$.

The computation of $f(2, 0, 3)$ in a Turing machine that computes a ternary number theoretic function f begins with the machine configuration

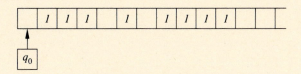

If $f(2, 0, 3) = 4$ the computation terminates with the configuration

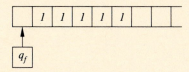

A total number theoretic function $r: \mathbf{N} \times \mathbf{N} \times \cdots \times \mathbf{N} \to \{0, 1\}$ defines an n-ary relation R on the domain of the function. The relation is defined by

$$[n_1, n_2, \ldots, n_k] \in \mathbf{R} \text{ if } r(n_1, n_2, \ldots, n_k) = 1$$
$$[n_1, n_2, \ldots, n_k] \notin \mathbf{R} \text{ if } r(n_1, n_2, \ldots, n_k) = 0.$$

The function r is called the **characteristic function** of the relation R. A relation is Turing computable if its characteristic function is Turing computable.

Turing machines that compute several simple, but important, number theoretic functions are given below. The functions are denoted by lowercase letters and the corresponding machines with capital letters.

The successor function: $s(n) = n + 1$.

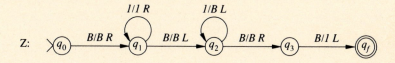

The zero function: $z(n) = 0$.

The empty function: $e(n) \uparrow$.

The machine that computes the successor simply adds a *1* to the right end of the input string. The zero function is computed by erasing the input and writing *1* in tape position one. The empty function is undefined for all arguments; the machine moves indefinitely to the right in state q_1.

The zero function is also computed by the machine

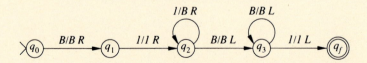

That two machines compute the same function illustrates the difference between functions and algorithms. A function relates elements in the domain to elements in the range. A Turing machine mechanistically computes the value of the function whenever the function is defined. The difference is that of definition and computation. In Section 12.5 we will see that there are number theoretic functions that cannot be computed by any Turing machine.

The value of the *k*-variable projection function $p_i^{(k)}$ is defined as the *i*th argument of the input, $p_i^{(k)}(n_1, n_2, \ldots, n_i, \ldots, n_k) = n_i$. The superscript *k* specifies the number of arguments, and the subscript designates the argument that defines the result of the projection. The superscript is placed in parentheses so it is not mistaken for an exponent. The machine that computes $p_1^{(k)}$ leaves the first argument unchanged and erases the remaining arguments.

$$P_1^{(k)}:$$

The function $p_1^{(1)}$ maps a single input to itself. This function is also called the identity function and is denoted *id*.

Machines $P_i^{(k)}$ that compute $p_i^{(k)}$ will be designed in Example 12.3.1.

Example 12.2.1

The Turing machine A computes the binary function defined by the addition of natural numbers.

$$A:$$

The unary representations of natural numbers *n* and *m* are 1^{n+1} and 1^{m+1}. The sum of these numbers is represented by 1^{n+m+1}. This string is generated by replacing the blank between the arguments with a *1* and erasing two *1*'s from the right end of the second argument.   □

12.3   Sequential Operation of Turing Machines

Turing machines designed to accomplish a single task can be combined to construct machines that perform complex computations. Intuitively, the combination is obtained by running the machines sequentially. The result of one computation becomes the input for the succeeding machine. A machine that computes the constant function $c(n) = 1$ can be constructed by combining the machines that compute the successor and the zero functions. Regardless of the input, a computation of the machine Z terminates with the value zero on the tape. Running the machine S on this tape configuration produces the number one.

The computation of Z terminates with the tape head in position zero scanning a blank. These are precisely the input conditions for the machine S. The initiation and termination conditions of Definition 12.1.1 were introduced to facilitate this coupling of machines. The handoff between machines is accomplished by identifying the final state of Z with the initial state of S. Except for this handoff, the states of the two machines are assumed to be distinct. This can be accomplished by subscripting each state of a component machine with the name of the machine.

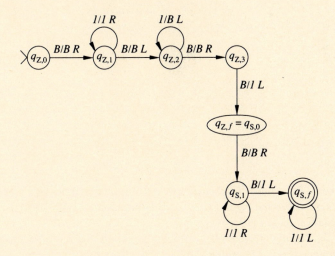

The sequential combination of two machines is represented by the diagram

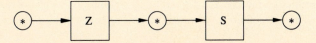

The state names are omitted from the initial and final nodes in the diagram since they may be inferred from the constituent machines.

There are certain sequences of actions that frequently occur in a computation of a Turing machine. Machines can be constructed to perform these recurring tasks. These machines are designed in a manner that allows them to be used as components in more complicated machines. Borrowing terminology from assembly language programming, a machine constructed to perform a single simple task is called a **macro**.

The computations of a macro adhere to several of the restrictions introduced in Definition 12.1.1. The initial state q_0 is used strictly to initiate the computation. Since these machines are combined to construct more complex machines, we do not assume that a computation must begin with the tape head at position zero. We do assume, however, that each computation begins with the machine scanning a blank and that the segment of the tape to the immediate right of the tape head contains the input for the computation. A macro may contain several states in which a computation may terminate. As with machines that compute functions, a macro is not permitted to contain a transition of the form $\delta(q_f, B)$ from any halting state q_f.

A family of macros is often described by a schema. The macro MR_i moves the tape head to the right through i consecutive natural numbers (sequences of I's) on the tape. MR_1 is defined by the machine

$$MR_1: \quad \times \!\!-\!\! q_0 \xrightarrow{B/B\ R} q_f \quad \circlearrowright 1/1\ R$$

MR_k is constructed by adding states to move the tape head through the sequence of k natural numbers.

$$MR_k: \quad \times \!\!-\!\! q_0 \xrightarrow{B/B\ R} q_1 \xrightarrow{B/B\ R} q_2 \cdots \xrightarrow{B/B\ R} q_{k-1} \xrightarrow{B/B\ R} q_f$$

The move macros do not affect the tape to the left of the initial position of the tape head. A computation of MR_2 that begins with the configuration $B\bar{n}_1 q_0 B\bar{n}_2 B\bar{n}_3 B\bar{n}_4 B$ terminates in the configuration $B\bar{n}_1 B\bar{n}_2 B\bar{n}_3 q_f B\bar{n}_4 B$.

Macros, like Turing machines that compute functions, expect to be run with the input having a specified form. The move right macro MR_i requries a sequence of at least i natural numbers to the immediate right of the tape at the initiation of a computation. The design of a composite machine must ensure the appropriate input to each macro.

Several families of macros are defined by describing the results of a computation of the machine. The computation of each macro remains within the segment of the tape defined by the initial and final blank in the description. The application of the macro will neither access nor alter any portion of tape outside of these bounds. The location of the tape head is indicated by the underscore. The double arrows indicate identical tape positions in the before and after configurations.

ML_k (move left):

$$B\bar{n}_1B\bar{n}_2B \ldots B\underline{\bar{n}_kB} \qquad k \geqslant 0$$
$$\updownarrow \qquad\qquad\qquad \updownarrow$$
$$\underline{B}\bar{n}_1B\bar{n}_2B \ldots B\bar{n}_kB$$

FR (find right):

$$\underline{B}B^i\bar{n}B \qquad i \geqslant 0$$
$$\updownarrow \quad \updownarrow$$
$$B^i\underline{B}\bar{n}B$$

FL (find left):

$$B\bar{n}B^i\underline{B} \qquad i \geqslant 0$$
$$\updownarrow \quad \updownarrow$$
$$\underline{B}\bar{n}B^iB$$

E_k (erase):

$$\underline{B}\bar{n}_1B\bar{n}_2B \ldots B\bar{n}_kB \qquad k \geqslant 1$$
$$\updownarrow \qquad\qquad\qquad \updownarrow$$
$$\underline{B}B \quad \ldots \quad BB$$

CPY_k (copy):

$$\underline{B}\bar{n}_1B\bar{n}_2B \ldots B\bar{n}_kBBB \quad \ldots \quad BB \qquad k \geqslant 1$$
$$\updownarrow \qquad\qquad\quad \updownarrow \qquad\qquad\quad \updownarrow$$
$$\underline{B}\bar{n}_1B\bar{n}_2B \ldots B\bar{n}_kB\bar{n}_1B\bar{n}_2B \ldots B\bar{n}_kB$$

$CPY_{k,i}$ (copy through i numbers):

$$\underline{B}\bar{n}_1B\bar{n}_2B \ldots B\bar{n}_kBn_{k+1} \ldots B\bar{n}_{k+i}BB \quad \ldots \quad BB \qquad k \geqslant 1$$
$$\updownarrow \qquad\qquad\quad \updownarrow \qquad\qquad\quad \updownarrow \qquad\qquad\quad \updownarrow$$
$$\underline{B}\bar{n}_1B\bar{n}_2B \ldots B\bar{n}_kB\bar{n}_{k+1} \ldots B\bar{n}_{k+i}B\bar{n}_1B\bar{n}_2B \ldots B\bar{n}_kB$$

T (translate):

$$\underline{B}B^i\bar{n}B \qquad i \geqslant 0$$
$$\updownarrow \quad \updownarrow$$
$$\underline{B}\bar{n}B^iB$$

The find macros move the tape head into a position to process the first natural number to the right or left of the current position. E_k erases a sequence of k natural numbers. The computation halts with the tape head in its original position.

The copy machines produce a copy of the designated number of integers. The segment of the tape on which the copy is produced is assumed to be blank. $\mathrm{CPY}_{k,i}$ expects a sequence of $k + i$ numbers followed by a blank segment large enough to hold a copy of the first k numbers. The translate macro changes the location of the first natural number to the right of the tape head. A computation terminates with the head in the position it occupied at the beginning of the computation with the translated string to its immediate right.

The input to the macro BRN (branch on zero) is a single number. The value of the input is used to determine the halting state of the computation. The branch macro is depicted

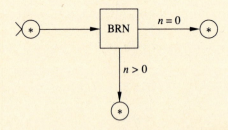

The computation of BRN does not alter the tape nor change the position of the tape head. Consequently, it may be run in any configuration $B\bar{n}B$. The branch macro is often used in the construction of loops in composite machines.

Additional macros can be created using those defined above. The machine

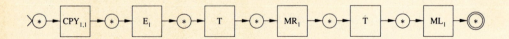

interchanges the order of two numbers. The tape configurations for this macro are

INT (interchange):

$$\begin{array}{cc} B\bar{n}B\bar{m}B \\ \updownarrow \quad \updownarrow \\ B\bar{m}B\bar{n}B \end{array}$$

Example 12.3.1

The computation of a machine that evaluates the projection function $p_i^{(k)}$ consists of three distinct actions: erasing the initial $i - 1$ arguments, translating the ith argument to tape position one, and erasing the remainder of the input. A machine to compute $p_i^{(k)}$ can be designed using the macros FR, FL, and E_i.

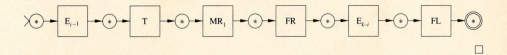

Turing machines defined to compute functions can be used like macros in the design of composite machines. Unlike the macros, there is no a priori bound on the amount of tape required by a computation of such a machine. Consequently, these machines should be run only when the input is followed by a completely blank tape.

Example 12.3.2

The macros and previously constructed machines can be used to design a Turing machine that computes the function $f(n) = 3n$.

The initial state of the complete machine is that of the macro CPY_1. The machine A, constructed in Example 12.2.1, adds two natural numbers. A computation with input $\bar{n}$ generates the following sequence of tape configurations.

Machine	Configuration
	$\underline{B}nB$
CPY_1	$B\bar{n}B\bar{n}B$
MR_1	$Bn\underline{B}nB$
CPY_1	$Bn\underline{B}nB\bar{n}B$
A	$Bn\underline{B}n+nB$
ML_1	$BnB\overline{n+nB}$
A	$\underline{B}n+n+nB$

Note that the addition machine A is run only when its two arguments comprise the rightmost nonblank symbols on the tape. □

Example 12.3.3

A Turing machine MULT is constructed to compute the multiplication of natural numbers. Macros can be mixed with standard Turing machine transitions when designing a composite machine. The conditions on the initial state of a macro permit the submachine to be entered upon the processing of a blank from any state. The identification of the start state of a macro with a state q_i is depicted

Since the macro is entered only upon the processing of a blank, transitions may also be defined for state q_i with the tape head scanning nonblank tape symbols.

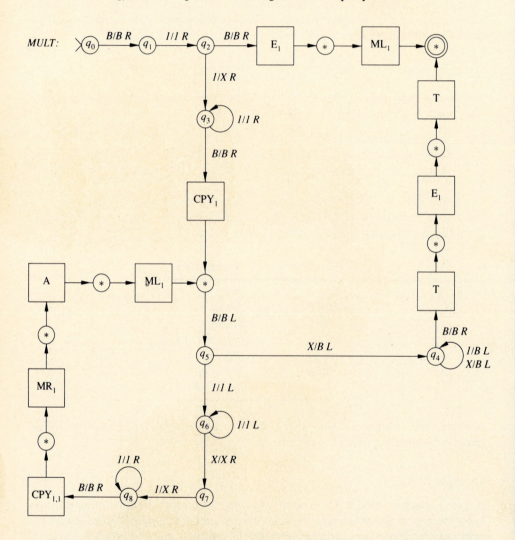

If the first argument is zero, the computation erases the second argument, returns to the initial position, and halts. Otherwise, a computation of MULT adds m to itself n times. The addition is performed by copying $\bar{m}$ and then adding the copy to the previous total. The number of iterations is recorded by replacing a *1* in the first argument with an *X* when a copy is made.   □

12.4   **Composition of Functions**

Using the interpretation of a function as a mapping from its domain to its range, the relations defined by the unary number theoretic functions *g* and *h* can be represented by the diagrams

A mapping from **N** to **N** can be obtained by identifying the range of *g* with the domain of *h* and sequentially traversing the arrows in the diagrams.

The function obtained by this combination is called the composition of *h* with *g*. The composition of unary functions is formally defined in Definition 12.4.1. Definition 12.4.2 extends the notion to *n*-variable functions.

Definition 12.4.1

Let *g* and *h* be unary number theoretic functions. The **composition** of *h* with *g* is the unary function $f: \mathbf{N} \to \mathbf{N}$ defined by

$$f(x) = \begin{cases} \uparrow & \text{if } g(x) \uparrow \\ \uparrow & \text{if } g(x) = y \text{ and } h(y) \uparrow \\ h(y) & \text{if } g(x) = y \text{ and } h(y) \downarrow. \end{cases}$$

The composite function is denoted $f = h \circ g$.

The value of the composite function $f = h \circ g$ for input *x* is written $f(x) = h(g(x))$. The latter expression is read "*h* of *g* of *x*." The value $h(g(x))$ is defined whenever $g(x)$ is defined and *h* is defined for the value $g(x)$. Consequently, the composition of total functions produces a total function.

From a computational viewpoint, the composition $h \circ g$ consists of the sequential evaluation of functions *g* and *h*. The computation of *g* provides the input for the computation of *h*.

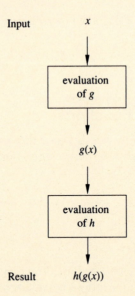

Input x

evaluation
of g

$g(x)$

evaluation
of h

Result $h(g(x))$

The composite function is defined only when the preceding sequence of computations can be successfully completed.

Definition 12.4.2

Let $g_1, g_2, \ldots, g_n$ be k-variable number theoretic functions and let h be an n-variable number theoretic function. The k-variable function f defined by

$$f(x_1, \ldots, x_k) = h(g_1(x_1, \ldots, x_k), \ldots, g_n(x_1, \ldots, x_k))$$

is called the **composition** of h with $g_1, g_2, \ldots, g_n$ and written $f = h \circ (g_1, \ldots, g_n)$. $f(x_1, \ldots, x_k)$ is undefined if either

i) $g_i(x_1, \ldots, x_k) \uparrow$ for some $1 \leq i \leq n$

ii) $g_i(x_1, \ldots, x_k) = y_i$ for $1 \leq i \leq n$ and $h(y_1, \ldots, y_n) \uparrow$.

The general definition of composition of functions also admits a computational interpretation. The input is provided to each of the functions g_i. These functions generate the arguments of h.

Example 12.4.1

Consider the mapping defined by the composite function

$$add \circ (c_2^{(3)}, add \circ (p_1^{(3)}, p_3^{(3)}))$$

where $add(n, m) = n + m$ and $c_2^{(3)}$ is the three-variable constant function defined by $c_2^{(3)}(n_1, n_2, n_3) = 2$. The composite is a three-variable function since the innermost functions of the composition, the functions that directly utilize the input, require three arguments. The function adds the sum of the first and third arguments to the constant two. The result for input 1, 0, 3 is

$$
\begin{aligned}
& add \circ (c_2^{(3)}, add \circ (p_1^{(3)}, p_3^{(3)}))(1, 0, 3) \\
= {}& add(c_2^{(3)}(1, 0, 3), add(p_1^{(3)}, p_3^{(3)})(1, 0, 3)) \\
= {}& add(2, add(p_1^{(3)}(1, 0, 3), p_3^{(3)}(1, 0, 3))) \\
= {}& add(2, add(1, 3)) \\
= {}& add(2, 4) \\
= {}& 6.
\end{aligned}
$$

$\square$

A function obtained by composing Turing computable functions is itself Turing computable. The argument is constructive; a machine can be designed to compute the composite function by combining the machines that compute the constituent functions and the macros developed in the previous section.

Let g_1 and g_2 be three-variable Turing computable functions and let h be a Turing computable two-variable function. Since g_1, g_2, and h are computable there are machines G_1, G_2, and H that compute them. The actions of a machine that computes the composite function $h \circ (g_1, g_2)$ are traced for input n_1, n_2, and n_3.

Machine	Configuration
	$\underline{B}\bar{n}_1B\bar{n}_2B\bar{n}_3B$
CPY_3	$\underline{B}\bar{n}_1B\bar{n}_2B\bar{n}_3B\bar{n}_1B\bar{n}_2B\bar{n}_3B$
MR_3	$B\bar{n}_1B\bar{n}_2B\bar{n}_3\underline{B}\bar{n}_1B\bar{n}_2B\bar{n}_3B$
G_1	$B\bar{n}_1B\bar{n}_2B\bar{n}_3\underline{B}g_1(n_1, n_2, n_3)B$
ML_3	$\underline{B}\bar{n}_1B\bar{n}_2B\bar{n}_3Bg_1(n_1, n_2, n_3)B$
$CPY_{3,1}$	$\underline{B}\bar{n}_1B\bar{n}_2B\bar{n}_3Bg_1(n_1, n_2, n_3)B\bar{n}_1B\bar{n}_2B\bar{n}_3B$
MR_4	$B\bar{n}_1B\bar{n}_2B\bar{n}_3Bg_1(n_1, n_2, n_3)\underline{B}\bar{n}_1B\bar{n}_2B\bar{n}_3B$
G_2	$B\bar{n}_1B\bar{n}_2B\bar{n}_3Bg_1(n_1, n_2, n_3)\underline{B}g_2(n_1, n_2, n_3)B$
ML_1	$B\bar{n}_1B\bar{n}_2B\bar{n}_3\underline{B}g_1(n_1, n_2, n_3)Bg_2(n_1, n_2, n_3)B$
H	$B\bar{n}_1B\bar{n}_2B\bar{n}_3\underline{B}h(g_1(n_1, n_2, n_3), g_2(n_1, n_2, n_3))B$
ML_3	$\underline{B}\bar{n}_1B\bar{n}_2B\bar{n}_3Bh(g_1(n_1, n_2, n_3), g_2(n_1, n_2, n_3))B$
E_3	$\underline{B}B \quad \ldots \quad Bh(g_1(n_1, n_2, n_3), g_2(n_1, n_2, n_3))B$
T	$\underline{B}h(g_1(n_1, n_2, n_3), g_2(n_1, n_2, n_3))B$

The computation copies the input and computes the value of g_1 using the newly created copy as the arguments. Since the machine G_1 does not move to the left of its starting position, the original input remains unchanged. If $g_1(n_1, n_2, n_3)$ is undefined, the computation of G_1 continues indefinitely. In this case the entire computation fails to terminate, correctly indicating that $h(g_1(n_1, n_2, n_3), g_2(n_1, n_2, n_3))$ is undefined. Upon the termination of G_1, the input is copied and G_2 is run.

If both $g_1(n_1, n_2, n_3)$ and $g_2(n_1, n_2, n_3)$ are defined, G_2 terminates with the input for H on the tape preceded by the original input. The machine H is run computing

$h(g_1(n_1, n_2, n_3), g_2(n_1, n_2, n_3))$. When the computation of H terminates, the result is translated to the correct position.

The preceding construction easily generalizes to the composition of functions of any number of variables, yielding Theorem 12.4.3.

Theorem 12.4.3
The Turing computable functions are closed under the operation of composition.

Theorem 12.4.3 can be used to show that a function f is Turing computable without explicitly constructing a machine that computes it. If f can be defined as the composition of Turing computable functions then, by Theorem 12.4.3, f is also Turing computable.

Example 12.4.2
The k-variable constant functions $c_i^{(k)}$ whose values are given by $c_i^{(k)}(n_1, \ldots, n_k) = i$ are Turing computable. The function $c_i^{(k)}$ can be defined by

$$c_i^{(k)} = \underbrace{s \circ s \circ \cdots \circ s}_{i \text{ times}} \circ z \circ p_1^{(k)}.$$

The projection function accepts the k-variable input and passes the first value to the zero function. The composition of i successor functions produces the desired value. Since each of the functions in the composition is Turing computable, the function $c_i^{(k)}$ is Turing computable by Theorem 12.4.3. □

Example 12.4.3
The binary function $smsq(n, m) = n^2 + m^2$ is Turing computable. The sum of squares function can be written as the composition of functions

$$smsq = add \circ (sq \circ p_1^{(2)}, sq \circ p_2^{(2)})$$

where sq is defined by $sq(n) = n^2$. The function add is computed by the machine constructed in Example 12.2.1 and sq by

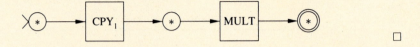

□

<hr>

12.5   Uncomputable Functions

A function is Turing computable only if there is a Turing machine that computes it. The existence of number theoretic functions that are not Turing computable can be demonstrated by a simple counting argument. We begin by showing that the set of computable functions is countably infinite.

A Turing machine is completely defined by its transition function. The states and tape alphabet used in computations of the machine can be extracted from the transitions. Consider the machines M_1 and M_2 defined by

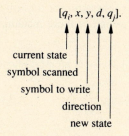

Both M_1 and M_2 compute the unary constant function $c_1^{(1)}$. The two machines differ only in the names given to the states and the markers used during the computation. These symbols have no effect on the result of a computation and hence the function computed by the machine.

Since the names of the states and tape symbols other than B and 1 are immaterial, we adopt the following conventions concerning the naming of the components of a Turing machine:

i) The set of states is a finite subset of $\overline{Q} = \{q_i \mid i \geq 0\}$.

ii) The input alphabet is $\{1\}$.

iii) The tape alphabet is a finite subset of the set $\overline{\Gamma} = \{B, 1, X_i \mid i \geq 0\}$.

iv) The initial state is q_0.

The transitions of a Turing machine have been specified using functional notation; the transition defined for state q_i and tape symbol x is represented by $\delta(q_i, x) = [q_j, y, d]$. This information can also be represented by the quintuple

$$[q_i, x, y, d, q_j].$$

current state
symbol scanned
symbol to write
direction
new state

Utilizing the naming conventions, a transition of a Turing machine is an element of the set $T = \overline{Q} \times \overline{\Gamma} \times \overline{\Gamma} \times \{L, R\} \times \overline{Q}$. The set T is countable since it is the Cartesian product of countable sets.

The transitions of a deterministic Turing machine comprise a finite subset of T in which the first two components of every element are distinct. There are only a countable number of such subsets. It follows that the number of Turing computable functions is at most countably infinite. On the other hand, the number of Turing computable functions is at least countably infinite since the constant functions are computable.

Theorem 12.5.1
The set of computable number theoretic functions is countably infinite.

In Section 1.3, the diagonalization technique was used to prove that there are uncountably many total unary number theoretic functions. Combining this with Theorem 12.5.1 we obtain Corollary 12.5.2.

Corollary 12.5.2
There is a total unary number theoretic function that is not computable.

Corollary 12.5.2 vastly understates the relationship between computable and uncomputable functions. The former comprise a countable set and the latter an uncountable set.

Exercises

1. Construct Turing machines with input alphabet $\{a, b\}$ that compute the specified functions. The symbols u and v represent arbitrary strings over $\{a, b\}^*$.

   a) $f(u) = aaa$

   b) $f(u) = \begin{cases} a & \text{if } length(u) \text{ is even} \\ b & \text{otherwise} \end{cases}$

   c) $f(u) = u^R$

   d) $f(u, v) = \begin{cases} u & \text{if } length(u) > length(v) \\ v & \text{otherwise} \end{cases}$

2. Construct Turing machines that compute the following number theoretic functions. Do not use macros in the design of these machines.

   a) $f(n) = 2n + 3$

   b) $half(n) = \lfloor n/2 \rfloor$ where $\lfloor x \rfloor$ is the greatest integer less than or equal to x

   c) $f(n_1, n_2, n_3) = n_1 + n_2 + n_3$

   d) $even(n) = \begin{cases} 1 & \text{if } n \text{ is even} \\ 0 & \text{otherwise} \end{cases}$

   e) $eq(n, m) = \begin{cases} 1 & \text{if } n = m \\ 0 & \text{otherwise} \end{cases}$

   f) $lt(n, m) = \begin{cases} 1 & \text{if } n < m \\ 0 & \text{otherwise} \end{cases}$

g) $n \div m = \begin{cases} n - m & \text{if } n \geq m \\ 0 & \text{otherwise} \end{cases}$

3. Use the macros and machines constructed in Sections 12.2–12.4 to design machines that compute the following functions:

   a) $f(n) = 2n + 3$

   b) $f(n) = n^2 + 2n + 2$

   c) $f(n_1, n_2, n_3) = n_1 + n_2 + n_3$

   d) $f(n, m) = m^2$

4. Design machines that compute the following relations. You may use the macros and machines constructed in Sections 12.2–12.4 and the machines constructed in Exercise 2.

   a) $gt(n, m) = \begin{cases} 1 & \text{if } n > m \\ 0 & \text{otherwise} \end{cases}$

   b) $persq(n) = \begin{cases} 1 & \text{if } n \text{ is a perfect square} \\ 0 & \text{otherwise} \end{cases}$

   c) $divides(n, m) = \begin{cases} 1 & \text{if } n > 0, m > 0, \text{ and } m \text{ divides } n \\ 0 & \text{otherwise} \end{cases}$

5. Trace the actions of the machine MULT for computations with input

   a) $n = 0, m = 4$

   b) $n = 1, m = 0$

   c) $n = 2, m = 2$.

6. Construct Turing machines that perform the actions specified by the following macros:

   a) FL

   b) E_2

   c) T

   d) BRN

7. Let F be a Turing machine that computes a total unary number theoretic function f. Design a machine that returns the first natural number n such that $f(n) = 0$. A computation should continue indefinitely if no such n exists. What will happen if the function computed by F is not total?

8. Let F be a Turing machine that computes a total unary number theoretic function f. Design a machine that computes the function

$$g(n) = \sum_{i=0}^{n} f(i).$$

9. Let F and G be Turing machines that compute total unary number theoretic functions f and g, respectively. Design a Turing machine that computes the function

$$h(n) = \sum_{i=0}^{n} eq(f(i), g(i)).$$

That is, $h(n)$ is the number of values in the range 0 to n for which the functions f and g assume the same value. You may assume the existence of a machine EQ that computes the function eq.

10. A unary relation R over **N** is Turing computable if its characteristic function is computable. Prove that every computable relation is a recursive set over **N**. Hint: Construct a machine that accepts R from the machine that computes its characteristic function.

11. Let $R \subseteq \{1\}^+$ be a recursive set. Prove that R is a computable relation.

12. Give examples of unary number theoretic functions that satisfy the following conditions:

    a) g is not one-to-one, h is not total, $h \circ g$ is total

    b) $g \neq e$, $h \neq e$, $h \circ g = e$, where e is the empty function

    c) $g \neq id$, $h \neq id$, $h \circ g = g \circ h$, where id is the identity function

    d) g is total, h is not one-to-one, $h \circ g = id$

13. Describe the mapping defined by each of the following composite functions:

    a) $add \circ (mult \circ (id, id), add \circ (id, id))$

    b) $p_1^{(2)} \circ (s \circ p_1^{(2)}, e \circ p_2^{(2)})$

    c) $mult \circ (c_2^{(3)}, add \circ (p_1^{(3)}, s \circ p_2^{(3)}))$

14. Let F be the set consisting of all total unary number theoretic functions that satisfy $f(i) = i$ for every even natural number i. Prove that there are functions in F that are not Turing computable.

15. Prove that there are unary relations over **N** that are not Turing computable.

CHAPTER 13

Mu-Recursive Functions

Computable functions have been introduced from a mechanical perspective. Turing machines provide a microscopic approach to computability; the elementary operations of the Turing machine define an effective procedure for computing the values of a function. Computability is now presented from a macroscopic viewpoint. Rather than focusing on elementary operations, the fundamental objects of study are the functions themselves. Two families of functions, the primitive recursive functions and μ-recursive functions, are introduced. The computability of the primitive and μ-recursive functions is demonstrated by outlining an effective method for generating the values of the functions. Because of the emphasis on computability, the arguments of a function are referred to as input and the evaluation of a function as a computation.

13.1 Primitive Recursive Functions

A family of functions is defined by a set of basic functions and operators. Operators are used to combine the basic functions to construct additional functions. The set of basic primitive recursive functions consists of

i) the successor function s: $s(x) = x + 1$

ii) the zero function z: $z(x) = 0$

iii) the projection functions $p_i^{(n)}$: $p_i^{(n)}(x_1, \ldots, x_n) = x_i$, $1 \le i \le n$.

The simplicity of the basic functions supports their intuitive computability. The successor function requires only the ability to add one to a natural number. Computing the zero function is even less complex; the value of function is zero for every argument. The value of the projection function $p_i^{(n)}$ is obtained directly from its ith argument.

The primitive recursive functions are constructed from the basic functions by applications of two operations that preserve computability. The first operation is functional composition. Let f be defined by the composition of the n-variable function h with the k-variable functions $g_1, g_2, \ldots, g_n$. If each of the components of the composition is computable, then the value of $f(x_1, \ldots, x_k)$ can be obtained from h and $g_1(x_1, \ldots, x_k)$, $g_2(x_1, \ldots, x_k), \ldots, g_n(x_1, \ldots, x_k)$. The computability of f follows from the computability of its constituent functions.

The second method of generating functions is primitive recursion. Taken together, composition and primitive recursion provide a powerful tool for the construction of functions.

Definition 13.1.1

Let g and h be total number theoretic functions with n and $n + 2$ variables, respectively. The $n + 1$-variable function f defined by

i) $f(x_1, \ldots, x_n, 0) = g(x_1, \ldots, x_n)$

ii) $f(x_1, \ldots, x_n, y + 1) = h(x_1, \ldots, x_n, y, f(x_1, \ldots, x_n, y))$

is said to be obtained from g and h by **primitive recursion.**

The x_i's are called the **parameters** of a definition by primitive recursion. The variable y is the **recursive variable.**

The operation of primitive recursion provides its own algorithm for computing the value of $f(x_1, \ldots, x_n, y)$ whenever g and h are computable. For a fixed set of parameters $x_1, \ldots, x_n, f(x_1, \ldots, x_n, 0)$ is obtained directly from the function g.

$$f(x_1, \ldots, x_n, 0) = g(x_1, \ldots, x_n)$$

The value $f(x_1, \ldots, x_n, y + 1)$ is obtained from the computable function h using

i) the parameters $x_1, \ldots, x_n$

ii) y, the previous value of the recursive variable

iii) $f(x_1, \ldots, x_n, y)$, the previous value of the function.

For example, $f(x_1, \ldots, x_n, y + 1)$ is obtained by the sequence of computations

$$f(x_1, \ldots, x_n, 0) = g(x_1, \ldots, x_n)$$
$$f(x_1, \ldots, x_n, 1) = h(x_1, \ldots, x_n, 0, f(x_1, \ldots, x_n, 0))$$
$$f(x_1, \ldots, x_n, 2) = h(x_1, \ldots, x_n, 1, f(x_1, \ldots, x_n, 1))$$
$$\vdots$$
$$f(x_1, \ldots, x_n, y + 1) = h(x_1, \ldots, x_n, y, f(x_1, \ldots, x_n, y)).$$

Since h is computable, this iterative process can be used to determine $f(x_1, \ldots, x_n, y + 1)$ for any value of the recursive variable y.

Definition 13.1.2

A function is **primitive recursive** if it can be obtained from the successor, zero, and projection functions by a finite number of applications of composition and primitive recursion.

A function defined by composition or primitive recursion from total functions is itself total. This is an immediate consequence of the definitions of the operations and is left as an exercise. Since the basic primitive recursive functions are total and the operations preserve totality, it follows that all primitive recursive functions are total.

Example 13.1.1

The constant functions $c_i^{(n)}(x_1, \ldots, x_n) = i$ are primitive recursive. Example 12.4.2 defines the constant functions as the composition of the successor, zero, and projection functions.   □

Example 13.1.2

Let add be the function defined by primitive recursion from the functions $g(x) = x$ and $h(x, y, z) = z + 1$. Then

$$add(x, 0) = g(x) = x$$
$$add(x, y + 1) = h(x, y, add(x, y)) = add(x, y) + 1.$$

The function add computes the sum of two natural numbers. The definition of $add(x, 0)$ specifies that the sum of any number with zero is the number itself. The latter condition defines the sum of x and $y + 1$ as the sum of x and y (the result of add for the previous value of the recursive variable) incremented by one.

The preceding definition establishes that addition is primitive recursive. Both g and h, the components of the definition by primitive recursion, are primitive recursive since $g = p_1^{(1)}$ and $h = s \circ p_3^{(3)}$.

The value of add can be obtained from the primitive recursive definition by repeatedly applying the condition $add(x, y + 1) = add(x, y) + 1$ to reduce the value of the recursive variable. For example,

$$
\begin{aligned}
add(2, 4) &= add(2, 3) + 1 \\
&= (add(2, 2) + 1) + 1 \\
&= ((add(2, 1) + 1) + 1) + 1 \\
&= (((add(2, 0) + 1) + 1) + 1) + 1 \\
&= (((2 + 1) + 1) + 1) + 1 \\
&= 6.
\end{aligned}
$$

When the recursive variable is zero, the function g is used to initiate the evaluation of the expression.   □

Example 13.1.3

Let g and h be the primitive recursive functions $g = z$ and $h = add \circ (p_3^{(3)}, p_1^{(3)})$. Multiplication can be defined by primitive recursion from g and h.

$$mult(x, 0) = g(x) = 0$$
$$mult(x, y + 1) = h(x, y, mult(x, y)) = mult(x, y) + x.$$

The infix expression corresponding to the primitive recursive definition is the identity $x \cdot (y + 1) = x \cdot y + x$, which follows from the distributive property of addition and multiplication.   □

Adopting the convention that a zero-variable function is a constant, Definition 13.1.1 can be used to define one-variable functions using primitive recursion and a two-variable function h. The definition of such a function f has the form

i) $f(0) = n_0$ where $n_0 \in \mathbf{N}$

ii) $f(y + 1) = h(y, f(y))$.

Example 13.1.4

The one-variable factorial function defined by

$$fact(y) = \begin{cases} 1 & \text{if } y = 0 \\ \prod_{i=1}^{y} i & \text{otherwise} \end{cases}$$

is primitive recursive. Let $h(x, y) = mult \circ (p_2^{(2)}, s \circ p_1^{(2)}) = y \cdot (x + 1)$. The factorial function is defined using primitive recursion from h by

$$fact(0) = 1$$
$$fact(y + 1) = h(y, fact(y)) = fact(y) \cdot (y + 1).$$

Note that the definition uses $y + 1$, the value of the recursive variable. This is obtained by applying the successor function to y, the value provided to the function h.

The evaluation of the function *fact* for the first five input values illustrates how the primitive recursive definition generates the factorial function.

$$fact(0) = 1$$
$$fact(1) = fact(0) \cdot (0 + 1) = 1$$
$$fact(2) = fact(1) \cdot (1 + 1) = 2$$
$$fact(3) = fact(2) \cdot (2 + 1) = 6$$
$$fact(4) = fact(3) \cdot (3 + 1) = 24.$$

□

The primitive recursive functions were defined as a family of intuitively computable functions. As one might expect, these functions are also computable using our mechanical approach to effective computation.

Theorem 13.1.3
Every primitive recursive function is Turing computable.

Proof   Turing machines that compute the basic functions were constructed in Section 12.2. To complete the proof it suffices to prove that the Turing computable functions are closed under composition and primitive recursion. The former was established in Section 12.4. All that remains is to show that the Turing computable functions are closed under primitive recursion; that is, if f is defined by primitive recursion from Turing computable functions g and h, then f is Turing computable.

Let g and h be Turing computable functions and let f be the function

$$f(x_1, \ldots, x_n, 0) = g(x_1, \ldots, x_n)$$
$$f(x_1, \ldots, x_n, y + 1) = h(x_1, \ldots, x_n, y, f(x_1, \ldots, x_n, y))$$

defined from g and h by primitive recursion. Since g and h are Turing computable, there are standard Turing machines G and H that compute them. A composite machine F is constructed to compute f. The computation of $f(x_1, x_2, \ldots, x_n, y)$ begins with tape configuration $B\bar{x}_1B\bar{x}_2B \ldots B\bar{x}_nB\bar{y}B$.

1. A counter, initially set to 0, is written to the immediate right of the input. The counter is used to record the value of the recursive variable for the current computation. The parameters and 0 are then written to the right of the counter, producing the tape configuration

$$B\bar{x}_1B\bar{x}_2B \ldots B\bar{x}_nB\bar{y}B\bar{0}B\bar{x}_1B\bar{x}_2B \ldots B\bar{x}_nB\bar{0}B.$$

2. The machine G is run on the final n values on the tape.

$$B\bar{x}_1B\bar{x}_2B \ldots B\bar{x}_nB\bar{y}B\bar{0}B\overline{g(x_1, x_2, \ldots, x_n)}B$$

   The computation of G generates $g(x_1, x_2, \ldots, x_n) = f(x_1, x_2, \ldots, x_n, 0)$.

3. The tape now has the form

$$B\bar{x}_1B\bar{x}_2B \ldots B\bar{x}_nB\bar{y}B\bar{i}B\overline{f(x_1, x_2, \ldots, x_n, i)}B.$$

If the counter i is equal to y, the computation of $f(x_1, x_2, \ldots, x_n, y)$ is completed by erasing the inital $n + 2$ numbers on the tape and translating the result to tape position one.

4. If $i < y$, the tape is configured to compute the next value of f.

$$B\bar{x}_1B\bar{x}_2B \ldots B\bar{x}_nB\bar{y}B\overline{i+1}B\bar{x}_1B\bar{x}_2B \ldots B\bar{x}_nB\bar{i}B\overline{f(x_1, x_2, \ldots, x_n, i)}B$$

The machine H is run on the final $n + 2$ values on the tape, producing

$$B\bar{x}_1B\bar{x}_2B \ldots B\bar{x}_nB\bar{y}B\overline{i+1}B\overline{h(x_1, x_2, \ldots, x_n, i, f(x_1, x_2, \ldots, x_n, i))}B.$$

The computation continues with the comparison in step 3. ∎

13.2   Some Primitive Recursive Functions

A function is primitive recursive if it can be constructed from the zero, successor, and projection functions by a finite number of applications of composition and primitive recursion. Composition permits g and h, the functions used in a primitive recursive definition, to utilize any function that has previously been shown to be primitive recursive.

Primitive recursive definitions are constructed for several common arithmetic functions. Rather than explicitly detailing the functions g and h, a definition by primitive recursion is given in terms of the parameters, the recursive variable, the previous value of the function, and other primitive recursive functions. Note that the definitions of addition and multiplication are identical to the formal definitions given in Examples 13.1.2 and 13.1.3 with the intermediate step omitted.

Because of the compatibility with the operations of composition and primitive recursion, the definitions in Tables 13.2.1 and 13.2.2 are given using the functional notation. The standard infix representations of the binary arithmetic functions, given below the function names, are used in the arithmetic expressions throughout the chapter. The notation '$+ 1$' denotes the successor operator.

TABLE 13.2.1   Primitive Recursive Arithmetic Functions

Description	Function	Definition
addition	$add(x, y)$ $x + y$	$add(x, 0) = x$ $add(x, y + 1) = add(x, y) + 1$
multiplication	$mult(x, y)$ $x \cdot y$	$mult(x, 0) = 0$ $mult(x, y + 1) = mult(x, y) + x$
predecessor	$pred(y)$	$pred(0) = 0$ $pred(y + 1) = y$
proper subtraction	$sub(x, y)$ $x \dotminus y$	$sub(x, 0) = x$ $sub(x, y + 1) = pred(sub(x, y))$
exponentation	$exp(x, y)$ x^y	$exp(x, 0) = 1$ $exp(x, y + 1) = exp(x, y) \cdot x$

A primitive recursive predicate is a primitive recursive function whose range is the set $\{0, 1\}$. Zero and one are interpreted as false and true, respectively. The first two predicates in Table 13.2.2, the sign predicates, specify the sign of the argument. The function sg indicates whether the argument is positive. The complement of sg, denoted $cosg$, is true when the input is zero. Binary predicates that compare the input can be constructed from the arithmetic functions and the sign predicates using composition.

Table 13.2.2   Primitive Recursive Predicates

Description	Predicate	Definition
sign	$sg(x)$	$sg(0) = 0$ $sg(y + 1) = 1$
sign complement	$cosg(x)$	$cosg(0) = 1$ $cosg(y + 1) = 0$
less than	$lt(x, y)$	$sg(y \mathbin{\dot{-}} x)$
greater than	$gt(x, y)$	$sg(x \mathbin{\dot{-}} y)$
equal to	$eq(x, y)$	$cosg(lt(x, y) + gt(x, y))$
not equal to	$ne(x, y)$	$cosg(eq(x, y))$

Predicates are functions that exhibit the truth or falsity of a proposition. The logical operations negation, conjunction, and disjunction are constructed using the arithmetic functions and the sign predicates. Let p_1 and p_2 be two primitive recursive predicates. Logical operations on p_1 and p_2 can be defined as follows:

Predicate	Interpretation
$cosg(p_1)$	not p_1
$p_1 \cdot p_2$	p_1 and p_2
$sg(p_1 + p_2)$	p_1 or p_2

Applying $cosg$ to the result of a predicate interchanges the values, yielding the negation of the predicate. This technique was used to define the predicate ne from the predicate eq. The disjunction is obtained by adding the truth values of the component predicates. Since the sum is two when both of the predicates are true, the disjunction is obtained by composing the addition with sg. The resulting predicates are primitive recursive since the components of the composition are primitive recursive.

Example 13.2.1

The equality predicates can be used to explicitly specify the value of a function for a finite set of arguments. For example, f is the identity function for all input values other than 0, 1, and 2.

$$f(x) = \begin{cases} 2 & \text{if } x = 0 \\ 5 & \text{if } x = 1 \\ 4 & \text{if } x = 2 \\ x & \text{otherwise} \end{cases} \qquad \begin{aligned} f(x) = {} & eq(x, 0) \cdot 2 \\ & + eq(x, 1) \cdot 5 \\ & + eq(x, 2) \cdot 4 \\ & + gt(x, 2) \cdot x \end{aligned}$$

The function f is primitive recursive since it can be written as the composition of primitive recursive functions eq, gt, $+$, and $\cdot$. The four predicates in f are exhaustive and mutually exclusive; that is, one and only one of them is true for any natural number. The value of f is determined by the single predicate that holds for the input.   □

The technique presented in the previous example, constructing a function from exhaustive and mutually exclusive primitive recursive predicates, is used to establish the following theorem.

Theorem 13.2.1

Let g be a primitive recursive function and f a total function that is identical to g for all but a finite number of input values. Then f is primitive recursive.

Proof   Let g be a primitive recursive and let f be defined by

$$f(x) = \begin{cases} y_1 & \text{if } x = n_1 \\ y_2 & \text{if } x = n_2 \\ \vdots & \\ y_k & \text{if } x = n_k \\ g(x) & \text{otherwise.} \end{cases}$$

The equality predicate is used to specify the values of f for input $n_1, \ldots, n_k$. For all other input values, $f(x) = g(x)$. The predicate obtained by the product

$$ne(x, n_1) \cdot ne(x, n_2) \cdots \cdots ne(x, n_k)$$

is true whenever the value of f is determined by g. Using these predicates, f can be written

$$\begin{aligned} f(x) = {} & eq(x, n_1) \cdot y_1 + eq(x, n_2) \cdot y_2 + \cdots + eq(x, n_k) \cdot y_k \\ & + ne(x, n_1) \cdot ne(x, n_2) \cdots \cdots ne(x, n_k) \cdot g(x). \end{aligned}$$

Thus f is also primitive recursive.   ■

The order of the variables is an essential feature of a definition by primitive recursion. The initial variables are the parameters and the final variable is the recursive variable. Combining composition and the projection functions permits a great deal of flexibility in specifying the number and order of variables in a primitive recursive function. This flexibility is demonstrated by considering alterations to the variables in a two-variable function.

Theorem 13.2.2

Let $g(x, y)$ be a primitive recursive function. Then the functions obtained by

  i) (adding dummy variables) $f(x, y, z_1, z_2, \ldots, z_n) = g(x, y)$

 ii) (permuting variables) $f(x, y) = g(y, x)$

iii) (identifying variables) $f(x) = g(x, x)$

are primitive recursive.

Proof Each of the functions is primitive recursive since it can be obtained from g and the projections by composition.

  i) $f = g \circ (p_1^{(n+2)}, p_2^{(n+2)})$

 ii) $f = g \circ (p_2^{(2)}, p_1^{(2)})$

iii) $f = g \circ (p_1^{(2)}, p_1^{(2)})$ ■

Dummy variables are used to make functions with different numbers of variables compatible for composition. The definition of the composition $h \circ (g_1, g_2)$ requires that g_1 and g_2 have the same number of variables. Consider the two-variable function f defined by $f(x, y) = (xy) + x!$. The constituents of the addition are obtained from a multiplication and a factorial operation. The former function has two variables and the latter has one. Adding a dummy variable to the function *fact* produces a two-variable function *fact'* satisfying $fact'(x, y) = fact(x) = x!$. Finally, we note that $f = add \circ (mult, fact')$ so that f is also primitive recursive.

13.3   **Bounded Operators**

The sum of a sequence of natural numbers can be obtained by repeated applications of the binary operation of addition. Addition and projection can be combined to construct a function that adds a fixed number of arguments. For example, the primitive recursive function

$$add \circ (p_1^{(4)}, add \circ (p_2^{(4)}, add \circ (p_3^{(4)}, p_4^{(4)})))$$

returns the sum of its four arguments. This approach cannot be used when the number of summands is variable. Consider the function

$$f(y) = \sum_{i=0}^{y} g(i) = g(0) + g(1) + \cdots + g(y).$$

The number of additions is determined by the input variable y. The function f is called the bounded sum of g. The variable i is the index of the summation. Computing a bounded sum consists of three actions: the generation of the summands, binary addition, and the comparison of the index with the input y.

We will prove that the bounded sum of a primitive recursive function is primitive recursive. The technique presented can be used to show that repeated applications of any primitive recursive operation is also primitive recursive.

Theorem 13.3.1

Let $g(x_1, \ldots, x_n, y)$ be a primitive recursive function. Then the functions

i) (bounded sum) $f(x_1, \ldots, x_n, y) = \displaystyle\sum_{i=0}^{y} g(x_1, \ldots, x_n, i)$

ii) (bounded product) $f(x_1, \ldots, x_n, y) = \displaystyle\prod_{i=0}^{y} g(x_1, \ldots, x_n, i)$

are primitive recursive.

Proof The sum

$$\sum_{i=0}^{y} g(x_1, \ldots, x_n, i)$$

is obtained by adding $g(x_1, \ldots, x_n, y)$ to

$$\sum_{i=0}^{y-1} g(x_1, \ldots, x_n, i).$$

Translating this into the language of primitive recursion, we get

$$f(x_1, \ldots, x_n, 0) = g(x_1, \ldots, x_n, 0)$$
$$f(x_1, \ldots, x_n, y+1) = f(x_1, \ldots, x_n, y) + g(x_1, \ldots, x_n, y+1). \qquad \blacksquare$$

The bounded operations just introduced begin with index zero and terminate when the index reaches the value specified by the function f. Bounded operations can be generalized by having the range of the index variable determined by two computable functions. The functions l and u are used to determine the lower and upper bounds of the index.

Theorem 13.3.2

Let g be an $n+1$-variable primitive recursive and let l and u be n-variable primitive recursive functions. Then the functions

i) $f(x_1, \ldots, x_n) = \displaystyle\sum_{i=l(x_1,\ldots,x_n)}^{u(x_1,\ldots,x_n)} g(x_1, \ldots, x_n, i)$

ii) $f(x_1, \ldots, x_n) = \displaystyle\prod_{i=l(x_1,\ldots,x_n)}^{u(x_1,\ldots,x_n)} g(x_1, \ldots, x_n, i)$

are primitive recursive.

Proof Since the lower and upper bounds of the summation are determined by the functions l and u, it is possible that the lower bound may be greater than the upper bound. When this occurs, the result of the summation is assigned the default value zero. The predicate

$$gt(l(x_1, \ldots, x_n), u(x_1, \ldots, x_n))$$

is true in precisely these instances.

   If the lower bound is less than or equal to the upper bound, the summation begins with index $l(x_1, \ldots, x_n)$ and terminates when the index reaches $u(x_1, \ldots, x_n)$. Let g' be the primitive recursive function defined by

$$g'(x_1, \ldots, x_n, y) = g(x_1, \ldots, x_n, y + l(x_1, \ldots, x_n)).$$

The values of g' are obtained from those of g and $l(x_1, \ldots, x_n)$.

$$g'(x_1, \ldots, x_n, 0) = g(x_1, \ldots, x_n, l(x_1, \ldots, x_n))$$
$$g'(x_1, \ldots, x_n, 1) = g(x_1, \ldots, x_n, 1 + l(x_1, \ldots, x_n))$$
$$\vdots$$
$$g'(x_1, \ldots, x_n, y) = g(x_1, \ldots, x_n, y + l(x_1, \ldots, x_n)).$$

By Theorem 13.3.1, the function

$$f'(x_1, \ldots, x_n, y) = \sum_{i=0}^{y} g'(x_1, \ldots, x_n, i)$$
$$= \sum_{i=l(x_1,\ldots,x_n)}^{y+l(x_1,\ldots,x_n)} g(x_1, \ldots, x_n, i)$$

is primitive recursive. The generalized bounded sum can be obtained by composing f' with the functions u and l.

$$f'(x_1, \ldots, x_n, (u(x_1, \ldots, x_n) \dot- l(x_1, \ldots, x_n)) = \sum_{i=l(x_1,\ldots,x_n)}^{u(x_1,\ldots,x_n)} g(x_1, \ldots, x_n, i)$$

Multiplying this function by the predicate that compares the upper and lower bounds ensures that the bounded sum returns the default value whenever the lower bound exceeds the upper bound. Thus

$$f(x_1, \ldots, x_n) = cosg(gt(l(x_1, \ldots, x_n), u(x_1, \ldots, x_n)))$$
$$\cdot f'(x_1, \ldots, x_n, (u(x_1, \ldots, x_n) \dot- l(x_1, \ldots, x_n))).$$

Since each of the constituent functions is primitive recursive, it follows that f is also primitive recursive.

A similar argument can be used to show that the generalized bounded product is primitive recursive. When the lower bound is greater than the upper, the bounded product defaults to one.   ∎

The value returned by a predicate p designates whether the input satisfies the property represented by p. For fixed values $x_1, \ldots, x_n$,

$$\mu z[p(x_1, \ldots, x_n, z)]$$

is defined to be the smallest natural number z such that $p(x_1, \ldots, x_n, z) = 1$. The notation $\mu z[p(x_1, \ldots, x_n, z)]$ is read "the least z satisfying $p(x_1, \ldots, x_n, z)$." This construction is called the **minimalization** of p, and μz is called the μ-operator. The minimalization of an $n + 1$-variable predicate defines an n-variable function

$$f(x_1, \ldots, x_n) = \mu z[p(x_1, \ldots, x_n, z)].$$

A function defined by minimalization can be thought of as a search procedure. Initially, the variable z is set to zero. The search sequentially examines the natural numbers until a value of z for which $p(x_1, \ldots, x_n, z) = 1$ is encountered.

Unfortunately, the function obtained by the minimalization of a primitive recursive predicate need not be primitive recursive. In fact, such a function may not even be total. Consider the function

$$f(x) = \mu z[eq(x, z \cdot z)].$$

If x is a perfect square, then $f(x)$ returns the square root of x. Otherwise, f is undefined.

By restricting the range over which the minimalization occurs, we obtain a bounded minimalization operator. An $n + 1$-variable predicate defines an $n + 1$-variable function

$$f(x_1, \ldots, x_n, y) = \overset{y}{\mu z}[p(x_1, \ldots, x_n, z)]$$
$$= \begin{cases} z & \text{if } p(x_1, \ldots, x_n, i) = 0 \quad \text{for } 0 \leqslant i < z \leqslant y \\ & \text{and } p(x_1, \ldots, x_n, z) = 1 \\ y + 1 & \text{otherwise.} \end{cases}$$

The bounded μ-operator returns the first natural number z less than or equal to y for which $p(x_1, \ldots, x_n, z) = 1$. If no such value exists, the default value of $y + 1$ is assigned. Limiting the search to the range of natural numbers between zero and y ensures the totality of the function

$$f(x_1, \ldots, x_n, y) = \overset{y}{\mu z}[p(x_1, \ldots, x_n, z)].$$

In fact, the bounded minimalization operator defines a primitive recursive function whenever the predicate is primitive recursive.

Theorem 13.3.3

Let $p(x_1, \ldots, x_n, y)$ be a primitive recursive predicate. Then the function

$$f(x_1, \ldots, x_n, y) = \overset{y}{\mu z}[p(x_1, \ldots, x_n, z)]$$

is primitive recursive.

Proof   The proof is given for a two-variable predicate $p(x, y)$. The technique presented easily generalizes to n-variable predicates. We begin by defining an auxiliary predicate

$$g(x, y) = \begin{cases} 1 & \text{if } p(x, i) = 0 \text{ for } 0 \leq i \leq y \\ 0 & \text{otherwise} \end{cases}$$

$$= \prod_{i=0}^{y} cosg(p(x, i)).$$

This predicate is primitive recursive since it is a bounded product of the primitive recursive predicate $cosg \circ p$.

The bounded sum of the predicate g produces the bounded μ-operator. To illustrate the use of g in constructing the minimalization operator, consider a two-variable predicate p with argument n whose values are given below.

$$p(n, 0) = 0 \qquad g(n, 0) = 1 \qquad \sum_{i=0}^{0} g(n, i) = 1$$

$$p(n, 1) = 0 \qquad g(n, 1) = 1 \qquad \sum_{i=0}^{1} g(n, i) = 2$$

$$p(n, 2) = 0 \qquad g(n, 2) = 1 \qquad \sum_{i=0}^{2} g(n, i) = 3$$

$$p(n, 3) = 1 \qquad g(n, 3) = 0 \qquad \sum_{i=0}^{3} g(n, i) = 3$$

$$p(n, 4) = 0 \qquad g(n, 4) = 0 \qquad \sum_{i=0}^{4} g(n, i) = 3$$

$$p(n, 5) = 1 \qquad g(n, 5) = 0 \qquad \sum_{i=0}^{5} g(n, i) = 3$$

$$\vdots \qquad\qquad \vdots \qquad\qquad \vdots$$

The value of g is one until the first number z with $p(n, z) = 1$ is encountered. All subsequent values of g are zero. The bounded sum adds the results generated by g. Thus

$$\sum_{i=0}^{y} g(n, i) = \begin{cases} y + 1 & \text{if } z > y \\ z & \text{otherwise.} \end{cases}$$

The first condition also includes the possibility that there is no z satisfying $p(n, z) = 1$. In this case, the default value is returned regardless of the specified range.

Formalizing the previous argument, the bounded minimalization of a primitive recursive predicate p, defined by the function

$$f(x, y) = \mu z[p(x, z)] = \sum_{i=0}^{y} g(x, i),$$

is primitive recursive.   ∎

Bounded minimalization can be generalized by generating the upper bound with a function u. When u is primitive recursive, so is the resulting function. The proof is similar to that of Theorem 13.3.2 and is left as an exercise.

Theorem 13.3.4
Let p be an $n + 1$-variable primitive recursive predicate and let u be an n-variable primitive recursive function. Then the function

$$f(x_1, \ldots, x_n) = \overset{u(x_1, \ldots, x_n)}{\mu z} [p(x_1, \ldots, x_n, z)]$$

is primitive recursive.

13.4 Division Functions

The fundamental operation of integer division, div, is not total. The function $div(x, y)$ returns the quotient, the integer part of x/y, when the second argument is nonzero. The function is undefined when y is zero. Since all primitive recursive functions are total, it follows that div is not primitive recursive. A primitive recursive division function quo is defined by assigning a default value when the denominator is zero.

$$quo(x, y) = \begin{cases} 0 & \text{if } y = 0 \\ div(x, y) & \text{otherwise} \end{cases}$$

The division function quo is constructed using the primitive recursive operation of multiplication. For values of y other than zero, $quo(x, y) = z$ implies that z satisfies $z \cdot y \leqslant x < (z + 1) \cdot y$. That is, $quo(x, y)$ is the smallest natural number z such that

$(z + 1) \cdot y$ is greater than x. The search for the value of z that satisfies the inequality succeeds before z reaches x since $(x + 1) \cdot y$ is greater than x. The function

$$\mu z[gt((z + 1) \cdot y, x)]^{x}$$

determines the quotient of x and y whenever the division is defined. The default value is obtained by multiplying the minimalization by $sg(y)$. Thus

$$quo(x, y) = sg(y) \cdot \mu z[gt((z + 1) \cdot y, x)]^{x}$$

where the bound is determined by the primitive recursive function $p_1^{(2)}$. The previous definition demonstrates that quo is primitive recursive since it has the form prescribed by Theorem 13.3.4.

The quotient function can be used to define a number of division related functions and predicates (Table 13.4.1). The function rem returns the remainder of the division of x by y whenever the division is defined. Otherwise, $rem(x, 0) = x$.

The predicate $divides$ is true whenever y divides x. By convention, zero is not considered to be divisible by any number. The factor $sg(x)$ enforces this condition. The default value of the remainder function guarantees that $divides(x, 0) = 0$.

The generalized bounded sum can be used to count the number of divisors of a number. The upper bound of the sum is computed from the input by the primitive recursive function $p_1^{(1)}$. This bound is satisfactory since no number greater than y is a divisor of y. A prime number is one whose only divisors are one and itself. The predicate $prime$ simply consults the function $ndivisors$.

The predicate prime and bounded minimalization can be used to construct a primitive recursive function pn that enumerates the primes. The value of $pn(i)$ is the ith prime. Thus, $pn(0) = 2$, $pn(1) = 3$, $pn(2) = 5$, $pn(3) = 7$, ... The $y + 1$st prime is the first prime number greater than $pn(y)$. Bounded minimalization is ideally suited for performing this type of search. To employ the bounded μ-operator, we must determine an upper

Table 13.4.1 Primitive Recursive Division Functions

$$quo(x, y) = sg(y) \cdot \mu z[gt((z + 1) \cdot y, x)]^{x}$$

$$rem(x, y) = x \div (y \cdot quo(x, y))$$

$$divides(x, y) = \begin{cases} 1 & \text{if } x > 0, y > 0, \text{ and } y \text{ is a divisor of } x \\ 0 & \text{otherwise} \end{cases}$$
$$= eq(rem(x, y), 0) \cdot sg(x)$$

$$ndivisors(y) = \sum_{i=0}^{y} divides(y, i)$$

$$prime(y) = eq(ndivisors(y), 2)$$

bound for the minimalization. By Theorem 13.3.4, the bound may be calculated using the input value y.

Lemma 13.4.1
Let $pn(y)$ denote the nth a prime. Then $pn(y + 1) \leqslant pn(y)! + 1$.

Proof   Each of the primes $pn(i)$, $i = 0, 1, \ldots, y$, divides $pn(y)!$. Since a prime cannot divide two consecutive numbers, either $pn(y)! + 1$ is prime or its prime decomposition contains a prime other than $pn(0), pn(1), \ldots, pn(y)$. In either case, $pn(y + 1) \leqslant pn(y)! + 1$. ∎

The bound provided by the preceding lemma is computed by the primitive recursive function $fact(x) + 1$. The yth prime function is obtained by primitive recursion as follows:

$$pn(0) = 2$$

$$pn(y + 1) = \overset{fact(pn(y))+1}{\mu z} \ [prime(z) \cdot gt(z, pn(y))].$$

Let us take a moment to reflect on the consequences of the relationship between the family of primitive recursive functions and Turing computability. By Theorem 13.1.3, every primitive recursive function is Turing computable. The bounded operators and bounded minimalization are powerful tools for constructing complex primitive recursive functions. Designing Turing machines that explicitly compute functions such as pn or $ndivisors$ would require a large number of states and a complicated transition function. Using the macroscopic approach to computation, these functions are easily shown to be computable. Without the tedium inherent in constructing complicated Turing machines, we have shown that many useful functions and predicates are Turing computable.

13.5 Gödel Numbering and Course-of-Values Recursion

Many common computations involving natural numbers are not number theoretic functions. Sorting a sequence of numbers returns a sequence, not a single number. However, there are many sorting algorithms that we consider effective procedures. We now introduce primitive recursive constructions that allow us to perform this type of operation. The essential feature is the ability to encode a sequence of numbers in a single value. The coding scheme utilizes the unique decomposition of a natural number into a product of primes. Such codes are called Gödel numberings after Kurt Gödel, who developed the technique.

A sequence $x_0, x_1, \ldots, x_n$ of length $n + 1$ is encoded by

$$pn(0)^{x_0+1} \cdot pn(1)^{x_1+1} \cdot \ldots \cdot pn(n)^{x_n+1} = 2^{x_0+1} \cdot 3^{x_1+1} \cdot \ldots \cdot pn(n)^{x_n+1}.$$

Since our numbering begins with zero, the elements of a sequence of length n are numbered $0, 1, \ldots, n - 1$.

Sequence	Encoding
1, 2	$2^2 3^3 = 108$
0, 1, 3	$2^1 3^2 5^4 = 11{,}250$
0, 1, 0, 1	$2^1 3^2 5^1 7^2 = 4{,}410$

An encoded sequence of length n is a product of powers of the first n primes. The choice of the exponent $x_i + 1$ guarantees that $pn(i)$ occurs in the encoding even when x_i is zero.

The definition of a function that encodes a fixed number of inputs can be obtained directly from the definition of the Gödel numbering. We let

$$gn_n(x_0, \ldots, x_n) = pn(0)^{x_0+1} \cdot \cdots \cdot pn(n)^{x_n+1} = \prod_{i=0}^{n} pn(i)^{x_i+1}$$

be the $n+1$-variable function that encodes a sequence $x_0, x_1, \ldots, x_n$. The function gn_{n-1} can be used to encode the components of an ordered n-tuple. The Gödel number associated with the ordered pair $[x_0, x_1]$ is $gn_1(x_0, x_1)$.

A decoding function is constructed to retrieve the components of an encoded sequence. The function $dec(i, x)$ returns the ith element of the sequence encoded in the Gödel number x. The bounded μ-operator is used to find the power of $pn(i)$ in the prime decomposition of x. The ith element in an encoded sequence is one less than the power of $pn(i)$ in the encoding.

$$dec(i, x) = \overset{x}{\mu z}[cosg(divides(x, pn(i)^{z+1}))] \;\dot-\; 1$$

The decoding function returns zero for every prime that does not occur the prime decomposition of x.

When a computation requires n previously computed values, the Gödel encoding function gn_{n-1} can be used to encode the values. The encoded values can be retrieved when they are needed by the computation.

Example 13.5.1

The Fibonacci numbers are defined as the sequence 0, 1, 1, 2, 3, 5, 8, 13, . . . , where an element in the sequence is the sum of its two successors. The function

$$f(0) = 0$$
$$f(1) = 1$$
$$f(y + 1) = f(y) + f(y - 1) \text{ for } y > 1$$

generates the Fibonacci numbers. This is not a definition by primitive recursion since the computation of $f(y + 1)$ utilizes both $f(y)$ and $f(y - 1)$. To show that the Fibonacci numbers are generated by a primitive recursive function, the Gödel numbering function

gn_1 is used to store the two values as a single number. An auxiliary function h encodes the ordered pair with first component $f(y - 1)$ and second component $f(y)$.

$$h(0) = gn_1(0, 1) = 2^1 3^2 = 18$$
$$h(y + 1) = gn_1(dec(1, h(y)), dec(0, h(y)) + dec(1, h(y)))$$

The initial value of h is the encoded pair $[f(0), f(1)]$. The calculation of $h(y + 1)$ begins by producing another ordered pair

$$[dec(1, h(y)), dec(0, h(y)) + dec(1, h(y))] = [f(y), f(y - 1) + f(y)].$$

Encoding the pair with gn_1 completes the evaluation of $h(y + 1)$. This process constructs the sequence of Gödel numbers of the pairs $[f(0), f(1)], [f(1), f(2)], [f(2), f(3)], \ldots$

The primitive recursive function $f(y) = dec(0, h(y))$ extracts the Fibonacci numbers from the first components of the ordered pairs.   □

The Gödel numbering functions gn_i encode a fixed number of arguments. A Gödel numbering function can be constructed in which the number of elements to be encoded is variable. The approach is similar to that taken in constructing the bounded sum and product operations. The values of a one-variable primitive recursive function f with input $0, 1, \ldots, n$ define a sequence $f(0), f(1), \ldots, f(n)$ of length $n + 1$. The bounded product

$$\prod_{i=0}^{y} pn(i)^{f(i)+1}$$

encodes the first $y + 1$ values of f. A Gödel numbering function $gn_f(x_1, \ldots, x_n, y)$ is defined from a total $n + 1$-variable function f. The relationship between a function f and its encoding function gn_f is established in Theorem 13.5.1.

Theorem 13.5.1

Let f be an $n + 1$-variable function and gn_f the encoding function defined from f. Then f is primitive recursive if, and only if, gn_f is primitive recursive.

Proof   If $f(x_1, \ldots, x_n, y)$ is primitive recursive, then the bounded product

$$gn_f(x_1, \ldots, x_n, y) = \prod_{i=0}^{y} pn(i)^{f(x_1, \ldots, x_n, i)+1}$$

computes the Gödel encoding function. On the other hand, the decoding function can be used to recover the values of f from the Gödel number generated by gn_f.

$$f(x_1, \ldots, x_n, y) = dec(y, gn_f(x_1, \ldots, x_n, y))$$

Thus f is primitive recursive whenever gn_f is.   ■

The primitive recursive functions have been introduced because of their intuitive computability. In a definition by primitive recursion, the computation is permitted to use the result of the function with the previous value of the recursive variable. Consider the function defined by

$$f(0) = 1$$
$$f(1) = f(0) \cdot 1 = 1$$
$$f(2) = f(0) \cdot 2 + f(1) \cdot 1 = 3$$
$$f(3) = f(0) \cdot 3 + f(1) \cdot 2 + f(2) \cdot 1 = 8$$
$$f(4) = f(0) \cdot 4 + f(1) \cdot 3 + f(2) \cdot 2 + f(3) \cdot 1 = 21$$
$$\vdots$$

Using the summation notation, f can be written

$$f(0) = 1$$
$$f(y + 1) = \sum_{i=0}^{y} f(i) \cdot (y + 1 - i).$$

The definition, as formulated, is not primitive recursive since the computation of $f(y)$ utilizes all of the previously computed values. The function, however, is intuitively computable; the definition itself outlines an algorithm by which any value can be calculated.

When the result of a function with recursive variable $y + 1$ is defined in terms of $f(0), f(1), \ldots, f(y)$, the function f is said to be defined by **course-of-values recursion.** Determining the result of a function defined by course-of-values recursion appears to utilize a different number of inputs for each value of the recursive variable. In the preceding example, $f(2)$ requires only $f(0)$ and $f(1)$, while $f(4)$ requires $f(0), f(1), f(2)$, and $f(3)$. No single function can be used to compute both $f(2)$ and $f(4)$ directly from the preceding values since a function has a fixed number of arguments.

Regardless of the value of the recursive variable $y + 1$, the preceding results can be encoded in the Gödel number $gn_f(y)$. This observation provides the framework for a formal definition of course-of-values recursion.

Definition 13.5.2

Let g and h be n and $n + 2$-variable total number theoretic functions, respectively. The $n + 1$-variable function f defined by

i) $f(x_1, \ldots, x_n, 0) = g(x_1, \ldots, x_n)$

ii) $f(x_1, \ldots, x_n, y + 1) = h(x_1, \ldots, x_n, y, gn_f(x_1, \ldots, x_n, y))$

is said to be obtained from g and h by course-of-values recursion.

Theorem 13.5.3

Let f be an $n + 1$-variable function defined by course-of-values recursion from primitive recursive functions g and h. Then f is primitive recursive.

Proof   We begin by defining gn_f by primitive recursion directly from the primitive recursive functions g and h.

$$gn_f(x_1, \ldots, x_n, 0) = 2^{f(x_1, \ldots, x_n, 0)+1}$$
$$= 2^{g(x_1, \ldots, x_n)+1}$$

$$gn_f(x_1, \ldots, x_n, y + 1) = gn_f(x_1, \ldots, x_n, y) \cdot pn(y + 1)^{f(x_1, \ldots, x_n, y+1)+1}$$
$$= gn_f(x_1, \ldots, x_n, y) \cdot pn(y + 1)^{h(x_1, \ldots, x_n, y, gn_f(x_1, \ldots, x_n, y))+1}$$

The evaluation of $gn_f(x_1, \ldots, x_n, y + 1)$ uses only

 i) the parameters $x_0, \ldots, x_n$
 ii) y, the previous value of the recursive variable
 iii) $gn_f(x_1, \ldots, x_n, y)$, the previous value of gn_f
 iv) the primitive recursive functions h, pn, $\cdot$, $+$, and exponentiation.

Thus, the function gn_f is primitive recursive. By Theorem 13.5.1, it follows that f is also primitive recursive.   ∎

In mechanical terms, the Gödel numbering gives computations the equivalent of unlimited memory. A single Gödel number is capable of storing any number of preliminary results. The Gödel numbering encodes the values $f(x_0, \ldots, x_n, 0)$, $f(x_0, \ldots, x_n, 1)$, $\ldots, f(x_0, \ldots, x_n, y - 1)$ that are required for the computation of $f(x_0, \ldots, x_n, y)$. The decoding function provides the connection between the memory and the computation. Whenever a stored value is needed by the computation, the decoding function makes it available.

Example 13.5.2

Let h be the primitive recursive function

$$h(x, y) = \sum_{i=0}^{x} dec(i, y) \cdot (x + 1 - i).$$

The function f, which was defined earlier to introduce course-of-values computation, can be defined by course-of-values recursion from h.

$$f(0) = 1$$
$$f(y + 1) = h(y, gn_f(y)) = \sum_{i=0}^{y} dec(i, gn_f(y)) \cdot (y + 1 - i)$$
$$= \sum_{i=0}^{y} f(i) \cdot (y + 1 - i)$$

□

13.6 Computable Partial Functions

The primitive recursive functions were defined as a family of intuitively computable functions. We have established that all primitive recursive functions are total. Conversely, are all computable total functions primitive recursive? Moreover, should we restrict our analysis of computability to total functions? In this section we will present arguments for a negative response to both of these questions.

Theorem 13.6.1

The set of primitive recursive functions is a proper subset of the set of effectively computable total number theoretic functions.

Proof The primitive recursive functions can be represented as strings over the alphabet $\Sigma = \{s, p, z, 0, 1, 2, 3, 4, 5, 6, 7, 8, 9, (,), \circ, :, \langle, \rangle\}$. The basic functions s, z, and $p_i^{(j)}$ are represented by $\langle s \rangle$, $\langle z \rangle$, and $\langle pi(j) \rangle$. The composition $h \circ g$ is encoded $\langle\langle h \rangle \circ \langle g \rangle\rangle$, where $\langle h \rangle$ and $\langle g \rangle$ are the representations of the constituent functions. A function defined by primitive recursion from functions g and h is represented by $\langle\langle g \rangle : \langle h \rangle\rangle$.

The strings in Σ^* can be generated by length: first the null string, followed by strings of length one, length two, and so on. A straightforward mechanical process can be designed to determine whether a string represents a correctly formed primitive recursive function. The enumeration of the primitive recursive functions is accomplished by repeatedly generating a string and determining if it is a syntactically correct representation of a function. The first correctly formed string is denoted f_0, the next f_1, and so on. In the same manner, we can enumerate the one-variable primitive recursive functions. This is accomplished by deleting all n-variable functions, $n > 1$, from the list generated above. This sequence is denoted $f^{(1)}_0, f^{(1)}_1, f^{(1)}_2, \ldots$.

The total one-variable function

$$g(i) = f^{(1)}_i(i) + 1$$

is effectively computable. The effective enumeration of the one-variable primitive recursive functions establishes the computability of g. The value $g(i)$ is obtained by

i) determining the ith one-variable primitive recursive function $f^{(1)}_i$

ii) computing $f^{(1)}_i(i)$

iii) adding one to $f^{(1)}_i(i)$.

Since each of these steps is effective, we conclude that g is computable. By the familiar diagonalization argument,

$$g(i) \neq f^{(1)}_i(i)$$

for any i. Consequently, g is total and computable but not primitive recursive. ∎

Theorem 13.6.1 uses a counting argument to demonstrate the existence of comput-able functions that are not primitive recursive. This can also be accomplished directly by constructing a computable function that is not primitive recursive. The two-variable number theoretic function, known as Ackermann's function, defined by

i) $A(0, y) = y + 1$

ii) $A(x + 1, 0) = A(x, 1)$

iii) $A(x + 1, y + 1) = A(x, A(x + 1, y))$,

is one such function. The values of A are defined recursively with the basis given in condition i). A proof by induction on x establishes that A is uniquely defined for every pair of input values (Exercise 14). The computations in Example 13.6.1 illustrate the computability of Ackermann's function.

Example 13.6.1

The values $A(1, 1)$ and $A(3, 0)$ are constructed from the definition of Ackermann's function. The column on the right gives the justification for the substitution.

a) $A(1, 1) = A(0, A(1, 0))$ iii)
$ = A(0, A(0, 1))$ ii)
$ = A(0, 2)$ i)
$ = 3$

b) $A(2, 1) = A(1, A(2, 0))$ iii)
$ = A(1, A(1, 1))$ ii)
$ = A(1, 3)$ a)
$ = A(0, A(1, 2))$ iii)
$ = A(0, A(0, A(1, 1)))$ iii)
$ = A(0, A(0, 3))$ a)
$ = A(0, 4)$ i)
$ = 5$ i)   □

The values of Ackermann's function exhibit a remarkable rate of growth. Fixing the first variable, Ackermann's function generates the one-variable functions

$$A(1, y) = y + 2$$
$$A(2, y) = 2y + 3$$
$$A(3, y) = 2^{y+3} - 3$$
$$A(4, y) = 2^{2^{\cdot^{\cdot^{\cdot^{2^{16}}}}}} - 3.$$

The number of twos in the exponential chain in $A(4, y)$ is y. The first variable determines the rate of growth of the function values. We state, without proof, the following theorem that compares the rate of growth of Ackermann's function with that of the primitive recursive functions.

Theorem 13.6.2

For every one-variable primitive recursive function f, there is some $i \in \mathbf{N}$ such that $f(i) < A(i, i)$.

Clearly, the one-variable function $A(i, i)$ is not primitive recursive. It follows that Ackermann's function is not primitive recursive. If it were, then $A(i, i)$, which can be obtained by the composition $A \circ (p_1^{(1)}, p_1^{(1)})$, would also be primitive recursive.

Regardless of the set of total functions that we consider computable, the diagonal argument presented in the proof of Theorem 13.6.1 can be used to show that there is no effective enumeration of these functions. Therefore, we must conclude that the computable functions cannot be effectively generated or that there are computable non-total functions. If we accept the latter proposition, the contradiction from the diagonalization argument disappears. The reason we can claim that g is not one of the f_i's is that $g(i) \neq f_i^{(1)}(i)$. If $f_i^{(1)}(i)\uparrow$, then $g(i) = f_i^{(i)}(i) + 1$ is also undefined. If we wish to be able to effectively enumerate the computable functions, it is necessary to include partial functions in the enumeration.

We now consider the computability of partial functions. Since composition and primitive recursion preserve totality, an additional operation is needed to construct partial functions from the basic functions. Minimalization has been informally described as a search procedure. Placing a bound on the range of the natural numbers to be examined ensured that the bounded minimalization operation produces total functions. Unbounded minimalization is obtained by performing the search without an upper limit on the set of natural numbers to be considered. The function

$$f(x) = \mu z[eq(x, z \cdot z)]$$

defined by unbounded minimalization returns the square root of x whenever x is a perfect square. Otherwise, the search for the first natural number satisfying the predicate continues ad infinitum. Although eq is a total function, the resulting function f is not, for example, $f(3)\uparrow$. A function defined by unbounded minimalization is undefined for input x whenever the search fails to return a value.

The introduction of partial functions forces us to reexamine the operations of composition and primitive recursion. The possibility of undefined values was considered in the definition of composition. The function $h \circ (g_1, \ldots, g_n)$ is undefined for input $x_1, \ldots, x_k$ if either

i) $g_i(x_1, \ldots, x_k)\uparrow$ for some $1 \leq i \leq n$

ii) $g_i(x_1, \ldots, x_k)\downarrow$ for all $1 \leq i \leq n$ and $h(g_1(x_1, \ldots, x_k), \ldots, g_n(x_1, \ldots, x_k))\uparrow$.

An undefined value propagates from any of the g_i's to the composite function.

The operation of primitive recursion required both of the defining functions g and h to be total. This restriction is relaxed to permit definitions by primitive recursion using partial functions. Let f be defined by primitive recursion from partial functions g and h.

$$f(x_1, \ldots, x_n, 0) = g(x_1, \ldots, x_n, 0)$$
$$f(x_1, \ldots, x_n, y + 1) = h(x_1, \ldots, x_n, y, f(x_1, \ldots, x_n, y)).$$

Determining the value of a function defined by primitive recursion is an iterative process. The function f is defined for recursive variable y only if the following conditions are satisfied:

i) $f(x_1, \ldots, x_n, 0) \downarrow$ if $g(x_1, \ldots, x_n, 0) \downarrow$

ii) $f(x_1, \ldots, x_n, y + 1) \downarrow$ if $f(x_1, \ldots, x_n, i) \downarrow$ for $0 \leqslant i \leqslant y$
$$\text{and } h(x_1, \ldots, x_n, y, f(x_1, \ldots, x_n)) \downarrow.$$

An undefined value for the primitive recursive variable causes f to be undefined for all the subsequent values of the primitive recursive variable.

With the conventions established for definitions with partial functions, a family of computable partial functions can be defined using the operations composition, primitive recursion, and unbounded minimalization.

Definition 13.6.3

The family of **μ-recursive functions** is defined as follows:

i) The successor, zero, and projection functions are μ-recursive.

ii) If h is an n-variable μ-recursive function and $g_1, \ldots, g_n$ are k-variable μ-recursive functions, then $f = h \circ (g_1, \ldots, g_n)$ is μ-recursive.

iii) If g and h are n and $n + 2$-variable μ-recursive functions, then the function f defined from g and h by primitive recursion is μ-recursive.

iv) If $p(x_1, \ldots, x_n, y)$ is a total μ-recursive predicate, then $f = \mu z[p(x_1, \ldots, x_n, z)]$ is μ-recursive.

v) A function is μ-recursive only if it can be obtained from i) by a finite number of applications of the rules in ii), iii), and iv).

Conditions i), ii), and iii) imply that all primitive recursive functions are μ-recursive. Notice that unbounded minimalization is not defined for all predicates. The unbounded μ-operator can be applied only to total μ-recursive predicates.

The notion of Turing computability encompasses partial functions in a natural way. A Turing machine computes a partial number theoretic function f if

i) the computation terminates with result $f(x_1, \ldots, x_n)$ whenever $f(x_1, \ldots, x_n) \downarrow$

ii) the computation does not terminate whenever $f(x_1, \ldots, x_n) \uparrow$.

The Turing machine computes the value of the function whenever possible. Otherwise, the computation continues indefinitely.

We will now establish the relationship between the μ-recursive and Turing computable functions. The first step is to show that every μ-recursive function is Turing computable. This is not a surprising result; it simply extends Theorem 13.1.3 to partial functions.

Theorem 13.6.4

Every μ-recursive function is Turing computable.

Proof   Since the basic functions are known to be Turing computable, the proof consists of showing that the Turing computable partial functions are closed under operations of composition, primitive recursion, and unbounded minimalization. The techniques developed in Theorems 12.4.3 and 13.1.3 demonstrate the closure of Turing computable total functions under composition and primitive recursion, respectively. These machines also establish the closure for partial functions. An undefined value in one of the constituent computations causes the entire computation to continue indefinitely.

The proof is completed by showing that the unbounded minimalization of a Turing computable total predicate is Turing computable. Let $f(x_1, \ldots, x_n) = \mu z[p(x_1, \ldots, x_n, y)]$ where $p(x_1, \ldots, x_n, y)$ is a total Turing computable predicate. A Turing machine to compute f can be constructed from P, the machine that computes the predicate p. The initial configuration of the tape is $Bx_1Bx_2B \ldots Bx_nB$.

1. A number $j,$ initially set to zero, is added to the right of the input.

$$B\bar{x}_1B\bar{x}_2B \ldots B\bar{x}_nB\bar{0}B$$

   The value of j is the index for the minimalization operator.

2. A working copy of the parameters and j is made, producing the tape configuration

$$B\bar{x}_1B\bar{x}_2B \ldots Bx_nB\bar{j}B\bar{x}_1B\bar{x}_2B \ldots Bx_nB\bar{j}B.$$

3. The machine P is run with the input consisting of the copy of the parameters and j.

$$B\bar{x}_1B\bar{x}_2B \ldots B\bar{x}_nB\bar{j}B\overline{p(x_1, x_2, \ldots, x_n, j)}B$$

4. If $p(x_1, x_2, \ldots, x_n, j) = 1$, the value of the minimalization of p is j. Otherwise, the $p(x_1, x_2, \ldots, x_n, j)$ is erased, j is incremented, and steps 2–4 are repeated.

A computation terminates at step 4 when the first j for which $p(x_1, \ldots, x_n, j) = 1$ is encountered. If no such value exists, the computation loops indefinitely, indicating that the function f is undefined.   ∎

13.7   Turing Computability and Mu-Recursive Functions

It has already been established that every μ-recursive function can be computed by a Turing machine. We now turn our attention to the opposite inclusion, that every Turing computable function is μ-recursive. A number theoretic function is designed to simulate the computations of a Turing machine. The construction of the simulating function requires moving from the domain of machines to the domain of natural numbers. The process of translating machine computations to functions is known as the arithmetization of Turing machines.

The arithmetization begins by assigning a number to a Turing machine configuration. Let $M = (Q, \Sigma, \Gamma, \delta, q_0, q_n)$ be a standard Turing machine that computes a one-variable number theoretic function f. The states and tape alphabet of M are denoted

$$Q = \{q_0, q_1, \ldots, q_n\}$$
$$\Gamma = \{B = a_0, 1 = a_1, \ldots, a_k\}.$$

A μ-recursive function is constructed to numerically simulate the computations of M. The construction easily generalizes to functions of more than one variable.

A configuration of the Turing machine M consists of the state, the position of the tape head, and the segment of the tape from the left boundary to the rightmost nonblank symbol. Each of these components must be represented by a natural number. The subscripts provide a numbering for the states and the tape alphabet. The tape symbols B and 1 are assigned zero and one, respectively. The location of the tape head can be encoded using the numbering of the tape positions.

	0	1	2	3	4	5	

The symbols on the tape to the rightmost nonblank square form a string over Σ^*. Encoding the tape uses the numeric representation of the elements of the tape alphabet. The string $x_{i_0} x_{i_1} \ldots x_{i_n}$ is encoded by the Gödel number associated with the sequence $i_0, i_1, \ldots, i_n$. The number representing the nonblank tape segment is called the **tape number.**

Representing the blank by the number zero permits the correct decoding of any tape position regardless of the segment of the tape encoded in the tape number. If $dec(i, z) = 0$ and $pn(i)$ divides z, then the blank is specifically encoded in the tape number z. On the other hand, if $dec(i, z) = 0$ and $pn(i)$ does not divide z, then position i is to the right of the encoded segment of the tape. Since the tape number encodes the entire nonblank segment of the tape, it follows that position i must be blank.

The tape number of the nonblank segment of the machine configuration

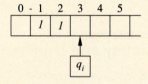

is $2^1 3^2 5^2 = 450$. Explicitly encoding the blank in position three produces $2^1 3^2 5^2 7^1 = 3150$, another tape number representing the tape. Any number of blanks to the right of the rightmost nonblank square may be included in the tape number.

A Turing machine configuration is defined by the state number, tape head position, and tape number. The configuration number incorporates these values into the single number

$$gn_2(\text{state number, tape head position, tape number})$$

where gn_2 is the Gödel numbering function that encodes ordered triples.

Example 13.7.1

The Turing machine S computes the successor function.

The configuration numbers are given for each configuration produced by the computation of the successor of one. Recall that the tape symbols B and 1 are assigned the numbers zero and one, respectively.

	State	Position	Tape Number	Configuration Number
q_0B11B	0	0	$2^1 3^2 5^2 = 450$	$gn_2(0, 0, 450)$
$\vdash Bq_111B$	1	1	$2^1 3^2 5^2 = 450$	$gn_2(1, 1, 450)$
$\vdash B1q_11B$	1	2	$2^1 3^2 5^2 = 450$	$gn_2(1, 2, 450)$
$\vdash B11q_1B$	1	3	$2^1 3^2 5^2 7^1 = 3150$	$gn_2(1, 3, 3150)$
$\vdash B1q_211B$	2	2	$2^1 3^2 5^2 7^2 11^1 = 242550$	$gn_2(2, 2, 242550)$
$\vdash Bq_2111B$	2	1	$2^1 3^2 5^2 7^2 11^1 = 242550$	$gn_2(2, 1, 242550)$
$\vdash q_2B111B$	2	0	$2^1 3^2 5^2 7^2 11^1 = 242550$	$gn_2(2, 0, 242550)$

□

A Turing machine transition need not alter the tape or the state, but it must move the tape head. The change in the tape head position and the uniqueness of the Gödel numbering ensure that no two consecutive configuration numbers of a computation are identical.

A function tr_M is constructed to trace the computations of a Turing machine M. Tracing a computation means generating the sequence of configuration numbers that correspond to the machine configurations produced by the computation. The value of $tr_M(x, i)$ is the number of the configuration after i transitions when M is run with input x. Since the initial configuration of M is $q_0B\bar{x}B$,

$$tr_M(x, 0) = gn_2(0, 0, 2^1 \cdot \prod_{i=1}^{x+1} pn(i)^2).$$

The value of $tr_M(x, y + 1)$ is obtained by manipulating the configuration number $tr_M(x, y)$ to construct the encoding of the subsequent machine configuration.

The state and symbol in the position scanned by the tape head determine the transition to be applied by the machine M. The primitive recursive functions

$$cs(z) = dec(0, z)$$
$$ctp(z) = dec(1, z)$$
$$cts(z) = dec(ctp(z), dec(2, z))$$

return the state number, tape head position, and the number of the symbol scanned by the tape head from a configuration number z. The position of the tape head is obtained by a direct decoding of the configuration number. The numeric representation of the scanned symbol is encoded as the $ctp(z)$th element of the tape number. The c's in cs, ctp, and cts stand for the components of the current configuration: current state, current tape position, and current tape symbol.

A transition specifies the alterations to the machine configuration and, hence, the configuration number. A transition of M is written

$$\delta(q_i, b) = [q_j, c, d]$$

where $q_i, q_j \in Q$; $b, c \in \Gamma$; and $d \in \{R, L\}$. Functions are defined to simulate the effects of a transition of M. We begin by listing the transitions of M.

$$\delta(q_{i_0}, b_0) = [q_{j_0}, c_0, d_0]$$
$$\delta(q_{i_1}, b_1) = [q_{j_1}, c_1, d_1]$$
$$\vdots$$
$$\delta(q_{i_m}, b_m) = [q_j, c_m, d_m]$$

The determinism of the machine ensures that the arguments of the transitions are distinct. The number assigned to the tape symbol a is denoted $n(a)$. A function that returns the number of the state entered by a transition from a configuration with configuration number z is

$$ns(z) = \begin{cases} j_0 & \text{if } cs(z) = i_0 \text{ and } cts(z) = n(b_0) \\ j_1 & \text{if } cs(z) = i_1 \text{ and } cts(z) = n(b_1) \\ \vdots & \quad\vdots \\ j_m & \text{if } cs(z) = i_m \text{ and } cts(z) = n(b_m) \\ cs(z) & \text{otherwise.} \end{cases}$$

The first condition can be interpreted "if the number of the current state is i_0 (state q_{i_0}) and the current tape symbol is b_0 then the new state has number j_0 (state q_{j_0})." This is a direct translation of the initial transition into the numeric representation. The conditions define a set of exhaustive and mutually exclusive primitive recursive predicates. Thus, $ns(z)$ is primitive recursive. A function nts that computes the number of the new tape symbol can be defined in a completely analogous manner.

A function that computes the new tape head position alters the number of the current position as specified by the direction in the transition. The transitions designate the directions as L (left) or R (right). A movement to the left subtracts one from the current position number and a movement to the right adds one. To numerically represent the direction we use the notation

$$n(d) = \begin{cases} 0 & \text{if } d = L \\ 2 & \text{if } d = R. \end{cases}$$

The new tape position is computed by

$$ntp(z) = \begin{cases} ctp(z) + n(d_0) \div 1 & \text{if } cs(z) = i_0 \text{ and } cts(z) = n(b_0) \\ ctp(z) + n(d_1) \div 1 & \text{if } cs(z) = i_1 \text{ and } cts(z) = n(b_1) \\ \quad \vdots & \qquad \vdots \\ ctp(z) + n(d_m) \div 1 & \text{if } cs(z) = i_m \text{ and } cts(z) = n(b_m) \\ ctp(z) & \text{otherwise.} \end{cases}$$

The addition of $n(d_i) \div 1$ to the current position number increments the value by one when the transition moves the tape head to the right. Similarly, one is subtracted on a move to the left.

We have almost completed the construction of the components of the trace function. Given a machine configuration, the functions ns and ntp compute the state number and tape head position of the new configuration. All that remains is to compute the new tape number.

A transition replaces the tape symbol occupying the position scanned by the tape head. In our functional approach, the location of the tape head is obtained from the configuration number z by the function ctp. The tape symbol to be written at position $ctp(z)$ is represented numerically by $nts(z)$. The new tape number is obtained by changing the power of $pn(ctp(z))$ in the current tape number. Before the transition, the decomposition of z contains $pn(ctp(z))^{cts(z)+1}$ encoding the value of the current tape symbol at position $ctp(z)$. After the transition, position $ctp(z)$ contains the symbol represented by $nts(z)$. The primitive recursive function

$$ntn(z) = quo(ctn(z), pn(ctp(z))^{cts(z)+1}) \cdot pn(ctp(z))^{nts(z)+1}$$

makes the desired substitution. The division removes the factor that encodes the current symbol at position $ctp(z)$ from the tape number $ctn(z)$. The result is then multiplied by $pn(ctp(z))^{nts(z)+1}$, encoding the new tape symbol.

The trace function is defined by primitive recursion from the functions that simulate the effects of a transition of M on the components of the configuration.

$$tr_M(x, 0) = gn_2\left(0, 0, 2^1 \cdot \prod_{i=1}^{x+1} pn(i)^2\right)$$

$$tr_M(x, y + 1) = gn_2(ns(tr_M(x, y)), ntp(tr_M(x, y)), ntn(tr_M(x, y)))$$

Since each of the component functions has been shown to be primitive recursive, we conclude that the tr_M is not only μ-recursive but also primitive recursive. The trace function is not the culmination of our functional simulation of a Turing machine; it does not return the result of a computation but rather a configuration number.

The result of the computation of the Turing machine M that computes the number theoretic function f with input x may be obtained from the function tr_M. We first note that the computation of M may never terminate; $f(x)$ may be undefined. The question of termination can be determined from the values of tr_M. If M specifies a transition for configuration $tr_M(x, i)$, then $tr_M(x, i) \neq tr_M(x, i + 1)$ since the movement of the head changes the Gödel number. On the other hand, if M halts after transition i, then $tr_M(x, i) = tr_M(x, i + 1)$. The functions *nts*, *ntp*, and *ntn* return the preceding value when the configuration number represents a halting configuration. Consequently, the machine halts after the zth transition where z is the first number that satisfies $tr_M(x, z) = tr_M(x, z + 1)$.

Since no bound can be placed on the number of transitions that occur before an arbitrary Turing machine computation terminates, unbounded minimalization is used to determine this value. The μ-recursive function

$$term(x) = \mu z[eq(tr_M(x, z), tr_M(x, z + 1))]$$

computes the number of the transition after which the computation of M with input x terminates. When a computation terminates, the halting configuration of the machine is encoded in the value $tr_M(x, term(x))$. Upon termination, the tape has the form $B\overline{f(x)}B$. The terminal tape number (*ttn*) is obtained from the terminal configuration number by

$$ttn(x) = dec(2, tr_M(x, term(x))).$$

The result of the computation is obtained by counting the number of 1's on the tape or, equivalently, determining the number of primes that are raised to the power of 2 in the terminal tape number. The latter computation is performed by the bounded sum

$$sim_M(x) = \left(\sum_{i=0}^{y} eq(1, dec(i, ttn(x))) \right) \div 1$$

where y is the length of the tape segment encoded in the terminal tape number. The bound y is computed by the primitive recursive function $gdln(ttn(x))$ (Exercise 12). One is subtracted from the bounded sum since the tape contains the unary representation of $f(x)$.

Whenever f is defined for input x, the computation of M and the simulation of M both compute the $f(x)$. If $f(x)$ is undefined, the unbounded minimalization fails to return a value and $sim_M(x)$ is undefined. The construction of sim_M completes the proof of the following theorem.

Theorem 13.7.1
Every Turing computable function is μ-recursive.

Theorems 13.6.4 and 13.7.1 establish the equivalence of the microscopic and macroscopic approaches to computation.

Corollary 13.7.2
A function is Turing computable if, and only if, it is μ-recursive.

13.8 The Church-Turing Thesis Revisited

The Church-Turing thesis, as presented in Chapter 11, asserted that every effectively solvable decision problem admits a Turing machine solution. We have subsequently designed Turing machines to compute number theoretic functions. In its functional form, the Church-Turing thesis associates the effective computation of functions with Turing computability.

The Church-Turing thesis A partial function is computable if, and only if, it is μ-recursive.

Turing machines that accept input by final state provided the formal framework for constructing solutions to decision problems. A functional approach to solving decision problems uses the computed values one and zero to designate affirmative and negative responses. The method of specifying the answer does not affect the set of decision problems that have Turing machine solutions (Exercises 12.10 and 12.11). The formulation of the Church-Turing thesis in terms of computable functions includes the assertion concerning decision problems presented earlier.

As before, no proof can be put forward for the Church-Turing thesis. It is accepted by the community of mathematicians and computer scientists because of the accumulation of evidence supporting the claim. Many attempts, employing a wide variety of techniques and formalisms, have been made to classify the computable functions. The approaches to computability fall into three general categories: mechanical, functional, and transformational. Turing computability and μ-recursive functions are examples of the first two categories. An example of the latter is provided by the computational scheme introduced by Markov that defines algorithmic computation as a sequence of string transformations. Each of these, and all other computational systems that have been constructed for this purpose, generate precisely the functions that can be computed by Turing machines, the μ-recursive functions.

Accepting the Church-Turing thesis is tantamount to bestowing the title "most general computing device" on the Turing machine. The thesis implies that any number theoretic function that can be effectively computed by any machine or technique can also be computed by a Turing machine. This contention extends to nonnumeric computation as well.

We begin by observing that the computation of any digital computer can be interpreted as a numeric computation. Character strings are often used to communicate with the computer, but this is only a convenience to facilitate the input of the data and the interpretation of the output. The input is immediately translated to a string over $\{0, 1\}$ using either the ASCII (American Standard Code for Information Interchange) or EBCDIC (Extended Binary Coded Decimal Interchange Code) encoding schemes. After the translation, the input string can be considered the binary representation of a natural number. The computation progresses, generating another sequence of 0's and 1's, again a binary natural number. The output is then translated back to character data because of our inability to interpret and appreciate the output in its internal representation.

Following this example, we can design effective procedures that transform a string computation to a number theoretic computation. The Gödel encoding can be used to translate strings to numbers. Let $\Sigma = \{a_0, a_1, \ldots, a_n\}$ and f be a function from Σ^* to Σ^*. The generation of a Gödel number from a string begins by assigning a unique number to each element in the alphabet. The numbering for Σ is defined by its subscript. The encoding of a string $a_{i_0} a_{i_1} \ldots a_{i_n}$ is generated by the bounded product

$$pn(0)^{i_0+1} \cdot pn(1)^{i_1+1} \cdot \cdots \cdot pn(n)^{i_n+1} = \prod_{j=0}^{y} pn(j)^{i_j+1}$$

where y is the length of the string to be encoded.

The decoding function retrieves the exponent of each prime in the prime decomposition of the Gödel number. The string can be reconstructed from the decoding function and the numbering of the alphabet. If x is the encoding of a string $a_{i_0} a_{i_1} \ldots a_{i_n}$ over Σ, then $dec(j, x) = i_j$. The original string is obtained by concatenating the results of the decoding. Once the elements of the alphabet have been identified with natural numbers, the encoding and decoding are primitive recursive and therefore Turing computable.

The transformation of a string function f to a numeric function is obtained by using the character to number encoding and number to character decoding.

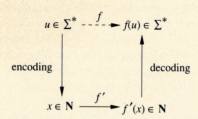

The numeric evaluation of f consists of three distinct computations: the transformation of the input string into a natural number, the computation of the number theoretic function f', and the translation of the result back to a string.

The Church-Turing thesis asserts that the function f' obtained from a computable nonnumeric function f is Turing computable. This can be established by observing that the encoding and decoding functions are reversible.

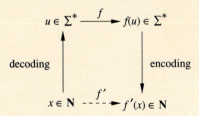

An effective procedure to compute f' consists of generating a string u from the input x, computing $f(u)$, and then encoding $f(u)$ to obtain the $f'(x)$. The Turing computability of f' follows from the Church-Turing thesis. Since f' is computable whenever f is, any nonnumeric function can be computed by a numeric function accompanied by encoding and decoding functions.

Example 13.8.1

Let Σ be the alphabet $\{a, b\}$. Consider the function $f: \Sigma^* \to \Sigma^*$ that interchanges the a's and the b's in the input string. A number theoretic function f' is constructed which, when combined with the functions that encode and decode strings over Σ, computes f. The elements of the alphabet are numbered by the function n: $n(a) = 0$ and $n(b) = 1$. A string $u = u_0 u_1 \ldots u_n$ is encoded as the number

$$pn(0)^{n(u_0)+1} \cdot pn(1)^{n(u_1)+1} \cdot \ldots \cdot pn(n)^{n(u_n)+1}.$$

The power of $pn(i)$ in the encoding is one or two depending upon whether the ith element of the string is a or b, respectively.

Let x be the encoding of a string u over Σ. Recall that $gdln(x)$ returns the length of the sequence encoded by x. The bounded product

$$f'(x) = \prod_{i=0}^{gdln(x)} (eq(dec(i, x), 0) \cdot pn(i) \cdot pn(i) + eq(dec(i, x), 1) \cdot pn(i))$$

generates the encoding of a string of the same length as the string u. When $eq(dec(i, x), 0) = 1$, the ith symbol in u is a. This is represented by $pn(i)^1$ in the encoding of u. The product

$$eq(dec(i, x), 0) \cdot pn(i) \cdot pn(i)$$

contributes the factor $pn(i)^2$ to $f'(x)$. Similarly, the power of $pn(i)$ in $f'(x)$ is one whenever the ith element of u is b. Thus f' constructs a number whose prime decomposition can be obtained from that of x by interchanging the exponents 1 and 2. The translation of $f'(x)$ to a string generates $f(u)$. ☐

Exercises

1. Using only the basic functions, composition, and primitive recursion, show that the following functions are primitive recursive. Give the functions g and h that comprise a definition by primitive recursion.

   a) $c_2^{(3)}$

   b) *pred*

   c) $f(x) = 2x + 2$

2. The functions below were defined by primitive recursion in Table 13.2.1. Explicitly, give the functions g and h that comprise the definition by primitive recursion.

   a) *sg*

   b) *sub*

   c) *exp*

3. a) Prove that a function f defined by the composition of total functions h and $g_1, \ldots, g_n$ is total.

   b) Prove that a function f defined by primitive recursion from total functions g and h is total.

   c) Conclude that all primitive recursive functions are total.

4. Show that the following functions are primitive recursive. You may use the functions and predicates from Tables 13.2.1 and 13.2.2. Do not use the bounded operations.

   a) $max(x, y) = \begin{cases} x & \text{if } x \geqslant y \\ y & \text{otherwise} \end{cases}$

   b) $min(x, y) = \begin{cases} x & \text{if } x \leqslant y \\ y & \text{otherwise} \end{cases}$

   c) $min(x, y, z) = \begin{cases} x & \text{if } x \leqslant y \text{ and } x \leqslant z \\ y & \text{if } y \leqslant x \text{ and } y \leqslant z \\ z & \text{if } z \leqslant x \text{ and } z \leqslant y \end{cases}$

   d) $even(x) = \begin{cases} 1 & \text{if } x \text{ is even} \\ 0 & \text{otherwise} \end{cases}$

   e) $half(x) = div(x, 2)$

   f) $sqrt(x) = \lfloor \sqrt{x} \rfloor$

5. Show that the following predicates are primitive recursive. You may use the functions and predicates from Tables 13.2.1 and 13.2.2 and Exercise 4. Do not use the bounded operators.

a) $le(x, y) = \begin{cases} 1 & \text{if } x \leqslant y \\ 0 & \text{otherwise} \end{cases}$

b) $ge(x, y) = \begin{cases} 1 & \text{if } x \geqslant y \\ 0 & \text{otherwise} \end{cases}$

c) $btw(x, y, z) = \begin{cases} 1 & \text{if } y < x < z \\ 0 & \text{otherwise} \end{cases}$

d) $prsq(x) = \begin{cases} 1 & \text{if } x \text{ is a perfect square} \\ 0 & \text{otherwise} \end{cases}$

6. Let g and h be a primitive recursive function. Use bounded operators to show that the following functions are primitive recursive. You may use any functions and predicates that have been shown to be primitive recursive.

a) $f(x, n) = \begin{cases} 1 & \text{if } g(i) < g(x) \text{ for all } 0 \leqslant i \leqslant y \\ 0 & \text{otherwise} \end{cases}$

b) $f(x, y) = \begin{cases} 1 & \text{if } g(i) = x \text{ for some } 0 \leqslant i \leqslant y \\ 0 & \text{otherwise} \end{cases}$

c) $f(y) = \begin{cases} 1 & \text{if } g(i) = h(j) \text{ for some } 0 \leqslant i, j \leqslant y \\ 0 & \text{otherwise} \end{cases}$

d) $f(y) = \begin{cases} 1 & \text{if } g(i) < g(i + 1) \text{ for all } 0 \leqslant i \leqslant y \\ 0 & \text{otherwise} \end{cases}$

e) $n(x, y) = $ the number of times $g(i) = x$ in the range $0 \leqslant i \leqslant y$

f) $thrd(x, y) = \begin{cases} 0 & \text{if } g(i) \text{ does not assume the value } x \text{ at least three times in the range } 0 \leqslant i \leqslant y \\ j & \text{if } j \text{ is the third integer in the range } 0 \leqslant i \leqslant y \text{ for which } g(i) = x \end{cases}$

g) $lrg(x, y) = $ the largest value in the range $0 \leqslant i \leqslant y$ for which $g(i) = x$

7. Show that the following functions are primitive recursive:

a) $gcd(x, y) = $ the greatest common divisor of x and y

b) $lcm(x, y) = $ the least common multiple of x and y

c) $pw2(x) = \begin{cases} 1 & \text{if } x = 2^n \text{ for some } n \\ 0 & \text{otherwise} \end{cases}$

8. Let g be a one-variable primitive recursive function. Prove that the function

$$f(x) = \min_{i=0}^{x} (g(i))$$
$$= \min\{g(0), \ldots, g(x)\}$$

is primitive recursive.

9. Prove that the function

$$f(x_1, \ldots, x_n) = \mu z^{u(x_1, \ldots, x_n)} [p(x_1, \ldots, x_n, z)]$$

is primitive recursive whenever p and u are primitive recursive.

10. Compute the Gödel number for the following sequences:

   a) 3, 0

   b) 0, 0, 1

   c) 1, 0, 1, 2

   d) 0, 1, 1, 2, 0

11. Determine the sequence encoded by the following Gödel numbers:

   a) 18,000

   b) 131,072

   c) 2,286,900

   d) 510,510

12. Prove that the following functions are primitive recursive:

   a) $gdn(x) = \begin{cases} 1 & \text{if } x \text{ is the Gödel number of some sequence} \\ 0 & \text{otherwise} \end{cases}$

   b) $gdln(x) = \begin{cases} n & \text{if } x \text{ is the Gödel number of a sequence of length } n \\ 0 & \text{otherwise} \end{cases}$

   c) $g(x, y) = \begin{cases} 1 & \text{if } x \text{ is a Gödel number and } y \text{ occurs in the sequence encoded in } x \\ 0 & \text{otherwise} \end{cases}$

13. Let g_1 and g_2 be one-variable primitive recursive functions. Also let h_1 and h_2 be four-variable primitive recursive functions. The two functions f_1 and f_2 defined by

$$f_1(x, 0) = g_1(x)$$
$$f_2(x, 0) = g_2(x)$$
$$f_1(x, y + 1) = h_1(x, y, f_1(x, y), f_2(x, y))$$
$$f_2(x, y + 1) = h_2(x, y, f_1(x, y), f_2(x, y))$$

are said to be constructed by simultaneous recursion from g_1, g_2, h_1, and h_2. The values $f_1(x, y + 1)$ and $f_2(x, y + 1)$ are defined in terms of the previous values of both of the functions. Prove that f_1 and f_2 are primitive recursive.

14. Let A be Ackermann's function (see Section 13.6).

   a) Compute $A(2, 2)$.

   b) Prove that $A(x, y)$ has a unique value for every $x, y \in \mathbf{N}$.

   c) Prove that $A(1, y) = y + 2$.

   d) Prove that $A(2, y) = 2y + 3$.

15. Prove that the following functions are μ-recursive. The functions g and h are assumed to be primitive recursive.

   a) $cube(x) = \begin{cases} 1 & \text{if } x \text{ is a perfect cube} \\ \uparrow & \text{otherwise} \end{cases}$

b) $root(c_0, c_1, c_2) =$ the smallest root of the quadratic polynomial $c_2 \cdot x^2 + c_1 \cdot x + c_0$

c) $r(x) = \begin{cases} 1 & \text{if } g(i) = g(i + x) \text{ for some } i \geq 0 \\ \uparrow & \text{otherwise} \end{cases}$

d) $l(x) = \begin{cases} \uparrow & \text{if } g(i) - h(i) < x \text{ for all } i \geq 0 \\ 0 & \text{otherwise} \end{cases}$

e) $f(x) = \begin{cases} 1 & \text{if } g(i) + h(j) = x \text{ for some } i, j \in \mathbf{N} \\ \uparrow & \text{otherwise} \end{cases}$

16. The unbounded μ-operator can be defined for partial predicates as follows:

$$\mu z[p(x_1, \ldots, x_n, z)] = \begin{cases} j & \text{if } p(x_1, \ldots, x_n, i) = 0 \text{ for } 0 \leq i < j \\ & \text{and } p(x_1, \ldots, x_n, j) = 1 \\ \uparrow & \text{otherwise.} \end{cases}$$

That is, the value is undefined if $p(x_1, \ldots, x_n, i) \uparrow$ for some i occurring before the first value j for which $p(x_1, \ldots, x_n, j) = 1$. Prove that the family of functions obtained by replacing the unbounded minimalization operator in Definition 13.6.3 with the preceding μ-operator is the family of Turing computable functions.

17. Construct the functions *ns, ntp,* and *nts* for the Turing machine S given in Example 13.7.1.

18. Let M be the machine

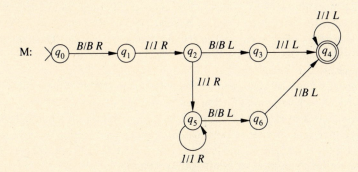

a) What one-variable number theoretic function does M compute?

b) Give the tape numbers for each configuration that occurs in the computation of M with input $\bar{0}$.

c) Give the tape numbers for each configuration that occurs in the computation of M with input $\bar{2}$.

19. Let f be the function from $\{a, b\}^*$ to $\{a, b\}^*$ defined by $f(u) = u^R$. Construct the primitive recursive function f' that, along with the encoding and decoding functions, computes f.

20. Let M be a Turing machine and tr_M the trace function of M.

   a) Show that the function

$$prt(x, y) = \begin{cases} 1 & \text{if the } y\text{th transition of M with input } x \text{ prints a blank} \\ 0 & \text{otherwise} \end{cases}$$

   is primitive recursive.

   b) Show that the function

$$fprt(x) = \begin{cases} y & \text{if } y \text{ is the number of the first transition of M} \\ & \text{with input } x \text{ that prints a blank} \\ \uparrow & \text{otherwise} \end{cases}$$

   is μ-recursive.

   c) In light of undecidability of the printing problem (Exercise 11.12), explain why *fprt* cannot be primitive recursive.

Bibliographic Notes

The functional and mechanical development of computability flourished in the 1930s. Gödel [1931] defined a method of computation now referred to as Herbrand-Gödel computability. The properties of Herbrand-Gödel computability and μ-recursive functions were developed extensively by Kleene. The equivalence of μ-recursive functions and Turing computability was established in Kleene [1936]. Post machines, Post, [1936], provide an alternative mechanical approach to numeric computation. The transformational work of Markov can be found in Markov [1961]. Needless to say, all these systems compute precisely the μ-recursive functions.

    Ackermann's function was introduced in Ackermann [1928]. An excellent exposition of the features of Ackermann's function can be found in Hennie [1977].

    The classic book by Kleene [1952] presents computability, the Church-Turing thesis, and recursive functions. A further examination of recursive function theory can be found in Hermes [1965], Péter [1967], and Rogers [1967]. Hennie [1977] develops computability from the notion of an abstract family of algorithms.

CHAPTER 14

Computational Complexity

A decision problem is solvable or a function computable if there is an effective procedure that determines the result. The objective of the preceding chapters was to characterize computability. We now shift our attention from exhibiting the existence of algorithms to analyzing their efficiency. The performance of an algorithm is measured by the resources required by a computation. A problem that is theoretically solvable may not have a practical solution; that is, there may be no algorithm that solves the problem without requiring an extraordinary amount of time or memory.

Since it is the inherent properties of the algorithm that are of interest to us, the analysis should be independent of any particular implementation. To isolate the features of the algorithm from those of the implementation, a single machine must be chosen for analyzing computational complexity. The choice should not place any unnecessary restrictions, such as limiting the time or memory available, upon the computation. These limitations are properties of the implementation and not of the algorithm itself. The standard Turing machine, which fulfills all of these requirements, provides the underlying computational framework for the analysis of algorithms. Moreover, the Church-Turing thesis assures us that any effective procedure can be implemented on such a machine.

14.1 Time Complexity of a Turing Machine

The time complexity of a computation measures the amount of work expended by the computation. The time of a computation of a Turing machine is quantified by the number of transitions processed. The issues involved in determining the time complexity of a

337

Turing machine are presented by analyzing the computations of the machine M that accepts the even-length palindromes over the alphabet $\{a, b\}$.

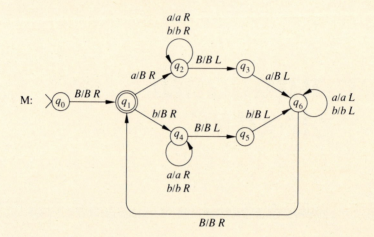

A computation of M consists of a loop that compares the first nonblank symbol on the tape with the last. The first symbol is recorded and replaced with a blank by the transition from state q_1. Depending upon the path taken from q_1, the final nonblank symbol is checked for a match in state q_3 or q_5. The machine then moves to the left through the nonblank segment of the tape, and the comparison cycle is repeated.

The computations of M are symmetric with respect to the symbols a and b. The upper path from q_1 to q_6 is traversed when processing an a and the lower path when processing a b. The computations in Table 14.1.1 contain all significant combinations of symbols in strings of length zero, one, two, and three.

TABLE 14.1.1 Computations of M

Length 0	Length 1	Length 2		Length 3	
q_0BB	q_0BaB	q_0BaaB	q_0BabB	q_0BabaB	q_0BaabB
$\vdash Bq_1B$	$\vdash Bq_1aB$	$\vdash Bq_1aaB$	$\vdash Bq_1abB$	$\vdash Bq_1abaB$	$\vdash Bq_1aabB$
	$\vdash BBq_2B$	$\vdash BBq_2aB$	$\vdash BBq_2bB$	$\vdash BBq_2baB$	$\vdash BBq_2abB$
	$\vdash Bq_3BB$	$\vdash BBaq_2B$	$\vdash BBbq_2B$	$\vdash BBbq_2aB$	$\vdash BBaq_2bB$
		$\vdash BBq_3aB$	$\vdash BBq_3bB$	$\vdash BBbaq_2B$	$\vdash BBabq_2B$
		$\vdash Bq_6BBB$		$\vdash BBbq_3aB$	$\vdash BBaq_3bB$
		$\vdash BBq_1BB$		$\vdash BBq_6bBB$	
				$\vdash Bq_6BbBB$	
				$\vdash BBq_1bBB$	
				$\vdash BBBq_4BB$	
				$\vdash BBq_5BBB$	

As expected, the computations show that the number of transitions in a computation depends upon the particular input string. Indeed, the amount of work may differ radically for strings of the same length. Rather than attempting to determine the exact number of transitions for each input string, the time complexity of a Turing machine measures the work required for strings of a fixed length.

Definition 14.1.1

Let M be a standard Turing machine. The **time complexity** of M is the function $tc_M: \mathbf{N} \rightarrow \mathbf{N}$ such that $tc_M(n)$ is the maximum number of transitions processed by a computation of M when initiated with an input string of length n.

When evaluating the time complexity of a Turing machine, we assume that the computations terminate for every input string. It makes no sense to attempt to discuss the efficiency, or more accurately the complete inefficiency, of a computation that continues indefinitely.

Definition 14.1.1 serves equally well for machines that accept languages and compute functions. The time complexity of deterministic multitrack and multitape machines is defined in a similar manner. The complexity of nondeterministic machines will be discussed in Section 14.4.

The time complexity gives the worst case performance of the Turing machine. In analyzing an algorithm, the worst case performance is chosen for two reasons. The first is that we are considering the limitations of algorithmic computation. The value $tc_M(n)$ specifies the minimum resources required to guarantee that the computation of M terminates when initiated with an input string of length n. The other reason is strictly pragmatic; the worst case performance is often easier to evaluate than the average performance.

The machine M accepting $\{uu^R \mid u \in \{a, b\}^*\}$ is used to demonstrate the process of determining the time complexity of a Turing machine. A computation of M terminates when the entire input string has been replaced with blanks or the first nonmatching pair of symbols is discovered. Since the time complexity measures the worst case performance, we need only concern ourselves with the strings whose computations contain the largest possible number of matching symbols. For even-length input, these are the strings accepted by M. The longest computation for odd-length input occurs when the string has the form uau^R and ubu^R where $u \in \{a, b\}^*$.

Using these observations, the initial values of the function tc_M can be obtained from the computations in Table 14.1.1.

$$tc_M(0) = 1$$
$$tc_M(1) = 3$$
$$tc_M(2) = 6$$
$$tc_M(3) = 10$$

Determining the remainder of the values of tc_M requires a detailed analysis of the computations of M. Consider the actions of M when processing an even-length input string. The computation alternates between sequences of right and left movements of the machine. Initially, the tape head is positioned to the immediate left of the nonblank segment of the tape.

- *Rightward movement:* The machine moves to the right, erasing the leftmost nonblank symbol. The remainder of the string is read and the machine enters state q_3 or q_5. This requires $k + 1$ transitions where k is the length of the nonblank portion of the tape.

- *Leftward movement:* M moves left, erasing the matching symbol, and continues through the nonblank portion of the tape. This requires k transitions.

The preceding actions reduce the length of the nonblank portion of the tape by two. The cycle of comparisons and erasures is repeated until the tape is completely blank. As previously noted, the worst case performance for an even-length string occurs when M accepts the input. A computation accepting a string of length n requires $n/2$ iterations of the preceding loop.

Iteration	Direction	Transitions
1	right	$n + 1$
	left	n
2	right	$n - 1$
	left	$n - 2$
3	right	$n - 3$
	left	$n - 4$
$\vdots$		$\vdots$
$n/2$	right	1

The total number of transitions of a computation can be obtained by adding those of each iteration. As indicated by the preceding table, the maximum number of transitions in a computation of a string of even-length n is the sum of the first $n + 1$ natural numbers. An analysis of odd-length strings produces the same result. Consequently, the time complexity of M is given by the function

$$tc_M(n) = \sum_{i=1}^{n+1} i = (n + 2)(n + 1)/2.$$

14.2 Rates of Growth

The time complexity of a Turing machine is often represented by the rate of growth of the function tc_M rather than the function itself. The rate of growth of a function measures

TABLE 14.2.1   Growth of Functions

n	0	5	10	25	50	100	1,000	10,000
$20n + 500$	500	600	700	1,000	1,500	2,500	20,500	200,500
n^2	0	25	100	625	2,500	10,000	1,000,000	100,000,000
$n^2 + 2n + 5$	5	40	125	680	2,605	10,205	1,002,005	100,020,005
$n^2/(n^2 + 2n + 5)$	0	.625	.800	.919	.960	.980	.998	.9999

the increase of the function values as the input gets arbitrarily large. Intuitively, the rate of growth is specified by the most significant contributor to the growth of the function.

The contribution of the individual terms to the values of a function can be seen by examining the growth of the functions n^2 and $n^2 + 2n + 5$ in Table 14.2.1. The contribution of n^2 to $n^2 + 2n + 5$ is measured by the ratio of the function values in the bottom row. The linear and constant terms of the function $n^2 + 2n + 5$ are called the lower-order terms. As n gets large, it is clear that the lower-order terms do not significantly contribute to the growth of the function values. In comparing the growth rates, the lower-order terms may exert undue influence on the initial values of the functions. Although n^2 grows faster than the linear function $20n + 500$, this is not exhibited for input values less than 25.

Definition 14.2.1

Let f and g be one-variable number theoretic functions. The function f is said to be of **order** g, written $f = O(g)$, if there is a positive constant c and a natural number n_0 such that

$$f(n) \leq c \cdot g(n)$$

for all $n \geq n_0$.

The order of a function provides an upper bound to the values of the function as the input increases. The function f is of order g if the growth of f is bounded by a constant multiple of the values of g. Because of the influence of the lower-order terms, the inequality $f(n) \leq c \cdot g(n)$ is required to hold only for input values greater than some specified number. The notation $f = O(g)$ is read "f is big oh of g."

Two functions f and g are said to have the same rate of growth if $f = O(g)$ and $g = O(f)$. When f and g have the same rate of growth, Definition 14.2.1 produces the two inequalities

$$f(n) \leq c_1 \cdot g(n) \qquad \text{for } n \geq n_1$$
$$g(n) \leq c_2 \cdot f(n) \qquad \text{for } n \geq n_2$$

where c_1 and c_2 are positive constants. Combining these inequalities, we see that each of these functions is bounded above and below by constant multiples of the other.

$$f(n)/c_1 \leq g(n) \leq c_2 \cdot f(n)$$
$$g(n)/c_2 \leq f(n) \leq c_1 \cdot g(n)$$

These relationships hold for all n greater than the maximum of n_1 and n_2. Because of these bounds, it is clear that neither f nor g can grow faster than the other.

Example 14.2.1

Let $f(n) = n^2 + 2n + 5$ and $g(n) = n^2$. Then $f = O(g)$ and $g = O(f)$. Since

$$n^2 \leqslant n^2 + 2n + 5$$

for all natural numbers, setting c to 1 and n_0 to 0 satisfies the conditions of Definition 14.2.1. Consequently, $g = O(f)$.

To establish the opposite relationship, we begin by noting that $2n \leqslant 2n^2$ and $5 \leqslant 5n^2$ for all $n \geqslant 1$. Then,

$$
\begin{aligned}
f(n) &= n^2 + 2n + 5 \\
&\leqslant n^2 + 2n^2 + 5n^2 \\
&= 8n^2 \\
&= 8 \cdot g(n)
\end{aligned}
$$

whenever $n \geqslant 1$. Using the big oh notation, the preceding inequality shows that $n^2 + 2n + 5 = O(n^2)$.   □

Example 14.2.2

Let $f(n) = n^2$ and $g(n) = n^3$. Then $f = O(g)$ and $g \neq O(f)$. Clearly, $n^2 = O(n^3)$ since $n^2 \leqslant n^3$ for all natural numbers.

Let us suppose that $n^3 = O(n^2)$. Then there are constants c and n_0 such that

$$n^3 \leqslant c \cdot n^2 \qquad \text{for all } n \geqslant n_0.$$

Choose n_1 to be the maximum of $n_0 + 1$ and $c + 1$. Then, $n_1^3 = n_1 \cdot n_1^2 > c \cdot n_1^2$ and $n_1 > n_0$, contradicting the inequality. Thus our assumption is false and $n^3 \neq O(n^2)$.   □

A **polynomial with integral coefficients** is a function of the form

$$f(n) = c_r \cdot n^r + c_{r-1} \cdot n^{r-1} + \cdots + c_1 \cdot n + c_0$$

where the $c_0, c_1, \ldots, c_{r-1}$ are arbitrary integers, c_r is a nonzero integer, and r is a natural number. The constants c_i are the coefficients of f and r is the degree of the polynomial. A polynomial with integral coefficients defines a function from the natural numbers into the integers. The presence of negative coefficients may produce negative values. For example, if $f(n) = n^2 - 3n - 4$ then $f(0) = -4$, $f(1) = -6$, $f(2) = -6$, and $f(3) = -4$. The values of the polynomial $g(n) = -n^2 - 1$ are negative for all natural numbers n.

The rate of growth has been defined only for number theoretic functions. The absolute value function can be used to transform an arbitrary polynomial into a number theoretic function. The absolute value of an integer i is the nonnegative integer defined by

$$|i| = \begin{cases} i & \text{if } i \geqslant 0 \\ -i & \text{otherwise.} \end{cases}$$

Composing a polynomial f with the absolute value produces a number theoretic function $|f|$. The rate of growth of a polynomial f is defined to be that of $|f|$.

The techniques presented in Examples 14.2.1 and 14.2.2 can be used to establish a general relationship between the degree of a polynomial and its rate of growth.

Theorem 14.2.2

Let f be a polynomial of degree r. Then

  i) $f = O(n^r)$

 ii) $n^r = O(f)$

iii) $f = O(n^k)$ for all $k > r$

iv) $f \neq O(n^k)$ for all $k < r$.

One of the consequences of Theorem 14.2.2 is that the rate of growth of any polynomial can be characterized by a function of the form n^r. The first two conditions show that a polynomial of degree r has the same rate of growth as n^r. Moreover, by conditions iii) and iv), its growth is not equivalent to that of n^k for any k other than r.

Other important functions used in measuring the performance of algorithms are the logarithmic, exponential, and factorial functions. A number theoretic logarithmic function with base a is defined by

$$f(n) = \lfloor \log_a(n) \rfloor.$$

Changing the base of a logarithmic function alters the value by a constant multiple. More precisely,

$$\log_a(n) = \log_b(n)\log_a(b).$$

This relationship indicates that the rate of growth of the logarithmic functions is independent of the base.

Theorem 14.2.3 compares the growth of these functions with each other and the polynomials. The proofs are left as exercises.

Theorem 14.2.3

Let r be a natural number and let a and b be real numbers greater than 1. Then

  i) $\log_a(n) = O(n)$

 ii) $n \neq O(\log_a(n))$

iii) $n^r = O(b^n)$

iv) $b^n \neq O(n^r)$

 v) $b^n = O(n!)$

vi) $n! \neq O(b^n)$.

A function f is said to be **polynomially bounded** if $f = O(n^r)$ for some natural number r. Although not a polynomial, it follows from condition i) that $n\log_2(n)$ is bounded by the polynomial n^2. The polynomially bounded functions, which of course include the polynomials, comprise an important family of functions that will be associated with the time complexity of efficiently solvable algorithms. Conditions iv) and vi) show that the exponential and factorial functions are not polynomially bounded. A big oh hierarchy can be constructed from the relationships outlined in Theorems 14.2.2 and 14.2.3. The elements in Table 14.2.2 are listed in the order of their rates of growth. It is standard practice to refer to a function f for which $2^n = O(f)$ as having exponential growth. With this convention, n^n and $n!$ are both said to exhibit exponential growth.

The efficiency of an algorithm is commonly characterized by its rate of growth. A polynomial time algorithm, or simply a polynomial algorithm, is one whose time complexity is polynomially bounded. That is, $tc_M = O(n^r)$, where M is a standard Turing machine that computes the algorithm. The distinction between polynomial and non-polynomial algorithms is apparent when considering the number of transitions of a computation as the length of the input increases. Table 14.2.3 illustrates the enormous resources required by an algorithm whose time complexity is not polynomial.

TABLE 14.2.2 A Big Oh Hierarchy

Big Oh	Name
$O(1)$	constant
$O(\log_a(n))$	logarithmic
$O(n)$	linear
$O(n\log_a(n))$	n log n
$O(n^2)$	quadratic
$O(n^3)$	cubic
$O(n^r)$	polynomial $r \geq 0$
$O(b^n)$	exponential $b > 1$
$O(n!)$	factorial

TABLE 14.2.3 Number of Transitions of Machine with Time Complexity tr_M with Input of Length n

n	$\log_2(n)$	n	n^2	n^3	2^n	$n!$
5	2	5	25	125	32	120
10	3	10	100	1,000	1,024	3,628,800
20	4	20	400	8,000	1,048,576	$2.4 \cdot 10^{18}$
30	4	30	900	27,000	$1.0 \cdot 10^9$	$2.6 \cdot 10^{32}$
40	5	40	1,600	64,000	$1.1 \cdot 10^{12}$	$8.1 \cdot 10^{47}$
50	5	50	2,500	125,000	$1.1 \cdot 10^{15}$	$3.0 \cdot 10^{64}$
100	6	100	10,000	1,000,000	$1.2 \cdot 10^{30}$	$> 10^{157}$
200	7	200	40,000	8,000,000	$1.6 \cdot 10^{60}$	$> 10^{374}$

14.3　Tractable and Intractable Decision Problems

The rate of growth was introduced to measure the efficiency of algorithms. We now shift our attention from algorithms to decision problems. A decision problem is said to be solvable in polynomial time, or simply polynomial, if there is at least one polynomially bounded algorithm that solves the problem. Since a decision problem may have many effective solutions, the effort required to solve it is characterized by the rate of growth of the most efficient solution. Because of the equivalence between solvable decision problems and recursive languages, we will also refer to the class of recursive languages recognized in polynomial time. The language of even-length palindromes over $\{a, b\}$ is polynomial since the machine M from Section 14.1 recognizes the language in $O(n^2)$ time.

Definition 14.3.1

A language L is **decidable in polynomial time** if there is a standard Turing machine M that accepts L with $tc_M = O(n^r)$ where r is a natural number independent of n. The family of languages decidable in polynomial time is denoted $\mathcal{P}$.

Computability theory is concerned with establishing whether decision problems are theoretically decidable. Complexity theory attempts to distinguish problems that are solvable in practice from those that are solvable in principle only. A solution to a decision problem may be impractical because of the resources required by the computations. Problems for which there is no efficient algorithm are said to be **intractable**. Because of the rate of growth of the time complexity, nonpolynomial decision problems are considered intractable. The division of the class of solvable decision problems into polynomial and nonpolynomial problems is generally considered to distinguish the efficiently solvable problems from the intractable problems.

The efficiency of an algorithm is measured by the time complexity of an implementation of the algorithm on a standard Turing machine. We could just as easily have chosen a multitrack, multitape, or two-way deterministic machine as the computational model on which algorithms are evaluated. The class $\mathcal{P}$ of polynomial decision problems is invariant under the choice of the deterministic Turing machine chosen for the analysis. A language accepted by a multitrack or two-way machine in time $O(n^r)$ is also accepted by a standard Turing machine in time $O(n^r)$. This follows immediately from the constructions presented in Theorems 9.3.1 and 9.4.1.

The transition from multitape to standard machine also perserves polynomial solutions. Let M be an k-tape machine that accepts the language L in $O(n^r)$. L is accepted in $O(n^{2r})$ time by a standard machine. This bound can be obtained by analyzing the simulation of a computation of M in the equivalent $2k + 1$-track machine M′ outlined in Theorem 9.5.1. The simulation of the $m + 1$st transition of M in M′

i) finds each of the markers on the even-numbered tapes and returns the tape head to the leftmost position (maximum of $2m$ transitions for each marker, yielding a total of $2 \cdot k \cdot m$ transitions)

ii) writes the appropriate symbols on the odd-numbered tracks and repositions the marker ($2k(m + 1)$ transitions).

The preceding analysis shows that the simulation of the mth transition of M requires fewer than $4k(m + 1)$ transitions of M'. Assume that M has time complexity tc_M. The summation

$$\sum_{i=0}^{tc_M(n)} 4k(i + 1) = 4k \left(\sum_{i=1}^{tc_M(n)+1} i \right) = 2k(tc_M(n) + 1)(tc_M(n) + 2)$$

is an upper bound on the number of transitions of M' needed in the simulation of a computation of M with input of length n. Thus, $tc_{M'} = O(n^{2r})$ whenever $tc_M = O(n^r)$.

The use of a nonpolynomial algorithm is impractical for all but the simplest cases of a problem. It is for this reason that solvable decision problems not in $\mathcal{P}$ are considered intractable. Nonpolynomial algorithms often do not provide insight into the nature of the problem but rather have the flavor of an exhaustive search. This type of behavior is exhibited by the machine constructed in Example 14.3.1 that solves the Hamiltonian circuit problem.

Let G be a directed graph with n vertices numbered 1 to n. An arc from vertex i to vertex j is represented by the ordered pair $[i, j]$. A Hamiltonian circuit is a path $i_0, i_1, \ldots, i_n$ in G that satisfies

i) $i_0 = i_n$

ii) $i_i \neq i_j$ for $i \neq j$ and $0 \leq i, j < n$.

That is, a Hamiltonian circuit is a path that visits every vertex exactly once and terminates at its starting point. A Hamiltonian circuit is frequently called a tour. Since each vertex is contained in a tour, we may assume that every tour begins and ends at vertex 1. The Hamiltonian circuit problem is to determine whether a directed graph has a tour.

Example 14.3.1

Let G be a directed graph with n vertices. The composition of a deterministic four-tape machine that solves the Hamiltonian circuit problem is outlined. A vertex of the graph is denoted by the unary representation of its subscript. The alphabet of the representation is $\{1, \#\}$. A graph with n vertices and m arcs is represented by the input string

$$\bar{x}_1 \# \bar{y}_1 \# \# \ldots \# \# \bar{x}_m \# \bar{y}_m \# \# \# \bar{n}$$

where $[x_i, y_i]$ are the arcs of the graph and $\bar{x}$ denotes the unary representation of the number x.

Throughout the computation, tape 1 maintains the representation of the arcs. The computation generates and examines sequences of $n + 1$ vertices $1, i_1, \ldots, i_{n-1}, 1$ to determine whether they form a cycle. The sequences are generated in numeric order on tape 2. The representation of the sequence $1, n, \ldots, n, 1$ is written on tape 4 and used to trigger the halting condition. The techniques employed by the machine in Fig. 9.1 can be used to generate the sequences on tape 2.

A computation is a loop that

1. generates a sequence $B\overline{1}B\overline{i}_1B\overline{i}_2B \ldots B\overline{i}_{n-1}B\overline{1}B$ on tape 2
2. halts if tapes 2 and 4 are identical
3. examines the sequence $1, i_1, \ldots, i_{n-1}, 1$ and halts if it comprises a tour of the graph.

If the computation halts in step 2, all sequences have been examined and the graph does not contain a Hamiltonian circuit.

The analysis in step 3 begins with the machine configuration

$$
\begin{array}{ll}
\text{Tape 4} & B\overline{1}(B\overline{n})^{n-1}B\overline{1} \\
\text{Tape 3} & B\overline{1}B \\
\text{Tape 2} & B\overline{1}B\overline{i}_1B \ldots B\overline{i}_{n-1}B\overline{1}B \\
\text{Tape 1} & B\overline{x}_1\#\overline{y}_1\#\# \ldots \#\#\overline{x}_m\#\overline{y}_mB
\end{array}
$$

The vertex i_j is added to the sequence on tape 3 if

i) $i_j \neq i_k$ for $1 \leq k \leq j - 1$
ii) there is an arc $[i_{j-1}, i_j]$ represented on tape 1;

that is, if $1, i_1, \ldots, i_j$ is an acyclic path in the graph. If every node in the sequence in tape 2 is added to tape 3, the path is a tour and the computation accepts the input.   □

The algorithm outlined in Example 14.3.1 is exponential. A computation examines and rejects each sequence $1, i_1, i_2, \ldots, i_{n-1}, 1$ when the input graph does not contain a tour. For a graph with n vertices, there are n^{n-1} such sequences. Disregarding the computations involved in checking a sequence, the number of sequences grows exponentially with the number of vertices of the graph. Since the unary representation is used to encode the vertices, adding a vertex (but no arcs) to a graph increases the length of the input string by a single character. Thus, incrementing the length of the input causes an exponential increase in the number of possible sequences that must be examined.

We have shown that the Hamiltonian circuit problem is solvable in exponential time. It does not follow that the problem cannot be solved in polynomial time. So far, no polynomial algorithm has been discovered. This may be because no such solution exists or maybe we have just not been clever enough to find one! The likelihood and ramifications of the discovery of a polynomial time solution are discussed in Section 14.5.

14.4 The Class $\mathcal{NP}$

Nondeterministic computations are fundamentally different from their deterministic counterparts. A deterministic machine often solves a decision problem by generating a solution. A nondeterministic machine need only determine if one of the possibilities is a solution. Consider the problem of deciding whether a natural number n is a composite (not a prime). A constructive, deterministic solution can be obtained by sequentially examining every number in the interval from 2 to $n - 1$. If a factor is discovered, then n is not prime. A nondeterministic computation begins by arbitrarily choosing a value in the designated range. A single division determines whether the guess is a factor. If n is a composite, one of the nondeterministic choices will produce a factor and that computation returns the affirmative response.

A string is accepted by a nondeterministic machine if at least one computation terminates in an accepting state. The acceptance of the string is unaffected by the existence of other computations that halt in nonaccepting states or do not halt at all. The worst case performance of the algorithm, however, measures the efficiency over all computations.

Definition 14.4.1
Let M be a nondeterministic Turing machine. The time complexity of M is the function $tc_M: \mathbf{N} \to \mathbf{N}$ such that $tc_M(n)$ is the maximum number of transitions processed by a computation, employing any choice of transitions, of an input string of length n.

This definition is identical to that of the time complexity of a deterministic machine. It is included to emphasize that the nondeterministic analysis must consider all possible computations for an input string. As before, our definition of time complexity assumes that every computation of M terminates. The time complexity of nondeterministic machines is used to define the class of languages accepted in nondeterministic polynomial time.

Definition 14.4.2
A language L is said to be accepted in **nondeterministic polynomial time** if there is a nondeterministic Turing machine M that accepts L with $tc_M = O(n^r)$ where r is a natural number independent of n. The family of languages accepted in nondeterministic polynomial time is denoted $\mathcal{NP}$.

The family $\mathcal{NP}$ is a subset of the recursive languages; the polynomial bound on the number of transitions ensures that all computations of M eventually terminate. Since every deterministic machine is also nondeterministic, $\mathcal{P} \subseteq \mathcal{NP}$. The status of the reverse inclusion is the topic of the remainder of this chapter.

Nondeterministic computations utilizing a guess and check strategy are generally simpler than their deterministic counterparts. The simplicity reduces the number of transitions required for a single computation. Employing this strategy, a nondeterministic machine is constructed that solves the Hamiltonian circuit problem in polynomial time.

Example 14.4.1
A three-tape nondeterministic machine that solves the Hamiltonian circuit problem in polynomial time is obtained by altering the deterministic machine constructed in Example 14.3.1. The fourth tape, which is used to terminate the computation when

the graph does not contain a tour, is not required in the nondeterministic machine. The computation

1. nondeterministically generates a sequence $1, i_1, \ldots, i_{n-1}, 1$ on tape 2
2. uses tapes 1 and 3 to determine whether the sequence on tape 2 defines a tour.

To show that the nondeterministic machine is polynomial, we construct an upper bound to the number of transitions in a computation. The maximum number of transitions occurs when the string defines a tour. Otherwise, the computation terminates without examining each of the symbols on tape 2.

The length of the input depends upon n, the number of nodes of the graph. A graph with n nodes contains at most n^2 arcs. We will show that the rate of growth of the number of transitions is polynomial in n. Since the length of the input cannot grow more slowly than n ($\bar{n}$ is a substring of the input), it follows that the time complexity is polynomial.

Generating the sequence on tape 2 and repositioning the tape head processes $O(n^2)$ transitions. Now assume that tape 3 contains the initial subsequence $B\bar{1}\#\bar{i}_1\#\ldots\#\bar{i}_{j-1}$ of the sequence on tape 2. The remainder of the computation consists of a loop that

i) moves tape heads 2 and 3 to the position of the first blank on tape 3 ($O(n^2)$ transitions)
ii) checks if the encoded vertex on tape 2 is already on tape 3 ($O(n^2)$ transitions)
iii) checks if there is an arc from i_{j-1} to i_j ($O(n^3)$ transitions examining all the arcs and repositioning the tape head)
iv) writes $\bar{i}_j$ on tape 3 and repositions the tape heads ($O(n^2)$ transitions).

A computation consists of the generation of the sequence on tape 2 followed by examination of the sequence. The loop that checks the sequence is repeated for each vertex $i_1, \ldots, i_{n-1}, 1$ on tape 2. The repetition of step iii) causes the number of transitions of the entire computation to grow at the rate $O(n^4)$. The rate of growth of the time complexity of the nondeterministic machine is determined by the portion of the computation that searches for the presence of a particular arc in the arc list. This differs from the deterministic machine in which the exhaustive search of the entire set of sequences of n vertices defines the rate of growth.   □

14.5 $\mathcal{P} = \mathcal{NP}?$

A language accepted in polynomial time by a deterministic multitrack or multitape machine is in $\mathcal{P}$. The construction of an equivalent standard Turing machine from one of these alternatives preserves polynomial time complexity. A technique for constructing an equivalent deterministic machine from the transitions of a nondeterministic machine was presented in Section 9.6. Unfortunately, this construction does not preserve polynomial time complexity.

Let L be a language accepted by a nondeterministic machine M and let k be the maximum number of alternative transitions for a state, symbol pair of M. The equivalent deterministic machine M′ sequentially examines all possible computations of M. The number of transitions in a computation of M′ with an input string of length n is at least k^{m-1} where $m = tc_M(n)$. When the nondeterministic machine M has alternative transitions, k is greater than one and the number of transitions of M′ grows exponentially with the length of the computation of M. Another strategy must be devised to show that a language accepted in nondeterministic polynomial time is also accepted in polynomial time.

One option is to examine the properties of each language or decision problem on an individual basis. For example, considerable effort has been expended attempting to develop a deterministic polynomial algorithm to solve the Hamiltonian circuit problem. On the face of it, finding such a solution would resolve the question for only one language. What is needed is a universal approach that answers the question for all languages in $\mathcal{NP}$ at once. To accomplish this we introduce the notion of the reducibility of languages.

Definition 14.5.1

Let Q and L be languages over alphabets Σ_1 and Σ_2, respectively. We say that Q is reducible to L in polynomial time if there is a polynomial time computable function $f: \Sigma_1^* \to \Sigma_2^*$ such that $u \in Q$ if, and only if, $f(u) \in L$.

A reduction of Q to L transforms the problem of recognizing Q to that of recognizing L. Let F be a machine that computes the function f. If L is accepted by a machine M, then Q is accepted by a machine that

i) runs F on an input string $u \in \Sigma_1^*$
ii) runs M on $f(u)$.

The resulting string $f(u)$ is accepted by M if, and only if, $u \in Q$. The time complexity of the composite machine can be obtained from those of F and M.

Theorem 14.5.2

Let Q be reducible to L in polynomial time and let $L \in \mathcal{P}$. Then $Q \in \mathcal{P}$.

Proof   As before, we let F denote the machine that computes the reduction and M the machine that recognizes L. Q is accepted by a machine that sequentially runs F and M. The time complexities tc_F and tc_M combine to produce an upper bound on the number of transitions of a computation of the composite machine. The computation of F with input string u generates the string $f(u) \in L$ which provides the input to M. The function tc_F can be used to establish an upper bound to the length of $f(u)$. If the input string $u \in L$ has length n, then the length of $f(u)$ cannot exceed the maximum of n and $tc_F(n)$.

The computation of M processes at most $tc_M(k)$ transitions, where k is the bound on the length of the input string. The number of transitions of the composite machine is bounded by the sum of the estimates of the two separate computations. If $tc_F = O(n^r)$ and $tc_M = O(n^t)$, then

$$tc_F(n) + tc_M(tc_F(n)) = O(n^{rt}).$$

■

Definition 14.5.3

A language L is called **NP-hard** if for every $Q \in \mathcal{NP}$, Q is reducible to L in polynomial time. An NP-hard language that is also in $\mathcal{NP}$ is called **NP-complete.**

One can consider an NP-complete language as a universal language in the class $\mathcal{NP}$. The discovery of a polynomial time machine that accepts an NP-complete language can be used to construct machines to accept every language in $\mathcal{NP}$ in deterministic polynomial time. This, in turn, yields an affirmative answer to the $\mathcal{P} = \mathcal{NP}$ question.

Theorem 14.5.4

If there is an NP-complete language that is also in $\mathcal{P}$, then $\mathcal{P} = \mathcal{NP}$.

Proof   Assume that L is an NP-complete language that is recognized in polynomial time by a deterministic Turing machine. Let Q be any language in $\mathcal{NP}$. Since L is NP-hard, there is a polynomial time reduction of Q to L. Now, by Theorem 14.5.2, Q is also in $\mathcal{P}$.   ∎

The definition of NP-completeness utilized the terminology of recursive languages and Turing computable functions because of the preciseness afforded by the concepts and notation of Turing computability. The duality between recursive languages and solvable decision problems permits us to speak of NP-hard and NP-complete decision problems. It is worthwhile to reexamine these definitions in the context of decision problems.

Reducibility of languages using Turing computable functions is a formalization of the notion reduction of decision problems that was developed in Chapter 11. A decision problem is NP-hard or NP-complete whenever the language accepted by a machine that solves the problem is. In an intuitive sense, an NP-complete problem **P** is a universal problem in the class $\mathcal{NP}$. Utilizing the reducibility to an NP-hard problem, a solution to any $\mathcal{NP}$ problem can be obtained by combining the reduction with the machine that solves **P**.

Regardless of whether we approach NP-completeness from the perspective of languages or decision problems, it is clear that these are an important class of problems. Unfortunately, we have not yet shown that such a universal problem exists. Although it requires a substantial amount of work, this omission is remedied in the next section.

14.6   The Satisfiability Problem

Historically, the satisfiability problem was the first decision problem shown to be NP-complete. The satisfiability problem is concerned with the truth values of formulas in propositional logic. The truth value of a formula is obtained from those of the elementary propositions occurring in the formula. The objective of the satisfiability problem is to determine whether there is an assignment of truth values to propositions that makes the formula true. Before demonstrating that the satisfiability problem is NP-complete, we will briefly review the fundamentals of propositional logic.

A **Boolean variable** is a variable that takes on values 0 and 1. Boolean variables are considered to be propositions, the elementary objects of propositional logic. The value of the variable specifies the truth or falsity of the proposition. The proposition x is true when the Boolean variable is assigned the value 1. The value 0 designates a false proposition. A **truth assignment** is a function that assigns a value 0 or 1 to every Boolean variable.

The logical connectives $\wedge$ (and) , $\vee$ (or), and $\sim$ (not) are used to construct propositions known as well-formed formulas from a set of Boolean variables. The symbols x, y, and z are used to denote Boolean variables while u, v, and w represent well-formed formulas.

Definition 14.6.1

Let V be a set of Boolean variables.

i) If $x \in$ V, then x is a well-formed formula.

ii) If x, $y \in$ V, then $(\sim x)$, $(x \wedge y)$, and $(x \vee y)$ are well-formed formulas.

iii) An expression is a well-formed formula over V only if it can be obtained from the Boolean variables in the set V by a finite number of applications of the operations in ii).

The expressions $((\sim(x \vee y)) \wedge z)$, $(((x \wedge y) \vee z) \vee \sim(x))$, and $(((\sim x) \vee y) \wedge (x \vee z))$ are well-formed formulas over the Boolean variables x, y, and z. The number of parentheses in a well-formed formula can be reduced by defining a precedence relation on the logical operators. Negation is considered the most binding operation, followed by conjunction and then disjunction. Additionally, the associativity of conjunction and disjunction permits the parentheses in sequences of these operations to be omitted. Utilizing these conventions, the preceding formulas may be written $\sim(x \vee y) \wedge z$, $x \wedge y \vee z \vee \sim x$, and $(\sim x \vee y) \wedge (x \vee z)$.

The truth values of the variables are obtained directly from the truth assignment. The standard interpretation of the logical operations can be used to extend the assignment of truth values to the well-formed formulas. The truth values of formulas $\sim u$, $u \wedge v$, and $u \vee v$ are obtained from the values of u and v according to the rules given in the following tables.

u	$\sim u$		u	v	$u \wedge v$		u	v	$u \vee v$
0	1		0	0	0		0	0	0
1	0		0	1	0		0	1	1
			1	0	0		1	0	1
			1	1	1		1	1	1

A formula u is satisfied by a truth assignment if the values of the variables cause u to assume the value 1. Two well-formed formulas are equivalent if they are satisfied by the same truth assignments.

A **clause** is a well-formed formula that consists of a disjunction of variables or the negation of variables. An unnegated variable is called a positive literal and a negated variable a negative literal. Using this terminology, a clause is a disjunction of literals. The formulas $x \vee \sim y$, $\sim x \vee z \vee \sim y$, and $x \vee z \vee \sim x$ are clauses over the set of Boolean variables $\{x, y, z\}$. A formula is in **conjunctive normal form** if it has the form

$$u_1 \wedge u_2 \wedge \cdots \wedge u_n$$

where each u_i is a clause. A classical theorem of propositional logic asserts that every well-formed formula can be transformed into an equivalent formula in conjunctive normal form.

Stated precisely, the **satisfiability problem** is the problem of deciding if a formula in conjunctive normal form is satisfied by some truth assignment. Let V be the set of variables $\{x, y, z\}$. The formulas u and v are satisfied by the truth assignment t.

$$u = (x \vee y) \wedge (\sim y \vee \sim z)$$
$$v = (x \vee \sim y \vee \sim z) \wedge (x \vee z) \wedge (\sim x \vee \sim y)$$
$$w = \sim x \wedge (x \vee y) \wedge (\sim y \vee x)$$

t	
x	1
y	0
z	1

The first clause in u is satisfied by x and the second by $\sim y$. The formula w is not satisfied by t. Moreover, it is not difficult to see that w is not satisfied by any truth assignment.

A deterministic solution to the satisfiability problem can be obtained by checking every truth assignment. The number of possible truth assignments is 2^n where n is the number of variables. An implementation of this strategy is essentially a mechanical method of constructing the complete truth table for the formula. Clearly, the complexity of this exhaustive approach is exponential. The work expended in checking a particular truth assignment, however, grows polynomially with the number of variables and the length of the formula. This observation provides the insight needed for designing a polynomial time nondeterministic machine that solves the satisfiability problem.

Theorem 14.6.2
The satisfiability problem is in $\mathcal{NP}$.

Proof We begin by developing a representation for the well-formed formulas over a set of Boolean variables $\{x_1, \ldots, x_n\}$. A variable is encoded by the unary representation of its subscript. The encoding of a literal consists of the encoded variable followed by #1 if the literal is positive and #0 if it is negative.

Literal	Encoding
x_i	$\bar{i}\#1$
$\sim x_i$	$\bar{i}\#0$

The number following the encoding of the variable specifies the Boolean value that satisfies the literal.

A well-formed formula is encoded by concatenating the literals with the symbols and representing disjunction and conjunction. The conjunctive normal form formula

$$(x_1 \vee \sim x_2) \wedge (\sim x_1 \vee x_3)$$

is encoded as

$$11\#1 \vee 111\#0 \wedge 11\#0 \vee 1111\#1.$$

Finally, the input to the machine consists of the encoding of the variables in the formula followed by ## and then the encoding of the formula itself. The input string representing the preceding formula is

$$11\#111\#1111\#\#11\#1 \vee 111\#0 \wedge 11\#0 \vee 1111\#1.$$
$$\underbrace{\qquad}_{\text{variables}} \quad \underbrace{\qquad\qquad}_{\text{formula}}$$

The representation of an instance of the satisfiability problem is a string over the alphabet $\{0, 1, \wedge, \vee, \#\}$. The language L_{SAT} consists of all strings over the alphabet that represent satisfiable conjunctive normal form formulas.

A two-tape nondeterministic machine M that solves the satisfiability problem is described below. M employs the guess and check strategy; the guess nondeterministically generates a truth assignment. Configurations corresponding to the computation initiated with the input string representing the formula $(x_1 \vee \sim x_2) \wedge (\sim x_1 \vee x_3)$ are given to illustrate the actions of the machine.

1. If the input does not have the anticipated form, the computation halts, rejecting the string.

   Tape 2   *BB*
   Tape 1   *B11#111#1111##11#1 $\vee$ 111#0 $\wedge$ 11#0 $\vee$ 1111#1B*

2. The encoding of the first variable on tape 1 is copied onto tape 2. This is followed by printing # and nondeterministically writing *0* or *1*. If this is not the last variable, ## is written and the procedure is repeated for the next variable. Nondeterministically choosing a value for each variable defines a truth assignment t. The value assigned to variable x_i is denoted $t(x_i)$.

   Tape 2   *B11#t(x_1)##111#t(x_2)##1111#t(x_3)B*
   Tape 1   *B11#111#1111##11#1 $\vee$ 111#0 $\wedge$ 11#0 $\vee$ 1111#1B*

The tape head on tape 2 is repositioned at the leftmost position. The head on tape 1 is moved past ## into a position to read the first variable of the formula.

The generation of the truth assignment is the only instance of nondeterminism of M. The remainder of the computation determines whether the formula is satisfied by the truth assignment.

3. Assume that x_i is the variable scanned on tape 1. The encoding of x_i is found on tape 2. The subsequent actions of the machine are determined by the result of comparing the value $t(x_i)$ on tape 2 with the Boolean value following x_i on tape 1.

4. If the values do not match, the current literal is not satisfied by the truth assignment. If the symbol following the literal is a B or $\wedge$, every literal in the current clause has been examined and failed. When this occurs, the truth assignment does not satisfy the formula and the computation halts, rejecting the string. If $\vee$ is read, the tape heads are positioned to examine the next literal in the clause (step 3).

5. If the values do match, the literal and current clause are satisfied by the truth assignment. The head on tape 1 moves to the right to the next $\wedge$ or B. If a B is encountered, the computation halts, accepting the input. Otherwise, the next clause is processed by returning to step 3.

The matching procedure in step 3 determines the rate of growth of the length of the computations. In the worst case, the matching requires comparing the variable on tape 1 with each of the variables on tape 2 to discover the match. This can be accomplished in $O(k \cdot n^2)$ time where n is the number of variables and k the number of literals in the input. ∎

We now must show that L_{SAT} is NP-hard, that is, that every language in $\mathcal{NP}$ is polynomial time reducible to L_{SAT}. At the outset, this may seem like an impossible task. There are infinitely many languages in $\mathcal{NP}$ and they appear to have little in common. They are not even restricted to having a common alphabet. The lone universal feature of the languages in $\mathcal{NP}$ is that they are all accepted by a polynomial time bounded nondeterministic Turing machine. Fortunately, this is enough. Rather than concentrating on the languages, the proof will exploit the properties of the machines that accept the languages. In this manner, a general procedure can be developed that can be used to reduce any $\mathcal{NP}$ language to L_{SAT}.

We begin with the following technical lemma. The notation

$$\bigwedge_{i=1}^{k} v_i \qquad \bigvee_{i=i}^{k} v_i$$

represents the conjunction and disjunction of the literals $v_1, v_2, \ldots, v_k$.

Lemma 14.6.3

Let $u = w_1 \vee w_2 \vee \cdots \vee w_n$ be the disjunction of conjunctive normal form formulas $w_1, w_2, \ldots, w_n$ over the set of Boolean variables V. Also let $V' = V \cup \{y_1, y_2, \ldots, y_{n-1}\}$ where the variables y_i are not in V. The formula u can be transformed into a formula u' over V' such that

i) u' is in conjunctive normal form

ii) u' is satisfiable over V' if, and only if, u is satisfiable over V

iii) the transformation can be accomplished in $O(m \cdot n^2)$ where m is the number of clauses in the w's.

Proof   The transformation of the disjunction of two conjunctive normal form formulas is presented. This technique may be repeated $n - 1$ times to transform the disjunction of n formulas. Let $u = w_1 \vee w_2$ where

$$w_1 = \bigwedge_{j=1}^{r_1} \left(\bigvee_{k=1}^{s_j} v_{j,k} \right)$$

$$w_2 = \bigwedge_{j=1}^{r_2} \left(\bigvee_{k=1}^{t_j} p_{j,k} \right)$$

Define

$$u' = \bigwedge_{j=1}^{r_1} \left(y \vee \bigvee_{k=1}^{s_j} v_{j,k} \right) \wedge \bigwedge_{j=1}^{r_2} \left(\sim y \vee \bigwedge_{k=1}^{t_j} p_{j,k} \right)$$

The formula u' is obtained by disjoining y to each clause in w_1 and $\sim y$ to each clause in w_2.

We now show that u' is satisfiable whenever u is. Assume that w_1 is satisfied by a truth assignment t over V. Then the truth assignment t'

$$t'(x) = \begin{cases} t(x) & \text{if } x \in \text{V} \\ 0 & \text{if } x = y \end{cases}$$

satisfies u'. When w_2 is satisfied by t, the truth assignment t' may be obtained by extending t by setting $t'(y) = 1$.

Conversely, assume that u' is satisfied by the truth assignment t'. Then the restriction of t' to V satisfies u. If $t'(y) = 0$ then w_1 must be true. On the other hand, if $t'(y) = 1$ then w_2 is true.

The transformation of

$$u = w_1 \vee w_2 \vee \ldots \vee w_n$$

requires $n - 1$ iterations of the preceding process. The repetition adds $n - 1$ literals to each clause in w_1, $n - 2$ literals to each clause in w_2, and so on. The transformation requires fewer than $m \cdot n^2$ steps where m is the total number of clauses in the formulas $w_1, w_2, \ldots, w_n$. ∎

Theorem 14.6.4
The satisfiability problem is NP-hard.

Proof   Let M be a nondeterministic machine whose computations are bounded by the polynomial p. Without loss of generality, we assume that all computations of M halt in one of two states. All accepting computations terminate in state q_A and rejecting computations in q_R. Moreover, we assume that there are no transitions leaving these states. An arbitrary machine can be transformed into an equivalent one satisfying these restrictions by adding transitions from every accepting configuration to q_A and from rejecting configurations to q_R. This alteration adds a single transition to every computation of the original machine. The transformation from computation to well-formed formula assumes that all computations with input of length n contain $p(n)$ configurations. The terminating configuration is repeated, if necessary, to ensure the correct number of configurations are present.

The states and elements of the alphabets of M are denoted

$$Q = \{q_0, q_1, \ldots, q_m\}$$
$$\Gamma = \{B = a_0, a_1, \ldots, a_s, a_{s+1}, \ldots, a_t\}$$
$$\Sigma = \{a_{s+1}, a_{s+2}, \ldots, a_t\}$$
$$F = \{q_m\}$$

The blank is assumed to be the tape symbol numbered 0. The input alphabet consists of the elements of the tape alphabet numbered $s + 1$ to t. The lone accepting state is q_m and the rejecting state is q_{m-1}.

Let $u \in \Sigma^*$ be a string of length n. Our goal is to define a formula $f(u)$ that encodes the computations of M with input u. The length of $f(u)$ depends on $p(n)$, the maximum length of computations of M with input of length n. The encoding is designed so that there is a truth assignment satisfying $f(u)$ if, and only if, $u \in L(M)$. The formulas are built from three classes of variables; each class is introduced to represent a property of a machine configuration.

Variable		Interpretation (When Satisfied)
$Q_{i,k}$	$0 \leq i \leq m$ $0 \leq k \leq p(n)$	M is in state q_i at time k
$P_{j,k}$	$0 \leq j \leq p(n)$ $0 \leq k \leq p(n)$	M is scanning position j at time k
$S_{j,r,k}$	$0 \leq j \leq p(n)$ $0 \leq r \leq t$ $0 \leq k \leq p(n)$	Tape position j contains symbol a_r at time k

The set of variables V is the union of the three sets defined above. A computation of M defines a truth assignment on V. For example, if tape position three initially contains symbol a_i then $S_{3,i,0}$ is true. Necessarily, $S_{3,j,0}$ must be false for all $i \neq j$. A truth assignment obtained in this manner specifies the state, position of the tape head, and the symbols on the tape for each time k in the range $0 \leq k \leq p(n)$. This is precisely the information contained in the sequence of configurations produced by the computation.

An arbitrary assignment of truth values to the variables in V need not correspond to a computation of M. Assigning 1 to both $P_{0,0}$ and $P_{1,0}$ specifies that the tape head is at two distinct positions at time 0. Similarly, an arbitrary assignment might specify that the machine is in several states at a given time or designate the presence of multiple symbols in a single position.

The formula $f(u)$ should impose restrictions on the variables to ensure that the interpretations of the variables are identical with those generated by the truth assignment obtained from a computation. Eight sets of formulas are defined from the input string and the transitions of M. Seven of the eight families of formulas are given directly in clause form. The clauses are accompanied by a brief description of their interpretation in terms of configurations and computations.

A truth assignment that satisfies the set of clauses defined in i) indicates that the machine is in a unique state at each time. Satisfying the first disjunction guarantees that at least one of the variables $Q_{i,k}$ holds. The pairwise negations specify that no two states are satisfied at a same time.

Clause	Conditions	Interpretation
i) State		
$\displaystyle\bigvee_{i=0}^{m} Q_{i,k}$	$0 \leqslant k \leqslant p(n)$	for each time k, M is in at least one state
$\sim Q_{i,k} \vee \sim Q_{i',k}$	$0 \leqslant i < i' \leqslant m$ $0 \leqslant k \leqslant p(n)$	M is in at most one state (not two different states at the same time)
ii) Tape head position		
$\displaystyle\bigvee_{j=0}^{p(n)} P_{j,k}$	$0 \leqslant k \leqslant p(n)$	for each time k, the tape head is in at least one position
$\sim P_{j,k} \vee \sim P_{j',k}$	$0 \leqslant j < j' \leqslant p(n)$ $0 \leqslant k \leqslant p(n)$	at most one position
iii) Symbols on tape		
$\displaystyle\bigvee_{r=0}^{t} S_{j,r,k}$	$0 \leqslant j \leqslant p(n)$ $0 \leqslant k \leqslant p(n)$	for each time k and position j, position j contains at least one symbol
$\sim S_{j,r,k} \vee \sim S_{j,r',k}$	$0 \leqslant j \leqslant p(n)$ $0 \leqslant r < r' \leqslant t$ $0 \leqslant k \leqslant p(n)$	at most one symbol

iv) Initial conditions for input string $u = a_{r_1} a_{r_2} \ldots a_{r_n}$

$Q_{0,0}$	computation begins reading
$P_{0,0}$	the leftmost blank
$S_{0,0,0}$	
$S_{1,r_1,0}$	the string u is in the input
$S_{2,r_2,0}$	position at time 0
$\vdots$	
$S_{n,r_n,0}$	
$S_{n+1,0,0}$	the remainder of the tape is
$\vdots$	blank at time 0
$S_{p(n),0,0}$	

v) Accepting condition

$Q_{m,p(n)}$	the halting state of the
	computation is q_m

A truth assignment that satisfies the clauses in i), ii), and iii) defines a machine configuration for each time between 0 and $p(n)$. The conjunction of the clauses i) and ii) indicates that the machine is in a unique state scanning a single tape position at each time. The clauses in iii) ensure that the tape is well defined, that is, the tape contains precisely one symbol in each position that may be referenced during the computation.

A computation, however, does not consist of a sequence of unrelated configurations. Each configuration must be obtained from its successor by the application of a transition. Assume that the machine is in state q_i, scanning symbol a_r in position j at time k. The final three sets of formulas are introduced to generate the permissible configurations at time $k + 1$ based on the variables that define the configuration at time k.

The effect of a transition on the tape is to rewrite the position scanned by the tape head. With the possible exception of position $P_{j,k}$, every tape position at time $k + 1$ contains the same symbol as at time k. Conditions must be added to the formula to ensure that the remainder of the tape is unaffected by a transition.

vi) Tape consistency

$$\sim S_{j,r,k} \vee P_{j,k} \vee S_{j,r,k+1} \qquad \begin{array}{l} 0 \leqslant j \leqslant p(n) \\ 0 \leqslant r \leqslant t \\ 0 \leqslant k \leqslant p(n) \end{array} \qquad \begin{array}{l} \text{symbols not at the position of} \\ \text{the tape head are unchanged} \end{array}$$

This clause is not satisfied if a change occurs to a tape position other than the one scanned by the tape head.

Now assume that for a given time k, the machine is in state q_i scanning symbol a_r in position j. These features of a configuration are designated by the assignment of 1 to the Boolean variables $Q_{i,k}$, $P_{j,k}$, and $S_{j,r,k}$. The clause

a) $\sim Q_{i,k} \vee \sim P_{j,k} \vee \sim S_{j,r,k} \vee Q_{i',k+1}$

is satisfied only when $Q_{i',k+1}$ is true. In terms of the computation, this signifies that M has entered state $q_{i'}$ at time $k + 1$. Similarly, the symbol in position j at time $k + 1$ and the tape head position are specified by the clauses

b) $\sim Q_{i,k} \vee \sim P_{j,k} \vee \sim S_{j,r,k} \vee S_{j,r',k+1}$

c) $\sim Q_{i,k} \vee \sim P_{j,k} \vee \sim S_{j,r,k} \vee P_{j+n(d),k+1}$

where $n(L) = -1$ and $n(R) = 1$. The conjunction of clauses of a), b), and c) is satisfied only if the configuration at time $k + 1$ is obtained from the configuration at time k by the application of the transition $[q_{i'}, a_{r'}, d] \in \delta(q_i, a_r)$.

The clausal representation of transitions is used to construct a formula whose satisfaction guarantees that the time $k + 1$ variables define a configuration obtained from the configuration defined by the time k variables by the application of a transition of M. Except for states q_m and q_{m-1}, the restrictions on M ensure that at least one transition is defined for every state, symbol pair.

The conjunctive normal form formula

$$(\sim Q_{i,k} \vee \sim P_{j,k} \vee \sim S_{j,r,k} \vee Q_{i',\ k+1}) \qquad \text{new state}$$
$$\wedge (\sim Q_{i,k} \vee \sim P_{j,k} \vee \sim S_{j,r,k} \vee P_{j+n(d),k+1}) \qquad \text{new tape head position}$$
$$\wedge (\sim Q_{i,k} \vee \sim P_{j,k} \vee \sim S_{j,r,k} \vee S_{j,r',k+1}) \qquad \text{new symbol at position } r$$

is constructed for every

$$0 \leqslant k \leqslant p(n) \qquad \text{time}$$
$$0 \leqslant i < m - 1 \qquad \text{nonhalting state}$$
$$0 \leqslant j \leqslant p(n) \qquad \text{tape head position}$$
$$0 \leqslant r \leqslant t \qquad \text{tape symbol}$$

where $[q_{i'}, a_{r'}, d] \in \delta(q_i, a_r)$ except when the position is 0 and the direction L is specified by the transition. The exception occurs when the application of a transition would cause the tape head to cross the left-hand boundary of the tape. In clausal form, this is represented by having the succeeding configuration contain the rejecting state q_{m-1}. This special case is encoded by the formulas

$$(\sim Q_{i,k} \vee \sim P_{0,k} \vee \sim S_{0,r,k} \vee Q_{m-1,k+1}) \qquad \text{enter the rejecting state}$$
$$\wedge (\sim Q_{i,k} \vee \sim P_{0,k} \vee \sim S_{0,r,k} \vee P_{0,k+1}) \qquad \text{same tape head position}$$
$$\wedge (\sim Q_{i,k} \vee \sim P_{0,k} \vee \sim S_{0,r,k} \vee S_{0,r,k+1}) \qquad \text{same symbol at position } r$$

for all transitions $[q_{i'}, a_{r'}, L] \in \delta(q_i, a_r)$.

Since M is nondeterministic, there may be several transitions that can be applied to a given configuration. The result of the application of any of these alternatives is a permissible succeeding configuration in a computation. Let $trans(i, j, r, k)$ denote disjunction of all the clauses that represent the alternative transitions for a configuration at time k in state q_i, tape head position j, and tape symbol r. The formula $trans(i, j, r, k)$ is satisfied only if the values of the variables encoding the configuration at time $k + 1$ represent a legitimate successor to the configuration encoded in the variables with time k.

vii) Generation of successor configuration

$trans(i, j, r, k)$

The formulas $trans(i, j, r, k)$ do not specify the actions to be taken when the machine is in state q_m or q_{m-1}, the halting states of the machine. In this case, the subsequent configuration is identical to its predecessor.

viii) Halted computation

$\sim Q_{i,k} \vee \sim P_{j,k} \vee \sim S_{j,r,k} \vee Q_{i,k+1}$	same state
$\sim Q_{i,k} \vee \sim P_{j,k} \vee \sim S_{j,r,k} \vee P_{j,k+1}$	same tape head position
$\sim Q_{i,k} \vee \sim P_{j,k} \vee \sim S_{j,r,k} \vee S_{j,r,k+1}$	same symbol at position r

These clauses are built for all j, r, k in the appropriate ranges and $i = q_{m-1}, q_m$.

Let $f'(u)$ be the conjunction of the formulas constructed in i) through viii). When $f'(u)$ is satisfied by a truth assignment on V, the variables define the configurations of a computation of M that accepts the input string u. The clauses in condition iv) specify that the configuration at time 0 is the initial configuration of a computation of M with input u. Each subsequent configuration is obtained from its successor by the result of the application of a transition. The string u is accepted by M since condition v) indicates that the final configuration contains the accepting state q_m.

A conjunctive normal form formula $f(u)$ can be obtained from $f'(u)$. This is accomplished by converting each formula $trans(i, j, r, k)$ into conjunctive normal form using the technique presented in Lemma 14.6.3. All that remains is to show that the transformation of a string $u \in \Sigma^*$ to $f(u)$ can be done in polynomial time.

The transformation of u to $f(u)$ consists of the construction of the clauses and the conversion of the formulas that comprise $trans$ into conjunctive normal form. The number of clauses is a function of

i) the number of states m and the number of tape symbols t

ii) the length n of the input string u

iii) the bound $p(n)$ on the length of the computation of M.

The values m and t obtained from the Turing machine M are independent of the input string. From the range of the subscripts, we see that the number of clauses is polynomial in $p(n)$. The development of $f(u)$ is completed with the transformation into conjunctive normal form, which is polynomial in the number of clauses in the formulas $trans(i, j, r, k)$.

We have shown that the conjunctive normal form formula can be constructed in a number of steps that grows polynomially with the length of the input string. What is really needed is the representation of the formula that serves as input to a Turing machine that solves the satisfiability problem. Any reasonable encoding, including the one developed in Theorem 14.6.1, requires only polynomial time to convert the high-level representation to the machine representation.   ■

14.7   Additional NP-Complete Problems

The proof that L_{SAT} is NP-complete was accomplished by associating Turing machine computations with conjunctive normal form formulas. If every proof of NP-completeness required the ingenuity of Theorem 14.6.4, the number of languages known to be NP-complete would not be very large. Fortunately, once one language has been shown to be NP-complete the reduction of languages provides a simpler technique to demonstrate that other languages are also NP-hard.

Theorem 14.7.1

Let Q be an NP-complete language. If Q is reducible to L in polynomial time, then L is NP-hard.

Proof   Let $f\colon Q \to L$ be the computable function that reduces Q to L. Since Q is NP-complete, there is a computable function $g_{Q'}\colon Q' \to Q$ for every language Q' in $\mathcal{NP}$. The composite function $f \circ g_{Q'}$ is a reduction of Q' to L. A polynomial bound to the reduction can be determined from the bounds on f and $g_{Q'}$.   ■

The reduction technique is used to show that several additional problems are NP-complete. We begin with a special case of the satisfiability problem known as the 3-satisfiability problem. A formula is said to be in **3-conjunctive normal form** if it is in conjunctive normal form and each clause contains precisely three literals. The objective of the 3-satisfiability problem is to determine whether a 3-conjunctive normal form formula is satisfiable.

Theorem 14.7.2

The 3-satisfiability problem is NP-complete.

Proof   Clearly, the 3-satisfiability problem is in $\mathcal{NP}$. The machine that solves the satisfiability problem for arbitrary conjunctive normal form formulas also solves it for the subclass of 3-conjunctive normal form formulas.

Now we must show that every conjunctive normal form formula can be transformed to a 3-conjunctive normal form formula. Each clause u whose length is not three is independently transformed into a 3-conjunctive form formula. The resulting formula u' is satisfiable if, and only if, there is a truth assignment that satisfies the original clause. The variables added in the transformation are assumed not to occur in the clause u.

Length 1: $u = v_1$
Transformation $u' = (v_1 \vee y \vee z) \wedge (v_1 \vee \sim y \vee z) \wedge (v_1 \vee y \vee \sim z) \wedge (v_1 \vee \sim y \vee \sim z)$

Length 2: $u = v_1 \vee v_2$
Transformation $u' = (v_1 \vee v_2 \vee y) \wedge (v_1 \vee v_2 \vee \sim y)$

Length $n > 3$: $u = v_1 \vee v_2 \vee \cdots \vee v_n$
Transformation $u' = (v_1 \vee v_2 \vee y_1) \wedge (v_3 \vee \sim y_1 \vee y_2) \wedge \cdots$
$$\wedge (v_{n-2} \vee \sim y_{n-4} \vee y_{n-3}) \wedge (v_{n-1} \vee v_n \vee \sim y_{n-3})$$

Establishing the relationship between satisfiability of clauses of length one and two and their transformations is left as an exercise. Let V be the variables in the clause $u = v_1 \vee v_2 \vee \cdots \vee v_n$ and let t be a truth assignment that satisfies u. Since u is satisfied by t, there is at least one literal satisfied by t. Let v_j be the first such literal. Then the truth assignment

$$t'(x) = \begin{cases} t(x) & \text{if } x \in V \\ 1 & \text{if } x = y_1, \ldots, y_{j-2} \\ 0 & \text{if } x = y_{j-1}, \ldots, y_{n-3} \end{cases}$$

satisfies u'.

Conversely, let t' be a truth assignment that satisfies u'. The truth assignment t obtained by restricting t' to V satisfies u. The proof is by contradiction. Assume that t does not satisfy u. Then the value of v_j is 0 for all $1 \leq j \leq n$. Since the first clause of u' has the value 1, it follows that $t'(y_1) = 1$. Now, $t'(y_2) = 1$ since the second clause also has the value 1. Employing the same reasoning, we conclude that $t'(y_k) = 1$ for all $1 \leq k \leq n - 3$. This implies that the final clause of u' has value 0, a contradiction since t' was assumed to satisfy u'.

The transformation of each clause into a 3-conjunctive normal form formula is clearly polynomial in the number of literals in the clause. The work required for the construction of the 3-conjunctive normal form formula is the sum of the work of the transformation of the individual clauses. Thus, the construction is polynomial in the number of clauses in the original formula. ∎

Let $G = (N, A)$ be an undirected graph. A subset VC of N is said to be a **vertex cover** of G if for every arc $[u, v]$ in A at least one of u and v is in VC. The vertex cover problem can be stated as follows: For an undirected graph G and an integer k, is there a vertex cover of G containing k vertices?

Theorem 14.7.3
The vertex cover problem is NP-complete.

Proof   The vertex cover problem can easily be seen to be in $\mathcal{NP}$. The nondeterministic solution strategy consists of choosing a set of k vertices and determining whether they cover the arcs of the graph. We show that the vertex cover problem is NP-hard by reducing the 3-satisfiability problem to it. Let

$$u = (u_{1,1} \vee u_{1,2} \vee u_{1,3}) \wedge \cdots \wedge (u_{m,1} \vee u_{m,2} \vee u_{m,3})$$

be a 3-conjunctive normal form formula where the $u_{i,j}$, $1 \leqslant i \leqslant m$ and $1 \leqslant j \leqslant 3$, are literals over the set $V = \{x_1, \ldots, x_n\}$ of Boolean variables. The reduction consists of constructing a graph G from the 3-conjunctive normal form formula. The satisfiability of u will be equivalent to the existence of a cover of G containing $n + 2m$ vertices.

The vertices of G consist of the sets

i) $\{x_i, \sim x_i \mid 1 \leqslant i \leqslant n\}$

ii) $\{u_{i,j} \mid 1 \leqslant i \leqslant m, 1 \leqslant j \leqslant 3\}$.

The arcs of G are obtained from the union of the sets

$$T = \{[x_i, \sim x_i] \mid 1 \leqslant i \leqslant n\}$$
$$C_k = \{[u_{k,1}, u_{k,2}], [u_{k,2}, u_{k,3}], [u_{k,3}, u_{k,1}]\} \quad \text{for } 1 \leqslant k \leqslant m$$
$$L_k = \{[u_{k,1}, v_{k,1}], [u_{k,2}, v_{k,2}], [u_{k,3}, v_{k,3}]\} \quad \text{for } 1 \leqslant k \leqslant m$$

where $v_{k,j}$ is the literal from $\{x_i, \sim x_i \mid 1 \leqslant i \leqslant n\}$ that occurs in position $u_{k,j}$ of the formula.

An arc in T connects a positive literal x_i to its corresponding negative literal $\sim x_i$. A vertex cover must include one of these two vertices. At least n nodes are needed to cover the arcs in T. Each clause $u_{j,1} \vee u_{j,2} \vee u_{j,3}$ generates a subgraph C_j. C_j can be pictured as a triangle connecting the literals $u_{j,1}$, $u_{j,2}$, and $u_{j,3}$. A set of vertices that covers C_j must contain at least two nodes. Thus a cover of G must contain $n + 2m$ vertices.

The arcs in L_j link the literal $u_{i,j}$ to the corresponding literal x_k or $\sim x_k$. Figure 14.1 gives the graph corresponding to the formula $(x_1 \vee \sim x_2 \vee x_3) \wedge (\sim x_1 \vee x_2 \vee \sim x_4)$. It is easy to show that the construction of the graph is polynomially dependent upon the number of variables and clauses in the formula. All that remains is to show that the formula u is satisfiable if, and only if, the associated graph has a cover of size $n + 2m$.

First we show that a cover VC of size $n + 2m$ defines a truth assignment on V that satisfies the formula u. By the previous remarks, we know that every cover must contain at least $n + 2m$ vertices. Consequently, exactly one vertex from each arc $[x_i, \sim x_i]$ and two vertices from each subgraph C_j are in VC. A truth assignment is obtained from VC by

$$t(x_i) = \begin{cases} 1 & \text{if } x_i \in VC \\ 0 & \text{otherwise.} \end{cases}$$

To see that t satisfies each clause, consider the covering of the subgraph C_j. Only two of the vertices $u_{j,1}$, $u_{j,2}$, and $u_{j,3}$ can be in VC. Assume $u_{j,k}$ is not in VC. Then the arc $[u_{j,k}, v_{j,k}]$ must be covered by $v_{j,k}$. This implies that $t(u_{j,k}) = 1$ and the clause is satisfied.

Now assume that $t: V \rightarrow \{0, 1\}$ is a truth assignment that satisfies u. A vertex cover VC of the associated graph can be constructed from the truth assignment. VC contains the vertex x_i if $t(x_i) = 1$ and $\sim x_i$ if $t(x_i) = 0$. Let $u_{j,k}$ be a literal in clause j that is satisfied by t. The arc $[u_{j,k}, v_{k,j}]$ is covered by $v_{k,j}$. Adding the two other vertices of C_j completes the cover. Clearly, $card(VC) = n + 2m$ as desired. ∎

We now return to our old friend, the Hamiltonian circuit problem. This problem has already been shown to be solvable in exponential time by a deterministic machine (Example 14.3.1) and in polynomial time by a nondeterministic machine (Example 14.4.1). A

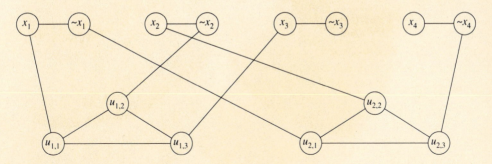

FIGURE 14.1   Graph representing reduction of $(x_1 \lor \sim x_2 \lor x_3) \land (\sim x_1 \lor x_2 \lor \sim x_4)$.

reduction of 3-satisfiability to the Hamiltonian circuit problem establishes that the latter is NP-complete.

Theorem 14.7.4
The Hamiltonian circuit problem is NP-complete.

Proof   Following the example of Theorem 14.7.3, a directed graph $G(u)$ is constructed from a 3-conjunctive normal form formula u. The construction is designed so that the presence of a Hamiltonian circuit in $G(u)$ is equivalent to the satisfiability of u.

Let $u = w_1 \land w_2 \land \cdots \land w_n$ be a 3-conjunctive normal form formula where $V = \{x_1, x_2, \ldots, x_s\}$ is the set of variables of u. The jth clause of u is denoted $u_{j,1} \lor u_{j,2} \lor u_{j,3}$ where each $u_{j,m}$ is a literal over V. For each variable x_i, let r_i be the maximum of the number of occurrences of x_i or $\sim x_i$ in u. A graph V_i is constructed for each variable x_i as illustrated in Fig. 14.2(a). Node e_i is considered the entrance to V_i and o_i the exit. There are precisely two paths through V_i that begin with e_i, end with o_i, and visit each node once. These are depicted in Fig. 14.2(b) and (c). The arc from e_i to $t_{i,0}$ or $f_{i,0}$ determines the remainder of the path through V_i.

The subgraphs V_i are joined to construct the graph G' depicted in Fig. 14.2(d). The two paths through each V_i combine to generate 2^n Hamiltonian circuits through the graph G'. A Hamiltonian circuit in G' represents a truth assignment on V. The value of x_i is specified by the arc from e_i. An arc e_i to $t_{i,0}$ designates a truth assignment of 1 to x_i. Otherwise, x_i is assigned 0. The graph in Fig. 14.3 is constructed from the formula

$$(x_1 \lor x_2 \lor \sim x_3) \land (\sim x_1 \lor x_2 \lor \sim x_4) \land (x_1 \lor \sim x_2 \lor x_4) \land (\sim x_1 \lor x_3 \lor x_4).$$

The tour highlighted in the graph defines the truth assignment

$$t(x_1) = 1$$
$$t(x_2) = 0$$
$$t(x_3) = 0$$
$$t(x_4) = 1.$$

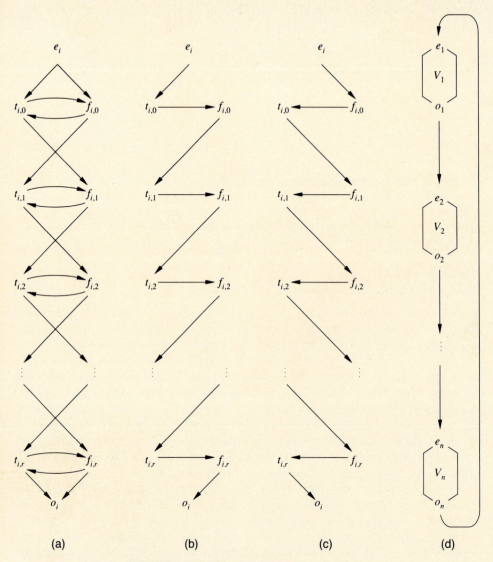

FIGURE 14.2   Subgraph for each variable x_i.

The Hamiltonian circuits of G′ encode the possible truth assignments of V. We now augment G′ with subgraphs that encode the clauses of the 3-conjunctive form formula.

For each clause w_j, we construct a subgraph C_j that has the form outlined in Fig. 14.4. The graph G(u) is constructed by connecting these subgraphs to G′ as follows:

i) If x_i is a literal in w_j, then pick some $f_{i,k}$ that has not previously been connected to a graph C. Add an arc from $f_{i,k}$ to a vertex $in_{j,m}$ of C_j that has not already been connected to G′. Then add an arc from $out_{j,m}$ to $t_{i,k+1}$.

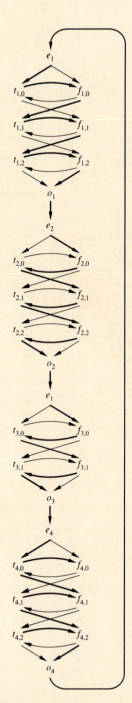

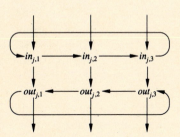

FIGURE 14.4 Subgraph representing clause w_j.

FIGURE 14.3 Truth assignment by Hamiltonian circuit.

ii) If $\sim x_i$ is a literal in w_j, then pick some $t_{i,k}$ that has not previously been connected to a graph C. Add an arc from $t_{i,k}$ to a vertex $in_{j,m}$ of C_j that has not already been connected to G'. Then add an arc from $out_{j,m}$ arc to $f_{i,k+1}$.

The graph in Fig. 14.5 is obtained by connecting the subgraph representing the clause $(x_1 \vee x_2 \vee \sim x_3)$ to the graph G' from Fig. 14.3.

A truth assignment is represented by a Hamiltonian circuit in the graph G'. If x_i is a positive literal in the clause w_j, then there is an arc from some vertex $f_{i,k}$ to one of the *in* vertices of C_j. Similarly, if $\sim x_i$ is in w_j, then there is an arc from some vertex $t_{i,k}$ to one of the *in* vertices of C_j. These arcs are used to extend the Hamiltonian circuit in G' to a tour of G(u) when the associated truth assignment satisfies u.

Let t be a truth assignment on V that satisfies u. We will construct a Hamiltonian circuit through G(u). Begin with the tour through the V_i's that represents t. We now detour the path through the subgraphs that encode the clauses. An arc $[t_{i,k}, f_{i,k}]$ in the path V_j indicates that the value of the truth assignment $t(x_i) = 1$. If the path reaches $f_{i,k}$ by an arc $[t_{i,k}, f_{i,k}]$ and $f_{i,k}$ contains an arc to a subgraph C_j that is not already in the path then connect C_j to the tour in G' as follows:

i) Detour to C_j via the arc from $f_{i,k}$ to $in_{j,m}$ in C_j.

ii) Visit each vertex of C_j once.

iii) Return to V_i via the arc from $out_{j,m}$ to $t_{i,k+1}$.

The presence of a detour to C_j indicates that the truth assignment encoded in G' satisfies the clause w_j.

On the other hand, a clause can also be satisfied by the presence of a negative literal $\sim x_i$ for which $t(x_i) = 0$. A similar detour can be constructed from a vertex $t_{i,k}$. Since $t(x_i) = 0$, the vertices $t_{i,k}$ are entered by an arc $[f_{i,k}, t_{i,k}]$. Choose a $t_{i,k}$ that has not already been connected to one of the subgraphs C_j. Construct the detour as follows:

i) Detour to C_j via the arc from $t_{i,k}$ to $in_{j,m}$ in C_j.

ii) Visit each vertex in C_j once.

iii) Return to V_i via the arc from $out_{j,m}$ to $f_{i,k+1}$.

In this manner, the Hamiltonian cycle of G' defined by a satisfying truth assignment can be extended to a tour of G(u).

Now assume that a graph G(u) contains a Hamiltonian circuit. We must show that u is satisfiable. The Hamiltonian circuit defines a truth assignment as follows:

$$t(x_i) = \begin{cases} 1 & \text{if the arc } [e_i, t_{i,0}] \text{ is in the tour} \\ 0 & \text{if the arc } [e_i, f_{i,0}] \text{ is in the tour.} \end{cases}$$

If $t(x_i) = 1$, then the arcs $[t_{i,k}, f_{i,k}]$ are in the tour. On the other hand, the tour contains the arcs $[f_{i,k}, t_{i,k}]$ whenever $t(x_i) = 0$.

Before proving that t satisfies u, we examine several properties of a tour that enters the subgraph C_j. Upon entering at the vertex $in_{j,m}$, the path may visit two, four, or all six

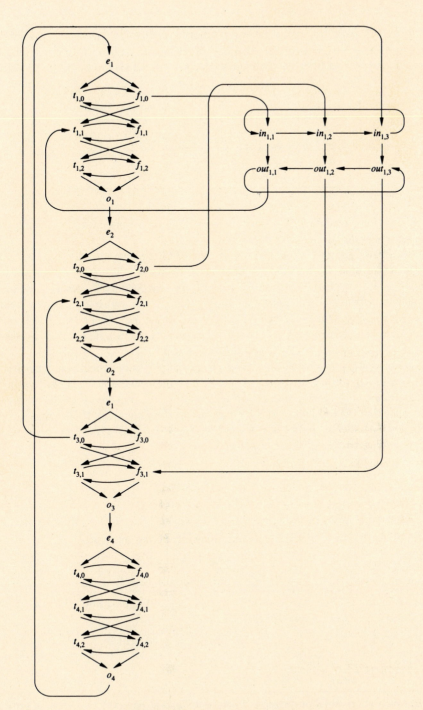

FIGURE 14.5   Connection of C_1 to G'.

vertices in C_j. A path that exits C_j at any position other than $out_{j,m}$, cannot be a subpath of a tour. Assume that C_j is entered at $in_{j,1}$, the following paths in C_j are not subpaths of a tour because the vertices listed cannot be reached without visiting some vertex twice.

Path	Unreachable Vertices
$in_{j,1}, in_{j,2}, in_{j,3}, out_{j,3}$	$out_{j,2}, out_{j,1}$
$in_{j,1}, in_{j,2}, in_{j,3}, out_{j,3}, out_{j,2}$	$out_{j,1}$
$in_{j,1}, in_{j,2}, out_{j,2}$	$out_{j,1}$
$in_{j,1}, in_{j,2}, out_{j,2}, out_{j,1}, out_{j,3}$	$in_{j,3}$

Thus the only paths entering C_j at $in_{j,1}$ that are subpaths of tours must exit at $out_{j,1}$. The same property holds for $in_{j,2}$ and $in_{j,3}$.

Each of the C_j's must be entered by the tour. If C_j is entered at node $in_{j,m}$ by an arc from a node $f_{i,k}$, then the tour exits C_j via the arc from $out_{j,m}$ to $t_{i,k+1}$. The presence of the arc $[f_{i,k}, in_{j,m}]$ in $G(u)$ indicates that w_j, the clause encoded by C_j, contains the literal x_i. Moreover, when C_j is entered by an arc $[f_{i,k}, in_{j,m}]$, the vertex $f_{i,k}$ must be entered by the arc $[t_{i,k}, f_{i,k}]$. Otherwise, the node $t_{i,k}$ is not in the tour. Since $[t_{i,k}, f_{i,k}]$ is in the tour, we conclude that $t(x_i) = 1$. Thus, w_j is satisfied by t. Similarly, if C_j is entered by an arc $[t_{i,k}, in_{j,m}]$ then $\sim x_i$ is in w_j and $t(x_i) = 0$.

Combining the previous observations, we see that the truth assignment generated by a Hamiltonian circuit through $G(u)$ satisfies each of the clauses of u and hence u itself. All that remains is to show that the construction of $G(u)$ is polynomial in the number of literals in the formula u. The number of nodes and arcs in a subgraph V_i increases linearly with the number of occurrences of the variable x_i in u. For each clause, the construction of C_j adds six vertices and 15 arcs to $G(u)$.   ∎

Exercises

1. Determine the time complexity of the following Turing machines.
   a) Example 9.2.1   b) Example 9.6.1
   c) Example 12.1.2   d) Example 12.2.1

2. For each of the functions below, choose the "best" big oh from Table 14.2.2 that describes the rate of growth of the function.
   a) $6n^2 + 500$ b) $2n^2 + n^2\log_2(n)$
   c) $\lfloor (n^3 + 2n)(n + 5)/n^2 \rfloor$ d) $n^2 \cdot 2^{n + n!}$
   e) $25 \cdot n \cdot sqrt(n) + 5n^2 + 23$

3. Let f be a polynomial of degree r. Prove that f and n^r have the same rate of growth.

4. Use Definition 14.2.1 to establish the following relationships.

   a) $n\log_2(n) = O(n^2)$ b) $n^r = O(2^n)$

   c) $2^n \neq O(n^r)$ d) $2^n = O(n!)$

   e) $n! \neq O(2^n)$

5. Let f and g be two unary functions such that $f = O(n^r)$ and $g = O(n^t)$. Give the best polynomial big oh that has the same rate of growth as the following functions.

   a) $f + g$ b) fg

   c) f^g d) $f \circ g$

6. Let M be a nondeterministic machine and p a polynomial. Assume that every string of length n in L(M) is accepted by at least one computation of $p(n)$ or fewer transitions. Note this makes no claim about the length of nonaccepting computations or other accepting computations. Prove that L(M) is in $\mathcal{NP}$.

7. Construct a deterministic Turing machine that reduces the language L_1 to L_2 in polynomial time. Using the big oh notation, give the time complexity of the machine that computes the reduction.

   a) $L_1 = \{a^i b^i a^j\}$ $L_2 = \{c^i d^i\}$

   b) $L_1 = \{a^i (bb)^i\}$ $L_2 = \{a^i b^i\}$

   c) $L_1 = \{a^i b^i a^i\}$ $L_2 = \{c^i d^i\}$

8. For each of the formulas below, give a truth assignment that satisfies the formula.

   a) $(x \vee y \vee \sim z) \wedge (\sim x \vee y) \wedge (\sim x \vee \sim y \vee \sim z)$

   b) $(\sim x \vee y \vee \sim z) \wedge (x \vee \sim y) \wedge (y \vee \sim z) \wedge (\sim x \vee \sim y \vee z)$

   c) $(x \vee y) \wedge (\sim x \vee \sim y \vee z) \wedge (x \vee \sim z) \wedge (\sim y \vee \sim z)$

9. Show that the formula $(x \vee \sim y) \wedge (\sim x \vee z) \wedge (y \vee \sim z) \wedge (\sim x \vee \sim y) \wedge (y \vee z)$ is not satisfiable.

10. Construct four clauses over $\{x, y, z\}$ such that the conjunction of any three is satisfiable but the conjunction of the four is unsatisfiable.

11. Prove that the formula u' is satisfiable if, and only if, u is satisfiable.

   a) $u = v$, $u' = (v \vee y \vee z) \wedge (v \vee \sim y \vee z) \wedge (v \vee y \vee \sim z) \wedge (v \vee \sim y \vee \sim z)$

   b) $u = v \vee w$, $u' = (v \vee w \vee y) \wedge (v \vee w \vee \sim y)$

12. A formula is in 4-conjunctive normal form if it is the conjunction of clauses consisting of the disjunction of four literals. Prove that the satisfiability problem for 4-conjunctive normal form formulas is NP-complete.

13. A clique in an undirected graph G is a subgraph of G in which every two vertices are connected by an arc. The clique problem is to determine, for an arbitrary graph G and integer k, whether G has a clique of size k. Prove that the clique problem is NP-complete. Hint: To show that the clique problem is NP-hard, establish a relationship between cliques in a graph G and vertex covers in the complement graph $\bar{G}$. There

is an arc between nodes x and y in $\bar{G}$ if, and only if, there is no arc connecting these nodes in G.

14. Let G be a weighted, directed graph. The cost of a path is the sum of the weights of the arcs that comprise the path. The traveling salesman problem can be formulated as follows: Is there a tour of G with cost k or less? Prove that the traveling salesman problem is NP-complete. Hint: Reduce the Hamiltonian circuit problem to the traveling salesman problem.

15. The integer linear programming problem is: Given an n by m matrix $\mathbf{A}$ and a column vector $\mathbf{b}$ of length n, does there exist a column vector $\mathbf{x}$ such that $\mathbf{Ax} \geq \mathbf{b}$? Use a reduction of 3-SAT to prove that the integer linear programming problem is NP-hard. (The integer linear programming problem is also in $\mathcal{NP}$; the proof requires knowledge of some of the elementary properties of linear algebra.)

Bibliographic Notes

The family $\mathcal{P}$ was introduced in Cobham [1964]. $\mathcal{NP}$ was first studied by Edmonds [1965]. The foundations of the theory of NP-completeness were presented in Cook [1971]. This work includes the proof that the satisfiability problem is NP-complete. Karp [1972] demonstrated the importance of NP-completeness by proving that several well-known problems are NP-complete. These include the 3-SAT, the vertex cover problem, and the Hamiltonian circuit problem.

An introduction to computational complexity can be found in the books by Machtey and Young [1977], Hopcroft and Ullman [1979], and Lewis and Papadimitriou [1981]. The first seven chapters of the book by Garey and Johnson [1979] give an entertaining introduction to the theory of NP-completeness. The remainder of the book is a virtual encyclopedia of NP-complete problems. Karp [1986], in the 1985 Association of Computing Machinery Turing Award Lecture, gives an interesting personal history of the development and directions of complexity theory.

We have introduced computational complexity in terms of the time of a computation. A similar analysis can be made for the memory required for a computation. An axiomatic approach to abstract complexity measures was introduced in Blum [1967] and developed further by Hartmanis and Hopcroft [1971]. Chapters 12 and 13 of Hopcroft and Ullman [1979] give an introduction to abstract complexity, as well as time and space complexity.

PART V

Deterministic Parsing

CHAPTER 15

LL(*k*) Grammars

The LL(*k*) grammars constitute the largest subclass of context-free grammars that permits deterministic top-down parsing using a *k*-symbol lookahead. The notation LL describes the parsing strategy for which these grammars are designed. The input string is scanned in a left-to-right manner and the parser generates a leftmost derivation.

Throughout this chapter, all derivations and rule applications are leftmost. We also assume that the grammars do not contain useless symbols. Techniques for detecting and removing useless symbols were presented in Section 5.3.

15.1 Lookahead in Context-Free Grammars

A top-down parser attempts to construct a leftmost derivation of an input string p. The parser extends derivations of the form $S \overset{*}{\Rightarrow} uAv$, where u is a prefix of p, by applying an A rule. "Looking ahead" in the input string can reduce the number of A rules that must be examined. If $p = uaw$, the terminal a is obtained by looking one symbol beyond the prefix of the input string that has been generated by the parser. Using the lookahead symbol, an A rule whose right-hand side begins with a terminal other than a can be eliminated from consideration. The application of any such rule generates a terminal string that is not a prefix of p.

Consider a derivation of the string *acbb* in the regular grammar

$$\text{G: } S \rightarrow aS \mid cA$$
$$A \rightarrow bA \mid cB \mid \lambda$$
$$B \rightarrow cB \mid a \mid \lambda.$$

The derivation begins with the start symbol *S* and lookahead symbol *a*. The grammar contains two *S* rules, $S \rightarrow aS$ and $S \rightarrow cA$. Clearly, applying $S \rightarrow cA$ cannot lead to a derivation of *acbb* since *c* does not match the lookahead symbol. It follows that the derivation must begin with an application of the rule $S \rightarrow aS$.

After the application of the *S* rule, the lookahead symbol is advanced to *c*. Again, there is only one *S* rule that generates *c*. Comparing the lookahead symbol with the terminal in each of the appropriate rules permits the deterministic construction of derivations in G.

Prefix Generated	Lookahead Symbol	Derivation	Rule
λ	*a*	$S \Rightarrow aS$	$S \rightarrow aS$
a	*c*	$\Rightarrow acA$	$S \rightarrow cA$
ac	*b*	$\Rightarrow acbA$	$A \rightarrow bA$
acb	*b*	$\Rightarrow acbbA$	$A \rightarrow bA$
acbb	λ	$\Rightarrow acbb$	$A \rightarrow \lambda$

Looking ahead one symbol is sufficient to construct derivations deterministically in the grammar G. A more general approach allows the lookahead to consist of the portion of the input string that has not been generated. An intermediate step in a derivation of a string *p* has the form $S \overset{*}{\Rightarrow} uAv$ where $p = ux$. The string *x* is called the **lookahead string** for the variable *A*. The lookahead set of *A* consists of all lookahead strings for that variable.

Definition 15.1.1

Let G $= (V, \Sigma, P, S)$ be a context-free grammar and $A \in V$.

i) The **lookahead set** of the variable *A*, LA(*A*), is defined by

$$LA(A) = \{x \mid S \overset{*}{\Rightarrow} uAv \overset{*}{\Rightarrow} ux \in \Sigma^*\}.$$

ii) For each rule $A \rightarrow w$ in P, the lookahead set of the rule $A \rightarrow w$ is defined by

$$LA(A \rightarrow w) = \{x \mid wv \overset{*}{\Rightarrow} x \in \Sigma^* \text{ where } S \overset{*}{\Rightarrow} uAv\}.$$

LA(*A*) consists of all terminal strings derivable from strings *Av* where *uAv* is a left sentential form of the grammar. LA($A \rightarrow w$) is the subset of LA(*A*) in which the subderivations $Av \overset{*}{\Rightarrow} x$ are initiated with the rule $A \rightarrow w$.

Let $A \rightarrow w_1, \ldots, A \rightarrow w_n$ be the A rules of a grammar G. The lookahead string can be used to select the appropriate A rule whenever the sets $\text{LA}(A \rightarrow w_i)$ partition $\text{LA}(A)$. That is, the sets $\text{LA}(A \rightarrow w_i)$ satisfy

i) $\text{LA}(A) = \displaystyle\bigcup_{i=1}^{n} \text{LA}(A \rightarrow w_i)$

ii) $\text{LA}(A \rightarrow w_i) \cap \text{LA}(A \rightarrow w_j) = \emptyset$ for all $1 \leq i < j \leq n$.

The first condition is satisfied for every context-free grammar; it follows directly from the definition of the lookahead sets. If the lookahead sets satisfy ii) and $S \overset{*}{\Rightarrow} uAv$ is a partial derivation of a string $p = ux \in \text{L}(G)$, then x is an element of exactly one set $\text{LA}(A \rightarrow w_k)$. Consequently, $A \rightarrow w_k$ is the only A rule whose application can lead to a successful completion of the derivation.

Example 15.1.1

The lookahead sets are constructed for the variables and the rules of the grammar

$$G_1: S \rightarrow Aabd \mid cAbcd$$
$$A \rightarrow a \mid b \mid \lambda.$$

$\text{LA}(S)$ contains all terminal strings derivable from S, that is, the entire language of G_1. Every terminal string derivable from the rule $S \rightarrow Aabd$ begins with a or b. On the other hand, derivations initiated by the rule $S \rightarrow cAbcd$ generate strings beginning with c.

$$\text{LA}(S) = \{aabd, babd, abd, cabcd, cbbcd, cbcd\}$$
$$\text{LA}(S \rightarrow Aabd) = \{aabd, babd, abd\}$$
$$\text{LA}(S \rightarrow cAbcd) = \{cabcd, cbbcd, cbcd\}$$

Knowledge of the first symbol of the lookahead string is sufficient to select the appropriate S rule.

To construct the lookahead set for the variable A we must consider derivations from all the left sentential forms of G_1 that contain A. There are only two such sentential forms, $Aabd$ and $cAbcd$. The lookahead sets consist of terminal strings derivable from $Aabd$ and $Abcd$.

$$\text{LA}(A \rightarrow a) = \{aabd, abcd\}$$
$$\text{LA}(A \rightarrow b) = \{babd, bbcd\}$$
$$\text{LA}(A \rightarrow \lambda) = \{abd, bcd\}$$

The substring ab can be obtained by applying $A \rightarrow a$ to $Abcd$ and by applying $A \rightarrow \lambda$ to $Aabd$. Looking ahead three symbols in the input string provides sufficient information to discriminate between these rules. A top-down parser with a three-symbol lookahead can deterministically construct derivations in the grammar G_1. $\square$

A lookahead string of the variable A is the concatenation of the results of two derivations, one from the variable A and one from the portion of the sentential form following A. Example 15.1.2 emphasizes the dependence of the lookahead set on the entire sentential form.

Example 15.1.2

A lookahead string of G_2 receives at most one terminal from each of the variables A, B, and C.

$$G_2: S \rightarrow ABCabcd$$
$$A \rightarrow a \mid \lambda$$
$$B \rightarrow b \mid \lambda$$
$$C \rightarrow c \mid \lambda$$

The only left sentential form of G_2 that contains A is $ABCabcd$. The variable B appears in $aBCabcd$ and $BCabcd$, both of which can be obtained by the application of an A rule to $ABCabcd$. In either case, $BCabcd$ is used to construct the lookahead set. Similarly, the lookahead set LA(C) consists of strings derivable from $Cabcd$.

$$LA(A \rightarrow a) = \{abcabcd, acabcd, ababcd, aabcd\}$$
$$LA(A \rightarrow \lambda) = \{bcabcd, cabcd, babcd, abcd\}$$
$$LA(B \rightarrow b) = \{bcabcd, babcd\}$$
$$LA(B \rightarrow \lambda) = \{cabcd, abcd\}$$
$$LA(C \rightarrow c) = \{cabcd\}$$
$$LA(C \rightarrow \lambda) = \{abcd\}$$

A string with prefix abc can be derived from the sentential form $ABCabcd$ using the rule $A \rightarrow a$ or $A \rightarrow \lambda$. One-symbol lookahead is sufficient for selecting the B and C rules. A four-symbol lookahead is required to parse the strings of G_2 deterministically.   □

The lookahead sets LA(A) and LA($A \rightarrow w$) may contain strings of arbitrary length. The selection of rules in the previous examples needed only finite-length prefixes of strings in the lookahead sets. The k-symbol lookahead sets are obtained by truncating the strings of the sets LA(A) and LA($A \rightarrow w$). A function $trunc_k$ is introduced to simplify the definition of the finite-length lookahead sets.

Definition 15.1.2

Let $G = (V, \Sigma, P, S)$ be a context-free grammar and let k be a natural number greater than zero.

i) $trunc_k$ is a function from $\mathcal{P}(\Sigma^*)$ to $\mathcal{P}(\Sigma^*)$ defined by

$$trunc_k(X) = \{u \mid u \in X \quad \text{with } length(u) \leqslant k \quad \text{or}$$
$$uv \in X \quad \text{with } length(u) = k\}$$

ii) The length-k lookahead set of the variable A is the set

$$LA_k(A) = trunc_k(LA(A)).$$

iii) The length-k lookahead set of the rule $A \rightarrow w$ is the set

$$LA_k(A \rightarrow w) = trunc_k(LA(A \rightarrow w)).$$

Example 15.1.3

The length-three lookahead sets are given for each of the rules of the grammar G_1 from Example 15.1.1.

$$LA_3(S \rightarrow Aabd) = \{aab, bab, abd\}$$
$$LA_3(S \rightarrow cAbcd) = \{cab, cbb, cbc\}$$
$$LA_3(A \rightarrow a) = \{aab, abc\}$$
$$LA_3(A \rightarrow b) = \{bab, bbc\}$$
$$LA_3(A \rightarrow \lambda) = \{abd, bcd\}$$

$\square$

Example 15.1.4

The language $\{a^i abc^i \mid i > 0\}$ is generated by each of the grammars G_1, G_2, and G_3. The minimal length lookahead sets necessary for discriminating between alternative productions are given for these grammars.

Rule	Lookahead Set
G_1: $S \rightarrow aSc$	$\{aaa\}$
$S \rightarrow aabc$	$\{aab\}$
G_2: $S \rightarrow aA$	
$A \rightarrow Sc$	$\{aa\}$
$A \rightarrow abc$	$\{ab\}$
G_3: $S \rightarrow aaAc$	
$A \rightarrow aAc$	$\{a\}$
$A \rightarrow b$	$\{b\}$

A one-symbol lookahead is insufficient for determining the S rule in G_1 since both of the alternatives begin with the symbol a. G_2 is constructed from G_1 by using the S rule to generate the leading a. The variable A is added to generate the remainder of the right-hand side of the S rules of G_1. This technique is known as **left factoring** since the leading a is factored out of the rules $S \rightarrow aSc$ and $S \rightarrow aabc$. Left factoring the S rule reduces the length of the lookahead needed to select the rules.

A lookahead of length one is sufficient to parse strings with the rules of G_3. The recursive A rule generates an a while the nonrecursive rule terminates the derivation by generating a b. $\square$

15.2   FIRST, FOLLOW, and Lookahead Sets

The lookahead set $LA_k(A)$ contains prefixes of length k of strings that can be derived from the variable A. If A derives strings of length less than k, the remainder of the lookahead string comes from derivations that follow A in the sentential forms of the grammar. For each variable A, sets $FIRST_k(A)$ and $FOLLOW_k(A)$ are introduced to provide the information required for constructing the lookahead sets. $FIRST_k(A)$ contains prefixes of terminal strings derivable from A. $FOLLOW_k(A)$ contains prefixes of terminal strings that can follow the strings derivable from A. For convenience, a set $FIRST_k$ is defined for every string in $(V \cup \Sigma)^*$.

Definition 15.2.1

Let G be a context-free grammar. For every string $u \in (V \cup \Sigma)^*$ and $k > 0$, the set $FIRST_k(u)$ is defined by

$$FIRST_k(u) = trunc_k(\{x \mid u \overset{*}{\Rightarrow} x, x \in \Sigma^*\}).$$

Example 15.2.1

FIRST sets are constructed for the strings S and ABC using the grammar G_2 from Example 15.1.2.

$$FIRST_1(ABC) = \{a, b, c, \lambda\}$$
$$FIRST_2(ABC) = \{ab, ac, bc, a, b, c, \lambda\}$$
$$FIRST_3(S) = \{abc, aba, aca, bca, bab, cab\} \qquad \square$$

Recall that the concatenation of two sets X and Y is denoted by juxtaposition, $XY = \{xy \mid x \in X \text{ and } y \in Y\}$. Using this notation, the following relationships can be established for the $FIRST_k$ sets.

Lemma 15.2.2

For every $k > 0$,

1. $FIRST_k(\lambda) = \{\lambda\}$
2. $FIRST_k(a) = \{a\}$
3. $FIRST_k(au) = \{av \mid v \in FIRST_{k-1}(u)\}$
4. $FIRST_k(uv) = trunc_k(FIRST_k(u)FIRST_k(v))$
5. if $A \to w$ is a rule in G, then $FIRST_k(w) \subseteq FIRST_k(A)$.

Definition 15.2.3

Let G be a context-free grammar. For every $A \in V$ and $k > 0$, the set $FOLLOW_k(A)$ is defined by

$$FOLLOW_k(A) = \{x \mid S \overset{*}{\Rightarrow} uAv \text{ and } x \in FIRST_k(v)\}.$$

The set $FOLLOW_k(A)$ consists of prefixes of terminal strings that can follow the variable A in derivations in G. Since the null string follows every derivation from the sentential form consisting solely of the start symbol, $\lambda \in FOLLOW_k(S)$.

Example 15.2.2

The FOLLOW sets of length one and two are given for the variables of G_2.

$$FOLLOW_1(S) = \{\lambda\} \qquad FOLLOW_2(S) = \{\lambda\}$$
$$FOLLOW_1(A) = \{a, b, c\} \qquad FOLLOW_2(A) = \{bc, ba, ca\}$$
$$FOLLOW_1(B) = \{a, c\} \qquad FOLLOW_2(B) = \{ca, ab\}$$
$$FOLLOW_1(C) = \{a\} \qquad FOLLOW_2(C) = \{ab\} \qquad \square$$

The FOLLOW sets of a variable B are obtained from the rules in which B occurs on the right-hand side. Consider the relationships generated by a rule of the form $A \rightarrow uBv$. The strings that follow B include those generated by v concatenated with all terminal strings that follow A. If the grammar contains a rule $A \rightarrow uB$, any string that follows A can also follow B. The preceding discussion is summarized in Lemma 15.2.4.

Lemma 15.2.4

For every $k > 0$,

1. $FOLLOW_k(S)$ contains λ, where S is the start symbol of G
2. if $A \rightarrow uB$ is a rule of G, then $FOLLOW_k(A) \subseteq FOLLOW_k(B)$
3. if $A \rightarrow uBv$ is a rule of G, then $trunc_k(FIRST_k(v)FOLLOW_k(A)) \subseteq FOLLOW_k(B)$.

The $FIRST_k$ and $FOLLOW_k$ sets are used to construct the lookahead sets for the rules of a grammar. Theorem 15.2.5 follows immediately from the definitions of the length-k lookahead sets and the function $trunc_k$.

Theorem 15.2.5

Let $G = (V, \Sigma, P, S)$ be a context-free grammar. For every $k > 0$, $A \in V$, and rule $A \rightarrow w = u_1u_2 \ldots u_n$ in P,

i) $LA_k(A) = trunc_k(FIRST_k(A)FOLLOW_k(A))$

ii) $LA_k(A \rightarrow w) = trunc_k(FIRST_k(w)FOLLOW_k(A))$
$$= trunc_k(FIRST_k(u_1) \ldots FIRST_k(u_n)FOLLOW_k(A)).$$

Example 15.2.3

The $FIRST_3$ and $FOLLOW_3$ sets for the symbols in the grammar

$$G_1: S \rightarrow Aabd \mid cAbcd$$
$$A \rightarrow a \mid b \mid \lambda$$

are given below.

$$\text{FIRST}_3(S) = \{aab, bab, abd, cab, cbb, cbc\}$$
$$\text{FIRST}_3(A) = \{a, b, \lambda\}$$
$$\text{FIRST}_3(a) = \{a\}$$
$$\text{FIRST}_3(b) = \{b\}$$
$$\text{FIRST}_3(c) = \{c\}$$
$$\text{FIRST}_3(d) = \{d\}$$
$$\text{FOLLOW}_3(S) = \{\lambda\}$$
$$\text{FOLLOW}_3(A) = \{abd, bcd\}$$

The set $\text{LA}_3(S \rightarrow Aabd)$ is explicitly constructed from the sets $\text{FIRST}_3(A)$, $\text{FIRST}_3(a)$, $\text{FIRST}_3(b)$, $\text{FIRST}_3(d)$, and $\text{FOLLOW}_3(S)$ using the strategy outlined in Theorem 15.2.5. The remainder of the length-three lookahead sets for the rules of G_1 can be found in Example 15.1.3.

$$
\begin{aligned}
\text{LA}_3(S \rightarrow Aabd) &= trunc_3(\text{FIRST}_3(A)\text{FIRST}_3(a)\text{FIRST}_3(b)\text{FIRST}_3(d)\text{FOLLOW}_3(S)) \\
&= trunc_3(\{a, b, \lambda\}\{a\}\{b\}\{d\}\{\lambda\}) \\
&= trunc_3(\{aabd, babd, abd\}) \\
&= \{aab, bab, abd\} \qquad\qquad\qquad\qquad\qquad\qquad\qquad \square
\end{aligned}
$$

15.3 **Strong LL(*k*) Grammars**

We have seen that the lookahead sets can be used to select the A rule in a top-down parse when $\text{LA}(A)$ is partitioned by the sets $\text{LA}(A \rightarrow w_i)$. This section introduces a subclass of context-free grammars known as the strong LL(*k*) grammars. The strong LL(*k*) condition guarantees that the lookahead sets $\text{LA}_k(A)$ are partitioned by the sets $\text{LA}_k(A \rightarrow w_i)$.

When employing a k-symbol lookahead, it is often helpful if there are k symbols to be examined. An endmarker $\#^k$ is concatenated to the end of each string in the language to guarantee that every lookahead string contains exactly k symbols. If the start symbol S of the grammar is nonrecursive, the endmarker can be concatenated to the right-hand side of each S rule. Otherwise, the grammar can be augmented with a new start symbol S' and rule $S' \rightarrow S\#^k$.

Definition 15.3.1

Let $G = (V, \Sigma, P, S)$ be a context-free grammar with endmarker $\#^k$. G is **strong LL(*k*)** if whenever there are two leftmost derivations

$$
\begin{aligned}
S &\stackrel{*}{\Rightarrow} u_1 A v_1 \stackrel{*}{\Rightarrow} u_1 x v_1 \stackrel{*}{\Rightarrow} u_1 z w_1 \\
S &\stackrel{*}{\Rightarrow} u_2 A v_2 \stackrel{*}{\Rightarrow} u_2 y v_2 \stackrel{*}{\Rightarrow} u_2 z w_2
\end{aligned}
$$

where $u_i, w_i, z \in \Sigma^*$ and $length(z) = k$, then $x = y$.

We now establish several properties of strong LL(k) grammars. First we show that the length-k lookahead sets can be used to parse strings deterministically in a strong LL(k) grammar.

Theorem 15.3.2
A grammar G is strong LL(k) if, and only if, the sets $LA_k(A \rightarrow w_i)$ partition $LA(A)$ for each variable $A \in V$.

Proof Assume that the sets $LA_k(A \rightarrow w_i)$ partition $LA(A)$ for each variable $A \in V$. Let z be a terminal string of length k that can be obtained by the derivations

$$S \overset{*}{\Rightarrow} u_1 A v_1 \Rightarrow u_1 x v_1 \overset{*}{\Rightarrow} u_1 z w_1$$
$$S \overset{*}{\Rightarrow} u_2 A v_2 \Rightarrow u_2 y v_2 \overset{*}{\Rightarrow} u_2 z w_2.$$

Then z is in both $LA_k(A \rightarrow x)$ and $LA_k(A \rightarrow y)$. Since the sets $LA_k(A \rightarrow w_i)$ partition $LA(A)$, $x = y$ and G is strong LL(k).

Conversely, let G be a strong LL(k) and let z be an element of $LA_k(A)$. The strong LL(k) condition ensures that there is only one A rule that can be used to derive terminal strings of the form uzw from the sentential forms uAv of G. Consequently z is in the lookahead set of exactly one A rule. This implies that the sets $LA_k(A \rightarrow w_i)$ partition $LA_k(A)$.   ∎

Theorem 15.3.3
If G is strong LL(k) for some k, then G is unambiguous.

Intuitively, a grammar that can be deterministically parsed must be unambiguous; there is exactly one rule that can be applied at each step in the derivation. The formal proof of this proposition is left as an exercise.

Theorem 15.3.4
If G has a left recursive variable, then G is not strong LL(k), for any $k > 0$.

Proof Let A be a left recursive variable. Since G does not contain useless variables, there is a derivation of a terminal string containing a left recursive subderivation of the variable A. The proof is presented in two cases.

Case 1: A is directly left recursive: A derivation containing direct left recursion uses A rules of the form $A \rightarrow Ay$ and $A \rightarrow x$ where the first symbol of x is not A.

$$S \overset{*}{\Rightarrow} uAv \Rightarrow uAyv \Rightarrow uxyv \overset{*}{\Rightarrow} uw \in \Sigma^*$$

The prefix of w of length k is in both $LA_k(A \rightarrow Ay)$ and $LA_k(A \rightarrow x)$. By Theorem 15.3.2, G is not strong LL(k).

Case 2: *A* is indirectly left recursive: A derivation with indirect recursion has the form

$$S \overset{*}{\Rightarrow} uAv \Rightarrow uB_1yv \Rightarrow \ldots \Rightarrow uB_nv_n \Rightarrow uAv_{n+1} \Rightarrow uxv_{n+1} \overset{*}{\Rightarrow} uw \in \Sigma^*.$$

Again, G is not strong LL(*k*) since the sets $LA_k(A \to B_1y)$ and $LA_k(A \to x)$ are not disjoint.   ∎

15.4   Construction of FIRST$_k$ Sets

We now present algorithms to construct the length-*k* lookahead sets for a context-free grammar with endmarker $\#^k$. This is accomplished by generating the FIRST$_k$ and FOLLOW$_k$ sets for the variables of the grammar. The lookahead sets can then be constructed using the technique presented in Theorem 15.2.5.

The initial step in the construction of lookahead begins with the generation of the FIRST$_k$ sets. Consider a rule of the form $A \to u_1u_2 \ldots u_n$. The subset of FIRST$_k(A)$ generated by this rule can be constructed from the sets FIRST$_k(u_1)$, FIRST$_k(u_2)$, . . . , FIRST$_k(u_n)$, and FOLLOW$_k(A)$. The problem of constructing FIRST$_k$ sets for a string reduces to that of finding the sets for the variables in the string.

Algorithm 15.4.1
Construction of FIRST$_k$ Sets

input: context-free grammar G = (V, Σ, P, *S*)

1. **for** each $a \in \Sigma$ **do** F'(*a*) := {*a*}

2. **for** each $A \in V$ **do** F(A) := $\begin{cases} \{\lambda\} & \text{if } A \to \lambda \text{ is a rule in P} \\ \varnothing & \text{otherwise} \end{cases}$

3. **repeat**
   3.1. **for** each $A \in V$ **do** F'(A) := F(A)
   3.2. **for** each rule $A \to u_1u_2 \ldots u_n$ with $n > 0$ **do**
        F(A) := F(A) $\cup$ $trunc_k$(F'(u_1)F'(u_2) . . . F'(u_n))

   until F(A) = F'(A) for all $A \in V$

4. FIRST$_k(A)$ = F(A)

The elements of FIRST$_k(A)$ are generated in step 3.2. At the beginning of each iteration of the repeat-until loop, the auxiliary set F'(A) is assigned the current value of F(A). Strings obtained from the concatenation F'(u_1)F'(u_2) . . . F'(u_n), where $A \to u_1u_2 \ldots u_n$ is a rule of G, are then added to F(A). The algorithm halts when an iteration fails to increment a set F(A) for some $A \in V$.

Example 15.4.1

Algorithm 15.4.1 is used to construct the FIRST$_2$ sets for the variables of the grammar

$$G: S \rightarrow A\#\#$$
$$A \rightarrow aAd \mid BC$$
$$B \rightarrow bBc \mid \lambda$$
$$C \rightarrow acC \mid ad.$$

The sets $F'(a)$ are initialized to $\{a\}$ for each $a \in \Sigma$. The action of the repeat-until loop is prescribed by the right-hand side of the rules of the grammar. Interpreting the rules of the grammar G, step 3.2 generates the assignment statements

$$F(S) := F(S) \cup trunc_2(F'(A)\{\#\}\{\#\})$$
$$F(A) := F(A) \cup trunc_2(\{a\}F'(A)\{d\}) \cup trunc_2(F'(B)F'(C))$$
$$F(B) := F(B) \cup trunc_2(\{b\}F'(B)\{c\})$$
$$F(C) := F(C) \cup trunc_2(\{a\}\{c\}F'(C)) \cup trunc_2(\{a\}\{d\}).$$

The generation of the FIRST$_2$ sets is traced by giving the status of the sets $F(S)$, $F(A)$, $F(B)$, and $F(C)$ after each iteration of the loop. Recall that the concatenation of the empty set with any set yields the empty set.

	F(S)	F(A)	F(B)	F(C)
0	$\emptyset$	$\emptyset$	$\{\lambda\}$	$\emptyset$
1	$\emptyset$	$\emptyset$	$\{\lambda, bc\}$	$\{ad\}$
2	$\emptyset$	$\{ad, bc\}$	$\{\lambda, bc, bb\}$	$\{ad, ac\}$
3	$\{ad, bc\}$	$\{ad, bc, aa, ab, bb, ac\}$	$\{\lambda, bc, bb\}$	$\{ad, ac\}$
4	$\{ad, bc, aa, ab, bb, ac\}$	$\{ad, bc, aa, ab, bb, ac\}$	$\{\lambda, bc, bb\}$	$\{ad, ac\}$
5	$\{ad, bc, aa, ab, bb, ac\}$	$\{ad, bc, aa, ab, bb, ac\}$	$\{\lambda, bc, bb\}$	$\{ad, ac\}$

□

Theorem 15.4.2

Let $G = (V, \Sigma, P, S)$ be a context-free grammar. Algorithm 15.4.1 generates the sets FIRST$_k(A)$, for every variable $A \in V$.

Proof   The proof consists of showing that the repeat-until loop in step 3 terminates and, upon termination, $F(A) = $ FIRST$_k(A)$.

i) Algorithm 15.4.1 terminates: The number of iterations of the repeat-until loop is bounded since there are only a finite number of lookahead strings of length k or less.

ii) $F(A) = $ FIRST$_k(A)$: First we prove that $F(A) \subseteq $ FIRST$_k(A)$ for all variables $A \in V$. To accomplish this we show that $F(A) \subseteq $ FIRST$_k(A)$ at the beginning of each iteration of the repeat-until loop. By inspection, this inclusion holds prior to the first iteration. Assume $F(A) \subseteq $ FIRST$_k(A)$ for all variables A after m iterations of the loop.

During the $m+1$st iteration, the only additions to F(A) come from assignment statements of the form

$$F(A) := F(A) \cup trunc_k(F'(u_1)F'(u_2) \ldots F'(u_n))$$

where $A \rightarrow u_1u_2 \ldots u_n$ is a rule of G. By the inductive hypothesis, each of the sets $F'(u_i)$ is a subset of $FIRST_k(u_i)$. If u is added to F(A) on the iteration then

$$\begin{aligned} u &\in trunc_k(F'(u_1)F'(u_2) \ldots F'(u_n)) \\ &\subseteq trunc_k(FIRST_k(u_1)FIRST_k(u_2) \ldots FIRST_k(u_n)) \\ &= FIRST_k(u_1u_2 \ldots u_n) \\ &\subseteq FIRST_k(A) \end{aligned}$$

and $u \in FIRST_k(A)$. The final two steps follow from parts 4 and 5 of Lemma 15.2.2.

We now show that $FIRST_k(A) \subseteq F(A)$ upon completion of the loop. Let $F_m(A)$ be the value of the set F(A) after m iterations. Assume the repeat-until loop halts after j iterations. We begin with the observation that if a string can be shown to be in $F_m(A)$ for some $m > j$ then it is in $F_j(A)$. This follows since the sets F(A) and F'(A) would be identical for all iterations of the loop past iteration j. We will show that $FIRST_k(A) \subseteq F_j(A)$.

Let x be a string in $FIRST_k(A)$. Then there is a derivation $A \overset{m}{\Rightarrow} w \in \Sigma^*$ where x is the prefix of w of length k. We show that $x \in F_m(A)$. The proof is by induction on the length of the derivation. The basis consists of terminal strings that can be derived with one rule application. If $A \rightarrow w \in P$, then x is added to $F_1(A)$.

Assume that $trunc_k(\{w \mid A \overset{m}{\Rightarrow} w \in \Sigma^*\}) \subseteq F_m(A)$ for all variables A in V. Let $x \in trunc_k(\{w \mid A \overset{m+1}{\Longrightarrow} w \in \Sigma^*\})$; that is, x is a prefix of terminal string derivable from A by $m + 1$ rule applications. We will show that $x \in F_{m+1}(A)$. The derivation of w can be written

$$A \Rightarrow u_1u_2 \ldots u_n \overset{m}{\Rightarrow} x_1x_2 \ldots x_n = w$$

where $u_i \in V \cup \Sigma$. Clearly, each subderivation $u_i \overset{*}{\Rightarrow} x_i$ has length less than $m + 1$. By the inductive hypothesis, the string obtained by truncating x_i at length k is in $F_m(u_i)$.

On the $m+1$st iteration, $F_{m+1}(A)$ is augmented with the set

$$trunc_k(F'_{m+1}(u_1) \ldots F'_{m+1}(u_n)) = trunc_k(F_m(u_1) \ldots F_m(u_n)).$$

Thus,

$$\{x\} = trunc_k(x_1x_2 \ldots x_n) \subseteq trunc_k(F_m(u_1) \ldots F_m(u_n))$$

and x is an element of $F_{m+1}(A)$. It follows that every string in $FIRST_k(A)$ is in $F_j(A)$ as desired.   ∎

15.5 Construction of FOLLOW$_k$ Sets

The inclusions in Lemma 15.2.4 form the basis of an algorithm to generate the FOLLOW$_k$ sets. FOLLOW$_k(A)$ is constructed from the FIRST$_k$ sets and the rules in which A occurs on the right-hand side. Algorithm 15.5.1 generates FOLLOW$_k(A)$ using the auxiliary set

FL(A). The set FL$'(A)$, which triggers the halting condition, maintains the value assigned to FL(A) on the preceding iteration.

Algorithm 15.5.1
Construction of FOLLOW$_k$ Sets

input: context-free grammar G $= (V, \Sigma, P, S)$
$\qquad$ FIRST$_k(A)$ for every $A \in V$

1. FL$(S) := \{\lambda\}$
2. **for** each $A \in V - \{S\}$ **do** FL$(A) := \emptyset$
3. **repeat**
$\qquad$ 3.1. **for** each $A \in V$ **do** FL$'(A) := $ FL(A)
$\qquad$ 3.2. **for** each rule $A \to w = u_1 u_2 \ldots u_n$ with $w \notin \Sigma^*$ **do**
$\qquad\qquad$ 3.2.1. L $:= $ FL$'(A)$
$\qquad\qquad$ 3.2.2. **if** $u_n \in V$ **then** FL$(u_n) := $ FL$(u_n) \cup$ L
$\qquad\qquad$ 3.2.3. **for** $i := n - 1$ **to** 1 **do**
$\qquad\qquad\qquad$ 3.2.3.1. L $:= trunc_k($FIRST$_k(u_{i+1})$L$)$
$\qquad\qquad\qquad$ 3.2.3.2. **if** $u_i \in V$ **then** FL$(u_i) := $ FL$(u_i) \cup$ L
$\qquad\qquad$ **end for**
$\qquad$ **end for**
$\qquad$ **until** FL$(A) = $ FL$'(A)$ for every $A \in V$
4. FOLLOW$_k(A) := $ FL(A)

The inclusion FL$(A) \subseteq$ FOLLOW$_k(A)$ is established by showing that every element added to FL(A) in statements 3.2.2 or 3.2.3.2 is in FOLLOW$_k(A)$. The opposite inclusion is obtained by demonstrating that every element of FOLLOW$_k(A)$ is added to FL(A) prior to the termination of the repeat-until loop. The details are left as an exercise.

Example 15.5.1

Algorithm 15.5.1 is used to construct the set FOLLOW$_2(A)$ for every variable A of the grammar G from Example 15.4.1. The interior of the repeat-until loop processes each rule in a right-to-left fashion. The action of the loop is specified by the assignment statements obtained from the rules of the grammar.

Rule	Assignments
$S \to A\#\#$	FL$(A) := $ FL$(A) \cup trunc_2(\{\#\#\}FL'(S))$
$A \to aAd$	FL$(A) := $ FL$(A) \cup trunc_2(\{d\}$FL$'(A))$
$A \to BC$	FL$(C) := $ FL$(C) \cup$ FL$'(A)$
	FL$(B) := $ FL$(B) \cup trunc_2($FIRST$_2(C)$FL$'(A))$
	$\qquad = $ FL$(B) \cup trunc_2(\{ad, ac\}FL'(A))$
$B \to bBc$	FL$(B) := $ FL$(B) \cup trunc_2(\{c\}$FL$'(B))$

The rule $C \to acC$ has been omitted from the list since the assignment generated by this rule is $FL(C) := FL(C) \cup FL'(C)$.

	FL(*S*)	FL(*A*)	FL(*B*)	FL(*C*)
0	$\{\lambda\}$	$\emptyset$	$\emptyset$	$\emptyset$
1	$\{\lambda\}$	$\{\#\#\}$	$\emptyset$	$\emptyset$
2	$\{\lambda\}$	$\{\#\#, d\#\}$	$\{ad, ac\}$	$\{\#\#\}$
3	$\{\lambda\}$	$\{\#\#, d\#, dd\}$	$\{ad, ac, ca\}$	$\{\#\#, d\#\}$
4	$\{\lambda\}$	$\{\#\#, d\#, dd\}$	$\{ad, ac, ca, cc\}$	$\{\#\#, d\#, dd\}$
5	$\{\lambda\}$	$\{\#\#, d\#, dd\}$	$\{ad, ac, ca, cc\}$	$\{\#\#, d\#, dd\}$

□

Example 15.5.2

The length-two lookahead sets for the rules of the grammar G are constructed from the $FIRST_2$ and $FOLLOW_2$ sets generated in Examples 15.4.1 and 15.5.1.

$$LA_2(S \to A\#\#) = \{ad, bc, aa, ab, bb, ac\}$$
$$LA_2(A \to aAd) = \{aa, ab\}$$
$$LA_2(A \to BC) = \{bc, bb, ad, ac\}$$
$$LA_2(B \to bBc) = \{bb, bc\}$$
$$LA_2(B \to \lambda) = \{ad, ac, ca, cc\}$$
$$LA_2(C \to acC) = \{ac\}$$
$$LA_2(C \to ad) = \{ad\}$$

G is strong LL(2) since the lookahead sets are disjoint for each pair of alternative rules.   □

The preceding algorithms provide a decision procedure to determine whether a grammar is strong LL(*k*). The process begins by generating the $FIRST_k$ and $FOLLOW_k$ sets using Algorithms 15.4.1 and 15.5.1. The techniques presented in Theorem 15.2.5 are then used to construct the length-*k* lookahead sets. By Theorem 15.3.2, the grammar is strong LL(*k*) if, and only if, the sets $LA_k(A \to x)$ and $LA_k(A \to y)$ are disjoint for each pair of distinct *A* rules.

15.6   A Strong LL(1) Grammar

The grammar AE was introduced in Section 4.3 to generate infix additive expressions containing a single variable *b*. AE is not strong LL(*k*) since it contains a directly left recursive *A* rule. In this section we modify AE to obtain a strong LL(1) grammar that generates the additive expressions. To guarantee that the resulting grammar is strong LL(1), the length-one lookahead sets are constructed for each rule.

The transformation begins by adding the endmarker # to the strings generated by AE. This ensures that the lookahead set does not contain the null string. The grammar

$$AE: S \to A\#$$
$$A \to T$$
$$A \to A + T$$
$$T \to b$$
$$T \to (A)$$

generates the strings in L(AE) concatenated with the endmarker $\#$. The direct left recursion can be removed using the techniques presented in Section 5.5. The variable Z is used to convert the left recursion to right recursion, yielding the equivalent grammar AE_1.

$$AE_1: S \to A\#$$
$$A \to T$$
$$A \to TZ$$
$$Z \to +T$$
$$Z \to +TZ$$
$$T \to b$$
$$T \to (A)$$

AE_1 still cannot be strong LL(1) since the A rules both have T as the first symbol occurring on the right-hand side. This difficulty is removed by left factoring the A rules using the new variable B. Similarly, the right-hand side of the Z rules begin with identical substrings. The variable Y is introduced by the factoring of the Z rules. AE_2 results from making these modifications to AE_1.

$$AE_2: S \to A\#$$
$$A \to TB$$
$$B \to Z$$
$$B \to \lambda$$
$$Z \to +TY$$
$$Y \to Z$$
$$Y \to \lambda$$
$$T \to b$$
$$T \to (A)$$

To show that AE_2 is strong LL(1), the length-one lookahead sets for the variables of the grammar must satisfy the partition condition of Theorem 15.3.2. We begin by tracing the sequence of sets generated by Algorithm 15.4.1 in the construction of the $FIRST_1$ sets.

	F(S)	F(A)	F(B)	F(Z)	F(Y)	F(T)
0	$\emptyset$	$\emptyset$	$\{\lambda\}$	$\emptyset$	$\{\lambda\}$	$\emptyset$
1	$\emptyset$	$\emptyset$	$\{\lambda\}$	$\{+\}$	$\{\lambda\}$	$\{b, (\}$
2	$\emptyset$	$\{b, (\}$	$\{\lambda, +\}$	$\{+\}$	$\{\lambda, +\}$	$\{b, (\}$
3	$\{b, (\}$	$\{b, (\}$	$\{\lambda, +\}$	$\{+\}$	$\{\lambda, +\}$	$\{b, (\}$
4	$\{b, (\}$	$\{b, (\}$	$\{\lambda, +\}$	$\{+\}$	$\{\lambda, +\}$	$\{b, (\}$

Similarly, the FOLLOW$_2$ sets are generated using Algorithm 15.5.1.

	FL(S)	FL(A)	FL(B)	FL(Z)	FL(Y)	FL(T)
0	$\{\lambda\}$	$\emptyset$	$\emptyset$	$\emptyset$	$\emptyset$	$\emptyset$
1	$\{\lambda\}$	$\{\#,)\}$	$\emptyset$	$\emptyset$	$\emptyset$	$\emptyset$
2	$\{\lambda\}$	$\{\#,)\}$	$\{\#,)\}$	$\emptyset$	$\emptyset$	$\emptyset$
3	$\{\lambda\}$	$\{\#,)\}$	$\{\#,)\}$	$\{\#,)\}$	$\emptyset$	$\emptyset$
4	$\{\lambda\}$	$\{\#,)\}$	$\{\#,)\}$	$\{\#,)\}$	$\{\#,)\}$	$\emptyset$
5	$\{\lambda\}$	$\{\#,)\}$	$\{\#,)\}$	$\{\#,)\}$	$\{\#,)\}$	$\{\#,)\}$
6	$\{\lambda\}$	$\{\#,)\}$	$\{\#,)\}$	$\{\#,)\}$	$\{\#,)\}$	$\{\#,)\}$

The length-one lookahead sets are obtained from the FIRST$_1$ and FOLLOW$_1$ sets generated above.

$$LA_1(S \to A\#) = \{b, (\}$$
$$LA_1(A \to TB) = \{b, (\}$$
$$LA_1(B \to Z) = \{+\}$$
$$LA_1(B \to \lambda) = \{\#,)\}$$
$$LA_1(Z \to +TY) = \{+\}$$
$$LA_1(Z \to \lambda) = \{\#,)\}$$
$$LA_1(Y \to Z) = \{+\}$$
$$LA_1(Y \to \lambda) = \{\#,)\}$$
$$LA_1(T \to b) = \{b\}$$
$$LA_1(T \to (A)) = \{(\}$$

Since the lookahead sets for alternative rules are disjoint, the grammar AE$_2$ is strong LL(1).

15.7   A Strong LL(k) Parser

Parsing with a strong LL(k) grammar begins with the construction of the lookahead sets for each of the rules of the grammar. Once these sets have been built, they are available for the parsing of any number of strings. The strategy for parsing strong LL(k) grammars presented in Algorithm 15.7.1 consists of a loop that compares the lookahead string with the lookahead sets and applies the appropriate rule.

Algorithm 15.7.1
Deterministic Parser for a Strong LL(k) Grammar

input: strong LL(k) grammar G = (V, Σ, P, S)
    string $p \in \Sigma^*$
    lookahead sets $LA_k(A \to w)$ for each rule in P

1. $q := S$
2. **repeat**
     Let $q = uAv$ where A is the leftmost variable in q and
     let $p = uyz$ where $length(y) = k$.
     2.1. **if** $y \in LA_k(A \to w)$ for some A rule **then** $q := uwv$
     until $q = p$ **or** $y \notin LA_k(A \to w)$ for all A rules
3. **if** $q = p$ **then** accept **else** reject

The presence of the endmarker in the grammar ensures that the lookahead string y contains k symbols. The input string is rejected whenever the lookahead string is not an element of one of the lookahead sets. When the lookahead string is in $LA_k(A \to w)$, a new sentential form is constructed by applying $A \to w$ to the current string uAv. The input is accepted if this rule application generates the input string. Otherwise, the loop is repeated for the sentential form uwv.

Example 15.7.1

Algorithm 15.7.1 and the lookahead sets from Section 15.6 are used to parse the string $(b + b)\#$ using the strong LL(1) grammar AE_2.

u	A	v	Lookahead	Rule	Derivation
λ	S	λ	$($	$S \to A\#$	$S \Rightarrow A\#$
λ	A	$\#$	$($	$A \to TB$	$\Rightarrow TB\#$
λ	T	$B\#$	$($	$T \to (A)$	$\Rightarrow (A)B\#$
$($	A	$)B\#$	b	$A \to TB$	$\Rightarrow (TB)B\#$
$($	T	$B)B\#$	b	$T \to b$	$\Rightarrow (bB)B\#$
$(b$	B	$)B\#$	$+$	$B \to Z$	$\Rightarrow (bZ)B\#$
$(b$	Z	$)B\#$	$+$	$Z \to +TY$	$\Rightarrow (b + TY)B\#$
$(b +$	T	$Y)B\#$	b	$T \to b$	$\Rightarrow (b + bY)B\#$
$(b + b$	Y	$)B\#$	$)$	$Y \to \lambda$	$\Rightarrow (b + b)B\#$
$(b + b)$	B	$\#$	$\#$	$B \to \lambda$	$\Rightarrow (b + b)\#$

□

15.8   LL(*k*) Grammars

The lookahead sets in a strong LL(*k*) grammar provide a global criterion for selecting a rule. When A is the leftmost variable in the sentential form being extended by the parser, the lookahead string generated by the parser and the lookahead sets provide sufficient information to select the appropriate A rule. This choice does not depend upon the sentential form containing A. The LL(*k*) grammars provide a local selection criterion; the choice of the rule depends upon both the lookahead and the sentential form.

Definition 15.8.1

Let $G = (V, \Sigma, P, S)$ be a context-free grammar with endmarker $\#^k$. G is **LL(*k*)** if whenever there are two leftmost derivations

$$S \overset{*}{\Rightarrow} uAv \Rightarrow uxv \overset{*}{\Rightarrow} uzw_1$$
$$S \overset{*}{\Rightarrow} uAv \Rightarrow uyv \overset{*}{\Rightarrow} uzw_2$$

where $u, w_i, z \in \Sigma^*$ and $length(z) = k$, then $x = y$.

Notice the difference between the derivations in Definitions 15.3.1 and 15.8.1. The strong LL(*k*) condition requires that there is a unique A rule that can derive the lookahead string z from any sentential form containing A. An LL(*k*) grammar only requires the rule to be unique for a fixed sentential form uAv. The lookahead sets for an LL(*k*) grammar must be defined for each sentential form.

Definition 15.8.2

Let $G = (V, \Sigma, P, S)$ be a context-free grammar and uAv a sentential form of G.

i) The lookahead set of the sentential form uAv is defined by $LA_k(uAv) = FIRST_k(Av)$.

ii) The lookahead set for the sentential form uAv and rule $A \to w$ is defined by
$LA_k(uAv, A \to w) = FIRST_k(wv)$.

A result similar to Theorem 15.3.2 can be established for LL(*k*) grammars. The unique selection of a rule for the sentential form uAv requires the set $LA_k(uAv)$ to be partitioned by the lookahead sets $LA_k(uAv, A \to w_i)$ generated by the A rules. If the grammar is strong LL(*k*), then the partition is guaranteed and the grammar is also LL(*k*).

Example 15.8.1

An LL(*k*) grammar need not be strong LL(*k*). Consider the grammar

$$G_1: S \to Aabd \mid cAbcd$$
$$A \to a \mid b \mid \lambda$$

whose lookahead sets were given in Example 15.1.1. G_1 is strong LL(3) but not strong LL(2) since the string ab is in both $LA_2(A \to a)$ and $LA_2(A \to \lambda)$. The length-two lookahead sets for the sentential forms containing the variables S and A are

$LA_2(S, S \to Aabd) = \{aa, ba, ab\}$
$LA_2(S, S \to cAbcd) = \{ca, cb\}$

$LA_2(Aabd, A \to a) = \{aa\}$ $LA_2(cAbcd, A \to a) = \{ab\}$
$LA_2(Aabd, A \to b) = \{ba\}$ $LA_2(cAbcd, A \to b) = \{bb\}$
$LA_2(Aabd, A \to \lambda) = \{ab\}$ $LA_2(cAbcd, A \to \lambda) = \{bc\}$

Since the alternatives for a given sentential form are disjoint, the grammar is LL(2). □

Example 15.8.2

A three-symbol lookahead is sufficient for a local selection of rules in the grammar

$$\text{G: } S \rightarrow aBAd \mid bBbAd$$
$$A \rightarrow abA \mid c$$
$$B \rightarrow ab \mid a.$$

The S and A rules can be selected with a one-symbol lookahead; so we turn our attention to selecting the B rule.

$$\text{LA}_3(aBAd, B \rightarrow ab) = \{aba, abc\}$$
$$\text{LA}_3(aBAd, B \rightarrow a) = \{aab, acd\}$$
$$\text{LA}_3(bBbAd, B \rightarrow ab) = \{abb\}$$
$$\text{LA}_3(bBbAd, B \rightarrow a) = \{aba, abc\}$$

The length-three lookahead sets for the two sentential forms that contain B are partitioned by the B rules. Consequently, G is LL(3). The strong LL(*k*) conditions can be checked by examining the lookahead sets for the B rules.

$$\text{LA}(B \rightarrow ab) = ab(ab)^*cd \cup abb(ab)^*cd$$
$$\text{LA}(B \rightarrow a) = a(ab)^*cd \cup ab(ab)^*cd$$

For any integer k, there is a string of length greater than k in both $\text{LA}(B \rightarrow ab)$ and $\text{LA}(B \rightarrow a)$. Consequently, G is not strong LL(*k*) for any k. □

Parsing deterministically with LL(*k*) grammars requires the construction of the local lookahead sets for the sentential forms generated during the parse. The lookahead set for a sentential form can be constructed directly from the FIRST_k sets of the variables and terminals of the grammar. The lookahead set $\text{LA}_k(uAv, A \rightarrow w)$, where $w = w_1 \ldots w_n$ and $v = v_1 \ldots v_m$, is given by

$$trunc_k(\text{FIRST}_k(w_1) \ldots \text{FIRST}_k(w_n)\text{FIRST}_k(v_1) \ldots \text{FIRST}_k(v_m)).$$

A parsing algorithm for LL(*k*) grammars can be obtained from Algorithm 15.7.1 by adding the construction of the local lookahead sets.

Algorithm 15.8.3
Deterministic Parser for an LL(*k*) Grammar

input: LL(*k*) grammar G = (V, Σ, P, S)
    string $p \in \Sigma^*$
    $\text{FIRST}_k(A)$ for every $A \in V$

1. $q := S$
2. **repeat**
   Let $q = uAv$ where A is the leftmost variable in q and
   let $p = uyz$ where $length(y) = k$.
   2.1. **for each** rule $A \to w$ construct the set $LA_k(uAv, A \to w)$
   2.2. **if** $y \in LA_k(uAv, A \to w)$ for some A rule **then** $q := uwv$
   until $q = p$ **or** $y \notin LA_k(uAv, A \to w)$ for all A rules
3. **if** $q = p$ **then** *accept* **else** *reject*

Exercises

1. Give the lookahead sets for each variable and rule of the following grammars.

   a) $S \to ABab \mid bAcc$
       $A \to a \mid c$
       $B \to b \mid c \mid \lambda$

   b) $S \to aS \mid A$
       $A \to ab \mid b$

   c) $S \to AB \mid ab$
       $A \to aA \mid \lambda$
       $B \to bB \mid \lambda$

   d) $S \to aAbBc$
       $A \to aA \mid cA \mid \lambda$
       $B \to bBc \mid bc$

2. Give the $FIRST_1$ and $FOLLOW_1$ sets for each of the variables of the following grammars. Which of these grammars are strong LL(1)?

   a) $S \to aAB\#$
       $A \to a \mid \lambda$
       $B \to b \mid \lambda$

   b) $S \to AB\#$
       $A \to aAb \mid B$
       $B \to aBc \mid \lambda$

   c) $S \to ABC\#$
       $A \to aA \mid \lambda$
       $B \to bBc \mid \lambda$
       $C \to cA \mid dB \mid \lambda$

   d) $S \to aAd\#$
       $A \to BCD$
       $B \to bB \mid \lambda$
       $C \to cC \mid \lambda$
       $D \to bD \mid \lambda$

3. Use Algorithms 15.4.1 and 15.5.1 to construct the $FIRST_2$ and $FOLLOW_2$ sets for variables of the following grammars. Construct the length-two lookahead sets for the rules of the grammars. Are these grammars strong LL(2)?

   a) $S \to ABC\#\#$
       $A \to aA \mid a$
       $B \to bB \mid \lambda$
       $C \to cC \mid a \mid b \mid c$

   b) $S \to A\#\#$
       $A \to bBA \mid BcAa \mid \lambda$
       $B \to acB \mid b$

4. Prove parts 3, 4, and 5 of Lemma 15.2.2.

5. Prove Theorem 15.3.3.

6. Show that each of the grammars defined below is not strong LL(k) for any k. Construct a deterministic PDA that accepts the language generated by the grammar.

a) $S \rightarrow aSb \mid A$
$A \rightarrow aAc \mid \lambda$

b) $S \rightarrow A \mid B$
$A \rightarrow aAb \mid ab$
$B \rightarrow aBc \mid ac$

c) $S \rightarrow A$
$A \rightarrow aAb \mid B$
$B \rightarrow aB \mid a$

7. Prove that Algorithm 15.5.1 generates the sets $FOLLOW_k(A)$.

8. Modify the grammars given below to obtain an equivalent strong LL(1). Build the lookahead sets to ensure that the modified grammar is strong LL(1).

a) $S \rightarrow A\#$
$A \rightarrow aB \mid Ab \mid Ac$
$B \rightarrow bBc \mid \lambda$

b) $S \rightarrow aA\# \mid abB\# \mid abcC\#$
$A \rightarrow aA \mid \lambda$
$B \rightarrow bB \mid \lambda$
$C \rightarrow cC \mid \lambda$

9. Parse the following strings with the LL(1) parser and the grammar AE_2. Trace the actions of the parser using the format of Example 15.7.1. The lookahead sets for AE_2 are given in Section 15.6.

a) $b+(b)\#$

b) $((b))\#$

c) $b+b+b\#$

d) $b++b\#$

10. Construct the lookahead sets for the rules of the grammar. What is the minimal k such that the grammar is strong LL(k)? Construct the lookahead sets for the combination of each sentential form and rule. What is the minimal k such that the grammar is LL(k)?

a) $S \rightarrow aAcaa \mid bAbcc$
$A \rightarrow a \mid ab \mid \lambda$

b) $S \rightarrow aAbc \mid bABbd$
$A \rightarrow a \mid \lambda$
$B \rightarrow a \mid b$

c) $S \rightarrow aAbB \mid bAbB$
$A \rightarrow ab \mid a$
$B \rightarrow aB \mid b$

11. Prove that a grammar is strong LL(1) if, and only if, it is LL(1).

12. Prove that a context-free grammar G is LL(k) if, and only if, the lookahead set $LA_k(uAv)$ is partitioned by the sets $LA_k(uAv, A \rightarrow w_i)$ for each sentential form uAv such that $S \underset{L}{\overset{*}{\Rightarrow}} uAv$.

Bibliographic Notes

Parsing with LL(*k*) grammars was introduced by Lewis and Stearns [1968]. The theory of LL(*k*) grammars and deterministic parsing was further developed in Rosenkrantz and Stearns [1970]. Relationships between the class of LL(*k*) languages and other classes of languages that can be parsed deterministically are examined in Aho and Ullman [1973]. The LL(*k*) hierarchy was presented in Kurki-Suonio [1969]. Foster [1968], Wood [1969], Stearns [1971], and Soisalon-Soininen and Ukkonen [1979] present techniques for modifying grammars to satisfy the LL(*k*) or strong LL(*k*) conditions.

The construction of compilers for languages defined by LL(1) grammars frequently employs the method of recursive descent. This approach allows the generation of machine code to accompany the syntax analysis. Several textbooks develop the relationships between LL(*k*) grammars, recursive descent syntax analysis, and compiler design. These include Lewis, Rosenkrantz, and Stearns [1976], Backhouse [1979], Barrett, Bates, Gustafson, and Couch [1986], and Pyster [1980]. A comprehensive introduction to syntax analysis and compiling can be found in Aho, Sethi, and Ullman [1986].

CHAPTER 16

LR(*k*) Grammars

A bottom-up parser generates a sequence of shifts and reductions to reduce the input string to the start symbol of the grammar. A deterministic parser must incorporate additional information into the process to select the correct alternative when more than one operation is possible. A grammar is LR(*k*) if a *k*-symbol lookahead provides sufficient information to make this selection. LR signifies that these strings are parsed in a left-to-right manner to construct a rightmost derivation. LR parsers generate right sentential forms, strings produced by derivations of the form $S \overset{*}{\underset{R}{\Rightarrow}} w$.

All derivations in this chapter are rightmost. We also assume that grammars have a nonrecursive start symbol and that all the symbols in a grammar are useful.

16.1 LR(0) Contexts

A deterministic bottom-up parser attempts to reduce the input string to the start symbol of the grammar. Nondeterminism in bottom-up parsing is illustrated by examining reductions of the string *aabb* using the grammar

$$\text{G: } S \rightarrow aAb \mid BaAa$$
$$A \rightarrow ab \mid b$$
$$B \rightarrow Bb \mid b.$$

The parser scans the prefix *aab* before finding a reducible substring. The suffixes *b* and *ab* of *aab* both constitute the right-hand side of a rule of G. Three reductions of *aabb* can be obtained by replacing these substrings.

Rule	Reduction
$A \rightarrow b$	$aaAb$
$A \rightarrow ab$	aAb
$B \rightarrow b$	$aaBb$

The objective of a bottom-up parser is to repeatedly reduce the input string until the start symbol is obtained. Can a reduction of *aabb* initiated with the rule $A \rightarrow b$ eventually produce the start symbol? Equivalently, is *aaAb* a right sentential form of G? Rightmost derivations of the grammar G have the form

$$S \Rightarrow aAb \Rightarrow aabb$$
$$S \Rightarrow aAb \Rightarrow abb$$
$$S \Rightarrow BaAa \Rightarrow Baaba \overset{i}{\Rightarrow} Bb^i aaba \Rightarrow bb^i aaba \qquad i \geq 0$$
$$S \Rightarrow BaAa \Rightarrow Baba \overset{i}{\Rightarrow} Bb^i aba \Rightarrow bb^i aba \qquad i \geq 0.$$

Successful reductions of strings in L(G) can be obtained by "reversing the arrows" in the preceding derivations. Since the strings *aaAb* and *aaBb* do not occur in any of these derivations, a reduction of *aabb* initiated by the rule $A \rightarrow b$ or $B \rightarrow b$ cannot produce S. With this additional information, the parser need only reduce *aab* using the rule $A \rightarrow ab$.

Successful reductions were obtained by examining rightmost derivations of G. A parser that does not use lookahead must decide whether to perform a reduction with a rule $A \rightarrow w$ as soon as a string *uw* is scanned by the parser.

Definition 16.1.1

Let G = (V, Σ, P, S) be a context-free grammar. The string *uw* is an **LR(0) context** of a rule $A \rightarrow w$ if there is a derivation

$$S \overset{*}{\underset{R}{\Rightarrow}} uAv \underset{R}{\Rightarrow} uwv$$

where $u \in (V \cup \Sigma)^*$ and $v \in \Sigma^*$. The set of LR(0) contexts of the rule $A \rightarrow w$ is denoted LR(0)-CONTEXT($A \rightarrow w$).

The LR(0) contexts of a rule $A \rightarrow w$ are obtained from the rightmost derivations that terminate with the application of the rule. In terms of reductions, *uw* is an LR(0) context of $A \rightarrow w$ if there is a reduction of a string *uwv* to S that begins by replacing *w* with *A*. If *uw* $\notin$ LR(0)-CONTEXT($A \rightarrow w$) then there is no sequence of reductions beginning with $A \rightarrow w$ that produces S from a string of the form *uwv* with $v \in \Sigma^*$. The LR(0) contexts, if known, can be used to eliminate reductions from consideration by the parser. The parser need only reduce a string *uw* with the rule $A \rightarrow w$ when *uw* is an LR(0) context of $A \rightarrow w$.

The LR(0) contexts of the rules of G are constructed from the rightmost derivations of G. To determine the LR(0) contexts of $S \to aAb$ we consider all rightmost derivations that contain an application of the rule $S \to aAb$.

$$S \Rightarrow aAb \Rightarrow aabb$$
$$S \Rightarrow aAb \Rightarrow abb$$

The only rightmost derivation terminating with the application of $S \to aAb$ is $S \Rightarrow aAb$. Thus LR(0)-CONTEXT($S \to aAb$) = $\{aAb\}$.

The LR(0) contexts of $A \to ab$ are obtained from the rightmost derivations that terminate with an application of $A \to ab$. There are only two such derivations. The reduction is indicated by the arrow from ab to A. The context is the prefix of the sentential form up to and including the occurrence of ab that is reduced.

$$S \Rightarrow aAb \Rightarrow aabb$$

$$S \Rightarrow BaAa \Rightarrow Baaba$$

Consequently, the LR(0) contexts of $A \to ab$ are aab and $Baab$. In a similar manner we can obtain the LR(0) contexts for all the rules of G.

Rule	LR(0) Contexts
$S \to aAb$	$\{aAb\}$
$S \to BaAa$	$\{BaAa\}$
$A \to ab$	$\{aab, Baab\}$
$A \to b$	$\{ab, Bab\}$
$B \to Bb$	$\{Bb\}$
$B \to b$	$\{b\}$

Example 16.1.1

The LR(0) contexts are constructed for the rules of the grammar

$$S \to aA \mid bB$$
$$A \to abA \mid bB$$
$$B \to bBc \mid bc.$$

The rightmost derivations initiated by the rule $S \to aA$ have the form

$$S \Rightarrow aA \overset{i}{\Rightarrow} a(ab)^i A \Rightarrow a(ab)^i bB \overset{j}{\Rightarrow} a(ab)^i bb^j Bc^j \Rightarrow a(ab)^i bb^j bcc^j$$

where $i, j \geq 0$. Derivations beginning with $S \to bB$ can be written

$$S \Rightarrow bB \overset{i}{\Rightarrow} bb^i Bc^i \Rightarrow bb^i bcc^i.$$

The LR(0) contexts can be obtained from the sentential forms generated in the preceding derivations.

Rule	LR(0) Contexts
$S \rightarrow aA$	$\{aA\}$
$S \rightarrow bB$	$\{bB\}$
$A \rightarrow abA$	$\{a(ab)^iA \mid i > 0\}$
$A \rightarrow bB$	$\{a(ab)^ibB \mid i \geq 0\}$
$B \rightarrow bBc$	$\{a(ab)^ibb^jBc,\ bb^jBc \mid i \geq 0, j > 0\}$
$B \rightarrow bc$	$\{a(ab)^ibb^jc,\ bb^jc \mid i \geq 0, j > 0\}$

$\square$

The contexts can be used to eliminate reductions from consideration by the parser. When the LR(0) contexts provide sufficient information to eliminate all but one action, the grammar is called an LR(0) grammar.

Definition 16.1.2

A context-free grammar $G = (V, \Sigma, P, S)$ with nonrecursive start symbol S is **LR(0)** if for every $u \in (V \cup \Sigma)^*$ and $v \in \Sigma^*$,

$$u \in \text{LR(0)-CONTEXT}(A \rightarrow w_1) \qquad \text{and} \qquad uv \in \text{LR(0)-CONTEXT}(B \rightarrow w_2)$$

implies $v = \lambda$, $A = B$, and $w_1 = w_2$.

The contexts of an LR(0) grammar provide the information needed to select the appropriate action. Upon scanning the string u, the parser takes one of three mutually exclusive actions:

1. If $u \in \text{LR(0)-CONTEXT}(A \rightarrow w)$, then u is reduced with the rule $A \rightarrow w$.
2. If u is not an LR(0) context but is a prefix of some LR(0) context, then the parser effects a shift.
3. If u is not the prefix of any LR(0) context, then the input string is rejected.

Since a string u is an LR(0) context for at most one rule $A \rightarrow w$, the first condition specifies a unique action. A string u is called a **viable prefix** if there is a string $v \in (V \cup \Sigma)^*$ such that uv is an LR(0) context. If u is a viable prefix and not an LR(0) context, a sequence of shift operations produces the LR(0) context uv.

Example 16.1.2

The grammar

$$G: S \rightarrow aA \mid aB$$
$$A \rightarrow aAb \mid b$$
$$B \rightarrow bBa \mid b$$

is not LR(0). The rightmost derivations of G have the form

$$S \Rightarrow aA \overset{i}{\Rightarrow} aa^iAb^i \Rightarrow aa^ibb^i$$
$$S \Rightarrow aB \overset{i}{\Rightarrow} ab^iBa^i \Rightarrow ab^iba^i$$

for $i \geq 0$. The LR(0) contexts for the rules of the grammar can be obtained from the right sentential forms in the preceding derivations.

Rule	LR(0) Contexts
$S \rightarrow aA$	$\{aA\}$
$S \rightarrow aB$	$\{aB\}$
$A \rightarrow aAb$	$\{aa^iAb \mid i > 0\}$
$A \rightarrow b$	$\{aa^ib \mid i \geq 0\}$
$B \rightarrow bBa$	$\{ab^iBa \mid i > 0\}$
$B \rightarrow b$	$\{ab^i \mid i > 0\}$

The grammar G is not LR(0) since ab is an LR(0) context of both $B \rightarrow b$ and $A \rightarrow b$.

$\square$

16.2   An LR(0) Parser

Incorporating the information provided by the LR(0) contexts of the rules of an LR(0) grammar into a bottom-up parser produces a deterministic algorithm. The input string p is scanned in a left-to-right manner. The action of the parser in Algorithm 16.2.1 is determined by comparing the LR(0) contexts with the string scanned. The string u is the prefix of the sentential form scanned by the parser, and v is the remainder of the input string. The operation $shift(u, v)$ removes the first symbol from v and concatenates it to the right end of u.

Algorithm 16.2.1
Parser for an LR(0) Grammar

input: LR(0) grammar $G = (V, \Sigma, P, S)$
     string $p \in \Sigma^*$

1. $u := \lambda, v := p$

2. dead-end $:= false$

3. **repeat**
     3.1. **if** $u \in$ LR(0)-CONTEXT$(A \rightarrow w)$ for the rule $A \rightarrow w$ in P
          where $u = xw$ **then** $u := xA$
          else if u is a viable prefix **and** $v \neq \lambda$ **then** $shift(u, v)$
               else dead-end $:= true$
    until $u = S$ **or** dead-end

4. **if** $u = S$ **then** accept **else** reject

The decision to reduce with the rule $A \rightarrow w$ is made as soon as a substring $u = xw$ is encountered. The decision does not use any information contained in v, the unscanned portion of the string. The parser does not look beyond the string xw; hence the zero in LR(0) indicating no lookahead is required.

One detail has been overlooked in Algorithm 16.2.1. No technique has been provided for deciding whether a string is a viable prefix or an LR(0) context of a rule of the grammar. This omission is remedied in the next section.

Example 16.2.1

The string *aabbbcc* is parsed using the rules and LR(0) contexts of the grammar presented in Example 16.1.1 and the parsing algorithm for LR(0) grammars.

u	*v*	Rule	Action
λ	*aabbbcc*		shift
a	*abbbcc*		shift
aa	*bbbcc*		shift
aab	*bbcc*		shift
aabb	*bcc*		shift
aabbb	*bcc*		shift
aabbbb	*cc*		shift
aabbbbc	*c*	$B \rightarrow bc$	reduce
aabbbB	*c*		shift
aabbbBc	λ	$B \rightarrow bBc$	reduce
aabbB	λ	$A \rightarrow bB$	reduce
aabA	λ	$A \rightarrow abA$	reduce
aA	λ	$S \rightarrow aA$	reduce
S			

□

16.3   The LR(0) Machine

A rule may contain infinitely many LR(0) contexts. Moreover, there is no upper bound on the length of the contexts. These properties make it impossible to generate the complete set of LR(0) contexts for an arbitrary context-free grammar. The problem of dealing with infinite sets was avoided in LL(*k*) grammars by restricting the length of the lookahead strings. Unfortunately, the decision to reduce a string requires knowledge of the entire scanned string (the context). The LR(0) grammars G_1 and G_2 demonstrate this dependence.

The LR(0) contexts of the rules $A \rightarrow aAb$ and $A \rightarrow ab$ of G_1 form disjoint sets that satisfy the prefix conditions. If these sets are truncated at any length k, the string a^k will be an element of both of the truncated sets. The final two symbols of the context are required to discriminate between these reductions.

Rule	LR(0) Contexts
G_1: $S \to A$	$\{A\}$
$A \to aAa$	$\{a^i Aa \mid i > 0\}$
$A \to aAb$	$\{a^i Ab \mid i > 0\}$
$A \to ab$	$\{a^i b \mid i > 0\}$

One may be tempted to consider only fixed-length suffixes of contexts, since a reduction alters the suffix of the scanned string. The grammar G_2 exhibits the futility of this approach.

Rule	LR(0) Contexts
G_2: $S \to A$	$\{A\}$
$S \to bB$	$\{bB\}$
$A \to aA$	$\{a^i A \mid i > 0\}$
$A \to ab$	$\{a^i b \mid i > 0\}$
$B \to aB$	$\{ba^i B \mid i > 0\}$
$B \to ab$	$\{ba^i b \mid i > 0\}$

The sole difference between the LR(0) contexts of $A \to ab$ and $B \to ab$ is the first element of the string. A parser will be unable to discriminate between these rules if the selection process uses only fixed-length suffixes of the LR(0) contexts.

The grammars G_1 and G_2 demonstrate that the entire scanned string is required by the LR(0) parser to select the appropriate action. This does not imply that the complete set of LR(0) contexts is required. For a given grammar, a finite automaton can be constructed whose computations determine whether a string is a viable prefix of the grammar. The states of the machine are constructed from the rules of the grammar.

Definition 16.3.1

Let $G = (V, \Sigma, P, S)$ be a context-free grammar. The **LR(0) items** of G are defined by

i) if $A \to uv \in P$, then $A \to u.v$ is an LR(0) item

ii) if $A \to \lambda \in P$, then $A \to .$ is an LR(0) item.

The LR(0) items are obtained from the rules of the grammar by placing the marker $.$ in the right-hand side of a rule. An item $A \to u.$ is called a **complete item**. A rule whose right-hand side has length n generates $n + 1$ items.

Definition 16.3.2

Let $G = (V, \Sigma, P, S)$ be a context-free grammar. The **nondeterministic LR(0) machine** of G is an NFA-λ $M = (Q, V \cup \Sigma, \delta, q_0, Q)$ where Q is the set of LR(0) items augmented with the state q_0. The transition function is defined by

i) $\delta(q_0, \lambda) = \{S \rightarrow .w \mid S \rightarrow w \in P\}$

ii) $\delta(A \rightarrow u.av, a) = \{A \rightarrow ua.v\}$

iii) $\delta(A \rightarrow u.Bv, B) = \{A \rightarrow uB.v\}$

iv) $\delta(A \rightarrow u.Bv, \lambda) = \{B \rightarrow .w \mid B \rightarrow w \in P\}$.

The computations of the nondeterministic LR(0) machine M of a grammar G completely process strings that are viable prefixes of the grammar. All other computations halt prior to reading the entire input. Since all the states of M are accepting, M accepts precisely the viable prefixes of the original grammar. A computation of M records the progress made toward matching the right-hand side of a rule of G. The item $A \rightarrow u.v$ indicates that the string u has been scanned and the automaton is looking for the string v to complete the match.

The symbol following the marker in an item defines the arcs leaving a node. If the marker precedes a terminal, the only arc leaving the node is labeled by that terminal. Arcs labeled B or λ may leave a node containing an item of the form $A \rightarrow u.Bv$. To extend the match of the right-hand side of the rule, the machine is looking for a B. The node $A \rightarrow uB.v$ is entered if the parser reads B. It is also looking for strings that may produce B. The variable B may be obtained by reduction using a B rule. Consequently, the parser is also looking for the right-hand side of a B rule. This is indicated by lambda transitions to the items $B \rightarrow .w$.

Definition 16.3.2, the LR(0) items, and the LR(0) contexts of the rules of the grammar G given below are used to demonstrate the recognition of viable prefixes by the associated NFA-λ.

Rule	LR(0) Items	LR(0) Contexts
$S \rightarrow AB$	$S \rightarrow .AB$ $S \rightarrow A.B$ $S \rightarrow AB.$	$\{AB\}$
$A \rightarrow Aa$	$A \rightarrow .Aa$ $A \rightarrow A.a$ $A \rightarrow Aa.$	$\{Aa\}$
$A \rightarrow a$	$A \rightarrow .a$ $A \rightarrow a.$	$\{a\}$
$B \rightarrow bBa$	$B \rightarrow .bBa$ $B \rightarrow b.Ba$ $B \rightarrow bB.a$ $B \rightarrow bBa.$	$\{Ab^iBa \mid i > 0\}$
$B \rightarrow ba$	$B \rightarrow .ba$ $B \rightarrow b.a$ $B \rightarrow ba.$	$\{Ab^iba \mid i \geq 0\}$

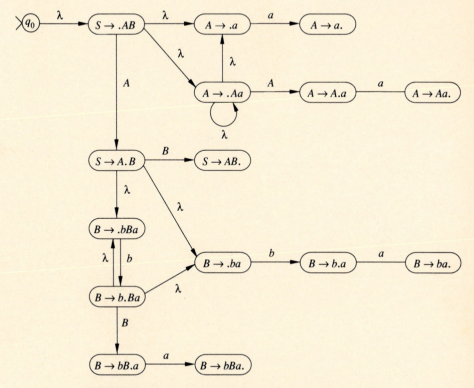

FIGURE 16.1   Nondeterministic LR(0) machine of G.

The NFA-λ in Fig. 16.1 is the LR(0) machine of the grammar G. A string w is a prefix of a context of the rule $A \rightarrow uv$ if $A \rightarrow u.v \in \hat{\delta}(q_0, w)$. The computation $\hat{\delta}(q_0, A)$ of the LR(0) machine in Fig. 16.1 halts in the states containing the items $A \rightarrow A.a$, $S \rightarrow A.B$, $B \rightarrow .bBa$, and $B \rightarrow .ba$. These are precisely the rules that have LR(0) contexts beginning with A. Similarly, the computation with input AbB indicates that AbB is a viable prefix of the rule $B \rightarrow bBa$ and no other.

The techniques presented in Chapter 6 can be used to construct an equivalent DFA from the nondeterministic LR(0) machine of G. This machine, the **deterministic LR(0) machine** of G, is given in Fig. 16.2. The start state q_s of the deterministic machine is the lambda closure of the q_0, the start state of the nondeterministic machine. The state that represents failure, the empty set, has been omitted. When the computation obtained by processing the string u successfully terminates, u is an LR(0) context or a viable prefix. Algorithm 16.3.3 incorporates the LR(0) machine into the LR(0) parsing strategy.

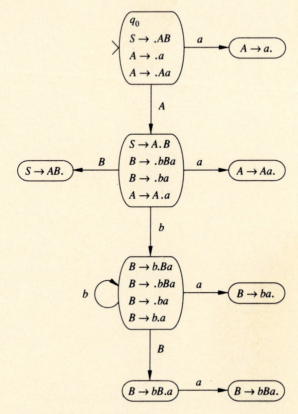

FIGURE 16.2   Deterministic LR(0) machine of G.

Algorithm 16.3.3
Parser Utilizing the Deterministic LR(0) Machine

input: LR(0) grammar $G = (V, \Sigma, P, S)$
     string $p \in \Sigma^*$
     deterministic LR(0) machine of G

1. $u := \lambda$, $v := p$
2. dead-end $:= \textit{false}$
3. **repeat**
       3.1. **if** $\hat{\delta}(q_s, u)$ contains $A \rightarrow w.$ where $u = xw$ **then** $u := xA$
             else if $\hat{\delta}(q_s, u)$ contains an item $A \rightarrow y.z$ and $v \neq \lambda$ **then** $\textit{shift}(u, v)$
                   else dead-end $:= \textit{true}$
       until $u = S$ or dead-end
4. **if** $u = S$ **then** accept **else** reject

Example 16.3.1

The string *aabbaa* is parsed using Algorithm 16.3.3 and the deterministic LR(0) machine in Fig. 16.2.

u	v	Computation		Action
λ	aabbaa	$\hat{\delta}(q_s, \lambda) =$	$\{S \rightarrow .AB,$ $A \rightarrow .a,$ $A \rightarrow .Aa\}$	shift
a	abbaa	$\hat{\delta}(q_s, a) =$	$\{A \rightarrow a.\}$	reduce
A	abbaa	$\hat{\delta}(q_s, A) =$	$\{A \rightarrow A.a,$ $S \rightarrow A.B,$ $B \rightarrow .bBa,$ $B \rightarrow .ba\}$	shift
Aa	bbaa	$\hat{\delta}(q_s, Aa) =$	$\{A \rightarrow Aa.\}$	reduce
A	bbaa	$\hat{\delta}(q_s, A) =$	$\{A \rightarrow A.a,$ $S \rightarrow A.B,$ $B \rightarrow .bBa,$ $B \rightarrow .ba\}$	shift
Ab	baa	$\hat{\delta}(q_s, Ab) =$	$\{B \rightarrow .bBa,$ $B \rightarrow b.Ba,$ $B \rightarrow .ba,$ $B \rightarrow b.a\}$	shift
Abb	aa	$\hat{\delta}(q_s, Abb) =$	$\{B \rightarrow .bBa,$ $B \rightarrow b.Ba,$ $B \rightarrow .ba,$ $B \rightarrow b.a\}$	shift
Abba	a	$\hat{\delta}(q_s, Abba) =$	$\{B \rightarrow ba.\}$	reduce
AbB	a	$\hat{\delta}(q_s, AbB) =$	$\{B \rightarrow bB.a\}$	shift
AbBa	λ	$\hat{\delta}(q_s, AbBa) =$	$\{B \rightarrow bBa.\}$	reduce
AB	λ	$\hat{\delta}(q_s, AB) =$	$\{S \rightarrow AB.\}$	reduce
S				

Upon processing the leading *a*, the machine enters the state $A \rightarrow a.$ specifying a reduction using the rule $A \rightarrow a$. Since $\hat{\delta}(q_s, A)$ does not contain a complete item, the parser shifts and constructs the string *Aa*. The computation $\hat{\delta}(q_s, Aa) = \{A \rightarrow Aa.\}$ indicates that *Aa* is an LR(0) context of $A \rightarrow Aa$ and that it is not a prefix of a context of any other rule. Having generated a complete item, the parser reduces the string using the rule $A \rightarrow Aa$. The shift and reduction cycle continues until the sentential form is reduced to the start symbol *S*.   □

16.4   Acceptance by the LR(0) Machine

The LR(0) machine has been constructed to decide whether a string is a viable prefix of the grammar. Theorem 16.4.1 establishes that computations of the LR(0) machine provide the desired information.

Theorem 16.4.1

Let G be a context-free grammar and M the nondeterministic LR(0) machine of G. The LR(0) item $A \to u.v$ is in $\hat{\delta}(q_0, w)$ if, and only if, $w = pu$ where puv is an LR(0) context of $A \to uv$.

Proof   Let $A \to u.v$ be an element of $\hat{\delta}(q_0, w)$. We prove, by induction on the number of transitions in the computation $\hat{\delta}(q_0, w)$, that wv is an LR(0) context of $A \to uv$.

The basis consists of computations of length one. All such computations have the form

where $S \to q$ is a rule of the grammar. These computations process the input string $w = \lambda$. Setting $p = \lambda$, $u = \lambda$, and $v = q$ gives the desired decomposition of w.

Now let $\hat{\delta}(q_0, w)$ be a computation of length $k > 1$ with $A \to u.v$ in $\hat{\delta}(q_0, w)$. Isolating the final transition, this computation can be written $\delta(\hat{\delta}(q_0, y), x)$ where $w = yx$ and $x \in V \cup \Sigma \cup \{\lambda\}$. The remainder of the proof is divided into three cases.

Case 1: $x = a \in \Sigma$: Then $u = u'a$. The final transition of the computation has the form

$$A \to u'.av \xrightarrow{a} A \to u'a.v$$

By the inductive hypothesis, $yu'av = wv$ is an LR(0) context of $A \to uv$.

Case 2: $x \in V$: The proof is similar to that of Case 1.

Case 3: $x = \lambda$: Then $y = w$ and the computation terminates at an item $A \to .v$. The final transition has the form

$$B \to r.As \xrightarrow{\lambda} A \to .v$$

The inductive hypothesis implies that w can be written $w = pr$ where $prAs$ is an LR(0) context of $B \to rAs$. Thus there is a rightmost derivation

$$S \overset{*}{\underset{R}{\Rightarrow}} pBq \underset{R}{\Rightarrow} prAsq.$$

The application of $A \to v$ yields

$$S \overset{*}{\underset{R}{\Rightarrow}} pBq \underset{R}{\Rightarrow} prAsq \underset{R}{\Rightarrow} prvsq.$$

The final step of this derivation shows that $prv = wv$ is an LR(0) context of $A \to v$.

To establish the opposite implication we must show that $\hat{\delta}(q_0, pu)$ contains the item $A \to u.v$ whenever puv is an LR(0) context of a rule $A \to uv$. First we note that if $\hat{\delta}(q_0, p)$ contains $A \to .uv$, then $\hat{\delta}(q_0, pu)$ contains $A \to u.v$. This follows immediately from conditions ii) and iii) of Definition 16.3.2.

Since puv is an LR(0) context of $A \to uv$, there is a derivation

$$S \overset{*}{\underset{R}{\Rightarrow}} pAq \underset{R}{\Rightarrow} puvq.$$

We prove, by induction on the length of the derivation $S \overset{*}{\underset{R}{\Rightarrow}} pAq$, that $\hat{\delta}(q_0, p)$ contains $A \to .uv$. The basis consists of derivations $S \Rightarrow pAq$ of length one. The desired computation consists of traversing the lambda arc to $S \to .pAq$ followed by the arcs that process the string p. The computation is completed by following the lambda arc from $S \to p.Aq$ to $A \to .uv$.

Now consider a derivation in which the variable A is introduced on the kth rule application.

$$S \overset{k-1}{\underset{R}{\Longrightarrow}} xBy \underset{R}{\Rightarrow} xwAzy$$

The inductive hypothesis asserts that $\hat{\delta}(q_0, x)$ contains the item $B \to .wAz$. Hence $B \to w.Az \in \hat{\delta}(q_0, xw)$. The lambda transition to $A \to .uv$ completes the computation. ∎

The relationships in Lemma 16.4.2 between derivations in a context-free grammar and the items in the nodes of the deterministic LR(0) machine of the grammar follow from Theorem 16.4.1. The proof of Lemma 16.4.2 is left as an exercise. Recall that q_s is the start symbol of the deterministic machine.

Lemma 16.4.2

Let M be the deterministic LR(0) machine of a context-free grammar G. Assume $\hat{\delta}(q_s, w)$ contains an item $A \to u.Bv$.

i) If $B \overset{*}{\Rightarrow} \lambda$, then $\hat{\delta}(q_s, w)$ contains an item of the form $C \to .$ for some variable $C \in V$.

ii) If $B \overset{*}{\Rightarrow} v \in \Sigma^+$, then there is an arc labeled by a terminal symbol leaving the node $\hat{\delta}(q_s, w)$ or $\hat{\delta}(q_s, w)$ contains an item of the form $C \to .$ for some variable $C \in V$.

Lemma 16.4.3

Let M be the deterministic LR(0) machine of an LR(0) grammar G. Assume $\hat{\delta}(q_s, u)$ contains the complete item $A \to w..$. Then $\hat{\delta}(q_s, ua)$ is undefined for all terminal symbols $a \in \Sigma$.

Proof By Theorem 16.4.1, u is an LR(0) context of $A \rightarrow w$. Assume that $\hat{\delta}(q_s, ua)$ is defined for some terminal a. Then ua is a prefix of an LR(0) context of some rule $B \rightarrow y$. This implies that there is a derivation

$$S \overset{*}{\underset{R}{\Rightarrow}} pBv \Rightarrow pyv = uazv$$

with $z \in (V \cup \Sigma)^*$ and $v \in \Sigma^*$. Consider the possibilities for the string z. If $z \in \Sigma^*$ then uaz is an LR(0) context of the rule $B \rightarrow y$. If z is not a terminal string, then there is a terminal string derivable from z.

$$z \overset{*}{\underset{R}{\Rightarrow}} rCs \Rightarrow rts \qquad r, s, t \in \Sigma^*$$

Combining the derivations shows that $uart$ is an LR(0) context of $C \rightarrow t$. In either case, u is an LR(0) context and ua is a viable prefix. This contradicts the assumption that G is LR(0). ∎

The previous results can be combined with Definition 16.1.2 to obtain a characterization of LR(0) grammars in terms of the structure of the deterministic LR(0) machine.

Theorem 16.4.4

Let G be a context-free grammar with a nonrecursive start symbol. G is LR(0) if, and only if, the extended transition function $\hat{\delta}$ of the deterministic LR(0) machine of G satisfies the following conditions:

i) If $\hat{\delta}(q_s, u)$ contains a complete item $A \rightarrow w$. with $w \neq \lambda$, then $\hat{\delta}(q_s, u)$ contains no other items.

ii) If $\hat{\delta}(q_s, u)$ contains a complete item $A \rightarrow .$, then the marker is followed by a variable in all other items in $\hat{\delta}(q_s, u)$.

Proof First we show that a grammar G with nonrecursive start symbol is LR(0) when the extended transition function satisfies conditions i) and ii). Let u be an LR(0) context of the rule $A \rightarrow w$. Then $\hat{\delta}(q_s, uv)$ is defined only when v begins with a variable. Thus, for all strings $v \in \Sigma^*$, $uv \in$ LR(0)-CONTEXT$(B \rightarrow x)$ implies $v = \lambda$, $B = A$, and $w = x$.

Conversely, let G be an LR(0) grammar and u an LR(0) context of the rule $A \rightarrow w$. By Theorem 16.4.1, $\hat{\delta}(q_s, u)$ contains the complete item $A \rightarrow w.$. The state $\hat{\delta}(q_s, u)$ does not contain any other complete items $B \rightarrow v.$ since this would imply that u is also an LR(0) context of $B \rightarrow v$. By Lemma 16.4.3, all arcs leaving $\hat{\delta}(q_s, u)$ must be labeled by variables.

Now assume that $\hat{\delta}(q_s, u)$ contains a complete item $A \rightarrow w.$ where $w \neq \lambda$. By Lemma 16.4.2, if there is an arc labeled by a variable with tail $\hat{\delta}(q_s, u)$ then $\hat{\delta}(q_s, u)$ contains a complete item $C \rightarrow .$ or $\hat{\delta}(q_s, u)$ has an arc labeled by a terminal leaving it. In the former case, u is an LR(0) context of both $A \rightarrow w$ and $C \rightarrow \lambda$ contradicting the assumption that G is LR(0). The latter possibility contradicts Lemma 16.4.3. Thus $A \rightarrow w.$ is the only item in $\hat{\delta}(q_s, u)$. ∎

Intuitively we would like to say that a grammar is LR(0) if a state containing a complete item contains no other items. This condition is satisfied by all states containing complete items generated by nonnull rules. The previous theorem permits a state containing $A \rightarrow$. to contain items in which the marker is followed by a variable. Consider the derivation using the rules $S \rightarrow aABc$, $A \rightarrow \lambda$, and $B \rightarrow b$.

$$S \underset{R}{\Rightarrow} aABc \underset{R}{\Rightarrow} aAbc \underset{R}{\Rightarrow} abc$$

The string a is an LR(0) context of $A \rightarrow \lambda$ and a prefix of aAb, which is an LR(0) context of $B \rightarrow b$. The effect of reductions by lambda rules in an LR(0) parser is demonstrated in Example 16.4.1.

Example 16.4.1

The deterministic LR(0) machine for the grammar

$$\text{G: } S \rightarrow BAAb$$
$$A \rightarrow \lambda$$
$$B \rightarrow b$$

is given below. The analysis of the string bb is traced using the computations of the machine to specify the actions of the parser.

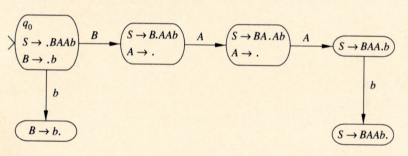

u	v	Computation		Action
λ	bb	$\hat{\delta}(q_s, \lambda) =$	$\{S \rightarrow .BAAb$ $B \rightarrow .b\}$	shift
b	b	$\hat{\delta}(q_s, b) =$	$\{B \rightarrow b.\}$	reduce
B	b	$\hat{\delta}(q_s, B) =$	$\{S \rightarrow B.AAb$ $A \rightarrow .\}$	reduce
BA	b	$\hat{\delta}(q_s, BA) =$	$\{S \rightarrow BA.Ab$ $A \rightarrow .\}$	reduce
BAA	b	$\hat{\delta}(q_s, BAA) = \{S \rightarrow BAA.b\}$		shift
$BAAb$	λ	$\hat{\delta}(q_s, BAAb) = \{S \rightarrow BAAb.\}$		reduce
S				

The parser reduces the sentential form with the rule $A \rightarrow \lambda$ whenever the LR(0) machine halts in a state containing the complete item $A \rightarrow$ .. This reduction adds an A to the end of the currently scanned string. In the next iteration, the LR(0) machine follows the arc labeled A to the subsequent state. An A is generated by a lambda reduction only when its presence adds to the prefix of an item being recognized. □

Theorem 16.4.4 establishes a procedure for deciding whether a grammar is LR(0). The process begins by constructing the deterministic LR(0) machine of the grammar. A grammar with a nonrecursive start symbol is LR(0) if the restrictions imposed by conditions ii) and iii) of Theorem 16.4.4 are satisfied by the LR(0) machine.

Example 16.4.2

The grammar AE augmented with the endmarker #

$$AE: S \rightarrow A\#$$
$$A \rightarrow A + T \mid T$$
$$T \rightarrow b \mid (A)$$

is LR(0). The deterministic LR(0) machine of AE is given in Fig. 16.3. Since each of the states containing a complete item is a singleton set, the grammar is LR(0). □

Example 16.4.3

The grammar

$$S \rightarrow A\#$$
$$A \rightarrow A + T \mid T$$
$$T \rightarrow F \cdot T \mid F$$
$$F \rightarrow b \mid (A)$$

is not LR(0). This grammar is obtained by adding the variable F (factor) to AE to generate multiplicative subexpressions. We show that this grammar is not LR(0) by constructing two states of the deterministic LR(0) machine.

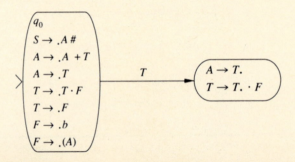

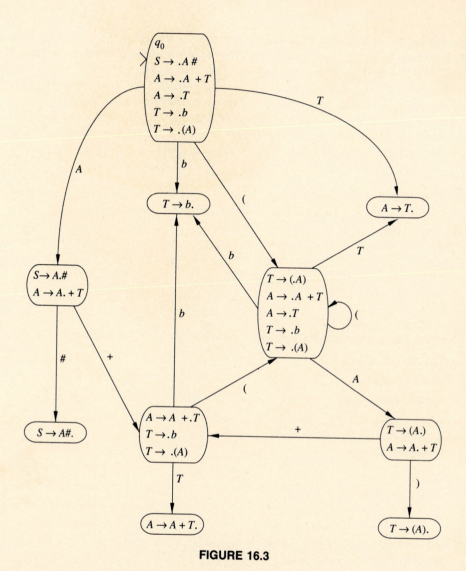

FIGURE 16.3

The computation generated by processing T contains the complete item $A \to T.$ and the item $T \to T. \cdot F$. When the parser scans the string T, there are two possible courses of action: reduce using $A \to T$ or shift in an attempt to construct the string $T \cdot F$.   □

16.5 LR(1) Grammars

The LR(0) conditions are generally too restrictive to construct grammars that define programming languages. In this section the LR parser is modified to utilize information obtained by looking beyond the substring that matches the right-hand side of the rule. The lookahead is limited to a single symbol. The definitions and algorithms, with obvious modifications, can be extended to utilize a lookahead of arbitrary length.

A grammar in which strings can be deterministically parsed using a one-symbol lookahead is called LR(1). The lookahead symbol is the symbol to the immediate right of the substring to be reduced by the parser. The decision to reduce with the rule $A \to w$ is made upon scanning a string of the form uwz where $z \in \Sigma \cup \{\lambda\}$. Following the example of LR(0) grammars, a string uwz is called an **LR(1) context** if there is a derivation

$$S \underset{R}{\overset{*}{\Rightarrow}} uAv \underset{R}{\Rightarrow} uwv$$

where z is the first symbol of v or the null string if $v = \lambda$. Since the derivation constructed by a bottom-up parser is rightmost, the lookahead symbol z is either a terminal symbol or the null string.

The role of the lookahead symbol in reducing the number of possibilities that must be examined by the parser is demonstrated by considering reductions in the grammar

$$G: S \to A \mid Bc$$
$$A \to aA \mid a$$
$$B \to a \mid ab.$$

When an LR(0) parser reads the symbol a, there are three possible actions:

i) Reduce with $A \to a$.

ii) Reduce with $B \to a$.

iii) Shift to obtain either aA or ab.

One-symbol lookahead is sufficient to determine the appropriate operation. The symbol underlined in each of the following derivations is the lookahead symbol when the initial a is scanned by the parser.

$S \Rightarrow A$	$S \Rightarrow A$	$S \Rightarrow Bc$	$S \Rightarrow Bc$
$\Rightarrow \underline{a}$	$\Rightarrow a\underline{A}$	$\Rightarrow a\underline{c}$	$\Rightarrow a\underline{b}c$
	$\Rightarrow aa\underline{A}$		
	$\Rightarrow aa\underline{a}$		

In the preceding grammar, the action of the parser when reading an a is completely determined by the lookahead symbol.

String Scanned	Lookahead Symbol	Action
a	λ	reduce with $A \to a$
a	a	shift
a	b	shift
a	c	reduce with $B \to a$

The action of an LR(0) parser is determined by the result of a computation of the LR(0) machine of the grammar. An LR(1) parser incorporates the lookahead symbol into the decision procedure. An LR(1) item is an ordered pair consisting of an LR(0) item and a set containing the possible lookahead symbols.

Definition 16.5.1

Let $G = (V, \Sigma, P, S)$ be a context-free grammar. The **LR(1) items** of G have the form

$$[A \rightarrow u.v, \{z_1, z_2, \ldots, z_n\}]$$

where $A \rightarrow uv \in P$ and $z_i \in \Sigma \cup \{\lambda\}$. The set $\{z_1, z_2, \ldots, z_n\}$ is the lookahead set of the LR(1) item.

The lookahead set of an item $[A \rightarrow u.v, \{z_1, \ldots, z_n\}]$ consists of the first symbol in the terminal strings y that follow uv in rightmost derivations

$$S \underset{R}{\overset{*}{\Rightarrow}} xAy \underset{R}{\Rightarrow} xuvy.$$

Since the S rules are nonrecursive, the only derivation terminated by a rule $S \rightarrow w$ is the derivation $S \Rightarrow w$. The null string follows w in this derivation. Consequently, the lookahead set of an S rule is always the singleton set $\{\lambda\}$.

As before, a complete item is an item in which the marker follows the entire right-hand side of the rule. The LR(1) machine, which specifies the actions of an LR(1) parser, is constructed from the LR(1) items of the grammar.

Definition 16.5.2

Let $G = (V, \Sigma, P, S)$ be a context-free grammar. The **nondeterministic LR(1) machine** of G is an NFA-λ $M = (Q, V \cup \Sigma, \delta, q_0, Q)$, where Q is a set of LR(1) items augmented with the state q_0. The transition function is defined by

i) $\delta(q_0, \lambda) = [\{S \rightarrow .w, \{\lambda\}\} \mid S \rightarrow w \in P]$

ii) $\delta([A \rightarrow u.Bv, \{z_1, \ldots, z_n\}], B) = \{[A \rightarrow uB.v, \{z_1, \ldots, z_n\}]\}$

iii) $\delta([A \rightarrow u.av, \{z_1, \ldots, z_n\}], a) = \{[A \rightarrow ua.v, \{z_1, \ldots, z_n\}]\}$

iv) $\delta([A \rightarrow u.Bv, \{z_1, \ldots, z_n\}], \lambda) = \{[B \rightarrow .w, \{y_1, \ldots, y_k\}] \mid B \rightarrow w \in P\}$
    where $y_i \in \text{FIRST}_1(vz_j)$ for some $j\}$

Disregarding the lookahead sets, the transitions of the LR(1) machine defined in i), ii), and iii) have the same form as those of the LR(0) machine. The LR(1) item $[A \rightarrow u.v, \{z_1, \ldots, z_n\}]$ indicates that the parser has scanned the string u and is attempting to find v to complete the match of the right-hand side of the rule. The transitions generated by conditions ii) and iii) represent intermediate steps in matching the right-hand side of a rule and do not alter the lookahead set. Condition iv) introduces transitions of the form

$$\boxed{[A \rightarrow u.Bv, \{z_1, \ldots, z_n\}]} \xrightarrow{\lambda} \boxed{[B \rightarrow .w, \{y_1, \ldots, y_k\}]}$$

Following this arc, the LR(1) machine attempts to match the right-hand side of the rule $B \rightarrow w$. If the string w is found, a reduction of uwv produces $uB.v$ as desired. The lookahead set consists of the symbols that follow w, that is, the first terminal symbol in strings derived from v and the lookahead set $\{z_1, \ldots, z_n\}$ if $v \overset{*}{\Rightarrow} \lambda$.

A bottom-up parser may reduce the string uw to uA whenever $A \rightarrow w$ is a rule of the grammar. An LR(1) parser uses the lookahead set to decide whether to reduce or to shift when this occurs. If $\delta(q_0, uw)$ contains a complete item $[A \rightarrow w., \{z_1, \ldots, z_n\}]$, the string is reduced only if the lookahead symbol is in the set $\{z_1, \ldots, z_n\}$.

The state diagrams of the nondeterministic and deterministic LR(1) machines of the grammar G are given in Figs. 16.4 and 16.5, respectively.

$$G: S \rightarrow A \mid Bc$$
$$A \rightarrow aA \mid a$$
$$B \rightarrow a \mid ab$$

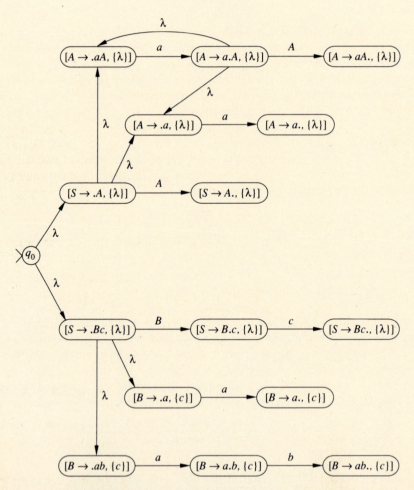

FIGURE 16.4 Nondeterministic LR(1) machine of G.

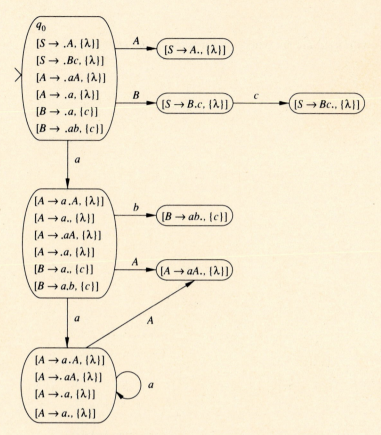

FIGURE 16.5   Deterministic LR(1) machine of G.

A grammar is LR(1) if the actions of the parser are uniquely determined using a single lookahead symbol. The structure of the deterministic LR(1) machine can be used to define the LR(1) grammars.

Definition 16.5.3

Let G be a context-free grammar with a nonrecursive start symbol. The grammar G is **LR(1)** if the extended transition function $\hat{\delta}$ of the deterministic LR(1) machine of G satisfies the following conditions:

i) If $\hat{\delta}(q_s, u)$ contains a complete item $[A \rightarrow w., \{z_1, \ldots, z_n\}]$ and $\hat{\delta}(q_s, u)$ contains an item $[B \rightarrow r.as, \{y_1, \ldots, y_k\}]$, then $a \neq z_i$ for all $1 \leq i \leq n$.

ii) If $\hat{\delta}(q_s, u)$ contains two complete items $[A \rightarrow w., \{z_1, \ldots, z_n\}]$ and $[B \rightarrow v., \{y_1, \ldots, y_k\}]$, then $y_i \neq z_j$ for all $1 \leq i \leq k$, $1 \leq j \leq n$.

Example 16.5.1

The deterministic LR(1) machine is constructed for the grammar AE.

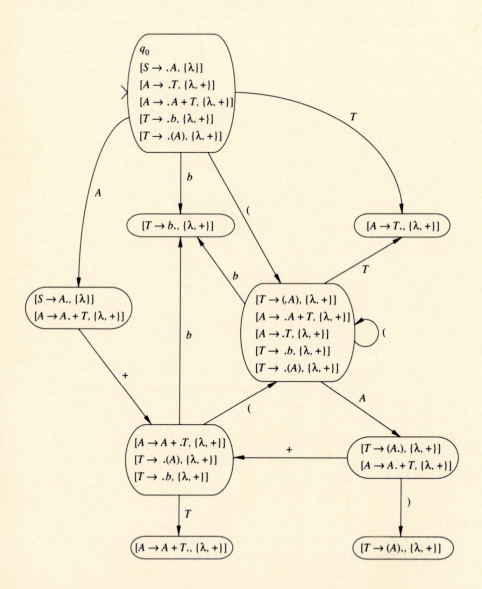

The state containing the complete item $S \to A.$ also contains $A \to A. + T$. It follows that AE is not LR(0). Upon entering this state, the LR(1) parser halts unsuccessfully unless the lookahead symbol is + or the null string. In the latter case, the entire input string has been read and a reduction with the rule $S \rightarrow A$ is specified. When the lookahead symbol is $+$, the parser shifts in an attempt to construct the string $A + T$.

□

The action of a parser for an LR(1) grammar upon scanning the string u is selected by the result of the computation $\hat{\delta}(q_s, u)$. Algorithm 16.5.4 gives a deterministic algorithm for parsing an LR(1) grammar.

Algorithm 16.5.4
Parser for an LR(1) Grammar

input: LR(1) grammar $G = (V, \Sigma, P, S)$
   string $p \in \Sigma^*$
   deterministic LR(1) machine of G

.1. let $p = zv$ where $z \in \Sigma \cup \{\lambda\}$ and $v \in \Sigma^*$
  (z is the lookahead symbol, v the remainder of the input)

2. $u := \lambda$

3. dead-end $:= \textit{false}$

4. **repeat**
  4.1. **if** $\hat{\delta}(q_s, u)$ contains $[A \rightarrow w., \{z_1, \ldots, z_n\}]$
    where $u = xw$ and $z = z_i$ for some $1 \leq i \leq n$ **then** $u := xA$
    else if $z \neq \lambda$ **and** $\hat{\delta}(q_s, u)$ contains an item $A \rightarrow p.zq$ **then**
      (shift and obtain new lookahead symbol)
      4.1.1. $u := uz$
      4.1.2. Let $v = zv'$ where $z \in \Sigma \cup \{\lambda\}$ and $v' \in \Sigma^*$
      4.1.3. $v := v'$
    end if
    else dead-end $:= \textit{true}$
 until $u = S$ **or** dead-end

5. **if** $u = S$ **then** accept **else** reject

For an LR(1) grammar, the structure of the LR(1) machine ensures that the action specified in step 4.1 is unique. When a state contains more than one complete item, the lookahead symbol specifies the appropriate operation.

Example 16.5.2

Algorithm 16.5.4 and the deterministic LR(1) machine in Fig. 16.4 are used to parse the strings *aaa* and *ac*.

u	z	v	Computation	Action
λ	a	aa	$\hat{\delta}(q_s, \lambda) = \{[S \to .A, \{\lambda\}],$ $[S \to .Bc, \{\lambda\}],$ $[A \to .aA, \{\lambda\}],$ $[A \to .a, \{\lambda\}],$ $[B \to .a \ \{c\}],$ $[B \to .ab \ \{c\}]\}$	shift
a	a	a	$\hat{\delta}(q_s, a) = \{[A \to a.A, \{\lambda\}],$ $[A \to a., \{\lambda\}],$ $[A \to .aA, \{\lambda\}],$ $[A \to .a, \{\lambda\}],$ $[B \to a., \{c\}],$ $[B \to a.b, \{c\}]\}$	shift
aa	a	λ	$\hat{\delta}(q_s, aa) = \{[A \to a.A, \{\lambda\}],$ $[A \to .aA, \{\lambda\}],$ $[A \to .a, \{\lambda\}],$ $[A \to a., \{\lambda\}]\}$	shift
aaa	λ	λ	$\hat{\delta}(q_s, aaa) = \{[A \to a.A, \{\lambda\}],$ $[A \to .aA, \{\lambda\}],$ $[A \to .a, \{\lambda\}],$ $[A \to a., \{\lambda\}]\}$	reduce
aaA	λ	λ	$\hat{\delta}(q_s, aaA) = \{[A \to aA., \{\lambda\}]\}$	reduce
aA	λ	λ	$\hat{\delta}(q_s, aA) = \{[A \to aA., \{\lambda\}]\}$	reduce
A	λ	λ	$\hat{\delta}(q_s, A) = \{[S \to A., \{\lambda\}]\}$	reduce
S				

u	z	v	Computation	Action
λ	a	c	$\hat{\delta}(q_s, \lambda) = \{[S \to .A, \{\lambda\}],$ $[S \to .Bc, \{\lambda\}],$ $[A \to .aA, \{\lambda\}],$ $[A \to .a, \{\lambda\}],$ $[B \to .a \ \{c\}],$ $[B \to .ab \ \{c\}]\}$	shift
a	c	λ	$\hat{\delta}(q_s, a) = \{[A \to a.A, \{\lambda\}],$ $[A \to a., \{\lambda\}],$ $[A \to .aA, \{\lambda\}],$ $[A \to .a, \{\lambda\}],$ $[B \to a., \{c\}],$ $[B \to a.b, \{c\}]\}$	reduce
B	c	λ	$\hat{\delta}(q_s, B) = \{[S \to B.c, \{\lambda\}]\}$	shift
Bc	λ	λ	$\hat{\delta}(q_s, Bc) = \{[S \to Bc., \{\lambda\}]\}$	reduce
S				$\square$

Exercises

1. Give the LR(0) contexts for the rules of the grammars below. Build the nondeterministic LR(0) machine. Use this to construct the deterministic LR(0) machine. Is the grammar LR(0)?

   a) $S \rightarrow AB$
   $A \rightarrow aA \mid b$
   $B \rightarrow bB \mid a$

   b) $S \rightarrow Ac$
   $A \rightarrow BA \mid \lambda$
   $B \rightarrow aB \mid b$

   c) $S \rightarrow A$
   $A \rightarrow aAb \mid bAa \mid \lambda$

   d) $S \rightarrow aA \mid AB$
   $A \rightarrow aAb \mid b$
   $B \rightarrow ab \mid b$

   d) $S \rightarrow BA \mid bAB$
   $A \rightarrow aA \mid \lambda$
   $B \rightarrow Bb \mid b$

   e) $S \rightarrow A \mid aB$
   $A \rightarrow BC \mid \lambda$
   $B \rightarrow Bb \mid C$
   $C \rightarrow Cc \mid c$

2. Build the deterministic LR(0) machine for the grammar

$$S \rightarrow aAb \mid aB$$
$$A \rightarrow Aa \mid \lambda$$
$$B \rightarrow Ac.$$

   Use the technique presented in Example 16.3.1 to trace the parse of the strings *aaab* and *ac*.

3. Show that the grammar AE without an endmarker is not LR(0).

4. Prove Lemma 16.4.2.

5. Prove that an LR(0) grammar is unambiguous.

6. Define the LR(k) contexts of a rule $A \rightarrow w$.

7. For each of the grammars defined below, construct the nondeterministic and deterministic LR(1) machines. Is the grammar LR(1)?

   a) $S \rightarrow Ac$
   $A \rightarrow BA \mid \lambda$
   $B \rightarrow aB \mid b$

   b) $S \rightarrow A$
   $A \rightarrow AaAb \mid \lambda$

   c) $S \rightarrow A$
   $A \rightarrow aAb \mid B$
   $B \rightarrow Bb \mid b$

   d) $S \rightarrow A$
   $A \rightarrow BB$
   $B \rightarrow aB \mid b$

   e) $S \rightarrow A$
   $A \rightarrow AAa \mid AAb \mid c$

8. Construct the LR(1) machine for the grammar introduced in Example 16.4.3. Is this grammar LR(1)?

9. Parse the strings below using the LR(1) parser and the grammar AE. Trace the actions of the parser using the format of Example 16.5.2. The deterministic LR(1) machine of AE is given in Example 16.5.1.

a) $b + b$

b) (b)

c) $b + + b$

Bibliographic Notes

LR grammars were introduced by Knuth [1965]. The number of states and transitions in the LR machine made the use of LR techniques impractical for parsers of computer languages. Korenjak [1969] and De Remer [1969, 1971] developed simplifications that eliminated these difficulties. The latter works introduced the SLR (simple LR) and LALR (lookahead LR) grammars.

The relationships between the class of LR(*k*) grammars and other classes of grammars that can be deterministically parsed, including the LL(*k*) grammars, are developed in Aho and Ullman [1972, 1973]. Additional information on syntax analysis using LR parsers can be found in the compiler design texts mentioned in the bibliographic notes of Chapter 15.

APPENDIX I

Index of Notation

Symbol	Page	Interpretation
$\in$	3	is an element of
$\notin$	3	is not an element of
N	4	the set of natural numbers
$\varnothing$	4	empty set
$\subseteq$	4	is a subset of
$\mathscr{P}(X)$	4	power set of X
$\cup$	4	union
$\cap$	5	intersection
$-$	5	$X - Y$: set difference
$\overline{X}$	5	complement
$\times$	6	$X \times Y$: Cartesian product
$[x, y]$	6	ordered pair
$f : X \to Y$	7	f is a function from X to Y
$f(x)$	7	the value assigned to x by the function f

Symbol	Page	Interpretation
$f(x)\uparrow$	8	$f(x)$ is undefined
$f(x)\downarrow$	8	$f(x)$ is defined
div	8	integer division
card	9	cardinality
s	13, 283	successor function
$\sum\limits_{i=n}^{m}$	22, 308	bounded summation
!	23	factorial
$\dot-$	27	proper subtraction
λ	30	null string
Σ^{*}	30	set of strings over Σ
length	30	length of a string
w^{R}	32	reversal of w
XY	33	concatenation of sets X and Y
X^{i}	33	concatenation of X with itself i times
X^{*}	33	strings over X
X^{+}	33	nonnull strings over X
∞	33	infinity
$\emptyset$	36	regular expression for the empty set
λ	36	regular expression for the null string
a	36	regular expression for the symbol a
$\cup$	36	regular expression union operation
$\rightarrow$	44, 237	rule of a grammar
$\Rightarrow$	45, 238	is derivable by one rule application
$\overset{*}{\Rightarrow}$	47, 238	is derivable from
$\overset{+}{\Rightarrow}$	47	is derivable by one or more rule applications
$\overset{n}{\Rightarrow}$	48	is derivable by n rule applications

Symbol	Page	Interpretation
$L(G)$	48	language of the grammar G
$g(G)$	75	graph of the grammar G
shift	90, 401	shift function
δ	134, 143, 186, 212	transition function
$L(M)$	135, 144, 187, 215	language of the machine M
$\vdash$	136, 187, 213	yields by one transition
$\vdash^{*}$	136, 187, 213	yields by zero or more transitions
$\hat{\delta}$	137	extended transition function
$\lambda\text{-}closure$	151	lambda closure function
B	211	blank tape symbol
z	283	zero function
e	283	empty function
$p_i^{(k)}$	284	k-variable projection function
id	284	identity function
$\circ$	291	composition
$c_i^{(k)}$	294	k-variable constant function
$\lfloor x \rfloor$	296	greatest integer less than or equal to x
$\prod_{i=0}^{n}$	308	bounded product
$\mu z[p]^{y}$	310	bounded minimalization
$pn(i)$	313	ith prime function
gn_k	315	k-variable Gödel numbering function
$dec(i, x)$	315	decoding function
gn_f	316	bounded Gödel numbering function
$\mu z[p]$	321	unbounded minimalization
tr_M	325	Turing machine trace function
tc_M	339, 348	time complexity function

Symbol	Page	Interpretation
O(f)	341	order of the function f
$\mathcal{P}$	345	polynomial languages
$\mathcal{NP}$	348	nondeterministically polynomial languages
LA(A)	376	lookahead set of variable A
LA($A \rightarrow w$)	376	lookahead set of the rule $A \rightarrow w$
$trunc_k$	378	length-k truncation function
$\text{FIRST}_k(u)$	380	FIRST_k set of the string u
$\text{FOLLOW}_k(A)$	380	FOLLOW_k set of the variable A

APPENDIX II

Backus-Naur Definition of Pascal

The programming language Pascal was developed by Niklaus Wirth in the late 1960s. The language was defined using the notation known as the Backus-Naur form (BNF). The metasymbol $\{u\}$ denotes zero or more repetitions of the string inside the brackets. Thus the BNF rule $A \rightarrow \{u\}$ is represented in a context-free grammar by the rules $A \rightarrow uA \mid \lambda$. The variables in the BNF definition are enclosed in ⟨ ⟩. The null string is represented by ⟨*empty*⟩. A BNF rule and its context-free counterpart are given to illustrate the conversion from one notation to the other.

BNF definition:

$$\langle unsigned\ integer \rangle \rightarrow \langle digit \rangle \{\langle digit \rangle\}$$

Context-free equivalent:

$$\langle unsigned\ integer \rangle \rightarrow \langle digit \rangle \mid \langle digit \rangle \langle digits \rangle$$
$$\langle digits \rangle \rightarrow \langle digit \rangle \langle digits \rangle \mid \lambda$$

The context-free rules can be simplified to

$$\langle unsigned\ integer \rangle \rightarrow \langle digit \rangle \langle unsigned\ integer \rangle \mid \langle digit \rangle.$$

The start symbol of the BNF definition of Pascal is the variable ⟨*program*⟩. A syntactically correct Pascal program is a string that can be obtained by a derivation initiated with the rule ⟨*program*⟩ → ⟨*program heading*⟩ ; ⟨*program block*⟩.

Reprinted from Kathleen Jensen and Niklaus Wirth, *Pascal: User Manual and Report,* 2nd ed., Springer Verlag, New York, 1974.

⟨*program*⟩ → ⟨*program heading*⟩ ; ⟨*program block*⟩

⟨*program block*⟩ → ⟨*block*⟩

⟨*program heading*⟩ → **program** ⟨*identifier*⟩ (⟨*file identifier*⟩ {, ⟨*file identifier*⟩}) ;

⟨*file identifier*⟩ → ⟨*identifier*⟩

⟨*identifier*⟩ → ⟨*letter*⟩ {⟨*letter or digit*⟩}

⟨*letter or digit*⟩ → ⟨*letter*⟩ | ⟨*digit*⟩

⟨*letter*⟩ → a | b | . . . | z

⟨*digit*⟩ → 0 | 1 | . . . | 9

⟨*block*⟩ → ⟨*label declaration part*⟩ ⟨*constant definition part*⟩ ⟨*type definition part*⟩
             ⟨*variable declaration part*⟩ ⟨*procedure and function declaration part*⟩
             ⟨*statement part*⟩

⟨*label declaration part*⟩ → ⟨*empty*⟩ | **label** ⟨*label*⟩ {, ⟨*label*⟩} ;

⟨*label*⟩ → ⟨*unsigned integer*⟩

⟨*constant definition part*⟩ → ⟨*empty*⟩ |
                              const ⟨*constant definition*⟩ {; ⟨*constant definition*⟩} ;

⟨*constant definition*⟩ → ⟨*identifier*⟩ = ⟨*constant*⟩

⟨*constant*⟩ → ⟨*unsigned number*⟩ | ⟨*sign*⟩ ⟨*unsigned number*⟩ | ⟨*constant identifier*⟩ |
             ⟨*sign*⟩ ⟨*constant identifier*⟩ | ⟨*string*⟩

⟨*unsigned number*⟩ → ⟨*unsigned integer*⟩ | ⟨*unsigned real*⟩

⟨*unsigned integer*⟩ → ⟨*digit*⟩ {⟨*digit*⟩}

⟨*unsigned real*⟩ → ⟨*unsigned integer*⟩ . ⟨*digit*⟩ {⟨*digit*⟩} |
                  ⟨*unsigned integer*⟩ . ⟨*digit*⟩ {⟨*digit*⟩} E ⟨*scale factor*⟩ |
                  ⟨*unsigned integer*⟩ E ⟨*scale factor*⟩

⟨*scale factor*⟩ → ⟨*unsigned integer*⟩ | ⟨*sign*⟩ ⟨*unsigned integer*⟩

⟨*sign*⟩ → + | −

⟨*constant identifier*⟩ → ⟨*identifier*⟩

⟨*string*⟩ → '⟨*character*⟩ {⟨*character*⟩}'

⟨*type definition part*⟩ → ⟨*empty*⟩ | **type** ⟨*type definition*⟩ {; ⟨*type definition*⟩} ;

⟨*type definition*⟩ → ⟨*identifier*⟩ = ⟨*type*⟩

⟨*type*⟩ → ⟨*simple type*⟩ | ⟨*structured type*⟩ | ⟨*pointer type*⟩

⟨*simple type*⟩ → ⟨*scalar type*⟩ | ⟨*subrange type*⟩ | ⟨*type identifier*⟩

⟨*scalar type*⟩ → (⟨*identifier*⟩ {, ⟨*identifier*⟩})

⟨*subrange type*⟩ → ⟨*constant*⟩ . . ⟨*constant*⟩

⟨*type identifier*⟩ → ⟨*identifier*⟩

⟨*structured type*⟩ → ⟨*unpacked structured type*⟩ | **packed** ⟨*unpacked structured type*⟩

⟨*unpacked structured type*⟩ → ⟨*array type*⟩ | ⟨*record type*⟩ | ⟨*set type*⟩ | ⟨*file type*⟩

⟨*array type*⟩ → **array** [⟨*index type*⟩ {, ⟨*index type*⟩}] **of** ⟨*component type*⟩

⟨*index type*⟩ → ⟨*simple type*⟩

⟨*component type*⟩ → ⟨*type*⟩

⟨*record type*⟩ → **record** ⟨*field list*⟩ **end**

⟨*field list*⟩ → ⟨*fixed part*⟩ | ⟨*fixed part*⟩ ; ⟨*variant part*⟩ | ⟨*variant part*⟩

⟨*fixed part*⟩ → ⟨*record section*⟩ {; ⟨*record section*⟩}

⟨*record section*⟩ → ⟨*field identifier*⟩ {, ⟨*field identifier*⟩} : ⟨*type*⟩ | ⟨*empty*⟩

⟨*variant part*⟩ → **case** ⟨*tag field*⟩ ⟨*type identifier*⟩ **of** ⟨*variant*⟩ {; ⟨*variant*⟩}

⟨*tag field*⟩ → ⟨*field identifier*⟩ : | ⟨*empty*⟩

⟨*variant*⟩ → ⟨*case label list*⟩ : (⟨*field list*⟩) | ⟨*empty*⟩

⟨*case label list*⟩ → ⟨*case label*⟩ {, ⟨*case label*⟩}

⟨*case label*⟩ → ⟨*constant*⟩

⟨*set type*⟩ → **set of** ⟨base type⟩

⟨*base type*⟩ → ⟨*simple type*⟩

⟨*file type*⟩ → **file of** ⟨*type*⟩

⟨*pointer type*⟩ → ↑ ⟨*type identifier*⟩

⟨*variable declaration part*⟩ → ⟨*empty*⟩ |
　　　　　　　　　　　　　　var ⟨*variable declaration*⟩ {; ⟨*variable declaration*⟩} ;

⟨*variable declaration*⟩ → ⟨*identifier*⟩ {, ⟨*identifier*⟩} : ⟨*type*⟩

⟨*procedure and function declaration part*⟩ → {⟨*procedure or function declaration*⟩ ;}

⟨*procedure or function declaration*⟩ → ⟨*procedure declaration*⟩ |
　　　　　　　　　　　　　　　⟨*function declaration*⟩

⟨*procedure declaration*⟩ → ⟨*procedure heading*⟩ ⟨*block*⟩

⟨*procedure heading*⟩ → **procedure** ⟨*identifier*⟩ ; |
　　　　　　　　procedure ⟨*identifier*⟩ (⟨*formal parameter section*⟩
　　　　　　　　{; ⟨*formal parameter section*⟩}) ;

⟨*formal parameter section*⟩ → ⟨*parameter group*⟩ | **var** ⟨*parameter group*⟩ |
　　　　　　　　function ⟨*parameter group*⟩ |
　　　　　　　　procedure ⟨*identifier*⟩ {, ⟨*identifier*⟩}

⟨*parameter group*⟩ → ⟨*identifier*⟩ {, ⟨*identifier*⟩} : ⟨*type identifier*⟩

⟨*function declaration*⟩ → ⟨*function heading*⟩ ⟨*block*⟩

⟨*function heading*⟩ → **function** ⟨*identifier*⟩ : ⟨*result type*⟩ ; |
　　　　　　　　function ⟨*identifier*⟩ (⟨*formal parameter section*⟩
　　　　　　　　{; ⟨*formal parameter section*⟩}) : ⟨*result type*⟩ ;

⟨*result type*⟩ → ⟨*type identifier*⟩

⟨*statement part*⟩ → ⟨*compound statement*⟩

⟨*statement*⟩ → ⟨*unlabeled statement*⟩ | ⟨*label*⟩ : ⟨*unlabeled statement*⟩

⟨*unlabeled statement*⟩ → ⟨*simple statement*⟩ | ⟨*structured statement*⟩

⟨*simple statement*⟩ → ⟨*assignment statement*⟩ | ⟨*procedure statement*⟩ |
⟨*go to statement*⟩ | ⟨*empty statement*⟩

⟨*assignment statement*⟩ → ⟨*variable*⟩ := ⟨*expression*⟩ |
⟨*function identifier*⟩ := ⟨*expression*⟩

⟨*variable*⟩ → ⟨*entire variable*⟩ | ⟨*component variable*⟩ | ⟨*referenced variable*⟩

⟨*entire variable*⟩ → ⟨*variable identifier*⟩

⟨*variable identifier*⟩ → ⟨*identifier*⟩

⟨*component variable*⟩ → ⟨*indexed variable*⟩ | ⟨*field designator*⟩ | ⟨*file buffer*⟩

⟨*indexed variable*⟩ → ⟨*array variable*⟩ [⟨*expression*⟩ {, ⟨*expression*⟩}]

⟨*array variable*⟩ → ⟨*variable*⟩

⟨*field designator*⟩ → ⟨*record variable*⟩ . ⟨*field identifier*⟩

⟨*record variable*⟩ → ⟨*variable*⟩

⟨*field identifier*⟩ → ⟨*identifier*⟩

⟨*file buffer*⟩ → ⟨*file variable*⟩ ↑

⟨*file variable*⟩ → ⟨*variable*⟩

⟨*referenced variable*⟩ → ⟨*pointer variable*⟩ ↑

⟨*pointer variable*⟩ → ⟨*variable*⟩

⟨*expression*⟩ → ⟨*simple expression*⟩ | ⟨*simple expression*⟩ ⟨*relational operator*⟩
⟨*simple expression*⟩

⟨*relational operator*⟩ → = | <> | < | <= | >= | > | **in**

⟨*simple expression*⟩ → ⟨*term*⟩ | ⟨*sign*⟩ ⟨*term*⟩ |
⟨*simple expression*⟩ ⟨*adding operator*⟩ ⟨*term*⟩

⟨*adding operator*⟩ → + | − | **or**

⟨*term*⟩ → ⟨*factor*⟩ | ⟨*term*⟩ ⟨*multiplying operator*⟩ ⟨*factor*⟩

⟨*multiplying operator*⟩ → * | / | **div** | **mod** | **and**

⟨*factor*⟩ → ⟨*variable*⟩ | ⟨*unsigned constant*⟩ | (⟨*expression*⟩) | ⟨*function designator*⟩ |
⟨*set*⟩ | **not** ⟨*factor*⟩

⟨*unsigned constant*⟩ → ⟨*unsigned number*⟩ | ⟨*string*⟩ | ⟨*constant identifier*⟩ | **nil**

⟨*function designator*⟩ → ⟨*function identifier*⟩ |
⟨*function identifier*⟩ (⟨*actual parameter*⟩ {, ⟨*actual parameter*⟩})

⟨*function identifier*⟩ → ⟨*identifier*⟩

⟨*set*⟩ → [⟨*element list*⟩]

⟨*element list*⟩ → ⟨*element*⟩ {, ⟨*element*⟩} | ⟨*empty*⟩

⟨*element*⟩ → ⟨*expression*⟩ | ⟨*expression*⟩ . . ⟨*expression*⟩

⟨*procedure statement*⟩ → ⟨*procedure identifier*⟩ |
                    ⟨*procedure identifier*⟩ (⟨*actual parameter*⟩
                    {, ⟨*actual parameter*⟩})

⟨*procedure identifier*⟩ → ⟨*identifier*⟩

⟨*actual parameter*⟩ → ⟨*expression*⟩ | ⟨*variable*⟩ |
                ⟨*procedure identifier*⟩ | ⟨*functional identifier*⟩

⟨*go to statement*⟩ → **goto** ⟨*label*⟩

⟨*empty statement*⟩ → ⟨*empty*⟩

⟨*empty*⟩ → λ

⟨*structured statement*⟩ → ⟨*compound statement*⟩ | ⟨*conditional statement*⟩ |
                ⟨*repetitive statement*⟩ | ⟨*with statement*⟩

⟨*compound statement*⟩ → **begin** ⟨*statement*⟩ {; ⟨*statement*⟩} **end**

⟨*conditional statement*⟩ → ⟨*if statement*⟩ | ⟨*case statement*⟩

⟨*if statement*⟩ → **if** ⟨*expression*⟩ **then** ⟨*statement*⟩ |
            if ⟨*expression*⟩ **then** ⟨*statement*⟩ **else** ⟨*statement*⟩

⟨*case statement*⟩ → **case** ⟨*expression*⟩ **of** ⟨*case list element*⟩ {; ⟨*case list element*⟩} **end**

⟨*case list element*⟩ → ⟨*case label list*⟩ : ⟨*statement*⟩ | ⟨*empty*⟩

⟨*case label list*⟩ → ⟨*case label*⟩ {, ⟨*case label*⟩}

⟨*repetitive statement*⟩ → ⟨*while statement*⟩ | ⟨*repeat statement*⟩ | ⟨*for statement*⟩

⟨*while statement*⟩ → **while** ⟨*expression*⟩ **do** ⟨*statement*⟩

⟨*repeat statement*⟩ → **repeat** ⟨*statement*⟩ {; ⟨*statement*⟩} **until** ⟨*expression*⟩

⟨*for statement*⟩ → **for** ⟨*control variable*⟩ := ⟨*for list*⟩ **do** ⟨*statement*⟩

⟨*for list*⟩ → ⟨*initial value*⟩ **to** ⟨*final value*⟩ | ⟨*initial value*⟩ **downto** ⟨*final value*⟩

⟨*control variable*⟩ → ⟨*identifier*⟩

⟨*initial value*⟩ → ⟨*expression*⟩

⟨*final value*⟩ → ⟨*expression*⟩

⟨*with statement*⟩ → **with** ⟨*record variable list*⟩ **do** ⟨*statement*⟩

⟨*record variable list*⟩ → ⟨*record variable*⟩ {, ⟨*record variable*⟩}

Bibliography

Ackermann, W. [1928], "Zum Hilbertschen Aufbau der reellen Zahlen," *Mathematische Annalen*, 99, pp. 118–133.

Aho, A. V., and J. D. Ullman [1972], *The Theory of Parsing, Translation and Compilation*, Vol. I: *Parsing*, Prentice-Hall, Englewood Cliffs, NJ.

Aho, A. V., and J. D. Ullman [1973], *The Theory of Parsing, Translation and Compilation*, Vol. II: *Compiling*, Prentice-Hall, Englewood Cliffs, NJ.

Aho, A. V., R. Sethi, and J. D. Ullman [1986], *Compilers: Principles, Techniques and Tools*, Addison-Wesley, Reading, MA.

Backhouse, R. C. [1979], *Syntax of Programming Languages: Theory and Practice*, Prentice-Hall, Englewood Cliffs, NJ.

Backus, J. W. [1959], "The syntax and semantics of the proposed international algebraic language of the Zurich ACM-GAMM conference," *Proceedings of the International Conference on Information Processing*, pp. 125–132.

Bar-Hillel, Y., M. Perles, and E. Shamir [1961], "On formal properties of simple phrase-structure grammars," *Zeitschrift für Phonetik, Sprachwissenschaft, und Kommunikationsforschung*, 14, pp. 143–177.

Barrett, W. A., R. M. Bates, D. A. Gustafson, and J. D. Couch [1986], *Compiler Construction: Theory and Practice*, Science Research Associates, Chicago, IL.

Bavel, Z. [1983], *Introduction to the Theory of Automata*, Reston Publishing Co., Reston, VA.

Blum, M. [1967], "A machine independent theory of the complexity of recursive functions," *J. ACM*, 14, pp. 322–336.

Bobrow, L. S., and M. A. Arbib [1974], *Discrete Mathematics: Applied Algebra for Computer and Information Science*, Saunders, Philadelphia, PA.

Bondy, J. A., and U. S. R. Murty [1977], *Graph Theory with Applications*, Elsevier, New York.

Brainerd, W. S., and L. H. Landweber [1974], *Theory of Computation*, Wiley, New York.

Busacker, R. G., and T. L. Saaty [1965], *Finite Graphs and Networks: An Introduction with Applications*, McGraw-Hill, New York.

Cantor, D. C. [1962], "On the ambiguity problems of Backus systems," *J. ACM*, 9, pp. 477–479.

Cantor, G. [1947], *Contributions to the Foundations of the Theory of Transfinite Numbers* (reprint), Dover, New York.

Chomsky, N. [1956], "Three models for the description of languages," *IRE Transactions on Information Theory*, 2, pp. 113–124.

Chomsky, N. [1959], "On certain formal properties of grammars," *Information and Control*, 2, pp. 137–167.

Chomsky, N. [1962], "Context-free grammar and pushdown storage," *Quarterly Progress Report* 65, M.I.T. Research Laboratory in Electronics, pp. 187–194.

Chomsky, N., and G. A. Miller [1958], "Finite state languages," *Information and Control*, 1, pp. 91–112.

Chomsky, N., and M. P. Schutzenberger [1963], "The algebraic theory of context free languages," in *Computer Programming and Formal Systems*, North-Holland, Amsterdam, pp. 118–161.

Church, A. [1936], "An unsolvable problem of elementary number theory," *American Journal of Mathematics*, 58, pp. 345–363.

Church, A. [1941], "The calculi of lambda-conversion," *Annals of Mathematics Studies*, 6, Princeton University Press, Princeton, NJ.

Cobham, A. [1964], "The intrinsic computational difficulty of functions," *Proceedings of the 1964 Congress for Logic, Mathematics and Philosophy of Science*, North-Holland, New York, pp. 24–30.

Cook, S. A. [1971], "The complexity of theorem proving procedures," *Proceedings of the Third Annual ACM Symposium on the Theory of Computing*, Association for Computing Machinery, New York, pp. 151–158.

Davis, M. D. [1965], *The Undecidable*, Raven Press, Hewlett, NY.

Davis, M. D., and E. J. Weyuker [1983], *Computability, Complexity and Languages: Fundamentals of Theoretical Computer Science*, Academic Press, New York.

Denning, P. J., J. B. Dennis, and J. E. Qualitz [1978], *Machines, Languages and Computation,* Prentice-Hall, Englewood Cliffs, NJ.

De Remer, F. L. [1969], "Generating parsers for BNF grammars," *Proceedings of the 1969 Fall Joint Computer Conference,* AFIPS Press, Montvale, NJ, pp. 793–799.

De Remer, F. L. [1971], "Simple LR(k) grammars," *Comm. ACM,* 14, pp. 453–460.

Edmonds, J. [1965], "Paths, trees and flowers," *Canadian Journal of Mathematics,* 3, pp. 449–467.

Evey, J. [1963], "Application of pushdown store machines," *Proceedings of the 1963 Fall Joint Computer Science Conference,* AFIPS Press, pp. 215–217.

Floyd, R. W. [1962], "On ambiguity in phrase structure languages," *Comm. ACM,* 5, pp. 526–534.

Floyd, R. W. [1964], *New Proofs and Old Theorems in Logic and Formal Linguistics,* Computer Associates, Inc., Wakefield, MA.

Foster, J. M. [1968], "A syntax improving program," *Computer J.,* 11, pp. 31–34.

Garey, M. R., and D. S. Johnson [1979], *Computers and Intractability: A Guide to the Theory of NP-completeness,* Freeman, New York.

Gersting, J. L. [1982], *Mathematical Structures for Computer Science,* W. H. Freeman, San Francisco, CA.

Ginsburg, S. [1966], *The Mathematical Theory of Context-Free Languages,* McGraw-Hill, New York.

Ginsburg, S., and H. G. Rice [1962], "Two families of languages related to ALGOL," *J. ACM,* 9, pp. 350–371.

Ginsburg, S., and G. F. Rose [1963a], "Some recursively unsolvable problems in ALGOL-like languages," *J. ACM,* 10, pp. 29–47.

Ginsburg, S., and G. F. Rose [1963b], "Operations which preserve definability in languages," *J. ACM,* 10, pp. 175–195.

Ginsburg, S., and J. S. Ullian [1966a], "Ambiguity in context-free languages," *J. ACM,* 13, pp. 62–89.

Ginsburg, S., and J. S. Ullian [1966b], "Preservation of unambiguity and inherent ambiguity in context-free languages," *J. ACM,* 13, pp. 364–368.

Gödel, K. [1931], "Uber formal unentscheidbare Sätze der Principia Mathematica und verwandter Systeme, I," *Monatschefte für Mathematik und Physik,* 38, pp. 173–198. (English translation in Davis [1965].)

Greibach, S. [1965], "A new normal form theorem for context-free phrase structure grammars," *J. ACM,* 12, pp. 42–52.

Halmos, P. R. [1974], *Naive Set Theory,* Springer-Verlag, New York.

Harrison, M. A. [1978], *Introduction to Formal Language Theory,* Addison-Wesley, Reading, MA.

Hartmanis, J., and J. E. Hopcroft [1971], "An overview of the theory of computational complexity," *J. ACM,* 18, pp. 444–475.

Hennie, F. C. [1977], *Introduction to Computability,* Addison-Wesley, Reading, MA.

Hermes, H. [1965], *Enumerability, Decidability, Computability,* Academic Press, New York.

Hopcroft, J. E. [1971], "An *n* log *n* algorithm for minimizing the states in a finite automaton," in *The Theory of Machines and Computation,* ed. by Z. Kohavi, Academic Press, New York, pp. 189–196.

Hopcroft, J. E., and J. D. Ullman [1979], *Introduction to Automata Theory, Languages and Computation,* Addison-Wesley, Reading, MA.

Jensen, K., and N. Wirth [1974], *Pascal: User Manual and Report,* 2nd ed., Springer-Verlag, New York.

Johnsonbaugh, R. [1984], *Discrete Mathematics,* Macmillan, New York.

Karp, R. M. [1972], "Reducibility among combinatorial problems," in *Complexity of Computer Computations,* Plenum Press, New York, pp. 85–104.

Karp, R. M. [1986], "Combinatorics, complexity and randomness," *Comm. ACM,* 29, no. 2, pp. 98–109.

Kleene, S. C. [1936], "General recursive functions of natural numbers," *Mathematische Annalen,* 112, pp. 727–742.

Kleene, S. C. [1952], *Introduction to Metamathematics,* Van Nostrand, Princeton, NJ.

Kleene, S. C. [1956], "Representation of events in nerve nets and finite automata," in *Automata Studies,* ed. by C. E. Shannon and J. McCarthy, Princeton University Press, Princeton, NJ., pp. 3–42.

Knuth, D. E. [1965], "On the translation of languages from left to right," *Information and Control,* 8, pp. 607–639.

Knuth, D. E. [1968], *The Art of Computer Programming:* Vol. 1: *Fundamental Algorithms,* Addison-Wesley, Reading, MA.

Kolman, B., and R. C. Busby [1984], *Discrete Mathematical Structures for Computer Science,* Prentice-Hall, Englewood Cliffs, NJ.

Korenjak, A. J. [1969], "A practical method for constructing LR(k) processors," *Comm. ACM,* 12, pp. 613–623.

Kurki-Suonio, R. [1969], "Notes on top-down languages," *BIT,* 9, pp. 225–238.

Kuroda, S. Y. [1964], "Classes of languages and linear-bounded automata," *Information and Control,* 7, pp. 207–223.

Landweber, P. S. [1963], "Three theorems of phrase structure grammars of type 1," *Information and Control,* 6, pp. 131–136.

Lewis, H. R., and C. H. Papadimitriou [1981], *Elements of the Theory of Computation,* Prentice-Hall, Englewood Cliffs, NJ.

Lewis, P. M. II, and R. E. Stearns [1968], "Syntax directed transduction," *J. ACM*, 15, pp. 465–488.

Lewis, P. M. II, D. J. Rosenkrantz, and R. E. Stearns [1976], *Compiler Design Theory*, Addison-Wesley, Reading, MA.

Machtey, M., and P. R. Young [1978], *An Introduction to the General Theory of Algorithms*, Elsevier North-Holland, New York.

Markov, A. A. [1961], *Theory of Algorithms*, Israel Program for Scientific Translations, Jerusalem.

McNaughton, R., and H. Yamada [1960], "Regular expressions and state graphs for automata," *IEEE Transactions on Electronic Computers*, 9, pp. 39–47.

Mealy, G. H. [1955], "A method for synthesizing sequential circuits," *Bell System Technical Journal*, 34, pp. 1045–1079.

Minsky, M. L. [1967], *Computation: Finite and Infinite Machines*, Prentice-Hall, Englewood Cliffs, NJ.

Moore, E. F. [1956], "Gendanken-experiments on sequential machines," in *Automata Studies*, ed. by C. E. Shannon and J. McCarthy, Princeton University Press, Princeton, NJ, pp. 129–153.

Myhill, J. [1960], "Linear bounded automata," WADD Technical Note 60-165, Wright Patterson Air Force Base, Ohio.

Naur, P., ed. [1963], "Revised report on the algorithmic language ALGOL 60," *Comm. ACM*, 6, pp. 1–17.

Nerode, A. [1958], "Linear automaton transformations," *Proc. AMS*, 9, pp. 541–544.

Oettinger, A. G. [1961], "Automatic syntax analysis and the pushdown store," *Proceedings on Symposia on Applied Mathematics*, 12, American Mathematical Society, Providence, RI.

Ogden, W. G. [1968], "A helpful result for proving inherent ambiguity," *Mathematical Systems Theory*, 2, pp. 191–194.

Ore, O. [1963], *Graphs and Their Uses*, Random House, New York.

Parikh, R. J. [1966], "On context-free languages," *J. ACM*, 13, pp. 570–581.

Péter, R. [1967], *Recursive Functions*, Academic Press, New York.

Post, E. L. [1936], "Finite combinatory processes—formulation I," *Journal of Symbolic Logic*, 1, pp. 103–105.

Post, E. L. [1946], "A variant of a recursively unsolvable problem," *Bulletin of the American Mathematical Society*, 52, pp. 264–268.

Post, E. L. [1947], "Recursive unsolvability of a problem of Thue," *Journal of Symbolic Logic*, 12, pp. 1–11.

Pyster, A. B. [1980], *Compiler Design and Construction*, Van Nostrand Reinhold, New York.

Rabin, M. O., and D. Scott [1959], "Finite automata and their decision problems," *IBM J. Res.*, 3, pp. 115–125.

Rogers, H., Jr. [1967], *Theory of Recursive Functions and Effective Computation*, McGraw-Hill, New York.

Rosenkrantz, D. J., and R. E. Stearns [1970], "Properties of deterministic top-down grammars," *Information and Control*, 17, pp. 226–256.

Sahni, S. [1981], *Concepts of Discrete Mathematics*, Camelot, Fridley, MN.

Salomaa, A. [1966], "Two complete axiom systems for the algebra of regular events," *J. ACM*, 13, pp. 156–199.

Salomaa, A. [1973], *Formal Languages*, Academic Press, New York.

Scheinberg, S. [1960], "Note on the Boolean properties of context-free languages," *Information and Control*, 3, pp. 372–375.

Schutzenberger, M. P. [1963], "On context-free languages and pushdown automata," *Information and Control*, 6, pp. 246–264.

Sheperdson, J. C. [1959], "The reduction of two-way automata to one-way automata," *IBM J. Res.*, 3, pp. 198–200.

Soisalon-Soininen, E., and E. Ukkonen [1979], "A method for transforming grammars into LL(k) form," *Acta Informatica*, 12, pp. 339–369.

Stearns, R. E. [1971], "Deterministic top-down parsing," *Proceedings of the Fifth Annual Princeton Conference on Information Sciences and Systems*, pp. 182–188.

Stoll, R. [1963], *Set Theory and Logic*, W. H. Freeman, San Francisco, CA.

Thue, A. [1914], "Probleme über Veränderungen von Zeichenreihen nach gegebenen Regeln," *Skrifter utgit av Videnskappsselskapet i Kristiana*, I., Matematisk-natur-videnskabelig klasse 10.

Tremblay, J. P., and R. Manohar [1975], *Discrete Mathematical Structures with Applications to Computer Science*, McGraw-Hill, New York.

Tremblay, J. P., and P. G. Sorenson [1984], *An Introduction to Data Structures with Applications*, 2nd ed., McGraw-Hill, New York.

Turing, A. M. [1936], "On computable numbers with an application to the Entscheidungsproblem," *Proceedings of the London Mathematical Society*, 2, no. 42, pp. 230–265; no. 43, pp. 544–546.

Wand, M. [1980], *Induction, Recursion and Programming*, North-Holland, New York.

Wilson, R. J. [1985], *Introduction to Graph Theory*, 3rd ed., American Elsevier, New York.

Wirth, N. [1971], "The programming language Pascal," *Acta Informatica*, 1, pp. 35–63.

Wood, D. [1969], "The theory of left factored languages," *Computer Journal*. 12, pp. 349–356.

Subject Index